Intonations

NEW AFRICAN HISTORIES SERIES

Series editors: Jean Allman and Allen Isaacman

David William Cohen and E. S. Atieno Odhiambo, *The Risks of Knowledge: Investigations into the Death of the Hon. Minister John Robert Ouko in Kenya, 1990*

Belinda Bozzoli, *Theatres of Struggle and the End of Apartheid*

Gary Kynoch, *We Are Fighting the World: A History of Marashea Gangs in South Africa, 1947–1999*

Stephanie Newell, *The Forger's Tale: The Search for Odeziaku*

Jacob A. Tropp, *Natures of Colonial Change: Environmental Relations in the Making of the Transkei*

Jan Bender Shetler, *Imagining Serengeti: A History of Landscape Memory in Tanzania from Earliest Times to the Present*

Cheikh Anta Babou, *Fighting the Greater Jihad: Amadu Bamba and the Founding of the Muridiyya in Senegal, 1853–1913*

Marc Epprecht, *Heterosexual Africa: The History of an Idea from the Age of Exploration to the Age of AIDS*

Marissa J. Moorman, *Intonations: A Social History of Music and Nation in Luanda, Angola, from 1945 to Recent Times*

Intonations

*A Social History of Music and Nation in
Luanda, Angola, from 1945 to Recent Times*

∽

Marissa J. Moorman

OHIO UNIVERSITY PRESS
ATHENS

Ohio University Press, Athens, Ohio 45701
www.ohioswallow.com
© 2008 by Ohio University Press
All rights reserved

To obtain permission to quote, reprint, or otherwise reproduce or distribute material from Ohio University Press publications, please contact our rights and permissions department at (740) 593-1154 or (740) 593-4536 (fax).

Printed in the United States of America
Ohio University Press books are printed on acid-free paper ∞ ™

15 14 13 12 11 10 09 08   5 4 3 2 1

Library of Congress Cataloging-in-Publication Data

Moorman, Marissa Jean.
 Intonations : a social history of music and nation in Luanda, Angola, from 1945 to recent times / Marissa J. Moorman.
     p. cm. — (New African histories series)
 Includes bibliographical references and index.
 ISBN 978-0-8214-1823-9 (hc : alk. paper) — ISBN 978-0-8214-1824-6 (pb : alk. paper)
 1. Music—Social aspects—Angola—Luanda (Luanda) 2. Music—Political aspects—Angola. 3. Nationalism in music. 4. Angola—History—Revolution, 1961–1975—Music and the revolution. 5. Angola—History—Civil War, 1975–2002—Music and the war. I. Title.
 ML3917.A65M66 2008
 306.4'8423096732—dc22

2008026805

For my parents, Carol and Michael Moorman

Contents

List of Illustrations	ix
Music on CD	xi
Acknowledgments	xiii
Abbreviations and Terms	xix
Timeline of Nationalism and Independence in Angola	xxiii
Timeline of Angolan Music	xxv
Introduction	1
Chapter 1 Musseques and Urban Culture	28
Chapter 2 In the Days of Bota Fogo: Culture and the Early Nationalist Struggle, 1947–61	56
Chapter 3 Dueling Bands and Good Girls: Gender and Music in Luanda's Musseques, 1961–75	81
Chapter 4 "Ngongo Jami" (My Suffering): Lyrics, Daily Life, and Musical Space, 1956–74	110
Chapter 5 Radios, Turntables, and Vinyl: Technology and the Imagined Community, 1961–75	140
Chapter 6 The Hiatus: Music, Dissent, and Nation Building after Independence, 1975–90s	165
Epilogue	190
Notes	197
Bibliography	255
Index	275

Illustrations

Map of Angola	xxvi
Map of Luanda's musseques, c. 1968	29
Women of Luanda	62
Rebita dance group performing, 2001	63
Housing in Bairro Indígena	69
Os Kiezos at a musseque club, early 1970s	99
Belita Palma album cover	104
Urbano de Castro album cover	105
Alba Clyngton album cover	115
Ngola Melodias album cover	116
"Traditional" Angolan dance	118
Map of radio stations in Angola, 1975	145
Ngola Ritmos album cover	158
Garda and Her Band album cover	159
Ngoleiros do Ritmo album cover	160
Paulo Pinheiro album cover	178
Emancipation of the Angolan Woman album cover	183

Music on CD

Track #	Title	Artist
1	Kia Lumingo	Urbano de Castro
2	N'ginda	Tony de Fumo
3	Semba Kassequel	Dina Santos
4	Muxima	Ngola Ritmos
5	Madya Kandimba	Garda e o Seu Conjunto
6	João Dumingu	Ngola Ritmos
7	Chofer de Praça	Luis Visconde
8	Milhorró	Os Kiezos
9	Diala Monzo	Elias dia Kimuezu
10	Bartolomeu	Prado Paim
11	Kaputu	N'zaji
12	Valódia	Santocas
13	Na Rua do São Paulo	Kaboko Meu
14	Amanhã Vamos à Procura da Chave	União Mundo
15	Poema do Semba	Paulo Flores

Acknowledgments

At the outset, this project looked like folly. It is thanks to many people, on many continents, and in many capacities that it has come to be a reality. To all of them I am deeply grateful. First and foremost, I offer heartfelt thanks to the men and women who shared their memories and stories with me. In the often harsh and crushing conditions of war-torn Angola, I never ceased to be amazed by the fact that men and women were eager to talk to me and patient with my queries. Indeed, they have given me something worth saying.

Ohio University Press senior editor Gillian Berchowitz offered wise counsel and was patient in the face of my health issues and shifting revision schedules. Her input, together with that of the series editors, Allen Isaacman and Jean Allman, and the anonymous readers of the book manuscript, made this a stronger and feistier book. Paul Mahern, Michael Casey, and Daniel Reed at the Indiana University Archives of Traditional Music produced the master CD for the book, and John Hollingsworth painstakingly drew the maps. In Angola, Lopito Feijó helped secure permission to reproduce the music and album cover images. An earlier version of chapter 3 appeared in the *International Journal of African Historical Studies*. Before it appeared it profited from a reading by David Schoenbrun's African Studies Graduate Seminar at Northwestern University in 2002 and a hearing at the Workshop on African Popular Music held at the University of California at San Diego on February 21, 2003, at the invitation of Benetta Jules Rossette. It received yet another reading at the University of Minnesota's ICGC Gender Consortium in 2005. Rudolph Ware and his graduate seminar at Northwestern read and discussed the entire manuscript and gave me encouragement at a critical moment in May 2007.

Several institutions and programs supported me and my research along the way. A University of Minnesota Department of History travel grant funded language study in summer 1995. The University of Minnesota Harold Leonard Memorial Film Study Grant and Fellowship funded ten months of predissertation research in 1997–98, and a University of Minnesota MacArthur Program grant supported dissertation research in Angola in 2000–2001. The Social Science Research Council's Dissertation Fellowship on the Arts and Social Science generously funded more research in 2001–2. A Doctoral Dissertation Fellowship from the University of Minnesota Graduate School allowed me to write my dissertation without distraction. Finally, a Summer Faculty Fellowship from Indiana University and grants from the Project on African Expressive Traditions (POAET) and the Office of International Programs at Indiana University made possible further research in Portugal and Angola in the summer of 2005.

At the University of Minnesota I profited from the direction and encouragement of professors Fernando Arenas, Amy Kaminsky, M. J. Maynes, John Mowitt, David Roediger, and Charlie Sugnet, and of Dr. Jim Johnson. In particular, my erstwhile advisers and current editors, Allen Isaacman and Jean Allman, helped me negotiate the worlds of academia and research. It would be difficult to find better mentors; their friendship and guidance have been priceless. Susan Geiger, a pioneering historian of African women and Tanganyikan nationalism, left an indelible mark on this book. Her confidence in me, along with Allen's and Jean's, often filled in for my own. I wish she were here to see this book.

In Portugal, Jorge Murteira cheered me with his sense of humor, offers of a place to stay, and early morning rides from the airport. Edmundo Rocha and Franz-Wilhelm Heimer provided important contacts. Dra. Maria Lurdes Henriques facilitated my work with the PIDE materials at the Torre do Tombo.

In Angola numerous people offered invaluable support. Dra. Rosa Cruz e Silva, the director of the Arquivo Histórico de Angola (Angolan Historical Archive), helped me negotiate the visa process. Dra. Maria Conceição Neto and Dra. Aurora Ferreira welcomed me and helped me find material. Indeed, São Neto suggested I look at music in the first place. She has been a constant source of insight and encouragement. All the staff at the Arquivo Histórico assisted me, despite the difficult conditions they often faced both in and outside the archive. In particular, and as the footnotes of this book should make amply clear, Tio (uncle) Carlos Lamartine, both a musician and a historian working at the archive, was a source of detailed and carefully recounted experience and information. António Fonseca, then at ENDIPU (Empresa Nacional do Disco e Publicações), generously offered me a selection of cassettes and CDs of Angolan music. Jorge Macedo and Jomo Fortunato shared their works in progress with me, and Jomo also let me scan a number of photographs. Dr. Filipe Zau, musician and scholar, has been a great source of information and intellectual exchange and a warm and generous friend. Virgílio Coelho, vice minister of culture, and Silva Candembo, associate editor of *Seminário Angolense*, helped me locate material in 2005. Ranca Tuba arranged an interview with Holden Roberto, and Todd Cleveland introduced me to Ranca and generously shared information on radio from his own interviews. I have been privileged to share time in Angola and time thinking about Angola with a cohort of other junior scholars: Jeremy Ball, Marcelo Bittencourt, Todd Cleveland, Roquinaldo Ferreira, Luena Nunes Pereira, Didier Peclard, Betty Rodriguez-Feo, and Yelmer Vos.

Dona Lucinda Costa, director of the music collection at Rádio Nacional de Angola (Angolan National Radio), allowed me to work there for two weeks in April 2002. During this time Maria Francisca Jacinta, a staff person in the music collection, translated the lyrics for a number of the songs in chapter 4. Dona Lucinda presented her to me as the person for the job; we sat together and listened to the music, which she then translated. I am grateful and indebted to her for this work. I would have liked to have been able to work with someone closely on interpretation of the lyrics but that was not possible. Madalena Afonso translated and interpreted the song "Muxima" and welcomed me in her home. For contacts and camaraderie I am indebted to Drumond Jaime from Rádio Nacional de Angola and to João das Chagas. Drumond was one of my very first contacts and he has always been solicitous, funny, and a source of sober assessments. Chagas invited me to events that he organized with musicians from the older generation and gave me translation work that helped keep me afloat in Luanda's unique economy.

Housing in Luanda is expensive. I am indebted to several people who helped house me and often accepted scones, cookies, carrot cake, pasta, sarcasm, and *boleias* (rides) in lieu of rent. A chance meeting in 1997 with Fernando Marques da Costa led to free housing on my first trip to Luanda. He put me into the hands of Maria Fernanda Vieira, to whom I am tremendously grateful for friendship, shared meals, and reflection on Angola's past. John Fleming, Carrie Manning, and Heidi Gengenbach facilitated my arrival in Luanda. On my second trip to Angola, Jennifer Press and James Moore offered friendship, food, yoga, and a roof in Luanda. François Burato, Heather and Bob Evans, Kara Greenblott, Karla Hershey, Luiza Moreira, Julie Nenon, Anna Richardson, and Lisa Williams-Ferreira and Claudio Ferreira all at one time or another provided a bed or sofa to sleep on, friendship, and *boleias*. Roquinaldo Ferreira and Julie Thompson lent me their scanner, their ears, and Roque's archival skill on more than one occasion. Maria Helena Correia Serra, Paulo Flores, Irina de Almeida, and Paulina Traça extended their unconditional friendship to me.

Gerald (Jerry) Bender, Tammy Bender, Domingos Coelho, Russell Hamilton, Anne Pitcher, and Jean-Michel Mabeko Tali have buoyed my spirits with their enthusiastic responses to and support of my work. I am particularly grateful to Jerry for taking time to help me with contacts, materials, and criticism. Angola lost an old friend with Tammy's passing. Domingos, interlocutor extraordinaire, is always quick with a story or clarification when I need it. Jean-Michel Mabeko Tali, like Jerry an honorary Angolan, is a great friend to me as well as a source of support and conversation about nationalism and all things Angolan. Anne Pitcher has been supportive, encouraging, and inspiring.

At Indiana University I have been warmly welcomed and supported by the History Department, the African Studies Program, and the Gender Studies Department. John Hanson is an exemplary colleague and friend: wise beyond his years, witty, and loyal. Phyllis Martin has been generous with her time, intellectual rigor, and friendship. Akin Adesokan, John Bodnar, Maria Bucur, Matt Guterl, Eileen Julien, Mark Roseman, and Jeff Wasserstrom have given wise counsel and encouragement. Gardner Bovingdon, Konstantin Dierks, and Lauren Morris MacLean helped me wrestle with writing this book and pushed me to refine my words and thoughts. Gardner and Kon along with Sara Friedman, Maddie Bovingdon-Friedman, and Sarah Knott provided an intellectual community and helped make Bloomington home. Kon made the finish line a reality.

In Minneapolis I shared graduate school and lively debate with my inimitable African history cohort: Amy Kaler, Peter Lekgoathi, Premesh Lalu, Wapulumuka Mulwafu, Derek Peterson, Guy Thompson, and Jacob Tropp. Heidi Gengenbach, Maanda Muladzi, Agnes Odinga, and Helena Pohlandt-McCormick were my *mais velhos* in the field. Florencia Belvedere, Sam Bullington, John Collins, Ana Margarita Gomez, Monika Mehta, Hans Nesseth, Amanda Swarr, and especially Mary Thomas offered laughter, meals, and engaging conversation.

To my parents Michael and Carol Moorman, my sister Daphne, my brother-in-law Leo, and my grandfather Sy (if only he were here to see this) for believing I could do this even when they did not understand it and for cheerfully countenancing my determination to trot off to war-torn Angola. To Augusto Cesar Wilson de Carvalho, *kamba do peito*, for being my first friend in Angola, for making me a part of his family, for transcribing and babysitting, and not least of all for teaching me how to dance. To my husband Leandro Lopes, who carried suitcases heavy with photocopies, CDs, and tapes, helped me transcribe, recorded music, and helped me manage negotiating the day-to-day work of teaching, research, and writing. And to Zola Kieza, a huge debt of gratitude for letting me share my attention with this project during her first years on this planet. I wish I could pass off some of the errors, lapses of logic, and debts owed that I have forgotten, but in the end the limitations of this work are all my responsibility.

Abbreviations and Terms

Anangola	Associação dos Naturais de Angola (Association of Natural-born Angolans)
B.O.	Bairro Operário
CITA	Centro de Informação e Turismo (Angolan Center for Information and Tourism)
DGS	Direcção Geral de Segurança (Directorate of General Security)
DIP	Departmento de Informação e Propaganda (Department of Information and Propaganda of the MPLA)
DISA	Direcção de Informação e Segurança de Angola (Angolan Directorate for Information and Security)
ENDIPU	Empresa Nacional do Disco e Publicações (National Company of Discs and Publications)
EOA	Emissora Oficial de Angola (Official Broadcasting Station of Angola)
FAPLA	Forças Armadas Populares de Libertação de Angola (Popular Armed Forces for the Liberation of Angola)
FNLA	Frente Nacional para a Libertação de Angola (National Front for the Liberation of Angola)
JMPLA	Juventude do Movimento Popular de Libertação de Angola (Youth of the MPLA)
LNA	Liga Nacional Africana (National African League)
MPLA	Movimento Popular de Libertação de Angola (Popular Movement for the Liberation of Angola)

OMA	Organização das Mulheres de Angola (Angolan Women's Organization)
PIDE	Polícia Internacional e de Defesa do Estado (International Police for Defense of the State, i.e., the Portuguese secret police)
RNA	Rádio Nacional de Angola (Angolan National Radio)
SCCIA	Serviços de Centralização e Coordenação de Informações de Angola (Angolan Services for the Centralization and Coordination of Information)
UNITA	União Nacional para a Independência Total de Angola (National Union for the Total Independence of Angola)
UNTA	União Nacional dos Trabalhadores de Angola (National Union of Angolan Workers)
angolanidade	Angolanness.
assimilado	Literally, assimilated person. Under the *indigenato* system instituted in the 1920s, assimilados were those mixed-race and African individuals who met the colonial government's criteria for Portuguese citizenship, exempting them from forced labor and taxation. One's status as an assimilado had to be proven and required evidence of the following: ability to speak and write Portuguese, gainful employment (supporting oneself and one's family), sleeping in a bed, and being a Christian (preferably a Catholic). This sector of colonial society was always less than 1 percent of the population, in large part because of the lack of education provided by the colonial system.
baixa	The lower part of the city of Luanda where the port, commercial services, and government ministries are located. In the late colonial period it was called the asphalt city or the European city.
bessangana	A woman of Luanda's urban elite. Bessanganas had a distinctive way of dressing comprising a series of undergarments, four layers of *panos* over a long-sleeved blouse, and a smaller *pano* wrapped around the head.

dikanza	The musicological term for this instrument is scraper. In Brazil it is called a *reco-reco*.
fubeiro	Shopkeeper in the musseques.
hungu	The musicological term for this instrument is gourd-resonated musical bow. In Brazil it is known as a *berimbau*.
indígena	Literally, indigenous person. The majority of the population that could not prove assimilado status were referred to as indígenas. They had no rights and were subject to coercive taxation and forced labor. The *indigenato* system was abolished in 1961 following the rebellions.
lusotropicalism	Brazilian sociologist Gilberto Freyre's theory (*lusotropicalismo*) to explain Brazilian national difference, which argued that the Portuguese were skilled at creating harmonious multiracial societies in the tropics. António Salazar's Estado Novo used this notion to defend its practice of holding onto Portugal's African territories long after most African colonies had achieved independence.
mais velho	Older one. Not necessarily an elder in the sense of someone of a different generation, but a person who is wiser and more experienced. It is a term of respect. In Luanda one also hears the word *kota*, meaning the same thing.
mestiço	Culturally mixed African.
musseque	Urban shantytown. Musseques ringed around the urban periphery are home to the majority of Africans living in Angolan cities, especially Luanda.
pano	A large colorful cloth used as a wrapper.
portugalidade	Portugueseness.
poder popular	People's power. A form of neighborhood organization adopted by the MPLA as strategy and slogan after independence.
quintal	Walled outside area of a home, typically behind the home.

rebita	A dance originating in the mid-eighteenth century that reached its heyday in the first half of the twentieth century. It includes a mix of African and European elements both in the music and with respect to the dress, movements, and behavior of the dancers.
rumba	A Congolese style of music developed in the 1950s and 1960s. Although it was particular to the Congo, rumba was inspired by Cuban rhythms of the 1930s and 1940s that circulated around the globe. It has had an impact on popular music throughout the African continent.
semba	In musicological terms, the beat that defines the rhythm of this particular kind of music. But in general Angolan parlance it refers to the new form of popular urban music produced in Angola in the 1960s and 1970s.
turma	Informal group of friends who would gather to play music in the musseques, especially in the 1950s and 1960s. Turmas were sometimes initially associated with carnaval groups but later had a discrete existence.

Timeline of Nationalism and Independence in Angola

Late 1950s	MPLA and FNLA are founded
1959	"Trial of 50": more than fifty people involved in nationalist organizing are arrested, tried, and jailed for conspiring against the state
1961	In the cotton-producing areas of the north central region, workers rebel against forced cotton production (January)
	In an effort to free political prisoners, Africans attack the Luanda prison where those arrested in the 1959 sweep are jailed (February)
	In the northern coffee-growing area, workers on coffee plantations demonstrate to demand payment of wages in arrears (March)
1961	MPLA and FNLA, independently of one another, take up armed struggle in exile
1966	Jonas Savimbi leaves the FNLA and founds UNITA
1974	A military coup (the Revolution of Carnations) overthrows the Portuguese fascist state
1975	Angola gains independence
1977	Alleged attempted coup by Nito Alves, known as 27 de Maio; MPLA declares itself a Workers' Party at the end of the year
1991	MPLA opens to political and economic reform
1992	War resumes after Savimbi refuses to accept MPLA victory in the first elections
2002	Angolan Armed Forces kill Savimbi. MPLA and UNITA sign Luena Peace Accord.

Timeline of Angolan Music

Late 1950s	The band Ngola Ritmos forms (also Estrela Canora and Grupo Teatral Gexto)
1959	Arrest and imprisonment of Carlos "Liceu" Vieira Dias and Amadeu Amorim (founder and band member respectively of Ngola Ritmos) in Tarrafal prison in Cape Verde; arrest and imprisonment of José Maria dos Santos (Ngola Ritmos band member) in 1960
1961–74	"Golden Age" of Angolan music
1975–89	"Hiatus" in Angolan music

Map of Angola

Introduction

> Em Angola, até o passado é imprevisível.
> (In Angola, even the past is unpredictable.)
>
> —*Christine Messiant*

IN MAY 1998, Alberto Teta Lando, a musician and local businessman in the capital Luanda, told me that three of the most popular musicians from the late 1960s and early 1970s had been killed by the government of independent Angola in 1977.[1] They had too much power over the people, he said. Teta Lando implied that these musicians were more popular and better-known among the populations of Luanda's *musseques*, or urban shantytowns, than were the new leaders of the ruling MPLA (Popular Movement for the Liberation of Angola). In fact, these three were among thousands of people massacred in the repression that followed an alleged coup attempt against the leadership of the ruling party in 1977.[2] Civil war had broken out with independence in 1975, and in 1977 contention within the ruling party erupted into a violent purge when the attempted coup was squelched. Most people I asked later about the murders of the three musicians claimed that the men had been involved with the coup plotters. But it was Teta Lando's suggestion that their demise was related to their music and to their power as musicians that intrigued me.

A few months after that interview, on August 8, 1998, Fernando Martins, a Luandan journalist, opined in the local press that "it is unpatriotic (with all the excesses that the expression implies) to be Angolan and over the age of 15 and to never have heard of Os Kiezos. Perhaps it would be easier to tolerate someone who did not know the name of the ocean that bathes the Angolan coast."[3] Os Kiezos was a band formed in the late 1960s. It was one of the most popular bands, if not the most popular, during the period in which David Zé, Urbano de Castro, and Artur Nunes, the three murdered musicians to whom Teta Lando referred, were also at the height of their popularity. Martins's claim appeals to the cultural bases of the nation more than to the politics of nationalism. He humbles the bombast of nationalist politics by locating patriotism not on the battlefield or in the political arena but in the practices and sounds that permeate everyday life, such as music. He is concerned with what makes the residents of the country Angolans. It is not enough, Martins implies, to be born in the territory. To be Angolan is located somewhere beyond the happenstance of birth and geography, if not in having heard this band then at least in having heard *of* them, and in knowing their style of music and the context of its creation and performance. In other words, one's *angolanidade,* or Angolanness, is less about knowing where one is located physically than about knowing where one is historically and culturally. And, in Martins's estimation, that place is fundamentally defined by the music of the 1960s and 1970s.

Lando's sketch of the political power of musicians and Martins's evocation of Os Kiezos and its milieu summon a history normally associated with the nationalist armed struggle for independence waged between 1961 and 1974. Their comments link music and nation, culture and politics, and in doing so they force us to reconsider the dominant nationalist narrative of Angolan history. In temporal terms, the dominant narrative reduces culture to a protonationalist moment of "discovering our identity" and to a postindependence nation-building project. In spatial terms the narrative pivots on the actions and thoughts of political leaders, primarily men, who were in exile or were part of the guerrilla forces based along Angola's borders. It is a curious feature of the narrative of Angolan history that the story of nationalism unfolds almost entirely outside and on the margins of the country.[4] The absence of activity with political consequence within the Angolan territory is improbable. Therefore, at the simplest level this book tries to answer the questions that emerge from the contradictions between Lando's and Martins's comments on the one hand and the dominant historical narrative on the other. What was the relationship between politics and culture inside Angola while the war for independence, for political sovereignty, was being waged primarily along the country's borders and in the international public sphere? What purchase does culture give us on politics in this period? And what is the relationship between the cultural nation and state formation?

I argue that it is in and through popular urban music, produced overwhelmingly in Luanda's musseques, that Angolan men and women forged the nation and developed expectations about nationalism and political, economic, and cultural sovereignty. They did this through the social relations that developed around the production and consumption of music. Lyrical content and musical sound mattered, but audiences and musicians gave them meaning in context. In other words, music in late colonial Angola moved people into nation and toward nationalism because it brought them together in new ways: across lines of class and ethnicity, through the intimate yet public politics of gender, and in new urban spaces.[5] Music created an experience of cultural sovereignty that served as a template for independence. The spread of radio technology and the establishment of a recording industry in the early 1970s, and the complex ways in which Angolans used these media, reterritorialized an urban-produced sound and cultural ethos across the whole territory, far beyond the capital city. This story of cultural practice with political import is barely glimpsed in standard historical accounts of Angolan nationalism.

Even if the cultural sovereignty achieved in the musseques remained invisible to colonial authorities, political agitation did not escape notice. As the independence movements waged armed struggle outside Angola and along its borders, colonial authorities occasionally recognized that the music scene inside the country was politicizing Angolans and feeding a generalized sense of revolt. The colonial police archives contain reports of disruptive parties and music festivals in the musseques,[6] but police also turned a watchful eye on secret meetings, plots to attack military patrols,[7] individuals suspected of supporting guerrillas,[8] and liberation-movement acronyms painted on the walls of homes and shops.[9] Anticolonial agitation and sentiment lurked inside the capital city—inside the musseques—and not only at the country's distant borders. Indeed, it was present inside the music scene. One night in 1967, for instance, the police broke up a drumming session in the musseque Marçal in which the drummers shouted the familiar admonition, "Go back to your land because this here is ours!"[10] Along with guerrilla radio broadcasts from abroad, the music scene in Luanda aroused the concern of colonial authorities. Even if they did not recognize the creation of cultural sovereignty by way of music, the police certainly deemed the musseques worthy of surveillance and found even the smallest moments of political expression worthy of note. This book recuperates what colonial authorities and liberation movements both failed to recognize in the 1960s and 1970s: the direct and the indirect ways that music created nation from inside as well as outside Angola.

AN OVERVIEW OF THE STANDARD NARRATIVE OF NATIONALISM AND INDEPENDENCE

The standard narrative of Angolan nationalism begins in the 1950s, though it locates fraternity in precolonial states and kingdoms, in resistance to Portuguese incursions that began in the fifteenth century, and in the development of a distinct Angolan identity among late nineteenth-century urban intelligentsia. António Salazar's fascist regime, the Estado Novo (New State), rose to power in Lisbon in 1932 and promoted a new wave of Portuguese immigration to Angola in the 1940s.[11] With this influx of immigrants to Angolan cities, especially Luanda, many African civil servants lost their jobs to Portuguese less qualified than they were. As colonial society became more racially segregated and racist, these African elites, known as *assimilados* or assimilated persons, turned away from metropolitan culture. They became increasingly identified with African cultural practices and the Angolan territory and with the majority of Africans, referred to as *indígenas*, that is, indigenous persons or natives.

The colonial government accorded no political representation to Africans either locally or in the metropole, and it banned all political activity that did not support the state. Clandestine political cells in Luanda, Benguela, and Malanje began to develop in the 1950s.[12] In Lisbon, Angolan students gathered with other African students from the Portuguese colonies of Mozambique, Cape Verde, Guinea-Bissau, and São Tomé and Príncipe to form organizations that began to push, often clandestinely, for independence from colonial rule.[13]

In 1959, in what is known as the Processo de 50 (Trial of 50), the colonial government arrested, tried, and jailed fifty-seven Angolans and a handful of Portuguese whom it accused of "activities against the external security of the state."[14] Most were civil servants, nurses, workers, and students from the most educated strata of Africans, although many of them lived or spent their free time in the musseques where the majority of Africans in Luanda lived. Both in Angola and in Lisbon, the authorities targeted with repression all the activities of organizations that had been formed earlier in the decade. Many of the individuals involved fled into exile on the African continent or in European countries other than Portugal.[15]

Armed struggle broke out in 1961 when the colonial state responded violently to three otherwise unrelated rebellions in the Angolan territory.[16] The two existing liberation movements, the Movimento Popular de Libertação de Angola (Popular Movement for the Liberation of Angola, MPLA) and the Frente Nacional para a Libertação de Angola (National Front for the Liberation of Angola, FNLA), saw no alternative but to take up arms against the colonial state.[17] By 1966 a third movement, the União Nacional para a Independência Total de Angola (National Union for the Total Independence of Angola, UNITA), joined the fray.

Division of the nationalist movement into three groups generally followed social, cultural, regional, and political lines drawn in the colonial period.[18] The armed struggle continued until April 1974. In all three cases, the movements' leaderships were based in neighboring countries (in the Congos and Zambia). They waged war primarily from bases in these countries although the MPLA, in particular, and UNITA had bases inside Angola as well (in the Dembos and the far east for the MPLA and in the southeast for UNITA, who in the 1970s began to fight against the MPLA with the support of the Portuguese army). Contact between internal bases and external leadership was notoriously poor.[19] A military coup in Portugal in 1974 toppled the fascist government and set in motion the transition to independence. The three armed movements returned to Angola to become political parties and negotiate joint rule. Negotiations foundered and fighting erupted between the groups, becoming particularly heated in Luanda in July and August 1975.

Shortly after the MPLA declared Angola's independence on November 11, 1975, a civil war began in earnest. The FNLA was quickly eliminated as a viable contender. The next twenty-seven years saw the MPLA, which controlled the new state, fighting UNITA, the rebel forces. As a socialist-oriented ruling party, the MPLA attempted to implement policies that addressed the grievances and divisions created by colonial rule, but with limited success. The civil war unfolded in the context of the Cold War: Cuban troops, doctors, and teachers and Soviet military advisers supported the MPLA, while the United States and apartheid South Africa backed UNITA. Despite the end of the Cold War and of external support, attempts to broker a durable peace, and elections in 1992, the war continued until February 2002 when state military forces shot and killed the rebel leader, Jonas Savimbi, in battle. The two parties signed a peace accord in April of that year. As of this writing in 2008, Angolans still await the first round of postwar elections.

Since the opening afforded by the cease-fire and elections in 1992, revisionist scholars have been contesting the official narrative of the MPLA and, to a lesser extent, those of the FNLA and UNITA. In particular, they have developed a much more nuanced understanding of dissent and struggles within the MPLA, reflected in the large number of individuals whom the party has excluded or who have left over the last quarter century.[20] They point to the diversity of groups and activities, like church-related and messianic movements, in the 1950s, which the official MPLA historical narrative omits.[21] This new scholarly work has been important in chipping away at the party's hegemonic hold on the history of struggle, a hegemony that, as Christine Messiant has pointed out, the party has used not just against the other political parties but also against those within its own ranks.[22] These studies have not, in general, looked beyond political elites, mostly men, or the realm of formal politics to ask questions about popular consciousness, mobilization, or culture. An exception is Inge Brinkman's work, which focuses on the experiences of civilians in southeast Angola during the anticolonial and civil wars. She asserts that "'popular support,' or the lack of it, for the nationalist movements in Angola has been

mentioned only from the perspective of the nationalist movements themselves
... The motives of civilians for supporting or not supporting the nationalist
groups do not become clear. Their views have remained by and large unstudied."[23] That is the historical terrain this book seeks to open up.

THE ARGUMENT

This book offers a different reading of Angolan history from 1945 to 1990. It is
a social history of culture and politics, more specifically of music and nation,
that takes the everyday cultural practices of urban Angolan men and women
as the very essence of the nation's political life.[24] It is a history of the relationship between culture and politics in two critical periods of Angola's history,
namely the late colonial and postindependence periods. In the late colonial
era, culture thrived separate from politics but was often intertwined with it. In
the postindependence period, while politics did not completely erode cultural autonomy, the independent state attempted to use culture to its own
ends in a way that the exiled liberation struggles never could. The conditions
that had converged to create the vibrant urban cultural world of the 1960s and
early 1970s changed quickly after independence. The new state attempted to
culturally engineer the nation, thus reconfiguring the connection between
culture and politics. Developments in the postindependence period underscore the historically contingent relationship between culture and politics
and highlight the distinction between popular intonations and intimations of
nation, on the one hand, and a state-driven project of nation building, on the
other. During the period of the liberation struggle, popular music helped Angolans create an autonomous cultural domain outside the realm of formal
politics, and through that space, it helped politicize them. After independence,
however, the state usurped both autonomous cultural spaces and politicization, thereby attempting to contain and redirect music's previous dynamism.

Popular music emerged as first among cultural practices during the period
in which the nationalist movements were waging an anticolonial war for liberation. Gage Averill, in discussing music in twentieth-century Haiti, has argued: "Emerging in the context of power relations, popular music bears the
traces of those relations."[25] In Angola, too, popular music carried the imprint
of power. However, the meaning of that imprint is not straightforward. In Angola, music was not a cipher for nationalist politics. At least until independence,
it was an autonomous realm, the site of what James Scott calls "infrapolitics":
"the immense political terrain that lies between quiescence and revolt."[26]
This terrain is often misrecognized or misunderstood as apolitical or protopolitical. In late colonial Angola, men's and women's production and con-

sumption of music politicized them and informed their expectations of what politics in independent Angola would look like. When independence arrived, they were not just putty, infinitely malleable in the hands of their leaders; rather, they pushed back with their own hopes and desires.

Music was not simply resistance or cultural distraction from economic and political oppression. Above all, culture inflamed political imagination. Culture in late colonial Angola did not merely reflect social, political, and economic relations and ideas; it produced them.[27] As Laura Fair frames it, "pastimes and politics were not discrete categories of experience . . . they were intimately connected."[28] Music was where the nation was imagined and even lived.[29] So it was that in 1974, before the official arrival of the MPLA in Luanda, a number of musicians and club-goers began organizing in support of the MPLA, translating their cultural savvy and autonomy into political will and mobilization.

I use the term "cultural sovereignty" to denote the autonomy and sense of self-rule that urban Angolans experienced in relation to the production of music and a music scene centered in Luanda's musseque-based clubs. The music scene was not so much outside the gaze of the colonial state as it was misapprehended by it. Attempts by colonial administrators to co-opt music or direct it to colonial or commercial purposes served instead to propel Angolan music further beyond state control. To the degree that clubs and the music scene represented a dynamic the state did not understand and could not capture, it was an autonomous space. But it was more than that. Angolan musicians and audiences transformed autonomous spaces into an experience of sovereignty as they began to imagine an Angola in and on their own terms.[30] This dynamism was the product of urban men and women who created an *angolanidade*, a sense of identity both rooted and cosmopolitan, and who secured it in the beat of a song, the lilt of a dance step, or the fold of a headscarf—and in the shuffle of bills and the ring of coins in the club's cashbox. Riffing on Benedict Anderson, I argue that "sonorous capitalism" was the motor that circulated this new sound and sensibility throughout the territory. Unmoored from the strictures of literacy, the cultural coordinates of nation traveled on the airwaves and on the vinyl singles manufactured in Angola.

Angolans refer to the music from this period as *semba*. They employ it as an umbrella term that gathers other musical rhythms and covers them with its imprimatur of authenticity: "made in Angola by Angolans." However, ethnomusicologists, musicians, and astute music lovers define semba as the unique beat that gives this music its distinctive Angolan sound. In a 2000 article in the Angolan press, António Venâncio asserted that "semba is not the music itself. Semba is simply the rhythm. The rhythm is a part and not the whole of a piece of music. Music is the combination of lyrics, rhythm, voices, melody, and all the other remaining ingredients. A music can be played or sung on the base of semba and it is in this case that we can say that we are in the presence of a music played in semba."[31] With all due respect to musicological precision, the word *semba* in this book refers to the first, more popular definition, and indexes a more ample social meaning. In this iteration, semba includes other genres of popular urban music (rumba, *kabetula*, *kazekuta*, and *rebita*, among others) that were played and refined in the 1960s and 1970s. Semba symbolizes that crucial moment in Angolan history, in the late colonial period, when a new conception of *angolanidade* emerged and engaged the nation. That is why Angolan musician Paulo Flores, in the song entitled "Poema do Semba" or Semba Poem, sings that "semba is our flag."[32] Semba is not only a musical genre to be parsed by ethnomusicologists, but a cultural style with historical depth and purpose that should interest historians.

Intonations is a story about Angolan men and women bringing the nation into being through cultural practice. "Intonations" as a title works at three levels. First, it invokes the musical sense of the word—"the utterance or production (by the voice, or an instrument, etc.) of musical tones"[33]—to underscore the agency of Angolans in singing, dancing, and imagining their nation. Second, it plays on the word's other sense, of variations in tone—"manner of utterance of the tones of the voice in speaking; modulation of the voice; accent"[34]—to suggest that the same word, "nation," or the same words, in lyrics for example, can have different meanings depending on who is speaking or intoning. Put another way, the story told in *Intonations* contests and cohabits with other narratives, like the standard narrative of nationalism and independence. Third, with a tap of the space bar, intonations becomes "into nations." Angolan musicians and audiences in part developed their politics and sense of nation in and through the activity of producing and consuming music: buying records, hanging out with friends and family, and dancing in clubs moved them "into nation." And there is yet another shade of meaning: at its most colloquial in American English, being "into" the nation means insertion, involvement, and investment in the nation. Coming from the U.S. youth context, this may at first seem irrelevant to Angola in the 1970s, but I mention it here to recall the significance Angolans placed on the question of style and the aesthetics of being hip, hot, or cool as they went about imagining their nation and producing *angolanidade*. In other words, as Robin D. G. Kelley suggests, "what might also be at stake here are aesthetics, style, and pleasure."[35] Young, urban Angolans invested their time, money, energy, and talent in the music scene because they enjoyed it and not only because it was an outlet for sorrow or oppression, although it was that too.

Created in clubs by an emergent musseque elite, popularized in street festivals, and massified and reterritorialized through the technological developments of radio and recorded sound, music in late colonial Angola produced an experience of nation in which urban men and women crafted their investments in and expectations of state independence, political nationalism, and cultural sovereignty. This experience, in part, generated both adherence to and critiques of the MPLA's own nationalist project. The resonance between the internal cultural scene in Angola and the external political movement had more to do with the activities and consciousness that ordinary people developed than with exiled movement leaders' attempts to reach out to them with news of the struggle, encouragements to resist, and the limited clandestine organizing that occurred in urban areas.[36] While the liberation movement leaders had heard this new music, they were oblivious to its power to rally urban Angolans. Even as the music scene and music itself informed popular mobilization around those movements when the exiles arrived back home, the movement leaders did not recognize that music had nourished a politics inside Angola that resonated with their own politics while not being entirely of it. For instance, musseque residents organized themselves for self-defense in the name of the MPLA, long before the party returned to Luanda. They put their consciousness and organizational skills to work for the party and for themselves without being asked to do so.

Thus, when musicians in today's Angola remember the late colonial period, their memories of cultural and economic self-sufficiency do not only critique the failures of the present regime to deliver the promises of independence; they also assert that the participants in the musseque world of cultural production created and defined their nation in terms of cultural and economic, not only political, sovereignty.

Although the book centers on the music scene in Luanda's musseques, the argument is of national relevance. From the late 1950s on, Luanda and its musseques grew rapidly, drawing people from the rural areas and from other cities in the territory. The city's young musseque population hailed from throughout the territory, and the new *angolanidade* in the musseques was created as much by them as by city residents with a deeper urban history.[37] While the musseques were defined in opposition to the *baixa*—the European city center—in the Manichean divisions between black and white, sand and asphalt, they were in no sense hermetically sealed off from the modernity that the baixa symbolized. Nor were they cut off from the rural world of agricultural production and colonial exploitation. Luanda's population represented the nation in terms of both its geographic mobility and its cultural vibrancy. Musseque residents put this diversity of experience to work in music, especially in semba, where they created a new political consciousness and cultural glue called nation.

NATION AND NATIONALISM

In order to recount the history of music and nation in Angola and in order to make sense of the comments by Lando and Martins that open this chapter, we need to linger on the distinction between nation and nationalism. In the simplest terms, nation refers to a sense of "we-ness" that is mapped both territorially and culturally. Nationalism takes this collective sensibility of being distinct to the political level and makes a claim for sovereignty and the establishment of a state based on this difference. Scholarly literature distinguishes between nation, the cultural formation, and nationalism, the political project. In Eric Hobsbawm's rendering, nationalism presupposes, and usually even forges in its own image, nation: "Nationalism comes before nations. Nations do not make states and nationalisms but the other way round."[38] Nation does not require nationalism, but nationalism's need to rewrite the past in the service of its teleology does shape the way we conceptualize nation. In Hobsbawm's telling, then, culture follows politics. Moving in the opposite direction, Benedict Anderson places cultural systems, technologies, and economic processes at the center of his study of the nation as an "imagined community." Anderson asks what it is that makes it possible to conceptualize the nation and, to a lesser extent, how it is produced officially once the institution of the nation-state is in place.[39]

Like Anderson's work, this book does not prioritize nationalism over nation but emphasizes the centrality of cultural practice to political imagination to assert that politics emerges as much from culture as vice versa. Like Partha Chatterjee, I argue that political imagination is culturally specific and is not exhausted by the Euro-American model Anderson proposed.[40] Indeed, the histories of nations in Africa and Asia emerging from and against the colonial yoke, and the study of these histories in a postcolonial analytic, point to the ways that nation is intertwined with histories of empire and colonialism.[41] One of the useful things this literature does is jettison a stable notion of "national consensus" in favor of a reading of the nation based on continuous contestation.[42]

Africanist scholars have placed the state, more than the nation, at the center of their analyses of postcolonial life and politics. While Basil Davidson bemoaned "the curse of the nation-state," Mahmood Mamdani emphasized state over nation in the continuity of authoritarianism produced both by colonial regimes and by their only partially reformed successors. Likewise, Achille

Mbembe and V. Y. Mudimbe further shift the terms away from the nation by subsuming the state in the production of knowledge. More frequently, the work of anthropologists and historians has brought the questions of nation and nationalism, culture and politics into focus.

Such work takes up the relation between music and popular politics to elaborate on Chatterjee's riposte to Anderson while also shifting from his emphasis on the intelligentsia to consider how both elites (colonial and postcolonial) and subalterns mark and make the nation in and through music and dance. Susan Geiger's work on gender and culture in Tanganyikan nationalism, Kelly Askew's work on Swahili music and cultural politics in Tanzania, and Thomas Turino's work on popular music and nationalism in Zimbabwe all demonstrate how cultural practices are constitutive of the politics of nationalism in African nations.[43] These three scholars build on work by other Africanists who have pioneered analysis of the connections between a variety of forms of cultural practice and different forms of political power.[44] This groundswell of scholarship creates the opportunity for an interrogation of the significance of popular music to liberation struggles and nationalist politics in Angola.

The historiography and the scholarly literature on Angola (whether in English, French, or Portuguese) is small relative to that written on other African countries, but work on nationalism in Angola is similar in that it focuses on nationalism, the political project, and not nation, the cultural formation.[45] Much of this work was produced around the time of independence. Some of these scholars were scholar activists, that is, people who were themselves involved in, directly or via solidarity work, the struggles to decolonize.[46] Here, the nation is subordinated to nationalism in terms of its political value.[47]

In Angola, the privileging of nationalism over nation, the political over the cultural, has a more specific provenance as well. Portugal's defense of its continued colonial relations long after most African nations had won their independence was based on the culturalist argument known as *lusotropicalismo*.[48] Cláudia Castelo argues that lusotropicalism never became official discourse but that the Estado Novo adopted it in the mid-1950s to counter global support for decolonization. In fact, the Estado Novo used lusotropicalist theories about the Portuguese personality to justify ongoing control of the "overseas territories" (as the colonies were called after 1951) as part and parcel of governance in a multi-continental nation.[49] Thus the Estado Novo used a culturalist argument and a nationalist one at the same time.

Lusotropicalismo was a theory produced by the Brazilian sociologist Gilberto Freyre to explain Brazilian national difference. He asserted that Portuguese culture was uniquely predisposed to produce multicultural, racially harmonious societies in the tropics. While his theories, circulated and debated in Portugal in the 1930s and 1940s, had a following among Portuguese cultural elites, they met with a hostile reception from Portuguese politicians in that era.[50] That changed in the 1950s. The state even went so far as to mail out copies of some of Freyre's books to foreign diplomats.

From then on, the use of culture to define Portuguese difference with respect to other colonizing powers, to distinguish Portuguese rule from the explicitly racially segregationist regimes in Southern Rhodesia and South Africa, and to justify ongoing colonial control made culture suspect as a term of analysis for those who opposed the regime. Social scientists and politicians critical of Portuguese overseas rule wanted to make a broad rational appeal to an international audience. They surmised that they required incontrovertible hard data to bring international pressure to bear on the Portuguese government and to counter Portuguese propaganda circulating in diplomatic circles that claimed that Portuguese colonization was culturally, not economically, driven.[51]

Literature written on the nationalist struggle sought to explain the history of Portuguese colonialism and the three different movements for national liberation to an international audience that knew little about them.[52] These were narratives centered on political figures and events and on the armed struggle. Scholarship produced since the early 1990s maintains this approach but has also sought to expand the history of nationalism beyond the official history of the MPLA, even as the focus has remained on that party.

Yet it would be incorrect to characterize work on Angola as completely ignoring cultural practices. Angolan literature has been the subject of a good deal of research and analysis.[53] Both historians and literary critics of Angola look to Luanda's creole elite of the late nineteenth century as the precursor of the nationalist politics that arose in the late 1950s.[54] But once this sort of backdating nationalism has occurred, most historians leave culture to the literary critics and return to their analyses of formal nationalist politics.

Culture surfaces in two other ways in the work on Angolan nationalism: as propaganda, that is, as an expression of political ends, or as camouflage, that is, as a cover for political activity. Both John Marcum and Jean-Michel Tali identify songs that explicitly supported one party or another as effective propaganda tools.[55] Examples of cultural practice as camouflaged political activity open a clearer trail for this book to tread. Marcelo Bittencourt suggests that creoles in the 1950s used their associations and some soccer clubs as avenues of political contestation.[56] He notes that literature and the press were particularly important in questioning colonialism and that with the passage of time this role was shared increasingly with "music, theatre and other cultural manifestations in an attempt at diversification and flight from repression."[57] Similarly, Christine

Messiant points to the need to clarify the role of groups and associations, like Bota Fogo and Ngola Ritmos (discussed in chapter 2 of this book), whose histories have been disregarded entirely or digested by official MPLA accounts.[58] Implying that culture has transformative qualities, Mário de Souza Clington, a participant in the early days of anticolonial struggle, points to recreational associations and, in particular, the Escola do Samba as having been critical sites of anticolonial sentiment that brought together urban elites and the dispossessed of the musseques before 1961.[59] Lúcio Lara, a key figure in the history of Angolan nationalism and the MPLA, contains the subversive impulses of culture within the confines of the party when he notes that sports and musical groups like Ngola Ritmos, Bota Fogo, and Ngongo, along with other more specifically politically defined groups, were involved in the origins of the MPLA.[60] While cultural practices may provide camouflage for political activity, they are not necessarily only proto-political in a directly institutional sense. If Messiant is right, and Angola's past is unpredictable, then more work remains to be done in formerly unexplored areas like the relation between politics and culture. Contributing to such a project, a study of cultural practice at close range shows that in late colonial Angola music generated cultural sovereignty, political consciousness, and even nationalist activism.

A social and cultural history of music and nation, looking at music in the context of daily life inside Angola during the period of the anticolonial struggle from 1961 to 1975, disturbs the standard nationalist narrative of Angolan history. It puts nonpolitical elites, everyday lives and cultural practices, and the memories of those who experienced late colonial life in Angola at the center of a political story. This book thus travels to politics through cultural practice, taking culture on its own terms and not simply as the handmaiden of politics. The anticolonial nationalist struggle was experienced not only in the bush, in the different politico-military regions established by the MPLA, and in the exile bases of the FNLA in Zaire and UNITA in Zambia, but in the day-to-day lives of those who "stayed behind." Their stories are not present in the nationalist narrative; they are represented only as grim figures of exploitation, as anonymous masses. By taking the experiences of life inside late colonial Angola seriously this book adds a different "nation-view," to borrow Prasenjit Duara's term, to those of the movements and parties typically represented in the literature.[61]

The "nation-view" or fragment of the nation, in Chatterjee's language, at the center of this book shifts the perspective of nation from outside to inside and from rural bases to urban ones. Anticolonial armed struggles, in particular, such as those in Algeria, Angola, Cape Verde and Guinea-Bissau, Kenya, Mozambique, and Zimbabwe are overwhelmingly represented in the literature as rurally based.⁶² Peasant and intellectual leaders, political parties, and international geopolitics drive the narrative. But the experiences of Luanda's musseque residents show that even if Angola's nationalist movements forfeited the urban areas as a terrain of struggle, residents of the cities did not.

This book thus offers a different angle on struggle by way of cultural practice in urban spaces and places. As the colonial state attempted to avert nationalist mobilization and consciousness by banning political engagement, Luanda's musseque residents generated novel political terrain when they imagined their nation in and around music. Their political imagination filled the spaces where the colonial state expected to distract them from their disenfranchisement with the accoutrements of modernization and development. And in so doing they made their nation and their city. As Martin Murray and Garth Myers argue, "Besides their morphological form, their built environment, and their physical infrastructure, cities also consist of an imaginary dimension through which urban residents define themselves and give meaning to their daily lives."⁶³ This book focuses on urban residents' imagination in the late colonial period and thereby brings a historical perspective to a growing literature on contemporary African urban life as well as to a more established body of work on shantytowns in colonial cities.⁶⁴ It brings together nation, city, musseque, and popular culture to limn the dynamics of cultural sovereignty and political nationalism in a decisive phase of Angola's contemporary history.

ON THE TRAIL OF MUSIC AND ON THE POLITICS OF MEMORY

My argument is born of a tension in oral testimonies in which the usual depiction of culture and its standard-bearers is both repeated and contested. In civil war-torn, independent Angola the authorized, if not yet official, history limits the discussion of music and politics to the story of the band Ngola Ritmos.⁶⁵ Everyone I spoke with noted the importance of this band. Indeed, historians of Angola, if they gesture to music at all, consistently refer to this group when they discuss the relationship of culture to nationalism. Formed in the late 1940s by a group of young men who were well-educated civil servants, Ngola Ritmos sought to recuperate, revalorize, and reimagine musical practices by singing in Kimbundu and other Angolan languages and by using local instruments and music drawn from a repertoire of songs sung at wakes, at work, and in worship. Many of the band members were politically active and the band's music had a message that was meant to awaken people to their oppressed condition and its colonial causes.⁶⁶ Because of the explicit involvement of some of the band's members in nationalist politics, and because they were one of the earliest bands to experiment with new forms of Angolan music, Ngola Ritmos is offered as the epitome of the relationship between music and politics. The band has become iconic, remembered in Agostinho Neto's poem "Içar da bandeira" (Raise the Flag), in José Luandino Vieira's novel *A vida verdadeira de Domingos Xavier* (The True Life of Domingos Xavier), and in Jorge Macedo's impressionistic memorial *Ngola Ritmos* (a pamphlet in a series entitled "Works on Angolan Nationalism"). It was also eloquently elegized and historicized in Angolan filmmaker António Ole's documentary *O Ritmo de Ngola Ritmos* (The Rhythm of Ngola Ritmos). In 1998, a journalist writing in the national daily paper proposed that the birthday of the band's founder, Carlos do Aniceto "Liceu" Vieira Dias, be made a national holiday.[67] These voices have all contributed to producing Ngola Ritmos as part of "dominant memory."[68]

But why was it, then, that Fernando Martins's article (quoted near the beginning of this chapter) made familiarity with Os Kiezos and not Ngola Ritmos a condition of being Angolan? In conversations and interviews with Angolans I began to notice a difference between the way people spoke about Ngola Ritmos and the way they spoke about the music from the period in which Os Kiezos, and bands like them, dominated the cultural scene. The women and men I interviewed were in no way dismissive of Ngola Ritmos, but it was not the music they associated with the club scene, the street festivals, and the radio. People became animated and enthusiastic when recounting their memories of the clubs, parties, street festivals, and music of the 1960s and 1970s—singing to me, describing in detail and with delight the dancing, the romantic intrigue, even the clothes they wore. The very things we are taught to distrust as romanticization of the past—vibrancy, nostalgia, and emotion—became impossible for me to dismiss as simply embellishments of memory. When I listened more closely I heard people speaking of their pride and a limited economic self-sufficiency that helped fuel a cultural world defined, owned, and produced by Angolans themselves.

This tension between asserting the foundational status of Ngola Ritmos in the late 1940s and an emotional investment in and attachment to what is considered the golden age of Angolan music in the late 1960s and early 1970s is part of a struggle over the history of nationalism and over politics. It is part of a larger process that scholars of oral history call the "social production of memory"—a process in which everyone participates, albeit unequally, and one that is structured by tensions produced between and within public representations and private memory.[69] In this case, public representations limit the history of music and politics to Ngola Ritmos, while private memory (which can also be collective) at once affirms that connection and uses it to contest the way that the broader narrative of nationalism overlooks the lives and practices of those Angolans who did not go to fight in the armed struggle.

Cultural producers including musicians, emcees, club owners, and dancers construct a genealogy in which the music of the 1960s and 1970s is heir to the practice of Ngola Ritmos. This is articulated in a chronology that places Ngola Ritmos at the beginning of Angolan popular music in the late 1940s and has their musical style adapted and elaborated in the late 1960s in what the scholar and musician Jomo Fortunato terms "the consolidation of semba."[70] But it is also apparent in the oft-repeated phrase "the music had a message." In saying this, Angolans claim not just a stylistic legacy for the music of the late 1960s but a political one as well.

However, between the heyday of Ngola Ritmos and the golden age of Angolan music the political atmosphere changed dramatically. Along with more than fifty others, some Ngola Ritmos band members were jailed for nationalist activities in 1959 and 1960 in the notorious Processo de 50. When three armed rebellions broke out in various parts of the country in 1961, the colonial government responded with extreme violence, napalming villages and beheading insurgents, and heightened political repression. Part of the counterinsurgency policy attempted to improve the day-to-day lives of Angolans in hopes that this would win their loyalty to the Portuguese state. The kind of politico-cultural involvement symbolized by Ngola Ritmos, that kind of music with a message, was simply no longer possible.

Angolan cultural producers today reaffirm the foundational status of Ngola Ritmos and lay claim to that legacy in order to assert that their own music, and their own cultural activities, were politically relevant even in the more stringent and severe political conditions of the 1960s and 1970s. The outbreak of armed struggle dislocated nationalism from its cultural bases in Luanda's musseques to guerrilla bases mainly along the country's borders and to metropolitan centers of exile activity. The narrative of nationalism also left the country, trailing political elites from Lisbon to Paris, from Kinshasa to Brazzaville, from Algiers to Dar es Salaam, and detecting the pulse of the masses in the troops and among the few civilians at guerrilla bases. Those who "stayed behind" were largely absent from the standard nationalist narrative—but not, I argue, from the politics of the 1960s and 1970s, nor from the popular memory of that era.[71]

In my conversations with musicians and other cultural producers I began to hear a narrative of Angolan music that ran deeper and wider than the story of Ngola Ritmos and that could not fit neatly within the narrative of Angolan nationalism. The musicians and other cultural producers I interviewed formally, as well as the countless friends, acquaintances, and colleagues I spoke with informally, all waxed lyrical and nostalgic about the music and the music scene of the late 1960s and early 1970s. Often in interviews my informants would unravel the present and rethink it with the past—either in their careful reconstruction of seemingly trivial details or in their claims on and critiques of the ruling party and its political elite. What came out of these conversations had as much to do with economic hardship in the present as with nostalgia for the past. Most crucial for Angolans was remembering a time when they were able to construct a thriving cultural scene despite material hardship. They crafted a cultural sovereignty in clubs and around the production of music that helped point them toward an imagined future of national independence.

Angolan cultural producers claim the legacy of Ngola Ritmos in order to enter the narrative of nationalism. Once there, they unfurl memories rich in detail and emotion that contest the silence in the standard nationalist narrative that leaps from Ngola Ritmos to the politically engaged music of post-1974 independent Angola. Not content just to fill in a lacuna, these musicians then go on to disrupt the chronology again by claiming that in the history of Angolan music, independence marks a "hiatus" or "moment of crisis" for music.[72] According to their narrative, the music of the 1960s and 1970s, music that for them defined the nation, should have become the national music at independence. Instead that music stopped at independence. The hiatus was marked by the official deployment of music as a means to build the nation under unstable conditions that included civil war and the control of dissent in the wake of the attempted coup in 1977. The state took over all musical production. Musicians from the earlier period found work performing and recording music for state institutions. But the music was different. It had to be music that sang about the new nation, taking up the socialist-inspired themes of yearly or biennial production goals and extolling the MPLA heroes and martyrs as the only true nationalists.[73] Many musicians joined the ruling party and undertook this work with enthusiasm. But they all mentioned that the tenor of the music had changed and that the music of this period did not embody *angolanidade* as had the music of the late 1960s and early 1970s.

When Angolan cultural producers recounted the past and talked about the history of music, they both affirmed the official narrative of Angolan nationalism and disputed it by insisting that the cultural world of the musseques was as important to independence as was the armed struggle in the bush. In other words, when cultural producers decoupled the history of music from that of nationalism, they insisted on the irreducibility of music to politics while also showing that the cultural world of late colonial Angola was politically significant: they offered a political history in cultural terms. And to a certain extent, they challenged a narrative of nation sanctimonious with sacrifice by offering one leavened with pleasure.

COSMOPOLITANISM

Musicians and audiences alike often described themselves and their scene as cosmopolitan. The music scene in Angola was composed of a set of cosmopolitan practices, no less African for incorporating modes of articulation and ideas considered to be European.[74] This was true both at the level of music, where European instruments were adopted, and at the level of politics, where ideas like nationalism took hold.[75] With cosmopolitanism Angolans moved toward nation and not away from it. They claimed national sovereignty through worldliness, instead of opposing one to the other.[76] In particular, Angolans used cosmopolitanism to situate themselves beyond the bounds of the fascist Portuguese colonial state and in a world upon which they could make claims and that they hoped would makes claims on them. Discussing music, cosmopolitanism, and nationalism in Zimbabwe, Thomas Turino argues that musical and political forms become internalized and integral to the people in the group: "This is part of who they are."[77] Pushing this one step further, Bob W. White asserts that "unlike 'globalization' or 'modernity,' cosmopolitanism is not something that happens to people, it is something that people do."[78] This doing is at the center of James Ferguson's discussion of cosmopolitanism as a style that is "motivated, intentional, and performative but not simply chosen or lightly slipped into."[79] In such a reading, culture in the musseques is a dynamic mode of African self-articulation rather than a European imposition.

Cosmopolitanism thus opens up an analysis of cultural practice, change, and mixing that avoids both the pitfalls of Portuguese exceptionalism as proposed in lusotropicalism as well as the too-narrow sense of cultural nationalism offered in calls for African authenticity. In fact, if *angolanidade* was a rejoinder to colonialism's *portugalidade*, then cosmopolitanism was urban Angolans' riposte to lusotropicalism. Angolans living in the musseques drew upon European cultural resources in crafting their own way of being and in so doing saw themselves as part of something located both in and far beyond the musseques. In creating their own clubs, styles of music, ways of dressing and dancing, and their own scene, Angolans in the musseques conceptualized their own culture as on a par with those defined in discrete national units like Brazil, Cuba, France, and Zaire. They developed a cultural self-sufficiency, style, and independence that resonated with cultures beyond theirs and yet was particular to Angola.

In this way, Angolans not only imagined but in fact lived and created the conditions of the Angolan nation in cultural terms even as they were prohibited from actualizing it in the political realm. Aware of the guerrilla struggle and the fact of independence in almost all other African countries, they cultivated a latent nationalism in these practices. They achieved cultural sovereignty and political consciousness *before* gaining political independence. Looking at the music scene, that is, the social relations involved in the production and consumption of music, we can locate the cosmopolitan imaginings of the Angolan nation that became central to the ability of exiled nationalist parties to establish themselves as representatives of the nation when they returned to the country and specifically to Luanda in late 1974.

SOURCES AND METHODOLOGY

The afternoon I interviewed Teta Lando we met in his store just off the Marginal, the paved boulevard that skirts Luanda's bay and is the locale of many of the city's high-rises and government ministries. Here, in the shadows of political and commercial power, was a small music shop, its windows and doors covered with metal grating, its mirrored shelves graced with a few old LPs. Glass cases displayed neatly stacked CDs, and a single spinning rack of cassette tapes offered as much music from the Congo, Brazil, and Cape Verde as from Angola. In 1998 Lando operated one of only two such establishments in Luanda, but unlike the other (RMS) he was also reediting music from the 1960s and 1970s through his music production company Teta Lando Produções. As we sat in his office at the back of the store I worried that the whirr of the fan that kept us comfortable in the otherwise stifling heat was going to drown out our voices on my low-tech tape recording. That worry was soon overshadowed by another as the fan suddenly slowed, then stopped, and the hush of a power outage settled upon us. This is but one small example of how the exigencies of life in war-torn, infrastructure-stressed Angola shaped my research.

The evidentiary bases of this book are interviews, colonial social science studies, the popular press of the late colonial period, music obtained from the National Radio Station collection, record album covers, and material from the archive of the PIDE (Polícia International e de Defesa do Estado, or International Police for Defense of the State—that is, the Portuguese secret police).[80] Over the course of the time in which I did my research, the music from the late colonial period started to become more available. It was played more frequently on the radio, and collections and reissues of music from the golden age began to appear.[81] Forthcoming works by Angolan scholars who are also musicians—Jorge Macedo, Jomo Fortunato, and Mário Rui Silva—elaborate the technical elements of urban popular music, known as semba, as well as the history of its primary innovators and its social insertion.[82] The musician and historian Carlos Lamartine and the musician and cultural worker Dionísio

Rocha, though they have not published on music, regularly appear on television and radio as authorities on the history of popular Angolan music. But, by and large, the airwaves and the turntables of disc jockeys at parties and at clubs still do not highlight this music except for programs and shows directed to aficionados and devotees.

The written record offers rather paltry resources for the researcher interested in cultural questions. The collection at the Angolan Historical Archives is richest for the distant past, that is, the sixteenth through nineteenth centuries. The archive has material on the twentieth century, but for the most part it is not catalogued and is therefore inaccessible.[83] What is available, mainly government-sponsored bulletins and colonial social science material, speaks only elliptically if at all about culture. Other potential sources that I identified as useful to my study are no longer available, having been either destroyed by the war or removed because of political paranoia. Specifically, the archives of record companies,[84] a crucial musseque newspaper,[85] and documents pertaining to the colonial Angolan Center for Information and Tourism[86] that oversaw many cultural events have all disappeared.

A small body of work on the musseques, mostly social science tracts and journalistic accounts, exists and forms the basis for the analysis in chapter 1. They are all, to varying degrees, imbued with the racism and paternalism that characterized colonialism in general and Portuguese colonialism in particular. For example, when it comes to talking about culture, none fails to note the timeless love of "the African" for song and dance. Popular magazines produced in Luanda for a territory-wide readership in the late colonial period (*Semana Ilustrada, Noite e Dia*, and *Notícia*) take a more colloquial approach to urban Angolan culture but offer little sense of what cultural practices meant to most Angolans. Articles about African performers and performances in the musseques, and about music festivals, cinemas, and local clubs in the baixa, all provide a window onto a young white Angolan world that complicates and disaggregates the notion of a singular "white" or "Portuguese" or even "colonial" perspective. Furthermore, these magazines had a readership, or at least an audience, far beyond their target audience of white urban youth. Almost everyone I spoke to was familiar with the magazines and had perused them at barber shops, newsstands, or homes of friends. As a result they constituted one of the ways in which the music scene of the musseques garnered an urban and cosmopolitan profile in a nationally distributed medium.

Much of the evidence for my discussion of the radio and its uses by the colonial state and the anticolonial movements derives from material I found in the PIDE archive at the Torre do Tombo in Lisbon. As many scholars have pointed out, although this archive contains a wealth of material, researchers must approach it with great care.[87] Commentaries by PIDE agents often involved much speculation, trials included feints and dodges by arrested activists, and original pieces of evidence are usually only available at one remove—photocopied or transcribed. Finally, these archives, only recently made available, have been used to defame prominent political and social figures, resurrect sullied reputations, and cast new stones. To the extent that such moves generate polemics and debate, this fascist colonial institution still shapes politics in independent Angola. With all this in mind, I looked carefully at the files of people I had interviewed as well as other prominent nationalist figures. Very little of this material enters my analysis because, for the most part, PIDE files only repeated what the people I interviewed had told me about their own activities. I found the richest material on radio and the counterinsurgency program in general. The files on the musseques, largely reports on incidents that punctuated daily life, depict a sense of generalized revolt and support for the nationalist cause among musseque residents that no secondary source has yet recognized.

Interviews helped me plot my navigation of the PIDE archives. But more than that, the interviews are at the center of my argument and of the story I tell. In particular, to get at the meaning and experience of cultural practices, to fill in details about the development of a new musical form including structural aspects related to the growth of a small recording industry, and to understand the significance of radio broadcasting, I rely predominantly on material from interviews I conducted. In total, I interviewed forty-one different people, speaking with ten of them more than once.[88]

I spent roughly three and a half years in Angola over the period 1997–2002 and made a return visit in the summer of 2005. This entire period was marked by the vicissitudes of civil war: failed peace accords, a return to active fighting, a tremendous humanitarian crisis throughout the country, and finally the death of the UNITA leader Jonas Savimbi and a cease-fire, signed one month before my departure from Angola in 2002. The poor condition of local infrastructure—frequent cuts in water and electricity, shabby health care services in a country with rampant malaria, unreliable transport—created daily crises for the people whom I sought to interview (and for me). These, together with the constant struggle to make ends meet, resulted in frequent cancellations and postponements. I had initially thought that given such conditions, people would be reluctant to speak with me. But to my initial surprise, the cultural producers I sought out to interview were welcoming and enthusiastic. However, the daily struggle to put food on the table, pay school fees, find or maintain employment, and preserve the integrity of body, family, and domicile often foiled the best-laid plans for scheduling conversation.

When I did manage to meet with someone, the interview generally began with a set of questions about when and where he or she was born, grew up, and went to school, and family background: this could include material conditions, racial, ethnic, and religious designations, marital status of parents, and educational history. I would then turn to music, if my interlocutor had not already moved our conversation in that direction, by asking how the person started playing and what the music scene was like at that time. Certain generic themes emerged in these conversations: the foundational status of the band Ngola Ritmos, the idea that music had a message that only Angolans understood and that duped the colonial state, the authenticity of music from the late 1960s and early 1970s, the injustice of five centuries of colonial rule, and the misfortune of Angolans to have been colonized by the Portuguese. I consider such repetitions both as "authorized texts"[89] that people use to narrate their lives and offer a common history and as a kind of established rhythm that people repeat, sometimes only in order to then contradict.

The conditions of daily life affected not only whether or not interviews came to pass but their content as well. Far from being grounds for dismissal of interviews as illegitimate historical sources, the presence of the present in interviews not only "speaks truth to power," as the past is mobilized to criticize current leaders and set the record straight, but yields meaningful historical material. The past and present were intricately interwoven in the narrative performances, making it impossible, if indeed it is even desirable, to untangle data from discourse. Here I follow Susan Geiger:

> While I assumed that the filter of present socioeconomic conditions and health would shape women's remembrances of past political activities, I had not considered the extent to which women's accounts of their own lives in the past, as well as in the present, expressed what nationalism in Tanzania was most significantly about.[90]

While nostalgia may be the form for reflection on the past, when musicians and other cultural producers talk about music and the music scene, they do not glorify colonial rule but instead remember their own ability to secure cultural sovereignty, make music a respectable profession, manage club affairs and daily life, and inspire political consciousness.[91]

Angolan men's and women's characterization of the late 1960s and early 1970s as a time when they could provide for themselves (albeit with a struggle) is in part a comment on the present, a criticism of the harsh material conditions created by civil war and economic and political mismanagement. Initially, I thought that was all it was. While these privations of the present throw the past into relief, they do not evacuate it of all meaning. When Angolans remember and reflect on the late colonial period, they do say something about the past, about what people valued in that earlier experience and what they hoped for from independence, even if today's difficult conditions tend to make the past look rosier than it was. I refer to what people valued as "cultural sovereignty," and I argue that it both produced the experience of nation and shaped urban Angolans' expectations about the dividends of national independence.

This book foregrounds the urban as an analytic for understanding the relationship between music and nation. Yet gender and class were dimensions of urban experience through which the nation was inflected and to which I therefore give distinct attention. My analysis of gender has two components. First, women were active in cultural organizations and in politics in the 1950s to a degree as yet unrecognized in current scholarship. Second, and by contrast, female musicians were few in the club scene during the 1960s and 1970s, even though women served as important figures in song lyrics and were critical members of audiences. For women to perform music on stage threatened to impugn their respectability, while for men, work in the music industry enhanced their status in society. Men dominated the production and commercialization of music, and audiences revered them as public figures. In a context where Angolans had no political representatives on the public scene, male musicians seized the limelight. With this newfound social prominence and prestige, male musicians came to symbolize as individuals what the music clubs symbolized as institutions: cultural sovereignty and national pride.

Often what gender differentiated, class put back together. Angolans of both sexes described themselves and their families as having been "middle class" in the late colonial period. This meant they had access to amenities like education, lived in modest cement or improvised homes but not huts, and occupied a social space between Europeans living in comfort and poorer Angolans recently arrived from rural areas. Such memories of economic well-being, no matter how modest, nevertheless have had no place in the official line of the different liberation struggles, which portrayed Portuguese economic exploitation of Angolan life and labor as a five-hundred-year constant. But these memories have been confirmed by scholars who point to economic improvements in the late colonial era, primarily to the benefit of an expanding social class labeled "petty bourgeois."[92] Most musicians and other cultural producers belonged to this petty bourgeoisie. They operated the businesses that drove the vibrant urban culture of the late 1960s and early 1970s: the music clubs, the recording studios, the radio stations, and all the other institutions of "sonorous capitalism." Significantly, members of this social class initiated the cultural activities and imagined the *angolanidade* that is still a vital point of reference today.

Class more than gender identity affected how I was received during my years of field research in Angola. No matter how many times I explained that I was a researcher studying history, many musicians and others I approached to talk about music referred to me as a journalist. Thus, I learned that in our conversations Angolans not only were educating me about musical and political history but were positioning me, in some cases, to speak out and speak for them. In other words, the people I interviewed had their own ideas about who our audience was or should be. My whiteness and foreignness (both unstable and shifting designations) marked me as a potential resource and a potential plunderer. People assumed that I was in Angola with support from my own government, and they were always shocked when I told them that I was not and that the folks at the U.S. embassy could not have cared less about my work. Some suspected that I was out to make money off what I was doing.[93] The asymmetries of global power and resource allocation could not help but shape my interviews at some level and quite possibly in ways still imperceptible to me.

With the exception of a few big-name figures, most musicians are worse off economically than they were prior to and just after independence. Many hold fond memories of the colonial period and of the early socialist republic (1975–91) of independent Angola. Interviews were often thick with sentimentality and nostalgia, particularly with reference to a nonpartisan national sentiment, but my conversations also revealed class, ethnic, political, and gender tensions that trouble any facile sense of unity in the past or the present. Musicians criticized the political elite, and those musicians who are a part of it, while simultaneously hoping for patronage from those same people. At the same time, memories of a common sense of purpose and a shared desire for independence superseded the identification of individuals with particular liberation movements.[94]

THE SHAPE OF THINGS TO COME

The book is divided into six chapters and a brief epilogue. Chapter 1, "Musseques and Urban Culture," decolonizes colonial social science material by reading it in light of interviews and secondary sources. Where colonial sources saw a cultural backwater and potential social crisis, I see an urban crucible that produced a distinctly Angolan culture that was neither purely African nor predominantly European. This chapter offers a modest social history of the musseques as a starting point for entering a more specific history of culture and politics.

Chapter 2, "'In the Days of Bota Fogo': Culture and the Early Nationalist Struggle, 1947–61," delves into the associations and political activities of the urban elite as they began to define *angolanidade* and sought common cause with the population of the musseques. Urban elites sought to revalorize Angolan cultural practice in the music, poetry, and theater they created in small groups and in larger associations. Here I introduce a discussion of gender by adopting the strategy of women's historians who seek to make women visible. The early involvement of women in politico-cultural organizing serves as a counterpoint to their engagement in the music scene in the later period. Why, if women were so central early on, did they become marginalized as cultural producers in the later period?

This question is a central concern in chapter 3, "Dueling Bands and Good Girls: Gender and Music in Luanda's Musseques, 1961–75." Here the focus is the music scene and the growth of clubs in Luanda's musseques as the war for independence was being waged by guerrilla fighters on the borders of the country. The music scene was gendered terrain. Women were central to the meanings of the scene but were sidelined as producers, marking a shift from earlier forms of cultural production. Masculinity came to define the musical nation-space through associations between sports, rivalry, and bands just as fame came to be measured in the number of girlfriends one had. Nonetheless, both women and men identified this music as truly Angolan and fondly remembered an experience of self-sufficiency or sovereignty—culturally and, to a limited degree, economically.

Chapter 4, "'Ngongo Jami' (My Suffering): Lyrics, Daily Life, and Social Space, 1956–75," takes a closer look at some popular song lyrics and at musical performance spaces. Conscious of the limitations that come with trying to freeze as text what was a dynamic performance, I look at song texts in order to show the different ways in which lyrics signified: they made individual suffering collective, they criticized colonialism, they offered social critique, and they very often told of loves lost and found. The new musical style itself became the national lingua franca. This novel style, called semba, and its companion style rumba,[95] represented and were used to construct an urban Angolan experience and sound that was locally rooted and internationally resonant. The music gained in popularity and range as it moved from the backyards of musseques to public festivals in the streets and cinemas of those same neighborhoods, and ultimately throughout the territory of Angola.

Chapter 5, "Radios, Turntables, and Vinyl: Technology and the Imagined Community, 1961–75," investigates the dissemination of music throughout the Angolan territory. How did music produced from Luanda's musseques make it to other areas of the country? Radio and the recording industry reterritorialized the musseque-produced music and made it national, not just by spreading it but by providing a means through which people could actively associate it with the armed struggle and with a wider world of independent nations and national cultures. Angolans used radio to actualize the "imagined community" of nation by connecting discrete "meanwhiles" across time and space.

Chapter 6, "The Hiatus: Music, Dissent, and Nation Building after Independence, 1975–1990s," examines the changes that occurred in the relationship between music and nation once independence was declared. I revisit the events of May 27, 1977, in light of what musicians told me about their involvement in turn-of-independence politics in Luanda's musseques. After a period in which music became politicized and implicated in the politics of the civil war, music in the 1990s and the first years of this millennium has again left party politics for the politics of daily life and the imagination of nation. The fact that musicians use the intertwined relation of music and nation to speak about and make claims on the current government and political leaders indicates how the formation of new elites is contested in cultural terms.[96] Music also continues to be a means of reflecting on daily life, transcending individual suffering, performing and thus constructing gendered roles and relations, and showing that fun can be subversive and subversion can be fun. At the same time, music continues to be a serious and sometimes deadly business, something I take up in the epilogue.

Before turning to the brief social history of the musseques, play and listen to at least some of the CD that accompanies this book. Imagine that it is a few days after payday in late colonial Luanda. You don the new duds commissioned from your tailor or seamstress—for men, low at the hip and wide at the ankle, and for women, a natty short-waisted jacket, big fabric buttons, an A-line skirt, and an African print head cloth to match. Outside the club you stand in line with others equally resplendent in new or newly pressed attire, undaunted by the dust of unpaved musseque streets. The air is tinged with the scent of grilling chicken and animated by the polite greetings of friends, cousins, and acquaintances (handshakes for the gentlemen, kisses on the cheeks for the ladies). You can hear the band inside checking their instruments as the great Franco's "On Entre OK, On Sort KO" (You Enter OK and Leave KO) plays in the background. Meanwhile, you wait for the bouncer's scrutiny to produce approval, registered only as he steps aside to let you in. As you pay the entrance fee with Portuguese tender and step across the lintel, you leave Portuguese rule behind. Nicely dressed couples sit with friends at well-appointed tables in this Angolan-owned and -run establishment. Young folks stand in small groups near the bar, sipping bottled Coca-Cola through waxy paper straws or drinking cold Cuca beer from brown glass bottles. Leaning against the bar, a musician, graying at the temples, lights a Caricoco cigarette, as much to dangle over his whiskey as to smoke. He tells his friend that he knows every James Brown hit by heart but that Tio Liceu ("Liceu" Vieira Dias of Ngola Ritmos) is his hero. He wonders aloud, though quietly, whether Tio Liceu is still composing even in jail in Cape Verde. By and large such *sotto voce* topics are drowned out by gregarious chatter—speculations about whether or not Urbanito's new single will go gold, invitations to picnic on Mussulo Island, gossip about how quickly Tia Lourdes will recover from the paraffin burns she recently suffered. Suddenly there is silence. Six band members leap onto the stage, clad in wide-lapelled suits, shiny shoes, and tailor-made shirts of tyrilene fabric. As they grab guitars, position a drum, and pick up a *dikanza*, the audience bursts into applause and whistles.

1 ∽ Musseques and Urban Culture

LUANDANS ASSERT AN imaginary of nation and contemporary history born of particular musseques. In casual conversations and in interviews, Luandans repeatedly offered me a meaningful map of their city. Bairro Operário was the birthplace of nationalism and the quintessence of musseque culture, Bairro Indígena (indicated as B.I. on the map of Luanda) was the home of future politicians, and Marçal was the cradle of Angolan music.[1] Luandans are known for being very neighborhood-centered in their identities: where you grew up, where you live, and the neighborhood with which you identify might say more about you than your political affiliation, your race, or your age.[2] And yet, the association of particular musseques with particular aspects of the Angolan nation—consciousness, political leadership, and culture—transcends individual ties. When people told me that such and such a neighborhood was the birthplace of this or that it was proffered as a national fact and not as an article of faith or a demonstration of loyalty to one's neighborhood. Of particular import to this book is the way these casual commentaries link culture, music, and nationalism to suggest a causal relationship. The musseques were the crucible where popular urban Angolan music was created, and within and around it a sense of nation.

Alternately damned and lauded, the musseques, while on the physical periphery of the ever-growing city, have always been at the center of urban discourse and life. They are where the majority of Africans (as well as a small number of poor whites) in colonial Luanda found housing when they came to the city to enter the colonial labor market. Tracts written in the late 1960s and early 1970s by social scientists in the employ of the Portuguese government

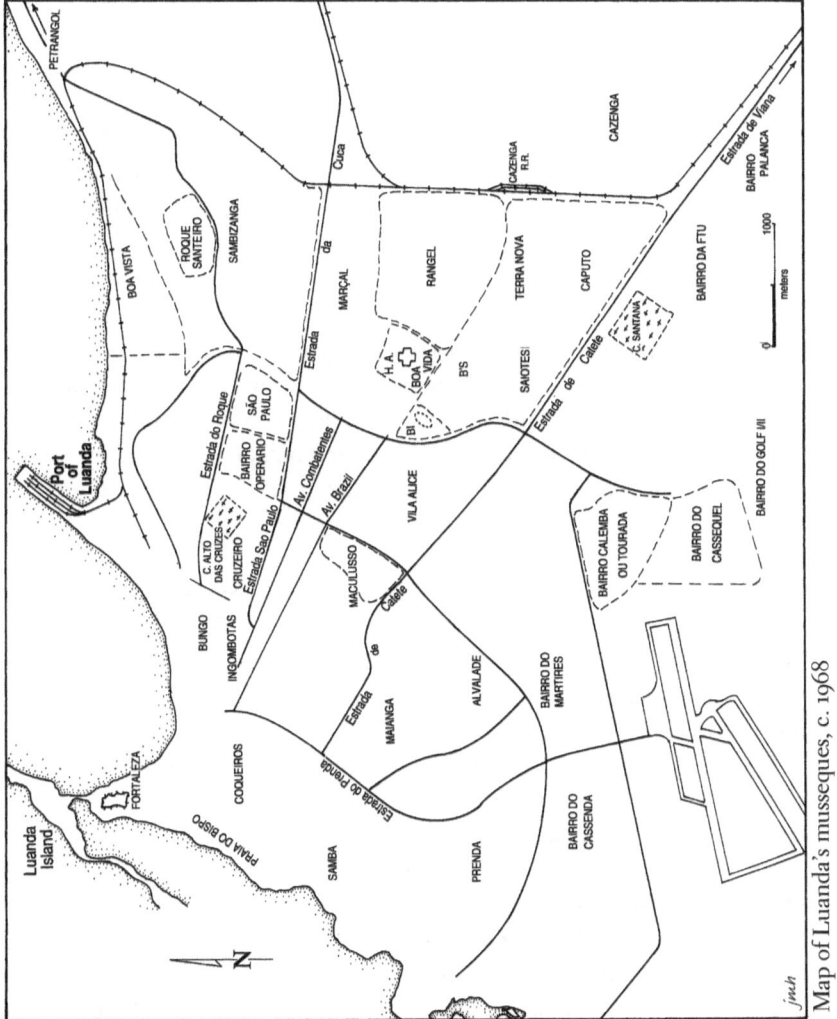

Map of Luanda's musseques, c. 1968

depict the musseques as peripheral urban spaces torn between the tradition, rules, and communal structures of rural life and the modernity, civility, and infrastructures of urban life. These works simultaneously reflect colonial government preoccupation with order and control (thanks to the Estado Novo's censorial clutch), refract it through the lenses of modernization and development current at the time, and unwittingly offer a host of information inimical to colonial ideology.

Based primarily on census data, police files, and information collected in interviews, colonial social science analyses sanitize the musseques. The rich histories recounted by the people I spoke with are nowhere to be found. Thus, the social science literature on the musseques is like much of the literature on urban Africa dating to the postwar period and continuing to the present in that its

> tendency to project fluid, contingent, and historically-specific situations into ahistorical indicators of a permanent condition of failed urbanism effectively substitutes assertion for critical investigation and analysis. . . . [It] tends to ignore the resourcefulness, inventiveness, and determination of the countless millions of ordinary people who somehow manage to successfully negotiate the perils of everyday life.[3]

While keeping those limitations in mind, we cannot and should not simply dismiss colonial social science studies of the musseques. This material contains important information about who lived in these urban shantytowns, how some people spent their money and time, and what concerns the colonial administration had about them.

For Angolan writers of the colonial period who championed nationalist cultural values and political rights, the musseques symbolized the exploitation of Africans by the colonial system and the resilience of African culture despite such conditions. Like Richard Rive's representation of Cape Town's District Six in *Buckingham Palace* and Don Mattera's descriptions of Sophiatown in *Gone with the Twilight*, works by Angolan writers located cultural rhythms that outpaced oppression in the musseques. They sketched three-dimensional characters where the colonial social scientists tabulated two-dimensional statistics. Along with a handful of social scientists sympathetic to the Angolan struggle for independence, they challenged the Estado Novo's representation of itself and its history of colonization.

In this chapter I engage three perspectives on the musseques: those of colonial social scientists, those of literary nationalists, and those of social scientists sympathetic to the Angolan cause. I use the latter two to reread the former. This has three outcomes. First, it reveals a struggle over representation of the musseques. Second, by bringing the musseques into focus, it takes the next step in a modest corrective to a literature on Angolan nationalism that centers on exiled leaders, guerrilla bases, and liberated zones. Third, the interface between the world of colonial policy and ideology and the world of the musseques comes into view. Nationalist leaders, and academics in solidarity with them, overturned what they considered the Estado Novo's flimsy cultural argument (lusotropicalism) with the hard facts of racial discrimination in colonial employment, education, and agricultural policy. But musseque residents offered a cultural riposte with a political direction. That riposte is the central concern of this book.

For the majority of Africans who lived there, the musseques were a rich cultural and social world limited but not entirely defined by the colonial order. People resident in the musseques in the 1950s through 1970s did not see themselves in the colonial social science depictions of social tragedy. Nor did they fully recognize themselves in the nationalist writers' poesy. They had little access to either, in fact. Their memories and music tell yet another story of the musseques. Here hardship and joy cohabitate. Here urban and African comingled to produce the urbane. Here *angolanidade* was a cosmopolitan practice that led into nation instead of away from it. But first, a more panoramic view of the history of the musseques.

ORIGINS AND SOCIAL COMPOSITION OF THE MUSSEQUES

For most of Angolan colonial history, from the days of the capital's founding in the late sixteenth century to the mid-twentieth century, Luanda's population grew in fits and starts, and with it, the city's boundaries and the musseques. Halting growth during the first three centuries of this period gave way to frenetic urbanization after World War II.[4] Founded in 1576, the city of Luanda, on the shores of the Atlantic Ocean, was the place from which the Portuguese conducted relations with kingdoms in the interior. It occupied a small space delimited by the bay on the west and rocky outcroppings to the north and south. Except for a small fishing population on the island across the bay, the area was uninhabited. Unpropitious agriculturally, it was, if nothing else, easily fortified and boasted a natural deepwater harbor. Until the independence of Brazil and the abolition of the slave trade in the first half of the nineteenth century, Luanda was first and foremost a port of dispatch in the slave trade. Africans captured in the interior were sent to Brazil as slaves from Luanda and Benguela, a coastal city further south.[5] The majority of Luanda's population in this period (including clergy and public servants) worked with the slave trade in some capacity.

With the abolition of the slave trade in 1836, Luanda's population stabilized and grew. The city's service sector and commerce developed accordingly.[6] Luanda garnered a novel political profile: no longer dependent on Brazil, it became a significant Portuguese colonial capital in its own right. By the late nineteenth century, a creole society and *mestiços* (culturally mixed Africans) held sway. Mestiços occupied positions of power in government, clergy, and military.[7] This new local elite expressed its self-consciousness as a group and as Angolans in the burgeoning local press.[8]

António Salazar's fascist Estado Novo ascended to power in Lisbon in 1932. Salazar centralized administrative power in the metropole and reinvigorated a policy of white occupation in Angola. These policies embodied a new political agenda that spelled the decline of Luanda's creole society and a shift in the colonial state.[9] White immigration combined with a boom in coffee production to create an "explosion," as Ilídio do Amaral described it, in Luanda's urban growth, beginning in the 1940s and increasing in the postwar period.[10] Luanda held an ever-larger proportion of the colony's population, and the white population in particular, while the centralization of power in Lisbon circumscribed the decision-making power exercised in the colonial capital. Racial stratification intensified. By the mid-twentieth century these social distinctions were mapped onto urban geography. A series of oppositions molded local discourse—between the baixa (lower city) and the musseques (periphery), between the asphalt city and the musseques (sandy places), and between the white city and the musseques (African townships)—and described the socio-economic, racial, and cultural divisions of the city.[11]

Musseque is a Portuguese word deriving from the Kimbundu *mu-seke* which means, literally, "sandy place."[12] It originally referred to areas of the city where the asphalt did not reach. In the work of Portuguese writers and social scientists the word's topographical meaning gave way to a sociological one, regardless of the meaning of musseque in the minds of the inhabitants.[13] Some scholars claim that ever since the Portuguese founded Luanda, musseques had existed to house enslaved Africans and free laborers (along with some Europeans). With time, these places moved farther and farther away from the city center (baixa), first to Ingombotas and Maculusso in the mid-nineteenth century and then to kilometers 3, 4, and 5 on the city limits.[14] Fernando Mourão points out that "plans of the city from the beginning of the [twentieth] century did not signal the existence of musseques on the periphery"; rather, huts were spread throughout nearly all city neighborhoods.[15] In the mid-1940s musseques still dotted the lower city neighborhoods, such as Ingombotas, Bungo, and Coqueiros, but by the 1960s only whites and a handful of African elites continued to reside in the baixa.[16] But in the context of the baixa, musseque describes a form of housing—huts—and not a place per se. When planners retrospectively applied the term musseques to conglomerations of huts occupied by African free and enslaved workers, they plied a definition of musseque that encompassed notions of labor and of race and not simply location.[17] Such assumptions followed the musseques to the urban periphery.

By the mid-twentieth century, concomitant with the post–World War II population explosion in Luanda, the musseques came to symbolize, for the colonial state, all that was problematic with urbanization. Ideas about labor, race, immigration, and living conditions combined to spell pathology in the minds of the colonizers. Between 1950 and 1970 the total population of the city more than tripled in size. The number of whites more than doubled between 1950 and 1960, increasing their percentage of Luanda's total population even though Africans continued to immigrate from the rural areas in large numbers.[18] The result was more pressure on urban infrastructure in general and on Africans who were displaced to the fringes of the city to accommodate whites in the city center. Despite these intertwined processes, the colonial government and the social scientists deemed African immigration to the city, and not white immigration from the metropole, to be the main problem and the reason for the growth of the musseques.[19] These outside observers characterized the musseques as disease ridden and socially addled, bursting with unemployed, underskilled young men with slack social and moral norms.

The memories of former musseque residents contrast with this image. They expressed concerns about similar issues—unsanitary conditions, unemployment, and social disarray—but ascribed them to the lack of infrastructure and not to the moral failings of the residents. In other words, they critiqued the colonial state. Residents also saw these shortcomings as part of daily life, woven into a broader context of struggles and successes related to work, recreation, and schooling.[20] These were conditions in which residents lived, managed, and even thrived.

Residential construction in the musseques physically proclaimed the improvisation and innovation through which residents transformed their situation. People often built their homes from salvaged materials: hubcaps, motor blocks, and wood taken from wine barrels were all recognizable in musseque dwellings.[21] Generally, walls were built of wood sticks and clay and roofs were fashioned from wood planks or, for those who could afford them, sheets of metal. Except in state-constructed neighborhoods like Bairro Indígena, running water was not available, and even in Bairro Indígena it was in a shared public space. Cooking and washing were done in a home's *quintal,* or walled outside area.²²

The labyrinthine streets were narrow, uneven, and dusty. Paved thoroughfares defined the musseque borders. April's heavy rains inundated the musseque streets, making them impassable to motor vehicles. Luiz Visconde's musical hit "Chofer de Praça" (Plaza Chauffeur) chronicles this situation and the urban social divisions it symbolized. The song's narrator is a young man who wants to take a cab to go visit his girlfriend in the musseque, which he calls the "suburb." The cab driver refuses, unwilling to sully his car or his dignity:

Mandei parar um carro de praça	I hailed a car from the plaza [taxi]
Ancioso em ver meu amor	Anxious to see my love
Chofer de praça então reclamou	The chauffeur then complained
Quando eu lhe disse que meu bem morava no subúrbio	When I told him my honey lived in the suburbs
"Tempo chuvoso no subúrbio, não vou Pois sou chofer de praça e não barqueiro"	"Rainy season in the suburbs, I won't go I am a plaza chauffeur, not a boatman"
Então emplorei	So I implored
"Peço o senhor chofer leve-me por favor	"I am asking you, Mr. Chauffeur, please take me
Ela não tem culpa de morar no subúrbio	It's not her fault she lives in the suburbs
Enquanto a chuva é obra de natureza"	And rain is the work of nature"

These lyrics highlight the social and physical divisions between baixa and musseque, contrast the driver's arrogance with the narrator's sunny determination, and elliptically point to colonial policy since "it's not her fault she lives in the suburbs."²³

The musseque population of the 1960s and early 1970s was quite diverse. The work of social scientists in the period shows that the majority of musseque residents in the 1960s had been born outside the city and that people from all areas of both Angola and Portugal were represented in the musseque population.²⁴ In the early 1970s, less than one-fifth of heads of households were born in Luanda.²⁵ For the part of the population not born in Luanda, "migratory movement toward the Capital is oriented by three important axes, whose departure points are situated in the large zones corresponding to the ethno-linguistic groups Ambundu-Kimbundu, Ovimbundu-Umbundu and Bakongo-Kikongo."²⁶ These are the three major ethno-linguistic groups in Angola, which together accounted for 75 percent of the population at the time.[27] Although new migrants tended to join family members already established in the city, rigid ethnic enclaves did not take shape, and each of these three groups (along with others) was represented in the various musseques.[28] The musseques were as ethnically diverse as the territory itself.

The same cannot be said for gender and age diversity. The musseque population in the 1960s and early 1970s was overwhelmingly young and male.[29] By the 1960s Luanda's white population demonstrated greater gender equity than the African population, though historically this had not been the case.[30] The unevenness of the data from this period makes it difficult to generalize but it appears that in the late nineteenth century the male-to-female ratio among the black population in Luanda was roughly equal; males only began to outnumber females in the mid-1920s.[31] From the city's founding in 1576, Luanda's white population was heavily male. The first white women only arrived in 1595, and then there were just twelve of them.[32] For the colony in general, gender ratios in the white population were a function of the colonial policy of white occupation of the territory, promoted initially at the end of the slave trade in the late nineteenth century and again in the mid-twentieth century after World War II. It was only at this latter point that Luanda's white population showed almost equal numbers of men and women. These demographic data were critical to the development of racial and social relations in Luanda over the long and short terms.

Christine Messiant argues that most migrants came to the city to escape the contract labor or compulsory work the state required of African males found to be unemployed or without a profession.[33] This helps to explain the greater presence of men than women in Luanda.[34] And it shows that what colonial administrators saw as a discrete economic motivation was, in fact, grounded in policies of the colonial administration.

Messiant describes the musseque population of the late 1950s as a "weakly industrialized proletariat" with the majority of the population employed as domestic laborers, manual laborers at the port and on the railroad, lower personnel in commerce, and apprentices to artisans.[35] By the early 1970s, 90 percent of the population worked for an employer and the majority worked in the private sector, where salaries were generally lower and more inconsistent than in the public sector. This was a striking shift from the 1950s, when only 68 percent of the population was employed by "others."[36] Ramiro Ladeiro Monteiro notes similar growth, however, in the number of those working as tailors, mechanics, barbers, furniture builders, and watch repairmen. People did this work mainly in their own shops, and increasingly they were able to employ someone other than just themselves.[37] The majority of women worked as laundresses or fruit and vegetable vendors.[38] Steady, salaried employment was a rarity for both men and women. Most people living in the musseques aspired to improve their lot, though low levels of education, due to the sparse and discriminatory colonial educational system in place until the early 1960s, made this exceedingly difficult.[39] Reforms in the educational system after 1961 led to an increase in schooling for Africans: enrollment increased by 375 percent in ten years, signaling the desire for education though not necessarily the effectiveness of the new program.[40]

The musseques mirrored the colonial territory in their ethnic diversity and in the way that their growth and population reflected the impact of colonial labor policies. While colonial-sponsored social science work does not remark this fact, it does attest it. But the musseques also presented novel living conditions and social relations that would give rise to new ways of conceptualizing that diversity and the experience of colonization in a nationalist sensibility. Thus the musseques were less spaces of transition from rural to urban in the social evolutionary sense, as social scientists in the period suggested, than they were an active interface between the two, enframed in part by colonial policy but reframed by musseque residents who produced an anticolonial ethic.[41]

COLONIAL SOCIAL SCIENCE, LUSOTROPICALISM, AND THE ESTADO NOVO

Working at institutes organized and patronized by the state, Portuguese social scientists (Ilídio do Amaral, José de Sousa Bettencourt, and Ramiro Ladeiro Monteiro) studied urbanization and the musseques. They endeavored to shape colonial policy with their work. But their analyses consistently denied the colonial administration's role as a causal factor in urban malaise. By focusing on the musseques and not on the city in general, by analyzing pathology at the level of individual behavior, by using the family as a unit of analysis, and by asserting, either explicitly or implicitly, that urbanization is synonymous with Europeanization, these works depict the musseques as unfortunate but inevitable byproducts of urbanization and industrialization, little related to colonial relations or policy.

Of the three colonial social scientists discussed here, Monteiro was the most closely linked to the colonial state. He was the head of the secret service known as Serviços de Centralização e Coordenação de Informações de Angola (Angolan Services for the Centralization and Coordination of Information, SCCIA). This agency was charged with collecting, analyzing, and distributing information (political, security, or administrative) of use to the state and the Armed Forces.[42] Theoretically, SCCIA's purview was within

Angola while the PIDE pursued investigations that crossed borders. Overlap in the work of these two organs, and tension between them, tugged at their combined objective of averting insurrection in the overseas provinces.[43] Amaral's and Bettencourt's connections to the colonial security apparatus were more attenuated. Their work was published by the scientific research institutes associated with the Overseas Ministry.[44]

The postwar Estado Novo was, like the French and British colonial states in the same period, a developmentalist state.[45] M. Anne Pitcher notes that "in much the same way as Britain and France had tried to do in the 1950s, Portugal appeared to be laying the economic foundations for a future neo-colonial relationship by constructing dams, devising hydroelectric and electrification schemes, and encouraging investment by Portuguese and foreign capital."[46] Insofar as Africans could be won over to Portugal through these reforms, the state saw itself advancing against the nationalist forces.

Ironically, while these researchers attempted to employ a universalist model of modernization and development current at the time, the Estado Novo was simultaneously laboring to convince the world of the exceptionalism of Portuguese colonial relations. The Brazilian sociologist Gilberto Freyre initially theorized *lusotropicalismo* in the early 1930s to explain and valorize the Brazilian nation and the pivotal role of Africans and Amerindians in its formation. The theory was adopted and adapted as ideology by the Portuguese Estado Novo in the postwar period.[47] In the face of intense international criticism and the pressure to decolonize,[48] the Portuguese state attempted to justify its continued presence in Africa and Asia in part by arguing that it had a unique ability to create harmonious racially egalitarian societies in the tropics.[49] The historian Cláudia Castelo notes that "from the middle of the 1950s a systematic effort by the Ministry of External Affairs to indoctrinate Portuguese diplomats in luso-tropicalismo is evident. The objective is to equip them with (supposedly) scientific arguments, based in history, sociology and anthropology that are capable of legitimizing the Portuguese presence in Africa, India, Macau and Timor."[50] Not only were diplomats educated about Freyre's theories but his books were translated and published (in Portuguese, French, and English) by the Ministry of Overseas Provinces and distributed in diplomatic circles, in particular to countries with seats at the United Nations.[51]

The discourse of lusotropicalism accompanied the transformation of the legal status of the colonies. In 1953 the Estado Novo instituted the Lei Orgânica do Ultramar Português (Organic Law of Overseas Portugal). This law, through legal and linguistic artifice, changed the colonies into overseas provinces of the Portuguese nation. Where there had been empire, now there was a single nation: spanning continents, one and indivisible, in the words of the state. The Estado Novo touted lusotropicalism to obscure this dubious legal tinkering. Giving defining power to Portuguese culture, it aimed to explain precisely why the overseas provinces were no different than continental Portugal. Finally, the Estado Novo spun lusotropicalism as Portugal's contribution to European security in the context of the Cold War: "The future of Europe could be safeguarded only by the creation of a Euro-African space, in which Portugal was seen to have blazed a trail, magically dispelling racism wherever its footprints were to be found."[52] The Estado Novo thus used lusotropicalism to smooth its way into the European community and to avert U.N. meddling.

Even as the language of lusotropicalism headlined in foreign-oriented public relations, Maria da Conceição Neto argues that

> *lusitanidade* and *portugalidade* were the preferred terms in the Portuguese colonies, especially after 1961. This was in part because *lusotropicalismo* could not but refer to the Brazilian paradigm, with the risk of independence as the final goal of "Portuguese integration in the tropics" . . . On the other hand, in the face of nationalisms in the African colonies, it was necessary to insist on the Portugalization of the populations rather than to exalt a patrimony common to the Portuguese, Brazilians and Africans.[53]

Flying in the face of lusotropicalism, social scientists disconnected the problems of the musseques from the particularity of Portuguese practices and linked them instead to a universal experience of urbanization. At times they acted as apologists for the state, airing universal theories of urbanization to rationalize what would otherwise look like contradictions in lusotropicalist assertions (for example, they argued that racialized residential segregation resulted from economic differentiation in the urban situation and not from colonial policy or settler racism). More often they maintained the *portugalidade* line that assumed Portuguese (and European) cultural superiority and saw assimilation and acculturation as a one-way process of the gradual adoption of this culture.[54] As Gerald Bender puts it: "They combined [Freyre's] concept of a harmonious and egalitarian multiracial society with their Social Darwinism and produced a bastardized version of lusotropicalism. This theoretical cross-fertilization did not yield a new hybrid society in Africa but a typical colonial society."[55] In the end, developmentalist policy belied lusotropicalism even as it tried to protect it. The Estado Novo's contradictory use of these two approaches exposed its struggle to shore up the political situation relative to the colonies.

SOCIAL SCIENTISTS, LITERARY NATIONALISTS, AND *ANGOLANIDADE*

Social science boomed in the postwar period. Its tools helped those who attacked the Estado Novo as well as those who defended it. Critics of the regime and its interpretation of lusotropicalism were not typically sanguine about the musseques, if and when they gave them any notice at all, but they were unflinching in attributing blame for urban misery on the Estado Novo and earlier colonial administrations.[56] Researchers like Perry Anderson, Gerald Bender, Charles Boxer, Basil Davidson, James Duffy, Franz-Wilhelm Heimer, John Marcum, and Thomas Okuma critiqued the then current and historical practices of Portuguese colonialism. These writers offered an economic and social indictment of Portuguese rule and explained the bases for the emergent national liberation movements. In the words of Bender's title, they exposed the reality behind the myth of Portuguese colonialism, the infrastructure of exploitation behind the façade of lusotropicalism.[57]

In doing so they followed the lead of Angolan nationalists. As Ronald Chilcote notes, the Angolan intellectual and political militant Mário Pinto de Andrade, in a 1955 article in *Présence Africaine*, was the first to call lusotropicalism a myth.[58] Américo Boavida's 1967 *Angola: Cinco séculos de exploração portuguesa* (Angola: Five Centuries of Portuguese Exploitation) led the way with a political economic critique.[59] Bender describes the challenge the nationalist thinkers posed:

> In short, while the liberation movements engaged the Portuguese army on the battlefield, they and their supporters challenged the Portuguese people and all concerned foreigners to measure the claims of lusotropicalism against the social, economic, and political realities of more than 95 per cent of the population who were not white. These partisans were no less confident than the Portuguese themselves that candid observers and historians would vindicate their claims.[60]

This was precisely what "candid observers and historians" did. They used social scientific method (especially quantitative and comparative analysis) to show that, in fact, in indicator after indicator, the numbers of schools, graduates, mixed-race individuals, and assimilados always fell short of Portuguese claims of assimilation, multiracialism, and equality. And they showed how white immigration and forced labor, while a boon for the colonizers, were a bane for the colonized.

Literary nationalists undid lusotropicalism in verse and prose. Beginning in 1948 under the banner "Vamos descobrir Angola!" (Let's discover Angola) and in the literary journal *Mensagem* (Message), this literary movement preceded but nurtured direct political action and nationalist consciousness. It countered *portugalidade* with an *angolanidade* rooted in local, African life and not in some diffuse notion of the lusotropical. In Basil Davidson's description: "If *assimilados* had a duty, *Mensagem* said implicitly in almost all its poems, it was to 'de-Portugalize' and 're-Africanize': to escape from Lusitanian isolation, to find contact with 'the natives,' whether in Luanda's festering slums or out there in the wild *sertão*, the backlands of the bush; and so, bridging the gulf, build an identity which should not be Portuguese but Angolan."[61]

Writers from the period included Mário Pinto de Andrade, Viriato da Cruz, Agostinho Neto, and António Jacinto. In *Mensagem*'s brief run (only four issues), they developed new forms of literary expression that valorized Angola's Africanness. But the message was out. The creation of *angolanidade* was reinitiated by the Sociedade de Cultura Angolana in their literary journal *Cultura* (Culture) published from 1957 to 1961. Writers including Costa Andrade, José Luandino Vieira, Domingos Van Dunem, Uanhenga Xitu, António Cardoso, and Arnaldo Santos placed the language and life of the musseques at the center of Angolan prose fiction.[62] They captured oral practices, African urban life, and the language and speech of the musseques self-consciously in the name of Angolan alterity.[63]

Fiction writers give us a different sense of the social reality of the musseques in the colonial period. In their work, lamentable social conditions are an indictment of colonial practices as well as a source of innovation, humor, and a new consciousness. In literature from the period, the musseques are not so much the location of pathology as they are the site of cultural richness, the re-creation of which, in fiction, constitutes a new cultural politics summed up in the word *angolanidade*.

COLONIAL SOCIAL SCIENCE REINTERPRETED

Unable to see colonial occupation as anything but a handmaiden to modernity, colonial social scientists analyzed social life in the musseques in isolation from its root causes. In the view of these scholars, the musseques' social problems flowed from the transition from rural to urban life. In their imaginations, the urban was synonymous with European culture and modernization while the rural idyll embodied African culture and tradition. Thus a concern with African immigration to urban areas spawned a preoccupation with migration, on the one hand, and detribalization, on the other. Just below these collective problems the colonial social scientists' gaze lingered on individual pathologies: the "double life" of heads of households and prostitution by young women.

But the central preoccupations, concepts, and data of the social scientists can be read in ways that lend a quite different interpretation to them. The rural-to-urban migration, the detribalization of musseque residents, the double life of those who worked in the city but lived in the musseques, and prostitution can have different meanings when seen with different eyes.

Those whose songs and works of literature were situated in the musseques present us with a world whose echo we barely perceive in the social science tracts unless we read them more closely. This section rereads the analyses of social scientists from the perspective of those who lived, worked, and agitated in the musseques and draws on the work of other social scientists to demystify late Portuguese colonialism. But it also engages the memories of some individuals who lived and participated in the cultural life of the musseques to reread moments of pathology in the social scientific texts as socially historically relevant and culturally novel. In these rereadings culture is not a static set of practices or behaviors, but a dynamic political resource.

Migration versus Immigration

According to the 1970 census, Luanda had a total population of 475,328, and nearly 40 percent of those people lived in the musseques.[64] Although the growth of the white population outpaced that of the African population, the social scientific gaze fell almost exclusively on the numbers of Africans present in the city.[65] José de Sousa Bettencourt's 1965 study, "Subsídio para o estudo sociológico da população de Luanda" (Elements for the Sociological Study of Luanda's Population), explains: "The situation of Luanda's African population constitutes a social problem if we pay attention to the fact that it shows itself as an enormous belt surrounding the European part of the population."[66] Amaral likewise describes the musseques as "neighborhoods of misery that surround and suffocate the urbanized city."[67] Both Bettencourt and Amaral portray the migrants as attracted by the city and "seduced" by its offerings, while Monteiro notes both the causes of attraction to the city and those of repulsion from the rural areas.[68] References to the urban anatomy and to physical dysfunction pose the problem succinctly: the musseques are threatening the very life of the city and perhaps the body politic.

For Portuguese social scientists, urban space was European space despite Luanda's history and despite the rural roots of recently arrived white residents. From the 1950s on, many of the white immigrants coming to Angola were from rural areas of northern Portugal, and though colonial policy makers dreamed that they would form agricultural communities, the majority wound up in urban centers and in Luanda in particular.[69] Despite the white immigrants' rural origins and the fact that they were thousands of miles from home, colonial social scientists ignored their cultural adaptation to a new urban environment. In Bettencourt's vision it was the African population that needed to "acculturate" and adjust to the Portuguese social system in Luanda (the most European city in all of Africa outside of South Africa, according to Bettencourt). He saw the increased postwar emigration from the rural areas to Luanda as nothing less than an "authentic invasion" of a city whose population was ethnically and culturally diverse but whose social patterns were Portuguese.[70]

The colonial social scientists deemed migration a primary cause of urban problems like unemployment, overcrowding, and unsanitary conditions in the musseques. They suggested that the city was a node of attraction for young males in search of work. Once there, they argued, many migrants would stay even without employment, seduced by urban novelties and freedoms. This narrow focus on migrant behavior kept the social scientists from noticing the deleterious effects of colonial labor practices and the impact of increased white immigration from the metropole on urban growth. A look at colonial policy suggests that the forces of repulsion were stronger than those of attraction. As Messiant notes, most workers said that their movement was motivated by the desire to escape recruitment into state service and contract labor.[71] Rural to urban migration certainly caused the urban population to expand in size and led to some degree of immiseration in the musseques, but so too did white immigration, a factor largely ignored by the social scientists.

Only Amaral acknowledges the effects of white immigration as of more than passing demographic interest. Rural Portuguese whites immigrating to Luanda after 1950 competed with the local African population for jobs as waiters, newspaper sellers, taxi drivers, porters at port warehouses, child care providers, laundresses, and market and street vendors.[72] Many Africans lost jobs and land to these new white immigrants. Despite the fact that the racist laws that separated the population into indígenas (indigenous) and assimilados (assimilated) were abolished after the uprisings in 1961, residential racial segregation and racial discrimination in labor practices and education continued.

Pointing to the racism practiced in Portuguese colonialism, Gerald Bender notes that Portuguese women took over the central marketplace, squeezing African women out completely.[73] Both Amaral and Bender suggest that increased white immigration following World War II led to an increase in "clandestine construction" by whites (i.e., against city codes, without permission, and on land not owned by the person building).[74] Much of this occurred in the musseques or along their borders. Because many of these white immigrants were poor and came to Angola seeking greater economic opportunities than they could find in the metropole, they rented inexpensive housing in the musseques, thereby displacing Africans from the few residential possibilities available to them. Articles in the local magazines *Semana Ilustrada* (Illustrated Weekly) and *Noite e Dia* (Night and Day) in the early 1970s criticized the government's lack of residential planning and published pictures of the musseques and other urban neighborhoods where whites had illegally built homes.[75]

The homes constructed by white immigrants contributed to the precariousness of housing and to crowding in the musseques. Moreover, these new immigrants were also largely responsible for illegal economic activities there. Amaral cites a 1964 study in the musseque Prenda that showed that 95 percent of black-market activities occurred in white-owned establishments (the remainder took places in the premises of Africans, primarily Cape Verdeans).[76] Bender used the evidence of white immigration and displacement of Africans from housing and jobs to demonstrate white domination of the urban African population. He countered Bettencourt's, Monteiro's, and Amaral's comparison of the musseques to U.S. and South African ghettos by asserting that while a black middle class had emerged in the ghettos, the same could not be said of Luanda's musseques.[77] The effects of white immigration had only negative ramifications for economic conditions and housing for Africans in the musseques.

Detribalization versus Transethnicity

For musseque dwellers it was not Portuguese social patterns that created cohesion in the city. Instead, the lack of economic power and the new social relations emerging from urban migration in search of economic betterment created a common experience. When social scientists studying the musseques mapped cultural difference onto the process of migration with the language of detribalization, they obfuscated social and economic problems with narratives of cultural demise.[78] In Amaral's words: "Those arriving from the rural areas suffer, in the city, a profound change; new forces destroy the traditional hierarchies and put them in a state of imbalance between the patterns of a European urban life and those of their traditional rural one."[79] Migrants to the city trade the ties and obligations of structured society, that is, "tribe," for the negatively defined cohesion of the urban mass: "the lack of economic stability, professional insecurity, the imbalance between the number of men and women."[80]

In the end, the only hope for social unity among musseque residents, according to Bettencourt, is

> the patterns of behavior that are not genuinely theirs, but are those of the laws of the Portuguese Nation. . . . .the population of each

musseque lacks the principal human elements that define a simple rural community, in which the primary relations, inherent to relations and neighbors, are the main basis of social organization, however rudimentary.[81]

Echoing modernization and development literature from the period, Bettencourt proposes integration of Portuguese culture as the remedy for the social disjuncture occasioned by urban migration. Unlike lusotropicalism's narrative of Portuguese adaptability, this emphasis on African acquisition of European culture is reminiscent of much colonial literature. In the ideal trajectory, urban migration meant losing the tribe to gain the (Portuguese) nation. The social problems that social scientists identified in the musseques were therefore the byproducts of rural cultural hangover or incomplete acculturation, not those of colonial rule. Using anthropological concepts then in vogue (detribalization, acculturation), these social scientists depoliticized the colonial situation and its social conditions in Luanda.

If detribalization threatened the average African migrant to the city, Bettencourt also worried that urban African elites were threatened by the déclassé behavior of the new and, in his estimation, culturally liminal migrants. What he saw as downward social mobility might instead be seen as a radicalizing form of education for those more privileged among the African population (assimilados) who now lived side by side with those considered to be on the bottom of the totem pole, the indígenas. In much scholarly work written since independence, the moment in the 1940s when Africans of every social status were pushed out of the city center and into the musseques was fundamental to the identification of urban elites with the mass of exploited Africans both in the city and in the countryside. While assimilado elites had defended the rights of the indígenas and provided some modest social uplift programs through the official channels of Anangola (Association of Natural-born Angolans) and the Liga Nacional Africana (National African League), two government-approved associations of assimilados, the relationship was one of elites to inferiors.[82]

Having lost their homes and with their positions in the civil service threatened by Portuguese immigrants, assimilados suddenly experienced a colonial racism from which their education, manners, and culture did not protect them.[83] The mixing of the traditional urban elites with families in the musseques engendered a contact and cultural exchange that proved fundamental to the burgeoning of clandestine nationalist politics and to the eventual development of cultural practices that imagined the nation.[84] At the same time, it is incorrect to suggest that all elites responded kindly and with interest to their new neighbors. Many continued to distinguish themselves from the average musseque residents in terms of education, employment, and family lineage.[85]

Finally, Messiant contends that from the time of the Second World War, a group emerged that she terms "les nouveaux assimilados" or the new assimilated.[86] Many lived in the musseques, were Protestants, and tended to be more connected to their areas of origin (predominantly Mbundu) and less connected to Portuguese culture than those she calls "les anciens assimilados." Unlike the old assimilated they identified themselves culturally as Africans.[87] From the perspective of nationalists, the approximation between the economically and more socially advantaged Africans and their poorer urban brethren permitted a radicalization and cultural re-Africanization of some elites. This was precisely what the literary nationalists had advocated with their call to "descobrir Angola." When literary nationalists proclaimed "vamos descobrir Angola!" they sought to surmount the alienation effected by Portuguese culture and education through a discovery and celebration of local culture.

For the bulk of musseque residents relatively newly arrived in the city from other areas, the experience of urban life did not necessarily strip them of their ethnic associations or practices. The Angolan writer and sociologist Pepetela argues that the musseques represented an experience of transethnicity and not necessarily one of ethnic erasure. Using Monteiro's data on the rising percentage of interethnic marriages in the musseques, he argues:

> This very important piece of data reinforces the idea that the musseque (and everything leads us to believe that this continues today) was a transethnic space where, in fact, the idea of nation was born and where it was constantly reinforced by the integration of elements that continually arrived from the rural areas.[88]

In this reading, Africans did not shed ethnicity but instead reinterpreted it. The musseques constituted a space where residents made and lived the nation as a kaleidoscope of ethnicities and cultures.

For the nationalist writers the diversity of the musseques was a source of great potential. Ethnicity was one among many ways of connecting with neighbors. The basis for an imaginary of self and other, defined in relation to something other than ethnicity or even race, might emerge from seeing that one's neighbors of a different ethnicity also suffered the same conditions and discrimination.[89] Agostinho Neto's expression "de Cabinda ao Cunene, um só povo, uma só nação" (from Cabinda to Cunene, one people, one nation), referring to the northernmost and southernmost provinces of Angola, nationalized this mix of ethnicities and origins present in the musseques.

Duplicity versus Dignity

Social scientists worried about the "double life" or duplicity of male household heads in the musseques, who were perceived as being Portuguese by day and African at night. They deemed this double life evidence of an incomplete acculturation that impeded modernization and development, postponing a Rostowian "takeoff." The military and police further suspected that the musseque environment contributed to a sense of misery that might nurture nationalist sympathizers.

Bettencourt wrote about the double life of hard-working upstanding types in the musseques. Pointing out that there are "workers, low-level functionaries and individuals with a certain financial freedom that does not justify their placement in poor neighborhoods," he suggests that they live in a "false misery" caused by their surroundings.[90] According to Bettencourt, the lowest common denominator sets the pace and stunts ambition in musseque society (his foil is the Portuguese sociocultural system). This lowest common denominator, he argues, manifests in the troubling behavior of household heads with jobs who act like well-integrated Portuguese citizens at work and like typical musseque residents, gossiping with neighbors, when at home. Under such circumstances it is not enough, Bettencourt argues, to have "functioning organs of conduct control aimed at the desired assimilation. We must take into account the mental resistance of individuals that are subjected to this acculturative process."[91] Hence, the failure redounds onto the residents themselves.

For Bettencourt, this double life or duplicity results from social pressures that compel a certain kind of behavior from all residents. Given the poverty of the bulk of the musseque population, he suggests that peer pressure pulls down the more upstanding, economically able families. These families try to identify with their poorer neighbors by wearing the same type of clothing, having similar homes, speaking in a similar way, and participating in neighborhood politics (by which he seems to mean the goings-on between people and not formal politics). As they engage in such déclassé behavior they change from being individuals into members of the horde:

> In the morning he puts on his nice suit, leaves home, catches the *maximbombo* [bus], and presents himself at the office, factory, or shop as a true individual perfectly integrated, distinguishing himself through his courtesy, cultured ways, and intelligence in social relations. When he returns home, he takes off his suit, puts on some old pants, a tattered pajama, some sandals and he goes and sits in the shade of the matchwood tree in the yard, immediately integrating himself in the life of the musseque, greeting this one and that one, listening

and commenting on the intrigues of others, like an authentic musseque resident. This mimesis is the dominant note. This duplicity of social life is a curious and peculiar phenomenon among the people of the musseques.[92]

In Portuguese, the first meaning of *duplicidade* (duplicity) is having two characteristics at the same time. Only secondarily does it connote the sense, as in English, of dissimulation or deception.[93] While Bettencourt seems to be using the first definition, the taint of the second lingers in his attribution of this as "curious and peculiar" and his assessment that this is a negative aspect of musseque life with "grave repercussions" for the family.

Amaral repeats this charge, though not with as much detail or judgment. And it surfaces again in Monteiro in the figure of the shirtless musseque resident who hardly resembles the nattily clad office worker he was before arriving home.[94] Monteiro sees musseque women as subject to a similar sartorial, and by implication behavioral, transformation: "This piece of clothing [the *pano* or wrapper] defines a woman's social status and its absence in certain social strata is noticed. That is why the laundress we see in her boss's house dressed as a European troubles herself with putting a *pano* around her waist when returning to the *musseque*."[95] While Bettencourt saw the doubleness in more sinister terms, as the result of negative peer pressure that was thwarting proper acculturation, Monteiro sees the phenomenon as evidence of incomplete integration into the urbanized world.

For those Africans employed in colonial bureaucracies and businesses, leading a so-called double life was a matter of maintaining one's dignity. Many civil servants, tired from the abuses and discrimination they experienced in the offices of the baixa, found relief in returning home to the musseques to enjoy bits of leisure time in which their bodies, their labor, and their language were not so closely monitored. Less a question of peer pressure than of maintaining one's social practices, this practice did not appear contradictory to the people who traveled between the two realms. The musician Amadeu Amorim remembers that when a man "went to work he was an assimilado but when he was in his own home he was an African," meaning he could speak his own language, go out to parties, or visit friends in the neighborhood.[96] Musseque residents dismissed neither the habits of the "acculturated" nor those of the "rural areas." Nor did they treat them as an act that one had to put on to survive. Instead, together these practices or behaviors constituted a new kind of urban *angolanidade*.

It was under these circumstances and because of the pressure to adopt Portuguese culture that some people began to actively procure and proclaim their

Africanness. What Bettencourt read as doubleness and duplicity, writers like António Jacinto, Mário António, António Cardoso, Agostinho Neto, Alda Lara, Luandino Vieira, Uanhenga Xitu, and Mário Pinto de Andrade, among others, read as the contradictions of colonialism and the stuff of everyday life that made Angola Angola. For these writers, the musseques were the essence of a new Angolan culture and not a hotbed of pathology. But that interpretation and their involvement in clandestine nationalist politics landed many of them in jail or in exile by the early 1960s.

Prostitution versus Procurement

If incomplete acculturation marks the lack of male integration into the urban world, prostitution and promiscuity are the urban social malaise that burdens women. Bettencourt is most exercised about promiscuity, which to him is a form of generalized prostitution. Because no money changes hands, the causes are not economic but social and cultural.[97] For Monteiro, the factors compelling prostitution are largely economic, whereas for Amaral the demographic gender imbalance is the primary cause. These factors all result from urbanization, according to these scholars.

Contrast this with a piece from the late 1940s that emphasizes colonial policy as the cause of female decadence. An early popular text, Julio de Castro Lopo's 1948 "Alguns aspectos dos musseques de Luanda" prefigures the later social scientific preoccupation with the musseques. Although not a social science tract, it demonstrates how the debate over colonial policy was changing and explains the stakes involved. Unlike social science studies that focus on male heads of household and urban workers, Lopo's work is solely preoccupied with the misery of the musseques as exemplified in *mulata*, or mixed-race, women.

This is a treatise on what Lopo calls the "woman problem." Until 1930 there were only a few white women in Angola, and Lopo must have been seeing this situation change only slowly.[98] Prostitution, in this reading, results from the conditions of colonization—from white men having relations with African and mixed-race women but then not assuming responsibility for the children that result. In this short anecdotal rendering of musseque life, he depicts the tragic *mulata* women who must turn to prostitution when abandoned to the musseques by their white fathers. Lopo sketches the sad lives of three young women, fictitious composites of women he met. He notes the characteristics that mark their potentially civilized nature—one's predilection for Lucky Strike cigarettes, another's dedicated reading of the French fashion magazine *La Femme*, still another's well-positioned kin in Lisbon society. The progeny of Portuguese men who failed to resist the seduction of the "three s's"—*sol* (sun), *sereno* (serenity), and *saias* (skirts)—that the musseques offered, these *mulatas* were left to defend themselves against the meanness and dissipation of the shantytowns.[99] Lopo blames their white fathers (he writes off their African mothers, whether mixed-race or black) and also faults the colonial immigration policy (or lack thereof) for the sorry state of these young women. Although he mentions that white women in the musseques are not exempt from the same "epidemic of immorality," he is particularly concerned with mixed-race women and children and entirely excludes mixed-race men from his discussion.

By the time Amaral, Bettencourt, and Monteiro are writing, some twenty-plus years after Lopo, the white population has not only grown significantly but has stabilized in terms of male-to-female ratios. Prostitution is still associated with the misery of the musseques, but it is blamed on African migration from rural to urban areas and the universal process of urbanization rather than on white immigrants. Amaral thinks that prostitution and concubinage result from the urban migration of young men, the general youth of the musseque population, and the "insufficient number of women."[100] But how then is the "polygamy"[101] that troubles him even viable, if men outnumber women and so many of the available women are prostitutes? Perhaps it results from migrants leaving their wives in rural areas and taking on new ones in urban areas. But if this is the case, why does he not also apply the same term to identical behavior by Portuguese men? Amaral was well aware of the Portuguese men who left wives behind in the metropole and lived with African women, producing the musseque "tragedy" that preoccupied Lopo.[102]

Unlike Amaral, Monteiro recognized that it is difficult to talk about prostitution in the musseques in isolation from the rest of the city. He is careful to point out that his discussion of prostitution has implications for Luanda in general and not just the musseques. This made sense since most prostitutes ("European, Euro-African, and African"[103]) did not practice in their own neighborhoods and since johns hailed from all parts of the city. For Monteiro the causes of an increase in prostitution since 1960 are economic, moral, social, and family-related. However, he also points to a problem posed by urban acculturation: women recently arrived from rural areas desire luxury goods and such consumerist desires propel them into prostitution.[104]

Unlike the sources on detribalization, those on prostitution are thin, and its discussion is generally charged since the subject is intertwined with racial and gender relations. When colonial policy makers and propagandists in the Estado Novo took up Gilberto Freyre's theory of lusotropicalism they offered miscegenation and the high number of *mulatos* in the population, relative to other colonies, as evidence of racial mixing and harmony. But, as James Duffy pointed out in the early 1960s, we dare not confuse "erotic expediency" due to demographic conditions with racial equality and harmonious coexistence.[105] Lopo's anecdotal piece on the musseques and what he calls the "woman problem" indicates one result of such "erotic expediency": young women unrecognized by their Portuguese fathers who are left to prostitute themselves in the musseques of Luanda. From early on in Angola's history, living with Portuguese men was sometimes an avenue to social and economic advancement for African women.[106] But Portuguese men rarely married the African women with whom they had relationships and fathered children.

Prostitution also troubled Africans living in the musseques. As Monteiro notes, most prostitutes did not practice their trade in their own neighborhoods, and so Bairro Operário and Marçal had houses of prostitution that employed women from other parts of the city. These businesses attracted, among others, soldiers from the Portuguese army. José Luandino Vieira's novel *Nosso musseque* described soldier visits:

> There were families complaining that [the soldiers] were always knocking on their doors to see if they had women for sale; mothers hurried to get their young girls inside earlier than usual, because those men would pass by and grope them, abuse them, whether they were old or young. And then they spoke of the case of an older man, from *Terra Nova*, who went out to defend his daughter, was beaten with a belt, and fled off in the grass and was never seen again.[107]

In this reading, from the perspective of the musseques, white soldiers and white men in general were the problem, not prostitution.

Prostitution attracted not only Portuguese patrons and practitioners, but locals as well. Monteiro noted that prostitutes came from all racial groups. Jacques dos Santos's literary rendering of the lives of prostitutes and pimps in Bairro Operário gives a brief glimpse of prostitution in the life of the neighborhood and underscores the diversity of prostitutes and johns. From both dos Santos and Monteiro we learn that prostitution afforded women some economic autonomy; indeed most houses of prostitution were female-owned and -operated.[108] Some musicians recalled that prostitutes attended musseque clubs in the late 1960s and early 1970s. They could afford to dress well and met the entrance requirements.[109] At the same time, clubs had to guard against prostitutes using their spaces as pickup joints and battled to keep things "clean" so as not to sully their reputations with the bulk of the musseque population.[110] Because prostitution occurred not only in certain areas of the city but in certain kinds of bars—what Monteiro refers to as cabaret bars—there was an association between women, nightlife, and prostitution that female performers and other young women had to guard against.[111]

CULTURAL PRACTICES

Social scientists read the adoption of Portuguese cultural practices as the mark of a successful if incomplete transition from rural to urban life. Culture, in this reading, is a static set of customs and behaviors. Insofar as Africans can shed the cultural practices associated with a rural lifestyle and adopt those of their European colonizers, they will have managed to adapt to life in the city. Change, in this way of thinking, is unidirectional, from African ways to European ones. For colonial social science, social diseases such as detribalization, prostitution, and duplicity attested to the failures of new urban residents to acculturate.

Bettencourt and Amaral dismissed the cultural practices in which nationalist writers found a rich source of urban Angolan culture. But Bettencourt did not dismiss cultural and recreational practices altogether. He points to sports, dance, and music groups as musseque institutions that could have a beneficial and integrative effect on the lives of musseque residents. He deems these groups "a magnificent vehicle of acculturation."[112] In discussing soccer clubs he suggests that the competition on the field as well as rivalry within the groups around leadership positions was beneficial in creating social mobility among people and establishing new norms of social behavior. Bettencourt notes that it was rare to find a musseque without a soccer team and that by the mid-1960s nearly six dozen clubs existed in these neighborhoods.[113] For women, he argues, dance and music groups could promote cooperation and limited competition and ultimately provide the same social benefit of introducing new forms of conduct and behavior (this regardless of the fact that many of the groups he identified would have practiced African dance).[114]

Monteiro discusses soccer and dance briefly, the latter mostly in the context of parties and clubs. In both cases, the keyword for him is "Westernization," evident in the names of soccer clubs (which follow the naming practices of Portuguese soccer teams) and in the parties and clubs so popular among musseque youth. In reference to dance, he notes that "traditional" and "genuine" forms are fast disappearing.[115] Yet this form of recreation combines neatly with the "strong and traditional inclination of these people for music and dance."[116] Mentioning only the already recognized importance of soccer to the phenomenon of "Westernization," and placing the discussion of these practices alongside the other diversions of cinema, radio, and the press, Monteiro paints a picture of a "westernizing" population.

These depictions of what entertainment looked like from the outside are not far from the one I developed by talking to people who lived in the musseques and participated in these forms of entertainment. But people's descriptions of what these practices meant to them differed sharply from what the social scientists imagined. Simply put, what the latter saw as "Westernization" were really practices that returned musseque residents to their Africanness and through which they imagined an independent Angola.[117] Literary treatments of life in the musseques emphasize the African and specifically Angolan aspects of urban life.[118] In the clubs and at parties where music was played, the scene may have looked or even sounded somewhat "Western," but that did not mean that those in attendance saw themselves as good Portuguese citizens. Amadeu Amorim, in a radio interview celebrating twenty years of independence, put it succinctly: "People felt an *angolanidade*; they would get together to hear the music of Ngola Ritmos [of which he was a part] and they would feel Angolan. . . . since their songs woke up people's consciousness, they woke up many who were politically distracted and inspired nationalism."[119] Music was a practice in which people came to see themselves as Angolans. Music and clubs brought people together in spaces where they celebrated a specificity that refused the urban/rural and Western/African dichotomies: Western instruments like guitars could be made to play Angolan rhythms, and Western-style dress could be combined with local dressing practices or could proclaim an African cosmopolitanism that looked beyond the colonial metropole.[120]

Even that most apparently Western of pastimes, soccer, could have a different meaning in people's lives from that anticipated by the social scientists. Alberto Jaime, a longtime member and administrator of Club Maxinde, one of the most popular dance clubs in the musseques, remembered that Maxinde started out as a soccer club and then grew to include other forms of recreation. In his mind, the work that he and his fellow members did in running the club was immensely important and had implications for the emerging nation:

> Leave politics to the politicians. And we'll deal with, we'll work on, the social part—which is the more important—of educating people. Because if we had had this a long time ago Angola would have been prepared for independence.[121]

Jaime suggests that the work of running an organization was a kind of training for independence, albeit an incomplete one or one not widely experienced in Angola. He said this in the context of a broader discussion about those nationalists who had returned from exile and who thought they had won independence with a handful of people like themselves. Jaime defended those who stayed behind, the majority in fact, who had to learn to work with the government even as they opposed it; in so doing they gained skills important for an independent Angola. Thus, the dance and soccer clubs of the musseques, far from producing the docile, "Westernized" urban citizens desired by government administrators and social scientists, created instead young men and women who gained a sense of self-sufficiency and autonomy through those very clubs. This gave them a taste of an independent, self-ruled Angola. In the meantime, the content of the music and dance in these clubs created an *angolanidade* that gave them some purchase on the imaginary of nation.

Mourão argues that historically Luanda was a *mestiço* city with a unique culture whose development toward *angolanidade* was ruptured by a spike in white immigration in the 1940s.[122] However, he continues, if Luanda as a whole was characterized by rupture, the musseques evidenced a continuity of increasing Africanization that was ever more apparent in the articulation of *angolanidade*.[123] Hence, urban space was also always African space. The musseques have always been considered an African part of the urban landscape, but by emphasizing their dynamism, Mourão, like the novelists and poets of the 1960s and 1970s, overturns the colonial social scientific depiction of the musseques as cultural backwaters and places them at the center of national history. The writer, scholar, and ethnomusicologist Jorge Macedo specifies this argument in relationship to music:

> In the dance hall, in the enclosure of the musseque, it can be said that Latin American sounds, the twin of African rhythm, fed a climate of Africanization of the assimilados (or those Europeanized individuals with citizenship). At dawn one would return drunk from the atmosphere of a nostalgia for an Africa lived in the rhythm and melody, and the country to be conquered remained stamped within each person, with patterns of adhesion to cultural roots, which did not tarry in giving birth to the baobob of feelings of solidarity and deep sensations of belonging to the African family that in that period strengthened the politically spiritual ties of shared blood.[124]

In this passage Macedo poeticizes the ways in which music is critical to political consciousness and new cultural forms. It is the Africanness of the music that will embolden nationalist action and bring assimilados closer to their African kin in the musseques.

MUSIC AND A REINTERPRETATION OF THE MUSSEQUES

For the social scientists the musseques were a space of pathology. For Angolan writers of the 1960s and 1970s, and for literary critics and social scientists writing since independence, they were the location of a new *angolanidade*. Though beset by social problems, the musseques nourished this kernel of an emerging difference.

An analysis of the music scene opens up new ways of looking at and interpreting the musseques of the 1950s, 1960s, and 1970s and this emerging difference. Analyses of music have generally been interpreted in the framework of *angolanidade*. Musicians themselves as well as musician-intellectuals like Jorge Macedo, Carlos Lamartine, Mário Rui Silva, and Jomo Fortunato all note the central role of the musseques in the development of popular urban Angolan music.[125] The musseques, these writers argue, were a new space where the musical traditions of the rural areas met and mixed with music of a European tradition to form a unique new urban popular music. Indeed, glimpses of this cultural mixing are evident in Monteiro, Bettencourt, and Amaral, the latter two viewing it negatively and the former treating it as a dying oddity. Instead of denigrating the mixing of cultures as syncretic, a station stop on a developmental train chugging toward modernity, or claiming it as an example of the Portuguese skill in creating racially harmonious societies (à la lusotropicalism), the more recent writings on music celebrate the innovation of local cultural producers who demonstrated an adaptability and creativity beyond that of their colonizers. The new musical styles were less a mark of transition than a way of expressing new conditions and experiences.

Angolan literature of the 1960s and 1970s may have situated its soul and stories in the musseque, but literary expression and communication were not woven into musseque life to the same extent that music was. By focusing on music and the music scene, this book investigates the relationship between music and politics in such a way that the everyday lives of Africans residing in the musseques are given new historical value.

Music had a constant presence in the musseques, heard on radios, amplified on home stereos, performed live in clubs, or played in a circle in the *quintal* (backyard) of people's homes. Tunes reverberated in the singing of *lavadeiras* (washerwomen) and the cries of *peixeiras* (fish saleswomen). As one colonial writer described it, "In the musseque one lives based on happiness. One hears radios turned on from 6 a.m. until midnight! And on the weekends, the music doesn't stop."[126] Imbued with colonial paternalism and racism, this article nonetheless attempted to present a different side to the musseques as a place where people suffered but survived, in part thanks to cultural resourcefulness.

Even though social science tracts only glanced at music, the popular Luandan press of the late 1960s and early 1970s, mainly serving the local white population, ran many articles on daily life and nightlife in the musseques. These articles suggested that those who did not know the musseques did not know Luanda. Articles on local artists prominent in the musseque club scene, as well as stories by reporters who spent a night partying at one of these clubs, painted the musseques as a required stop on the urban nightlife circuit. Musicians, club owners, and others who were part of the scene remembered that the musseque clubs attracted large crowds of not only musseque residents but whites as well. By the early 1970s, whites were leaving the bars and shows of the baixa behind for the scene at Maxinde, or Giro-Giro, or Salão dos Anjos, three musseque clubs of particular renown.[127]

With the growth of a locally based recording industry and an explosion of radio stations in the same period, the music produced in Luanda was available and played throughout the country. Musical talent from other Angolan cities also made it to Luanda stages, both directly and via those who lived in the musseques. In this way, music had a much greater reach than literature and was more intimately a part of everyday life. Indeed, more than a few pieces of literature mention music and *farras* (parties), the struggle to dress well despite limited means, and the fights and romances associated with the clubs.[128]

An analysis of the music scene, its precursors, the lyrics, and the spread of music throughout the country reveals the musseques as a complicated cosmopolitan social space where the national imaginary was made and remade as the guerrilla war raged on in the distance. More than just a stop on the way to modernity or urbanization, the musseques were a place where various generations, classes, ethnic groups, races, and genders met and imagined a new world for themselves in the practices of everyday life. Let us turn now to the earliest rumblings and manifestations of nationalist sentiments and cultural practices in the musseques.

2 ~ In the Days of Bota Fogo

Culture and the Early Nationalist Struggle, 1947–61

THIS CHAPTER EXPLORES the connection between culture and nationalist political activity in the 1950s. It offers a perspective on life and cultural activities in the musseques unavailable either in the social science tracts of colonial origin or in the literary treatments by nationalist writers. Opening up an interior view of the relationship between culture and nationalism grounded in everyday life, this chapter brings class and gender to the surface. As aspects of the urban experience, class and gender do not displace or rend nation but rather inflect it. Although grounded in the urban quotidian, the primary objective of this chapter is to interrogate and complicate the teleological narrative of nation that leaps from the literary cultural flourish of the 1950s and its interest in representing the musseques, to the organization of underground political cells, to exile politics, and finally to independence. The unnamed narrative center of that teleology is male political elites in exile and in rural guerrilla bases. It otherwise ignores the participation and practices of urban residents, both male and female, elite and nonelite.[1] An investigation of everyday cultural practice in the musseques reveals that female and male residents of the musseques imagined the nation sometimes in quite different ways than did the leaders of political movements. Nevertheless it was the urban residents' "ethos of nationalism," as Susan Geiger termed it, that male political elites scrambled to appropriate after 1974.[2]

Cultural practice mattered for a longer period of time and in different ways than the existing metanarrative of Angolan nationalism concedes. Historians and other analysts locate the cultural basis of Angolan nationalism in the writing of a small number of urban-based intellectuals in the 1950s. In this standard historical interpretation, culture is read as immature politics. It receives scholarly attention only insofar as it leads to formal political activity. Scholarly analyses of Angolan history and nationalism describe assimilado associations (the Liga Nacional Africana and Anangola) as proto-nationalist organizations. Their ambivalent relation to the Portuguese colonial state and their valorization of a specifically Angolan culture and history (expressed in the cultural departments and predominantly literary cultural undertakings of these associations) give rise to the contradictions that impel a younger generation to engage in more explicitly nationalist anticolonial politics.[3]

Alongside these associations some scholars have noted, in passing, the appearance and importance of recreational and cultural associations, notably soccer clubs and music bands.[4] Lúcio Lara, an MPLA leader, remarks that the MPLA had its origins, in part, in groups like Bota Fogo and Ngola Ritmos. He thereby subordinates their histories to and folds them into that of the party.[5] Other scholars have suggested that these groups were formed autonomously by urban residents connected to Angolans in the rural areas and have pointed to their importance in mobilizing both urban and rural residents for all three nationalist parties (MPLA, FNLA, and UNITA).[6] Yet even in this perspective these cultural and recreational groups are of interest only to the extent that they result in nationalist political organizing. Edmundo Rocha, like other scholars of nationalism in Angola, concludes that

> what characterized the period from 1955 to 1959, the period of the genesis of Angolan nationalism, in Luanda was the qualitative passage from a cultural and associative movement—one based on positions of compromise with the colonial authorities, but also affirming specific values that would come to be expressed as "Vamos descobrir Angola!"—to the initial organizational phase of the nationalist movements.[7]

Like Rocha's writing, Douglas Wheeler's historical work and Marcelo Bittencourt's *Dos jornais às armas* (From Newspapers to Arms) emphasize the literary cultural movements of the 1950s as a breeding ground for nationalist thinking. For most historians of Angola, culture is a good enough explanation for the antecedents of nationalist politics but it is not taken up again in its own right. It leads to politics and that is where the interest in culture ends.

The study of cultural practice in Angola has generally been the bailiwick of literary critics.[8] Yet here too, it is mostly strictly literary texts and movements that receive attention. As in the historical material, when musical or theatrical groups appear they are quickly marginalized. Music typically receives short shrift:

> The 1940s in Angola saw the revival of African and Creole cultural expression. One of the important events of that period was the creation in 1947 of Ngola Ritmos . . . With its original compositions in Kimbundu, Ngola Ritmos was more than a mere vehicle for a musical renaissance. Indeed for the first time in Angola music and politics were intimately connected. The success of Ngola Ritmos was a portent of things to come. However, it was in literature that the search for the culture of *Angolanidade* was to develop most fully.[9]

The intention of this chapter is not to dismiss the scholarly work, both historical and literary-critical, on this period but to extend an analysis to the politico-cultural groups of the 1950s that other scholars have only glanced at and in so doing begin to broaden our understanding of the relationship between culture and nationalism. Cultural practice is not just a basis for nationalism but is intimately intertwined with and productive of nationalism throughout the struggle for independence and afterwards.[10] In the late 1950s in Luanda's musseques, culture was sometimes a cover for nationalist politics, sometimes a stepping-stone to it, and sometimes the creation of a space parallel to politics but political in its own right. While not ignoring the work of exile intellectuals and poets, this and the following chapters focus on the cultural practices of male and female residents of the musseques.

This shift in the angle of vision offers three analytical advantages. First, it returns our attention to urban spaces and urban culture. The musseques were the site of cultural production, not just a symbol of it. While many of the writers of the late colonial period lived or spent time in the musseques, their literary works represented life there but were not a part of it. By the early 1960s, a good number of these writers (António Cardoso, António Jacinto, Luandino Vieira, Uanhenga Xitu) had been sent off to the Tarrafal prison in the Cape Verde islands for their political activities. While their literature spoke in solidarity with the poor and disenfranchised of the musseques, their main reading audience was the local and metropolitan elite. In contrast, the cultural practices discussed in this chapter were part of the fabric of everyday life in the musseques and represented the quotidian experience there. Looking at cultural producers and the groups and activities in which they were involved yields a sharper image of the musseques' social composition and of the conditions of cultural production there. In stark contrast to the social science vision of the musseques as dangerous sites of social disease, cultural disarray, and poverty, where European culture maintained only a tenuous foothold, the memories of cultural producers from the musseques open up a world characterized by the constitution of new social relations, cultural renaissance, the reconfiguration of European cultural forms in African cultural practices, and the politics of memory. Thus the significance of the musseques to the relationship between politics and culture is not limited to the moment preceding the exile of writers and intellectuals but spills over to the period of the guerrilla struggle as well.

Second, looking at daily cultural practice in the musseques allows us to revisit the nature of late colonialism in Angola. Taken collectively, the memories of people who lived in the musseques in this period suggest that they experienced an improvement in their living conditions and quality of life. Part of this book's argument is that urban residents enjoyed a degree of cultural and economic self-sufficiency in the late colonial period and that this experience prepared them for the politics of nationalism that returned with the exiled liberation movements in 1974. While some scholars have analyzed the lack of substantial changes created by the reforms of the late colonial period, others have highlighted economic growth in both the colonies and the metropole.[11] No one has studied the subjective bases for the general sense among urban residents that their lives had improved.[12] In the memories of musicians and other cultural producers, the musseque world of cultural production was a world of cultural and limited economic sovereignty. In this chapter these changes are accessible through the language and optic of class. Cultural producers referred to themselves as middle class when remembering this period. While the categories of assimilado or indígena continued to define one's civil status under colonial law, people's own definitions of themselves were shifting. Increasingly, assimilados and indígenas were finding themselves in the same places, having similar experiences. In Luanda's musseques they shared in creating a new cultural world while living the vicissitudes of the colonial economy. The coffee boom and increased white immigration spurred construction in Luanda's baixa, thus displacing Africans to the musseques and pushing the musseques further out. Beginning in 1953, a series of development plans intended to direct economic growth disproportionately benefited white settlers, white immigrants, and Portuguese oligopolies.[13] Thus, as Michael O. West has argued for the African middle class in the Zimbabwean context, "The aspirations and achievements of elite Africans amounted to a subversion of colonial will."[14]

Third, and in a modest way, looking at everyday cultural practices in the musseques enables an investigation of the gendered nature of nationalism. Studying formerly marginalized or dismissed cultural groups and practices reveals the involvement of women in this early period of nationalist activity. This adds women's voices to the narrative of nationalism and illuminates the ways in which both nationalism and the cultural production of nation are gendered.[15] After 1961, as music became the salient cultural practice associated with the nation, moving from backyards to clubs and public stages, women's relationship to cultural production became circumscribed while the representation of women in music and their role in the music scene grew in importance. The metanarrative of Angolan nationalism simultaneously ghettoizes and glorifies the role of women, limiting its focus to the Angolan Women's Organization (Organização das Mulheres de Angola, OMA) and to the figure of the heroine.[16] An analytical focus on men's and women's experiences of cultural production opens up nationalism and the cultural production of nation as sites of gendered contestation and power.[17]

BAIRRO OPERÁRIO, NGOLA RITMOS, AND GINÁSIO FUTEBOL CLUBE: EARLY EXPRESSIONS OF MUSIC AND POLITICS, 1947–59

The Bairro Operário neighborhood and the band Ngola Ritmos are closely associated with Angolan nationalism. When I told people that I was doing research on music and politics they referred me repeatedly to the members of Ngola Ritmos, as if to say that they were the first and last word on the issue. The band is generally credited with creating a new musical genre, semba, associated with the emergent nation.[18] Ngola Ritmos symbolizes the link between music and politics because many of the band members were jailed in a crackdown on nationalist activity in 1959 and because these band members used music as a cover for politics and as a way to wake up the masses to their situation. In this sense they were unlike the bands that flourished in the late 1960s and early 1970s. Nonetheless, by looking at this band in the context of the Bairro Operário neighborhood and next to other clubs, like Ginásio Futebol Clube and Bota Fogo, we begin to see how cultural practice fit into everyday life and how the musseques were a site of cultural production. The explicit link between music and nationalist politics that emerges in Ginásio and Ngola Ritmos is the beginning and not the end of the story of the relationship between culture and nationalism, a story not limited to literary texts and political leaders.

In the 1940s, the African assimilado families living in Luanda's baixa were pushed out to the musseques to make room for high-rises and for new Portuguese immigrants chasing the profits of the coffee boom. By the early 1950s, Luanda's musseques had a thriving cultural scene that revolved around soccer clubs, backyard parties, Saturday lunches, and the annual celebration of carnival. Bairro Operário or B.O., whose name means workers' neighborhood, was an old quarter, home to the city's African elite, and it was the center of much of this cultural activity. Although the neighborhood appeared on city maps as early as 1926, its heyday was in the 1940s, 1950s, and 1960s.[19]

As the memories of Albina Assis, Efigénia Mangueira, Armando Correia de Azevedo, and Alberto Jaime will demonstrate, many assimilado families moved to B.O. and then on to other musseques where housing was less expensive or land more available. While a good number of the families that lived in B.O. were considered elites because they worked in the colonial bureaucracy and had access to education, their economic situations were often quite precarious.[20] This new fragility of the *assimilados'* social and economic situation vis-à-vis the colonial state and the fact that they now lived side by side with working class Angolans meant that they more intimately experienced the injustices of the colonial system. In a newly fragile social and economic relation to the colonial state, and now living side by side with working-class Angolans, the assimilados experienced the injustices of the colonial system in a way they never had before. Amadeu Amorim, a longtime resident of B.O. in this period and a member of the band Ngola Ritmos, described the neighborhood as a "kind of ghetto that ended up being where the African or Angolan intellectuals connected with the specialized laborers and other folks. Therefore, that's where they started to mix . . . It was because of this that it was the cradle of revolutionary struggle here."[21]

Agostinho Neto, the first president of independent Angola, lived in B.O. The neighborhood was also home to the Casa dos Panfletos, the "pamphlet house" where early nationalist figures like Beto Van Dunem and Amorim gathered to talk politics and produce political tracts for distribution throughout the musseques.[22] And B.O. is where Ngola Ritmos formed. The band rehearsed there in a house rented by two prominent figures in the anticolonial struggle.[23]

Some of the earliest musical and cultural groups, groups that came both before and after Ngola Ritmos, are associated with B.O. By promoting an African aesthetic in their music, dance, and presentation, these groups ran counter to the cultural politics of colonialism that urged the assimilation of Portuguese culture and traditions. In the 1940s, *rebita* and carnival groups were the predominant form of such cultural activity in the musseques.[24] *Rebita*, a dance originating in the mid-eighteenth century, was popular among Luanda's Africans in the 1930s, and workers formed *rebita* groups in the musseques.[25] *Rebita* is danced in a large circle formed by couples. It includes European elements (including instructions called out in French by the emcee)[26] as well as African ones (particular dance steps like the *umbigada* or stomach thrust). The dress code similarly reflected a mix of influences: men wore European suits and ties and women dressed à la *bessangana*.[27] Women from the urban elite were referred to as *bessanganas* and their distinctive attire consisted of a series of undergarments, four layers of *panos* over a long-sleeved blouse, and a smaller *pano* wrapped around the head.[28] The emcee

Women of Luanda. Agência Geral do Ultramar. *Courtesy of Arquivo de Fotografia de Lisboa, Torre do Tombo*

vetted the dancers' attire. As much as some social scientists wanted to claim the presence of European dress as a sign of progressive acculturation,[29] *rebita* bespoke a sensibility more cosmopolitan than metropolitan. It did not elevate Portuguese culture and dress over African but wedded European cultural practices of salon dancing, dress, and language with African instruments, clothing, and social codes to create a novel local practice. *Carnaval* groups, most active once a year at the beginning of Lent, also included both men and women and used African rhythms, instruments, and costumes along with European whistles and forms of dress.

Inspired by these local cultural practices but also moving in a slightly different direction, groups including Fogo Negro, Xenda Hala, Ngoleiros do Ritmo, and Estrela Canora sang in Kimbundu, used local instruments, wore "typical" or folkloric dress, and included dancers as central figures in their performances.[30] Around the same time, in the 1950s, *turmas* (mostly male groups of friends) got together to play music and dance. By and large, the colonial authorities tolerated these groups as expressions of local folklore within the pluri-continental nationalist imaginary of the Estado Novo. In fact, some of the colonial social scientists thought it beneficial to promote such recreational activities.[31]

Unlike these other groups but like Bota Fogo, Ngola Ritmos had members who were directly involved in political cells and who saw their music as a

Novatos da Ilha Rebita dance group performing at União Mundo da Ilha, 2001

wake-up call for those Angolans who were not as educated or as politically conscious as they were. Ngola Ritmos formed in 1947 and continued until the 1970s with various combinations of musicians including two female vocalists, Belita Palma and Lourdes Van Dunem. In the early 1960s some founding members were sent off to prison or exiled from Luanda to other provinces on temporary work assignments. The band played in a variety of venues in the capital, from the birthday parties of friends and families to the Liga, the city's cinemas, and even the governor's palace, as well as in other provinces.

Carlos do Aniceto "Liceu" Vieira Dias was the group's founder. Despite the fact that he was not from Bairro Operário he grew up, in the words of Jacques dos Santos, in "the B.O. School."[32] His earliest musical endeavors were with European instruments like piano and guitar. In the late 1930s, with other young male assimilados, he formed the Grupo dos Sambas. They primarily played Brazilian music. It was Brazilian music, he claimed, "'that brought us to discover our culture and the value it has.'"[33] Through a foreign musical practice, Vieira Dias and others of his generation returned to their own culture. Cosmopolitan practice led them back home. They began to emphasize the Africanness of their cultural heritage that was so denigrated by colonial society.

Angolan musicologists credit Vieira Dias with translating songs of rural derivation into a popular music that was danceable and, in so doing, unleashing the development of urban popular music and in particular the form known as semba.[34] The technical innovation of semba is generally located in the transposition (or addition) of local instrumentation to European instruments: translating *dikanza* to guitar chords, or using local instruments in addition to

European ones.[35] But it also consists of borrowing from one's neighbors—the famous guitar solos of Congolese musicians like Franco were re-created and Angolanized (a technique pursued by later bands building on Ngola Ritmos).[36]

Vieira Dias took the songs he remembered his mother and grandmother singing at home and elaborated upon them. He transferred to guitar the musical rhythms he heard while accompanying his father, a civil servant, on work trips to different parts of Angola.[37] In this way he transformed local musical practices into music that was similar to the foreign music heard on the radio and at parties (Cuban rumbas and *sons*, Congolese rumba, and a variety of Brazilian forms). Ngola Ritmos used a combination of European and Angolan instruments. Their popularity with European audiences derived from playing Portuguese songs like "Timpanas" and "Maria Vai a Fonte" with Angolan instruments and rhythms (an ironic inversion of the lusotropicalist dictum that lauded Portuguese adaptability to the tropics since it was, in this case, Africans who were the agents of change). Band member Amorim described these as stylized songs, that is, Portuguese songs to which they added a tropical rhythm.[38] Their popularity won them access to the national radio station, which recorded their music under the rubric of "folklore" and broadcast it throughout Angola.

Typical of cultural activities at the time, which included a variety of artistic expressions, Ngola Ritmos's first public performance at the Liga was in the context of a musico-theatrical performance by the group Gexto, some of whose members were also involved in political cells. The two groups sometimes traveled together to Funda, a town in nearby Bengo province, where they would perform at picnics designed to politicize the local populations. Aside from the fact that the lyrics of the songs often carried a message, the band also served to attract people to the meetings. In Angolan filmmaker António Ole's film *O Ritmo do N'gola Ritmos* (The Rhythm of Ngola Ritmos), Gexto's founder Gabriel Leitão recalls:

> It was thanks to the music of Ngola Ritmos that we managed to mobilize, I can safely say, almost 90 percent of the town of Funda for this meeting. We also used Ngola Ritmos for clandestine work in Sambizanga [a Luanda musseque]. . . . There was a simulated party in a place where Ngola Ritmos was going to play and this was only a cover because this party was nothing more than a meeting with a Cuban man, Franciso Xavier Hernandez, who was the first Cuban journalist we met here in Angola.[39]

Ngola Ritmos band member José "Zé" Maria dos Santos also remembers doing political work—exchanging information, distributing pamphlets—in other towns and cities even farther away from the capital, especially towns in central-southern Angola like Gabela and Benguela. He recounted that their rehearsals, in the 1950s, often served as a cover for political conversations and meetings at the house in B.O. where they practiced.[40] Musical lyrics often had political implications. Songs in Kimbundu like "João Dumingu" were social critiques: "See how the stupid man will / End up dying in the contract [forced labor]" (track 6 on the CD; full lyrics to this song are in chapter 4). This song exhorted people to replace foot-dragging forms of resistance with hard work and education. Rather than lament colonial oppression, it foresaw the requirements of independence from the perspective of an educated elite, from the point of view of middle-class values that stressed hard work and respectability.

By the late 1950s the idea that music could be used to rouse the consciousness of the masses had other adherents in the nascent Luandan musical scene. The soccer club Ginásio, like Bota Fogo, had a cultural section and a group of politicized members. The club stood in the B.O./Sambizanga area. The musician Elias dia Kimuezu, considered the "king" of Angolan music, played soccer on their team. Elias, as he is popularly known, lived in Sambizanga, a musseque that was home to a diverse population from various parts of Angola along with Cape Verdeans and native Luandans.[41] Many of its inhabitants worked in the port or for the railroads, both located nearby. As a teenager Elias worked as a railroad mechanic's assistant to learn the trade. At the age of twelve, when his father fell ill, he stopped attending school in order to accompany his father to his home area north of Luanda, the Dembos. Following an ailing parent to his or her rural home was common practice among recent immigrants to the city, according to Elias. After his father's death, Elias remained in this area for a number of years. He lived with extended family and he adopted the name of a local Protestant pastor, Kimuezu, who looked after him. Experiencing the lifeways of the rural world proved pivotal to his musical success. Unlike the mostly assimilado musicians at the time, Elias spoke Kimbundu and knew firsthand the practices and stories of the Mbundu people living in the area around Luanda.[42]

Elias got involved in Ginásio's soccer team. The team was composed mainly of a group of friends who lived in various musseques (B.O., Marçal, Rangel, Sambizanga) but who knew each other from the Liceu Salvador Correia, the high school for Portuguese and African elites in Luanda. Elias did not come from this elite but he got on well with his teammates. He claims that they had political objectives for him beyond the soccer field: "They got me involved because they knew that I knew this national language [Kimbundu] and it was a way for me to be the messenger for certain work" that they were doing.[43] They went so far as to form a band named after the club and that included future MPLA politicians like Angola's second president, José Eduardo dos Santos, who succeeded Neto as president in 1979 and was still in power as of 2008.[44] Elias's talent for composing songs in Kimbundu that were rooted in local stories and that could also be read as social critiques earned him the adoration of his *mais velhos*—his more experienced companions.[45] Thus, while other bands tended to rehash the songs composed by Ngola Ritmos, Elias was opening up new areas musically.[46] His sense that other club members were using him for political purposes underscores both the clandestine nature of the political activity and its association with elites.

It was precisely this elite-organized clandestine nationalist actvity that put Ngola Ritmos members, Vieria Dias and Amorim, in jail in 1959. They were arrested and tried as part of the Processo de 50 after the Portuguese secret police infiltrated their political cell. Zé Maria dos Santos was arrested in January 1961, shortly before the attack on the prisons. Yet the band continued to work, albeit with some interruptions. Tremendous repression meant that their political activities had to be undertaken with even greater secrecy. Amorim, who was twenty when he was arrested, said that in his house, "No one could have imagined, no one thought, that I would have been involved in something," and thus his arrest came as a complete surprise.[47] What mattered among the elite was protecting one's position in the colonial bureaucracy. Civil servants were closely watched by their superiors and by each other. At the same time, it was the younger generation of this old elite that began to part ways with what they considered the collaborationist politics of the Liga and Anangola—first through literary expressions and groups like Ngola Ritmos and Gexto and then through the organization and proliferation of small political groups. According to Amorim, the need for secrecy meant that "society became increasingly closed and no one could think about anyone else. Within our band few people knew who was or wasn't involved and in what cell they were involved."[48] Politics was dangerous business and playing in a band could be simultaneously a political act for some members and an innocent cultural performance for others.

The social policing or censorship within families and between members of elite society that Amorim recounts also occurred on a broader social level. Dos Santos remembered that two band members quit the band because of social pressure and the desire to protect their personal prestige, since it was seen as uncultured, that is, not Portuguese, to sing in Kimbundu. The *hungu* player Kituxi remembers, even in the 1960s, suffering the same pressure from neighbors in the musseque who did not like to see him bare-chested and practicing in his backyard.[49] The attempt to valorize local cultural practices was still an incipient movement and political activity a limited and secret affair.

BAIRRO INDÍGENA, MARÇAL, AND THE CONTEXT OF BOTA FOGO: THE CHANGING SOCIAL COMPOSITION OF THE MUSSEQUES IN THE POSTWAR PERIOD

Bota Fogo Futebol Clube was located in Marçal, just across the street from Bairro Indígena. It opened in 1951 and, according to its last general secretary, Armando Correia de Azevedo, it had two distinct phases: 1951–55 and 1956–61.[50] As its name suggests, Bota Fogo Futebol Clube began as a sports club with a soccer team known by the same name.[51] Soccer clubs had proliferated in the musseques by the mid-1960s.[52] Clubs expanded their recreational activities to include holding dances, sponsoring carnival groups, and offering activities for children. Bota Fogo had all of this and more and in an earlier period. It also had a distinctly political character, or so its former adherents maintain.[53]

Although it was physically situated in Marçal, a musseque whose primary association is with the music of the 1960–70 period, Bota Fogo is more often associated with Bairro Indígena, a middle-class neighborhood across the street. The neighborhood is closely identified with contemporary MPLA political figures, including Fernando da Piedade dos Santos "Nandó," who became prime minister in 2002; Aristides Van Dunem, an original member of the MPLA central committee; Roberto de Almeida, longtime president of the National Assembly; and Lopo do Nascimento, an original member of the political bureau, the first prime minister for the MPLA government at independence, and a member of Parliament.[54]

Luandans remember Bairro Indígena as the neighborhood of politicians. Interviews with former residents, however, suggest that the neighborhood's social composition was more complex than that label implies and reflected the distinctions Christine Messiant makes between "old" and "new" assimilados.[55] These distinctions are represented in the experiences of new assimilados like Elias dia Kimuezu and Alberto Jaime and old assimilados like the members of Ngola Ritmos and the core members of the Ginásio Futebol Clube, as well as Albina Assis, Efigénia Mangueira, and Armando Correia de Azevedo, whose memories shape the rest of this chapter. Despite these differences and the resulting tensions around political participation, Bairro Indígena residents shared certain experiences: of living in planned government-built housing, of exploitation at the hands of local shopkeepers, and of daily cultural practices that included sports, storytelling, and music. It was in these cultural activities that the lives of musseque elites, including both old and new assimilados, intersected with those considered indígenas, who were migrating to the capital in increasing numbers after World War II.[56]

Efigénia Barroso Mangueira Van Dunem was born in Bairro Operário in 1943 but her family soon moved to Bairro Indígena, where she lived until 1962. Her father was a missionary preacher in the Catholic Church and was therefore considered an assimilado. Mangueira remembers the neighborhood and described it in detail, even drawing me a map. It was more or less a middle-class"[57] neighborhood, she said,

> but we had a little of everything—various life circumstances. There were lots of women who were domestic workers and had to raise their children on their own . . . And women who washed clothes for various families [European families from the city] in order to get by.[58]

In other words, this nominally middle-class quarter accommodated those who had already arrived, assimilados, and those who aspired to move up, indígenas. It is interesting to note, as Mangueira does, that many of those in the latter group were single women who would have had greater difficulty achieving assimilado status on their own.

The neighborhood was built by the government in the 1940s and consisted of two areas, each with an open space in the middle surrounded by houses. Bathrooms (one for every two families), washing bins, water pumps (houses had neither electricity nor water), and an area to play soccer occupied this courtyard. There were 114 houses in total. Mangueira's house, where she lived with her eleven brothers and sisters and her parents, consisted of three bedrooms, a veranda, a living room, and a kitchen inside the house, though she mentioned that most people preferred to cook outside using charcoal.[59] Families with some means and some education, like the Mangueiras, often had relatives living with them, typically young relatives who needed to live in the city in order to access the educational system.[60] The neighborhood housed families from Luanda as well as those arriving in the city from the interior.[61]

Although Bairro Indígena was more or less middle-class, it was not free of the hardships and discrimination associated with the musseques. Just behind Bairro Indígena was the neighborhood of Cacimba, built over a dry gulch that flooded during the rainy season. Across Avenida Brasil sat Marçal, one of the city's oldest musseques, and up that same street were the beginnings of Rangel, which by the mid-1960s was Luanda's most populous musseque.[62]

While Mangueira's family qualified as assimilado, Alberto Jaime's family, which had also moved to Bairro Indígena from B.O., was considered indígena. His father paid the *imposto indígena* (native tax) as much as five or six times a year to avoid the penalties of jail and forced labor. The neighborhood's residents were subject to police raids and to abuse by local shop own-

Housing in Bairro Indígena, Luanda. Agência Geral do Ultramar. *Courtesy of Arquivo de Fotografia de Lisboa, Torre do Tombo*

ers, known as *fubeiros*,[63] as were the residents of the other musseques. Underscoring the sense of Bairro Indígena as the home of politicians, Jaime describes it as a neighborhood

> with many patriots—young people who had already expressed their ideas and whom the government did not look kindly upon. There were a bunch of families—the Mangueiras, the Leitãos, some of whom were jailed in the Processo de 50—various families, and us, the poorest ones. But it was a neighborhood with class. The rents were 80, 60, 50 escudos per month, that is, they were for the classes that were economically weakest.... There were indígenas and assimilados.... We used to have this phrase, which described what it was like there. We called it a "firm trench" [space of strong resistance].[64] All that would enter, *eh, pá*, it was an authentic family.[65]

Bairro Indígena, despite its name, was thus a place where assimilados and indígenas lived side by side and created a single community, "an authentic family."

Shared experience and a sense of commonality often transcended the colonially imposed divide between indígena and assimilado mandated under the *indigenato* system established in 1926–33. If the system instituted was one of selective assimilation, the experience of everyday life by former residents of

Bairro Indígena suggests that the neighborhood actually brought assimilados and indígenas closer together. Aside from the shared experience of discrimination at the hands of the state and the *fubeiros* and the day-to-day struggle to survive economically, recreational and cultural practices in the neighborhood provided opportunities for residents to gather.

As the profits from the coffee boom began to accelerate Luanda's urbanization, the African populations in the 1940s and 1950s were pushed out of the baixa neighborhoods and into the musseques.[66] The musseque population grew through this displacement, through natural increase, and through immigrants arriving from rural areas. This propelled new immigrants and long-time Luanda residents into ever-closer contact.[67] It should be no surprise, then, that the former residents of Bairro Indígena thought of themselves as a "middle" class. On the edges of the white city, they were physically between—in the middle of—the urban and the rural. Socially, these upwardly mobile indígenas and downwardly mobile assimilados were a kind of middle between the white colonial elites and the poorer indígenas who had few prospects for improving their situation in colonial society. This self-defined, at least for some, middle class worked and went to school, or hoped to work and go to school, in the city. At the same time, they created and enjoyed the sounds and social practices associated with the rural areas.

One common pastime consisted of weekend "afternoon sessions" in which families, neighbors, and friends got together. Especially popular was the Saturday afternoon *funjada*, a typical Angolan meal. Jaime remembered dropping in at these events after playing soccer against the other neighborhood teams. Music played on gramophones, and jam sessions with guitars, drums, cans— whatever one could find—would erupt spontaneously. Music was embedded in the social experience of the musseques. In the afternoon sessions and other social events, music was part of a larger fabric that also included intergenerational exchange, storytelling, gossip, and recreation. And despite the colonial state's attempt to mold the behavior of the residents of this government-built neighborhood, life here, and particularly social life, looked much like that in the surrounding musseques.

For better or for worse, Bairro Indígena no longer exists. This colonial project to provide affordable homes to middle-class Africans was razed and its inhabitants displaced by the same government that built the homes in the first place. On the vacant site rose the imposing Estádio Nacional Cidadela Desportiva, the national stadium. In the song "Bairro Indígena" (1974), the musician Santocas laments:

> There where I was born, today there is nothing
> All that remains are memories of my friends from childhood

After thirty years of false promises
In which they promised to give us homes
Our parents paid rent in escudos [Portuguese currency]
And then they ran us off as if we were cattle
Pay 500 escudos for a neighborhood without electricity
For houses without yards
All of them run down.

BOTA FOGO FUTEBOL CLUBE: ASSIMILADO EXPERIENCE AND DAILY LIFE IN THE MUSSEQUES, 1951–61

While the young male and female members of Bota Fogo were, in general, de jure or de facto assimilados, they promoted cultural activities and engaged in cultural forms that sought out local roots. And they made these practices more accessible to their neighbors than the literary works of writers associated with the elite associations of the Liga and Anangola. In Luandans' memories, the association of Bota Fogo with Bairro Indígena and not Marçal (the neighborhood where the club was physically located) aligns the club with the more politically challenging culture of the 1950s and with the generation of Ngola Ritmos, rather than with the seemingly less political music of the late 1960s and early 1970s that was associated with Marçal's musicians and clubs. Identifying themselves with Bairro Indígena, the club's former members recuperate their own histories and cultural practices within the standard narrative of Angolan nationalism without challenging the subordination of culture to politics. Their stories show us the differing experiences, forms of politicization, and cultural activities in which young men and women in the musseques engaged. Bota Fogo is the place where the participation of young elite women initially becomes visible and where we see the tensions between old and new assimilados emerge in the degree of their political participation.

Bota Fogo grew out of the social mix that Bairro Indígena represented and addressed the conditions of daily life there. Like other clubs at the time, it started as a soccer club. Mangueira mentioned that her father had been an avid sportsman and had been involved in the Boa Vista soccer club, which predated Bota Fogo. And Jaime, Mangueira's senior by twelve years, founded a strictly soccer-oriented club called Baizinha. Even older clubs existed in the city. Sports clubs like Sporting and Benfica, based on the Portuguese sports teams, and the Clube Atlético de Luanda, whose members belonged to the old African urban aristocracy but were informally banned from Sporting and Benfica on racial grounds, dominated the baixa.[68] The musseques were likewise peppered with soccer and recreational clubs and other venues where neighborhood parties were held.

But Bota Fogo was different, insisted its last general secretary, Armando Correia de Azevedo. Not a resident of Bairro Indígena, Azevedo counted time spent there as honorary residence. He was born at roughly the same time as Alberto Jaime, in the early 1930s, and his family, like that of Jaime's, lived first in Ingombotas, a historically Angolan neighborhood (that is, African, inhabited by assimilados and indígenas, but located in the lower city). They moved first to B.O. and later to the area around Bairro Indígena.[69] Unlike Jaime, Azevedo got involved in Bota Fogo with the intent to produce politically relevant cultural activities. In Azevedo's mind the sports served as a distraction for more important work: "For the Portuguese authorities here in the country it was a soccer club, but for others the soccer was just a cover."

In the first phase, recreational activities arose around holidays and member-organized dances and parties. The club's cultural section organized afternoon performances and matinees on Sundays for children and young people from the area, because activities in the city created for youth (entertainment programs like *Chá das 6* and *Cazumbi*) catered only to European and assimilado children. Azevedo helped teach the musseque youth how to sing, dance regional dances, recite poetry, and play local instruments like drums and *dikanza*. The club consisted of dues-paying members. But club events were open to friends of members and others from the neighborhood for the price of a ticket.

According to Azevedo, Bota Fogo closed in 1955 when the older generation distanced itself from the club:

> Bota Fogo demanded a lot of a person—it was an authentic vocation! People dedicated themselves to it. They would leave work or school and go straight to Bota Fogo, not stopping at home. A part of your life then lacked attention . . . But then the younger group said "No sir! We are going to continue with Bota Fogo!"[70]

They reopened the club in 1956. Although Azevedo did not articulate the generational conflict as political in nature, it was around the same period that politicized generational tensions were unfolding at the Liga and Anangola as club members became increasingly engaged in political activities. A similar tension likely permeated the changes at Bota Fogo.

In the club's second phase, activities expanded to include adult literacy programs held at the club headquarters and in the various musseques. Club members who were students at the *liceu* or at the commercial and industrial schools in Luanda, like Albina Assis and Efigénia Mangueira, worked in these literacy programs. The club even had some members who worked full time at the headquarters helping younger students and those in the first years of the *liceu* with their homework. Bota Fogo's health section offered members free medical consultations with doctors who volunteered their services. A women's section conducted sewing and embroidering classes for young women as well as classes on child rearing. In this way, Bota Fogo provided some social services to a part of the growing urban population whose needs the colonial government did not address. This provided the club with some degree of official tolerance and thus gave them the space to practice clandestine politics, at least in the short term.[71]

The cultural section promoted and performed Angolan culture. Mangueira and Assis, aside from working on the literacy project and raising funds to help restart the club in 1956, participated in theatrical pieces and poetry readings. Azevedo was a central figure here as well. In an urban cultural environment overwhelmingly oriented to Europe and Portugal, especially for assimilados and anyone attending school, the use of Angolan practices and local themes was a way to protest colonial social and cultural control. Since most of these young people did not speak Kimbundu they had to take recourse to various sources: older family members like grandmothers; writers like Oscar Ribas, who had written about Angolan culture and recorded and translated stories told in Kimbundu; and Mário Pinto de Andrade, who wrote a series of short stories published in the Liga and Anangola's newspapers and magazines.[72] They recited the poetry of the "Vamos Descobrir Angola" generation of writers including that of Agostinho Neto, António Jacinto, Viriato da Cruz, and Alda Lara. This meant that the literature being produced by the next generation of writers in publications like *Cultura* and *Mensagem* spread by and to urban Angolan youth and beyond what was an otherwise limited reading public.

Theatrical pieces dramatized daily life. They might represent the disgraces of forced labor and alcoholism to which the average Angolan was subject or mock the African who had rejected African culture in favor of European ways.[73] Bota Fogo encouraged the formation of small musical groups that played Angolan instruments like the *dikanza*, the *hungu*, and various kinds of drums. People who later distinguished themselves as prominent musicians, including Dionísio Rocha, Tonito, Bonga, and Manuel Assis Faria (Albina Assis's brother), participated in performances at Bota Fogo. Rocha remembered that Faria's band, Kimbandas do Ritmo, was a regular act at Bota Fogo dance and theater performances.[74]

Individuals such as Mangueira, Albina Assis, and Azevedo (and other Bota Fogo members like Lopo do Nascimento, Aristides Van Dunem, Manuel dos Santos, and Contreiras da Costa) were conscious of the political implications of their work and used culture to awaken people to their political situation. Dos Santos and da Costa were eventually sent to the Tarrafal prison in Cape Verde following their arrests and trial in the Processo de 50.[75] Mangueira recalled that while they could not organize outright political events, they talked about "everything" in the cultural section, exchanging information they had heard on foreign radio broadcasts or from other sources, but only behind closed doors. Assis noted that at the age of thirteen she was already politicized. Her father was an early member of the Liga, and although they lived in Bungo, an old neighborhood in the lower city, he would take them to the musseques to visit family and to remind them of the reality in which most Angolans in the city lived:

> Even though we were born in a European environment, we always had a mentality oriented to our country, to our nation in terms of Africanness. At thirteen I was already going to visit political prisoners. I was friends with Noé de Saude and Amadeu Amorim is my cousin and both were jailed in the Processo de 50 . . . Why did we go to Bota Fogo? And Santa Cecília [girls' group]? Because we thought that given our education we could raise people's consciousness and convey a message. Because the problem was to explain to others the message: that we were in a situation of oppression and that they therefore shouldn't conform to or accept that situation.[76]

Assis's father died when she was young and the family ended up moving to Marçal, so by the time she was involved in Bota Fogo she was already living in that area and experiencing firsthand the downward mobility occasioned by white immigration. Like Assis, other assimilados pushed out of the baixa by increased Portuguese immigration in the post–World War II period began to articulate a politics that saw common cause with the indígena population residing in the musseques.

Assis and Mangueira frequented Bota Fogo after school and on the weekends. They never faced any restrictions from their parents regarding their attendance even if it meant they did not return home until nine at night, well after dark.[77] Despite the fact that they were young women, they did not experience restrictions on their activities or their political participation. While certainly in the minority numerically, these young women engaged in political and cultural activities that were patently nationalistic in character. In their minds, valorizing and creating the nation was part of an explicitly political agenda that they tried to spread to their neighbors who had less formal education than they did. The Portuguese educational system clearly discriminated against girls, but the social and cultural mores of the African elite allowed at least some young women the possibility to participate in cultural and political activities that were not deemed strictly recreational.[78]

Political activity was risky. In 1957 the Portuguese sent a contingent of the PIDE, the political secret police, to Angola. They attempted to infiltrate political groups and stymie anticolonial and antistate activity. Consequently, all political organizing was done on the basis of small secret cells, meeting in groups of not more than three to five people, in order not to attract the attention of the PIDE or of *fubeiros* (shopkeepers), many of whom were police informants. With public recruiting for political activity impossible, friendship became the preferred vehicle of mobilization. Assis recounted being given the task of making friends with Irene Cohen (killed in 1967 by FNLA forces and considered a national heroine) in order to draw her into the political movement. Assis invited Cohen to parties and to events at Bota Fogo, and offered to share books with her. They became close friends and political confidants. Men likewise remembered friendship as a vehicle for their involvement in politics. Azevedo and Aristides Van Dunem (Mangueira's future husband) were arrested in 1957 for *uma panfletada*, a mass distribution of pamphlets, after they dropped leaflets containing the conclusions on decolonization drafted at the 1955 Bandung Conference into the yards of musseque dwellers. Often ties of friendship or of age were used to persuade someone to unwittingly pass along political information. Jaime said he dropped pamphlets in the yards of his and surrounding neighborhoods several times without reading them. His *mais velhos* asked him to take a bundle of pamphlets and distribute them, saying they were to mobilize people for cultural activities, and he did not question their motives. One day, while on his way to visit his girlfriend, he read one of the pamphlets and was surprised by its political tone.

When I asked Jaime why he had not previously read the pamphlets he responded that he and his friends were much more interested in playing soccer, having a few drinks, chatting with friends, and going to parties. He said that it was those involved in political cells that were behind the activities of Bota Fogo:

> They were the ones who would do this kind of work [producing pamphlets] and deliver them to the "bases." Eh, *pá*, for the "bases," those of us who were living in the middle of these shopkeepers and I don't know what else—are you going to get involved in politics? That is some bad luck you are getting yourself into. If your mother found out she would scold you![79]

Jaime repeatedly emphasized the danger of political activity and how it was more suited to those better educated or better connected than he was. Unlike Assis, Azevedo, and Mangueira, Jaime was a first-generation assimilado. His father did not play a part in his life, his mother was a market vendor, and he only managed the identification card necessary for admittance to the *liceu* with the help of a neighbor. His brothers and sisters did not receive their cards until after 1961, when Portuguese citizenship was extended to all Angolans and the official division between assimilado and indígena was abolished. For Jaime, the stakes of political involvement in these early days were simply too high.

Political consciousness, however, was viable even if political activity was not. Jaime remembered the process of becoming more politically aware and committed to the idea of Angolan independence. In the late 1950s and early 1960s he was employed at the ABC newspaper. This newspaper belonged to the Portuguese opposition, and a number of his senior colleagues were imprisoned; one fled to join the liberation struggle in 1962.[80] Jaime noted that the rank and file workers at the paper were, for the most part, just interested in earning their daily bread. He worked in the printing section where he printed proofs that had to pass muster with government censors before he could paginate the final edition. It was here that Jaime came into contact with literature and the news. Jaime read the uncensored proofs, often including articles about Congolese independence or the Portuguese opposition, in order to educate himself.[81] But access to information could prove costly.

> When I was talking about Bota Fogo, since it was a sports club and all, they often asked me to play [soccer] for them. When I started to have contact with literature and the newspaper and all the news, like the revolution in the Congo, I started to look at this here. It started to open my eyes that the same thing was happening to us here. So when I would print the proofs to be edited and reviewed, I would print an extra copy or two and take it back to my neighborhood and drop it off at Bota Fogo. There were people there who were already involved—they had contacts. [MM: What were they proofs of?] Of the paper before it was censored; the news. We would print proofs of the paper and they would go to the censors at the palace.[82] Sometimes they would come back with entire pages cut out. Anyway, one of these times it almost cost me my job. An individual from Bota Fogo—when the PIDE started doing raids they caught him with this proof.[83] They went to ABC—they actually went there! It was a mess![84]

When questioned by his boss, Jaime explained that he was not involved in a political cell. He extricated himself from the situation by telling the police that the delivery boy had probably carelessly dropped a proof that a passerby then picked up. At the time Jaime was thirty years old, had a wife and five children, and, despite his convictions, was not prepared to risk his livelihood for political activity. In retrospect, he relishes recounting these stories of being on the margins of activism. He alternates between describing political activity as a luxury he could not afford and describing it as something beyond his station, as reserved for those with more education, those who were prepared.

It was not uncommon for political work to go on behind the scenes of other activities. In the case of Bota Fogo, the members were more or less aware of this. A range of politically charged activities took place there, from theatrical pieces with social critiques of colonial conditions to poetry readings to organizing pamphlet distributions and other actions. Young men as well as young women were involved and, as Jaime's story demonstrates, status within this new middle class (more than gender or residence) distinguished those who were willing to take political risks from those who were not. Nonetheless, Bota Fogo provided a way for some musseque residents to begin to reflect critically on their experiences, for others to revalorize local cultural practices, conscious of the political implications of such activities, and for a few to do the frankly political work of organizing and pamphlet distribution.

GRUPO FEMININO SANTA CECÍLIA: ELITE WOMEN'S EARLY NATIONALIST ACTIVITIES, 1958–61

If Bota Fogo represented the potentially powerful mix of different origins and social classes in the musseques, the Grupo Feminino Santa Cecília (Santa Cecília Girls Group) represented an arena of politico-cultural activity restricted to young female elites. This group shows the ways in which young women of the elite used socially acceptable relations like friendship and cultural activities like religious celebrations to educate themselves and others politically. Working in consonance with gendered norms of behavior, they garnered a nationalist consciousness that moved many of them into the arena of politics. This is where women become a visible part of the nationalist narrative, defining their participation in terms that distinguished them from their parents' (specifically, their fathers') generation and its activities at the Liga.

The Grupo Feminino was another manifestation of anticolonialist sentiment that expressed itself in cultural form. Assis and Mangueira both participated, along with Irene Cohen and Deolinda Rodrigues, official heroines of the Angolan revolution. So did many other women who were involved in the liberation movement, formed the Angolan Women's Organization (OMA), and later held positions in the new government, or who were the spouses of political figures.[85]

A Catholic priest from Kwanza Sul, Padre Vicente José Rafael, started the Grupo Feminino in 1958. Having just returned from four years of study at the Gregorian University in Rome, Padre Vicente was in charge of the chapel at the Liga, ministered in other urban churches, and taught at the Catholic seminary. Inspired by a course he took on the history of Italian lay movements, he began to think about "how to organize a Christian nation in such a way that the lay people under the orientation of the bishops, priests and others from the church could organize a democracy."[86] To this end he formed three groups: an association of Angolan priests, an association of ex-seminarians[87] who had not joined the priesthood, and an organization of young women, the Grupo Feminino Santa Cecília. He wanted to prepare Angolans for independence and particularly for a Christian Democratic future in which Christian men and women would shape a democracy under the guidance of Christian leaders.[88] Padre Vicente believed that independence was a historical inevitability given what was happening in other African countries. This put him in direct conflict with the position of the Catholic Church in Angola, which had been officially engaged since the 1940 Concordata in the project of promoting and facilitating Portuguese colonialism. In 1961 he was sent to Lisbon with another priest, Alexandre Nascimento, where they were placed under house arrest.[89]

The Grupo Feminino Santa Cecília was based on the Catholic celebration of Saint Cecília in November.[90] The group had a religious choir but also organized plays and poetry readings that celebrated African culture. They organized a girls' basketball team and held exhibitions to raise money for the families of political prisoners. They rehearsed and hosted events at the Liga but they were not part of the Liga, an organization that many younger nationalist deemed collaborationist since it was dependent on the colonial government.

Mangueira remembered that the association with the Liga created some conflicts because "our activities went beyond the inspirations of the Liga; their cultural activities were of a more recreational character whereas ours were more political. And our friends were people who had objectives that were different than those of the Liga . . . the majority of our friends were seminary students."[91] In Mangueira's estimation the Liga was merely a venue for events and not an institution that met the political needs of her generation. Her comment underscores the sentiments of many of the young writers and other youth who began to search for alternatives to the associational activities of their parents' generation.

Assis recalled that approximately forty young women were involved in Santa Cecília. What she called the "hard core"—Assis, Mangueira, Sílvia

Belo—were consciously involved in political issues, including clandestine meetings of political cells, and cultural activities like producing plays (either at Bota Fogo or with Santa Cecília) that critiqued the effects of colonialism on local society. According to Assis, those members who were not, at first, politically conscious became so later. Consciousness developed either in the course of their involvement with Santa Cecília or after the attack on the prisons on February 4, 1961, when the reprisal of the colonial police against the populations of the musseques made it unmistakably clear to everyone that "colonialism was on one side, and we were on the other."[92] The group continued briefly after the state imprisoned Padre Vicente but eventually disbanded. Some of its former participants helped form the musical theatrical group Ngongo with former members of Bota Fogo, while others, like Deolinda Rodrigues and Irene Cohen, fled the country to join the exiled liberation movements.[93]

The nationalist sensibilities of some of these educated young women brought them to the Grupo Feminino as well as to Bota Fogo. As Mangueira emphasized, this marked a break from the largely loyalist politics of the Liga and Anangola. Young women, as well as young men, were a part of this new generation and new vision. Young women involved in the group participated in cultural activities and in social support services for the political prisoners of the Processo de 50 and their families. For some, these activities provided a means to express their already nationalist intentions, while for others they offered an avenue for radicalization and led to a dawning consciousness of the desirability of independence. Unlike Bota Fogo, this group was not based in the musseques, but it nonetheless had connections to them through young women like Assis and Mangueira who worked with Bota Fogo and resided in the musseques, and through Padre Vicente's vision of a religiously inspired national community that would include all Angolans and direct educational programs at those left behind by the colonial system.

∽

This chapter has taken the first steps of unfettering culture from the narrative of Angolan nationalism, where it is otherwise confined to literary practice. By relocating cultural production in the musseques and making visible the politico-cultural activities of young men and women, it becomes apparent that the history of Angolan nationalism has neither a single source nor a single trajectory.[94] The explicit political use of music by Ngola Ritmos and by the Ginásio Futebol Clube and of other cultural forms like theater and poetry readings by Bota Fogo demonstrates the ways that cultural practices grounded in the musseques drew people in to politics and sometimes served as a cover for political activity. This is but one moment in the history of the relationship between popular culture, and of music in particular, and nationalism in urban Angola.

In the aftermath of the events of 1961, cultural producers had to break any explicit link between culture and politics. The metanarrative of Angolan nationalism privileges elite political activity so that before 1961 culture is relevant epiphenomenally in literary activity and in the form of Ngola Ritmos and Bota Fogo. After 1961 the story follows politics into exile and in so doing silences or trivializes cultural production completely. By looking at Ngola Ritmos, Bota Fogo, and the Grupo Feminino Santa Cecília in the context of the musseques and their cultural practices, it becomes possible to detach their history from the metanarrative and connect it to the cultural practices of the post-1961 period, namely the explosion of music. Not only does culture have a history and political sensibility that extends after 1961, but it generates a sense of nation and nationalism within the country.

The events of 1959 and of 1961 fundamentally altered the social and political scene of the musseques by squelching virtually all clandestine political activity. Even in the 1950s, as the memories recounted in this chapter demonstrate, musseque residents considered political activity dangerous, something to keep secret. Government repression of suspected or real political activity intensified following the events of 1961. However, the social and cultural needs of musseque residents to gather, socialize, and play music did not diminish. And while political activities were increasingly circumscribed, political consciousness became intertwined with cultural practice in ways that had an even greater reach among the populations of the musseques.

Changes in the musseque population, in colonial policy toward African culture, and in economic possibilities meant that music would become first among cultural practices and would take the lead in the continued revalorization of local culture. In this new socioeconomic and political context, music no longer served as an occasional cover for politics but constituted a new space that operated in parallel with exile politics, in which the nation was imagined in and through cultural sovereignty. This shift had gendered implications. Whereas young women had been vital to the activity of politico-cultural groups in the 1950s and to the development of nationalist sentiments, in the 1960s and 1970s they were not so much producers as consumers of the cultural scene.

3 ∽ Dueling Bands and Good Girls

Gender and Music in Luanda's Musseques,
1961-75

ONE PROMINENT HISTORIAN of Angola refers to 1961 as the pivot of Angola's contemporary history. The year signals a rupture in the Angolan historical narrative in relation to colonial rule and the metanarrative of Angolan nationalism. Three popular revolts occurred in 1961. In January cotton producers in the Baixa de Kassanje, east of Malanje, rebelled against the system of forced cotton production for the Cotonang cotton monopoly. In February musseque residents armed with machetes attacked Luanda prisons, hoping to free the political prisoners rounded up in the Processo de 50 and subsequent raids. And in March, primarily Bakongo coffee producers attacked the local colonial authority, white plantation owners, assimilados, mixed-race individuals, and Ovimbundu migrant workers after their demonstrations demanding payment of wages in arrears were met with gunfire. In all three instances the colonial government and white settlers responded with extreme violence and in all three instances the newly formed MPLA and FNLA nationalist movements scrambled to claim or deny authorship and tailor their interpretation of the events to their own interests. The Portuguese colonial government crushed each of these rebellions and intensified the repression of political activity both in the cities and in the rural areas. In this environment, and given the government's grisly response to these uprisings, the nationalist movements saw no alternative but to take up arms.

In order to wage war against the Portuguese colonial state, the MPLA and the FNLA moved to neighboring countries to set up guerrilla bases: first in Kinshasa, Zaire, then in Brazzaville, Republic of the Congo, and finally in Lusaka and along the border in Zambia. The metanarrative of Angolan nationalism followed along behind them. Those who stayed behind in the urban centers are, in the literature, reduced to the status of "the masses"—passive, faceless beings acted upon by the colonial state and later by the returning political leadership.[1] This characterization fails to specify the conditions of life in the musseques in the period between 1961 and 1974 and it inaccurately homogenizes the musseque population. Finally, the metanarrative insists that although nationalism may have been born in the musseques of Luanda (and secondarily Benguela), it grew up in the enclaves of guerrilla struggle.[2]

Angolan nationalism is more complex than this trajectory allows. Scholars recognize that there were three liberation struggles but they do not attend to the lived experience of urban residents in the musseques or explain how their practices, visions, and dreams figured prominently in creating a sense of the Angolan nation. The people who remained in the country, particularly in the impoverished urban neighborhoods, also shaped the history of Angolan nationalism through the music they played and listened to and the clubs they patronized. They rearranged relations between themselves and the colonial state, between urban and rural societies, among members of the urban milieu, and between and among men and women while forging a new sense of nation.

We have seen the often explicit link between culture and politics in early nationalism and the participation of women as cultural producers. This chapter complicates the relationship between culture and politics by focusing on the production of nation. Gender and class are two aspects of the urban experience through which this creation of nation is inflected. Here the discussion of class shifts from people's self-description as "middle class" to an analysis of economic changes that occasioned the growth of a petty bourgeoisie. In the last chapter, "middle class" referred to the consciousness some urban residents had of themselves and of their social position. In this chapter, the term "petty bourgeois" derives from scholarly work on Angola in this period. It describes the material conditions and cultural world of this emerging group. But the consciousness that emerges from that cultural world and the experiences of people from this group are more of nation than of class. Finally, this chapter shifts the focus from female and male participation in the nationalist political movement to a focus on the production of gendered subjectivities in the cultural practice of music in which Angolans imagined and made their nation.

The ways in which African residents of urban shantytowns shaped the cultural basis of nation, and hence involved themselves in the political project of nationalism after 1974, was facilitated, but by no means defined by, reforms in colonial policy instituted after the revolts of 1961. Urban Africans took advantage of these reforms to improve their daily lives, carve out new cultural spaces, and create new practices.

THE PROBLEM

What was life like for those who "stayed behind"? Why were the populations of Luanda's musseques spontaneously organizing behind the MPLA when the exiles returned in 1974, allowing the party to achieve the hegemony required to declare itself the leader of the independent Republic of Angola on November 11, 1975?[3] We will not find answers to these questions in the realm of explicit, even if clandestine, political activity. The extreme repression that began in 1959 and reached new heights after 1961 crushed political activity and fractured the relationship between politics and culture that existed in the politico-cultural groups of the 1950s.[4] Culture could no longer serve as a cover for politics or as a tool for deliberately sparking people's consciousness. But that does not mean, as the metanarrative holds, that culture became irrelevant. In fact, a new style of music boomed and local culture seemed more vibrant than ever. This new form of music, semba, and the cultural scene that grew up around it kept alive a spirit of insurgency, defined a different nation, and buoyed a sense of Angolan difference while refiguring the relationship of culture to politics. This was not a retreat from politics to culture by the nationalist underground, most of whom were imprisoned or went into exile, but a transformation of culture into politics by urban residents.

Just as the PIDE increased its pursuit of "enemies" and "terrorists," the Estado Novo instituted changes in colonial policy meant to assuage international criticism and convince the Angolan population that Portuguese rule was congenial to their needs. The colonial state used seemingly contradictory tools—political repression, on the one hand, and political and economic reforms, on the other—to arrive at the same end: averting insurrection and promoting identification with a pluri-continental Portuguese nation.

Economic and political reforms produced some palpable, if extraordinarily belated, changes in everyday life.[5] The colonial administration instituted nominal political representation, abolished the most egregious practices of colonial rule, and promoted a social agenda of African-centered entertainment and recreation, all aimed at winning the hearts and minds of Angolans.[6] Taking advantage of the colonial state's new receptivity to African cultural and recreational activities, some African civil servants opened more than two dozen clubs in the city's nine musseques.[7] These clubs helped spur the development of musicians and bands and they gave Luanda a new kind of nightlife and form of recreation, albeit one with strong cultural antecedents in the musseques of the 1940s and 1950s.

Angolan popular music exploded in this period and became the first among cultural practices. This resulted from African entrepreneurial initiative in opening clubs and the combined efforts of Africans and of European-financed activities in developing a series of street and cinema-based music festivals, a network of radio stations, and a nascent recording industry. The creation of amateur radio clubs and, eventually, a state broadcasting system meant that locally produced music could be broadcast to and from various places throughout the colonial territory. Street festivals in the musseques drew huge crowds from across the city, leading to a circulation of people between various neighborhoods that otherwise would not have occurred to the same extent. Bands traveled to other cities in Angola and most urban centers had clubs, although the Luanda scene was the largest and most vibrant. People came together and related to each other in new ways because of music.

While the then exiled political movements characterize the period from the outbreak of violence in 1961 to the 1974 revolt by the Portuguese military as politically repressive and violent, Luanda's residents remember it as a period of limited economic advancement and, more than anything else, fun. It was the golden age of Angolan music. Armando Correia de Azevedo described the music festival held at a musseque cinema as "packed full! It was applause, and happiness, it was a tremendous confusion to go to Ngola Cine — they called it the Olympia of Angola!"[8] Yet it was also the period in which the MPLA, the FNLA, and UNITA guerrilla forces were fighting the Portuguese military in northern and eastern Angola.[9] Therefore, the music of the golden age was music produced in the context of the struggle for independence. This is the music that many regard as "authentically" Angolan, free of the political sloganeering of music from the 1980s, when the postindependence civil war was tearing the fabric of the nation, and also different from what some people see as the overly foreign-influenced music of the 1990s. Musicians remember this period as one in which they were able to develop artistically, in which some of them could even live off their art, and in which everyone shared the same desire: Angolan independence.

Music brought people together and dignified them. Olga Baltazar remembers the pride associated with Angolan music as it conquered its own space alongside other "national" musics:

> A person would feel proud seeing the music of their land. Because it wasn't just *fado*, and Brazilian music, and American music — rock — and GVs (which were Cuban music) and Puerto-Rican music. Do you see? Our music started to claim its space. And it was people's first choice! And there were artists, well-known ones, who would go sing in various clubs and even in the bars [of the baixa].[10]

Everyone I interviewed, men and women alike, raved about the music of this period and the venues where it came to life: parties, clubs, and festivals. They spoke in animated terms punctuated by gestures, laughter, and snatches of song. These were the good old days, the salad days, but what made them glorious seemed to have little to do with the nationalist struggle. What counted was entertainment and fun. Even those who were politically active said it was generally too risky to discuss politics in clubs or at parties and festivals because they were frequented by PIDE agents and their informers. Besides, everyone just wanted to have a good time and escape day-to-day pressures and tragedies. Good music, good company, and dancing were the elements of a night well spent.[11] Distant from nationalism and from the guerrilla struggle as these desires might seem, they were, in fact, central to the nation because they produced multiple temporalities and alternative spaces that were parallel to the armed struggle and perpendicular to the colonial project.

Benedict Anderson asserts that the notion of "meanwhile" is critical to conceptualizing the nation. It expresses simultaneity: what is happening in one place is imagined to be connected to what is happening in another, no matter the distance.[12] For Anderson this new conception of time is embodied in the novel and newspaper and is accessible to a wide group of people through print capitalism. Through these technologies people come to imagine themselves as part of a community with a common past and common future. In Angola that "meanwhile" was actualized not so much by print capitalism as by what I call sonorous capitalism, transmitted by radio and made possible by shortwave broadcasting, on the one hand, and by recording technologies, on the other. For Angolans who remained in the country, both in the cities and in the rural areas, the radio opened up the "meanwhiles" of the guerrilla struggle. It gave them a window on developments in other towns and cities within the country and on the international and continental geopolitical scenes, where questions about Portugal's continuing colonialism were debated by the United Nations and by the Organization of African Unity.

While radio and recording technologies allowed for the imagined linkage of different spaces and scales of national significance, Luanda's music and the music scene signified in a special way within this spatio-temporal network. If the "meanwhile" of guerrilla struggle demanded political sovereignty, directly asserted independence in the place of colonial overrule, and propelled a narrative of patriotism based on suffering and sacrifice for the nation, the "meanwhile" of the music scene in Luanda forged cultural and economic sovereignty in the interstices of colonial subjugation while spinning a narrative of citizenship that was urbane, cosmopolitan, and "hot." The music scene created a space of "otherwise": it was an alternative space where the participants realized cultural sovereignty and economic self-sufficiency.[13] As Robin D. G. Kelley argues in relation to the mid-twentieth-century black working class in the United States:

> Black working-class culture was created more for pleasure, not merely to challenge or explain domination. But people thought before they acted, and what they thought shaped, and was shaped by, cultural production and consumption. Besides for a working class whose days consisted of backbreaking wage work, low income, long hours, and pervasive racism, these social sites were more than relatively free spaces in which the grievances and dreams of an exploited class could be openly articulated. They enabled African Americans to take back their bodies for their own pleasure rather than another's profit.[14]

Culture, Kelley argues, does not always read as a direct political challenge but this does not mean that it functions merely as an escape valve for the frustrations of the oppressed. Even as the colonial state promoted African cultural activities and recreation as a vent for frustration, the effects of those activities did not accommodate colonial desires. If, following Kelley, black working-class culture produced something of a ludic, anticapitalist ethos, musseque residents in late colonial Angola produced a ludic, anticolonial, pro-consumerist, *and* nationalist ethos in clubs and through music.

Despite the sometime presence and constant fear of PIDE agents or their informers, the clubs were African cultural spaces. In the name and act of entertainment, new relationships and sensibilities emerged between people that gave them a taste of nation.[15] Matemona Sebastião described his band Ritmo Jazz this way:

> It was mixed in languages—we spoke all the languages of the provinces. The members were Zé Manuel from Bembe, Pioca from Mbanza Congo, Mangololo from Malanje, Ambrósio Caetano from Luanda, Matemona [referring to himself] from Damba, and Petanga who played five Cuban drums and was from Matela. And since I had learned to speak Umbundu when I was living in the south I could also do translations of that, not to mention Portuguese and French.[16]

Matemona thus defined the band as a group of equals hailing from different parts of the country. Jorge Macedo portrayed clubs and parties in the following manner: "In these get-togethers there were romances, etc. There wasn't just recreation but also politics in the sense that at parties there was much exchange of affections—and not just romantic but political. The word *patrício*, my *patrício*, was used."[17] A *patrício* is a compatriot, someone from the same land. Ethnic and regional identifications were thus superseded in musical production and in the clubs. Other participants talked of being in the club ambiance as being with "family," even when the clubs were filled with as many as three hundred people.[18] The metaphor of family domesticated the novelty of the growing and changing urban population. In this sense, if music and partying were escapism, intended to help people "forget,"[19] they took people away from the solitude of their individual grievances and hardships and refocused them on the shared tribulations and aspirations of the musseques and of Angola more generally. Music was an experience of collectivity.

At the same time, and despite the haloed memories that men and women have of this period, the unity of feeling in the face of colonial oppression was built on and through the uneven ground of class and gender relations. Commenting on the relationship between gender and nation, Anne McClintock explains: "Nations are not simply phantasmagoria of the mind but are historical practices through which social difference is both invented and performed."[20] Angolans produced a sense of nation through music and the music scene but they often did so in gendered terms. As music became semi-professionalized and mass produced, it became the predominant form of cultural practice. Male musicians were first among equals, public figures who musicalized and transformed the woes of everyday life, embodied a "hot" cosmopolitan cool, and represented a common urban experience of work and struggle. The club-based music scene was where male musicians garnered notoriety as they rode the crest of masculinist tropes of sports, rivalry, and fame that became central to musical production. Thus they symbolized, in gendered terms, the economic self-sufficiency and cultural finesse associated with nation.

If the music scene was an "alternative" space, a kind of "provisional nation"[21] defined by cultural sovereignty and limited economic self-sufficiency, it was also one in which male producers dominated. Yet women were critical members of the audience insofar as the success of a particular song was measured in dance and dancing was done by couples. Women could be the mark of male success but their presence in the clubs was also the object of discussion and ambivalence. Female musicians found their ability to participate in the scene beyond performance constrained and therefore they did not emerge as admired public figures and representers of this provisional nation. Female audience members, on the other hand, had more space to maneuver and their attendance at the clubs evidenced changing class mores regarding gender. Finally, the growth of radio and recording technologies meant that women (and men as well) did not have to enter the clubs to hear the music.

Women, no less than men, remember the music of this period and associate it with nation.[22] If class more than gender distinguished those willing to take risks and participate politically in the 1950s, gender more than class characterized one's ability to represent the nation in the club scene.[23]

LATE COLONIAL REFORMS AND CHANGES IN EVERYDAY LIFE

What did the shared horizon of late colonial urban life look like? While numerous scholars writing around the time of the guerrilla struggle simply dismissed the reforms of the late colonial period as "too little too late,"[24] people's memories reconstruct, if not a period of prosperity, at least one in which people did better than scrape by and in which they began to imagine new possibilities for themselves.[25] Musicians took advantage of the reforms and they emerged, as a group, at the intersection of changes in education, economy, and culture.[26] In the 1961–74 period music became a culturally legitimate, if not totally respectable or economically viable, profession. Few musicians lived solely off their art, though the possibility of an independent musical livelihood in the future seemed real to them in the early 1970s.

Scholarship produced since Angolan independence has contested the view that the late colonial state's development projects and attempts at reform were ineffectual, though these studies tend to agree that white settlers benefited the most. Gervase Clarence-Smith points out that "although the regime claimed unrealistically high achievements, there can be no doubt that the nature of colonial rule changed greatly and that the guerillas' assertion that these were paper reforms cannot be sustained."[27] He argues that the Portuguese economy boomed in the 1960s and 1970s. In the colonies, foreign investment increased—Belgian investment was replaced with American and South African investments—in ways that reinforced the Portuguese oligopolies. Real wages rose, in particular for urban residents, and some rural producers prospered.[28] M. Anne Pitcher likewise argues that the development plans of the 1960s motivated growth in manufacturing and transportation infrastructure, in part afforded by new oil production revenue, and resulted in improved economic indicators for the two largest colonies, Angola and Mozambique.[29] She points to contradictory interests in the colonial state that, on the one hand, moved in the direction of integration into the European Economic Community and, on the other, promoted continued investment in the economies of the overseas territories.[30]

In Angola the Estado Novo pursued a two-pronged approach of reform and repression, or as Bender calls it, "development and control," to keep Angolans from joining the nationalist movements and to persuade them to invest their aspirations in the Portuguese system. Reforms instituted in September 1961 abolished the *indigenato* system, forced labor, and illegal land expropriation, and made all Angolans Portuguese citizens. As a result of reform and development initiatives, the colonial state recruited more Africans into the civil service in cities while promoting markets and agricultural extension services in rural areas.[31] Repression and control heightened with the increased efforts of the PIDE to ferret out political dissidents and with the implementation of a "psychosocial" counterinsurgency plan in 1967.[32] But while official colonial documents show increased spending in the areas of health, education, and rural social assistance, official decrees were often distant from the on-the-ground realities or had effects other than those intended, particularly in the rural areas.[33] When the colonial state removed one million rurally based Africans from their homes and lands, it caused social dislocation and damaged their economic situation.[34] This made the dislocated Africans more open to alliances with the nationalist forces.[35] At the same time, those peasants who were not dislocated and who actually benefited from the reforms often regarded white settlers and the colonial state as an obstacle to their ambitions.[36]

Relative to the urban populations, Franz-Wilhelm Heimer noted that the economy experienced real growth in the period and that musseque residents reported that exploitation had decreased.[37] Manuel Faria, a club owner and longtime resident of the musseque Sambizanga, confirmed this view: "The time after '61 was the [period] of greatest benefit we had. In terms of the country, because the *colono* [Portuguese settlers and colonizers] after '61 bet on Angola as part of Portugal. . . . And we also started moving around more."[38] Faria suggested that Portugal bet on Angola by introducing reforms that spurred economic growth and that Angolans took advantage of this to improve their social and economic circumstances. But as in the rural areas, this did not necessarily mean that Angolans were therefore betting on Portugal. Many began to see that the Portuguese presence stymied their economic plans and hopes.

Perhaps most significant for the economy in general was the growth of the industrial sector, which occurred largely via the investment of foreign capital in extractive industries (mining and oil) and in the establishment of factories geared toward import substitution (textiles, tire tubes, foodstuffs, chemical products, petroleum derivatives).[39] Most of these factories were located on the outskirts of Luanda, Benguela, and Lobito and provided jobs to people newly arrived in the musseques from rural areas. Nonetheless, they employed only a small segment of a growing urban population.[40]

Scholars of the period generally agree on the growth of an urban proletariat, many recently proletarianized and fresh from rural areas, and a petty bourgeoisie.⁴¹ The ranks of such professions as tailors, auto and motorcycle mechanics, watch repairmen, barbers, and carpenters expanded, and a good number of these people were able to open their own shops and sometimes hire one or two additional employees. Carlos Lamartine remembered that most musicians and club directors hailed from this group as well as from the ranks of civil servants.⁴² Many of them would have been what Messiant calls the new assimilados, whose numbers grew in the postwar period. Together this petty bourgeoisie constituted a small but growing fraction of the musseque population. But they had an overwhelming effect on the cultural scene, thanks to their organizational ambitions and their small disposable incomes.⁴³

The post-1961 reforms marginally improved life for people living in the musseques, though more for this emerging group than for others. Nonetheless, through these changes musseque residents, regardless of class, developed common desires about how to spend their free time and escape the poor material conditions that continued to characterize their neighborhoods. The way urban residents managed these reforms moved them closer to Angola (their imagined nation) and further from the colonial state. This was certainly not what the reforms were intended to do. Clarence-Smith noted that "the new elites were not necessarily won over to the cause of Portugal, for they saw the departure of the Portuguese as the key to even more rapid promotion and social advance. They formed a kind of alternative nationalist leadership to the exiles and the guerillas, a situation which was to create great problems at independence."⁴⁴

In the mid-1960s some Africans in the musseques, primarily from this new petty bourgeoisie, opened nightclubs and founded recreational clubs and associations. The colonial state provided a small monthly subsidy to clubs with a sports component to help defray their operating costs. In this way the state loosely supported such venues once they had been established through local initiative. The colonial state went so far as to sponsor street and cinema-based music and variety shows that had proven popular with the bulk of the musseque population. This was part of the government's counterinsurgency plan of reforms and associated measures instituted to conquer Angolan public opinion. One government decree called for "the promotion or stimulation of any kind of initiatives that will reinforce the ties of solidarity and neighborliness between the different classes or social or ethnic groups, particularly through athletic, folkloric or generally cultural means as well as through youth work camps, building one's own home, etc."⁴⁵ The colonial state could only imagine that this would bolster its position.

But Angolans used these clubs and venues to meet their own social and entertainment needs and thereby made them politically meaningful. By taking up the reforms they participated in colonial society while carving out their own nation. Armando Correia de Azevedo used political language to describe cultural endeavors in this period: "Portugal started to enact some reforms. But one couldn't talk of independence . . . this was prohibited . . . and so Angolans also started to be 'diplomats': we started to be 'good' Portuguese, etc., and exactly so that we could fight for the Angolan cause."[46] In other words, they learned how to say one thing and do another and how to use the language of colonial reform to build their own cultural world. This was particularly true for civil servants who worked in the administration during the day but returned home to the musseques at night.

Like the bulk of the musseque population, musicians were, by and large, young, male, and unmarried.[47] With few exceptions, they all had day jobs, usually as mechanics, tailors, welders, beer salesmen, factory workers, or low-level civil servants. Musical gigs allowed them to buy new instruments, strings for guitars, nice clothes for performances, and drinks at clubs when they were not playing.[48] The money musicians earned performing at clubs or at street and cinema-based music festivals and variety shows was not enough to cover all the costs of daily life, especially for those with families.[49] But if finances were well managed, musicians could purchase new clothing and instruments and even help pay the rent.[50] Changes in the economy instituted after 1961 allowed those with jobs, and someone willing to back them up, access to loans. Stores in the center of the city that sold instruments and clothing allowed musicians to purchase items on layaway, paid in monthly installments at a local bank.[51] Musicians dressed well and they followed the latest fashions in magazines and films, transforming them into symbols of Angolan urban identity. Chico Coio remembered that everyone had his own tailor or seamstress and that musicians (and many audience members as well) preferred personally tailored togs to those purchased ready-to-wear. In this way, musicians both emerged from and sustained this burgeoning subgroup of self-employed Africans, and consumption fueled the imagination of nation.

When Angolans attended clubs to hear Angolan music, they supported local entrepreneurs and neighborhood-based clubs. Clubs were either member-based or individually owned. Registration with the government made them visible to the colonial state but they were otherwise autonomous. Member-based clubs collected dues from their members, but the parties held there (in which bands featured) were, for the most part, self-sustaining. Partygoers, who could be club members or not, purchased tickets to gain entry. And the clubs paid the band or bands with revenue from ticket sales. Nonetheless, clubs functioned with a very narrow margin of profit and sometimes none at all. Indeed, Lamartine remembered that clubs often went into and out of bankruptcy and lived a precarious financial life. Monteiro, in his study on the musseques, similarly noted the financial instability of the clubs but pointed out that when the situation was desperate the necessary funds always seemed to appear.[52]

Despite this fragile financial situation, membership-based clubs imparted skills like budgeting, marketing, and management to those members involved in their administration. As Alberto Jaime, former president of the club Maxinde, remembered: "We wrote reports—annual reports, praised the work of the managing body, and presented balance sheets. We would have meetings and people would make accusations—'That budget is all lies!'—but that was all part of it. It was a way for people to participate."[53] In this sense, clubs were training grounds for independence where people could develop the skills needed to run their own lives and their own country. Since the majority of musseque residents worked for someone other than themselves, and even the emerging group of self-employed had probably worked for someone else at some point, the experience of participating in a club or of just spending one's limited disposable income there to hear a new and characteristically Angolan kind of music created a sense of sovereignty. Against the arrogance of those who had gone into exile, Jaime defended the work of those who remained in Angola, arguing that "the struggle is fought on various fronts." He worked through the clubs to bring people together so there would not be a dispersion of "Angolan patriots" and "progressive Angolan forces," that is, those who had grown up with the generation of Bota Fogo but had not headed off into exile.[54]

Access to the clubs was restricted by ticket prices and by the dress code, both of which presumed a certain financial liquidity. But even musseque residents who were not of the petty bourgeoisie were able to attend parties at clubs sometimes, if not regularly. In any case, the streets were filled with music. People who could not afford the ticket or the flashy togs required for admission to the clubs would gather outside them, as they did outside cinemas, to enjoy the festivities remotely, sometimes creating their own party in the street.[55] Bands played at music and variety shows held in the streets of the various musseques and at the Cine Ngola, a cinema located on the edge of the most populous musseque, Rangel. And the low cost of transistor radios made music increasingly available over the airwaves.

All of this represented a significant shift from cultural life in the musseques of the 1950s. In fact, everyday life in the musseques in the late colonial period was changing from what it had been. As Jean-Michel Mabeko Tali noted, those returning to Luanda from years in exile or in the guerrilla struggle did not recognize the city they had left behind in the early 1960s. "In that year, 1974, Luanda was the prosperous capital of a colony in the midst of economic development."[56]

But the division between the white city and the black city, the baixa and the musseque, still existed, and it had sharpened as both areas grew in size and the musseques were pushed further and further from the city center. Despite the censure of the PIDE and thanks in part to this de facto segregation, Africans in the musseques had been able to establish their own world. They took advantage of legal and social changes to secure their cultural sovereignty and a degree of economic well-being. One could walk down the street in the musseque and see African-owned businesses: barbers and tailors and mechanics plied their trade from their own homes or on adjacent properties. Parents could more easily educate their children and themselves. Employment, though still competitive and generally poorly remunerated, was more available. Recreational and sports associations and clubs flourished in the various musseques. Almost everywhere one went in the musseques one could hear the sounds of Angolan music on transistors glued to the ears of young Angolan men or on the home radios and record players of the emerging petty bourgeoisie. Despite the differences between this emerging class, the old elites, and the bulk of recently emigrated musseque residents, all three groups together created an urban culture in which the horizontal signifier *patrício*, compatriot, often superseded the vertical relations of class.

MASCULINITY AND MUSIC

Men, in particular, spoke with great animation about the rivalry between bands, their fame as musicians, and their friendships.[57] Male camaraderie characterized the music scene in the musseques from at least the late 1950s. Carlos Alberto Pimentel remembered rivalries between bands in that era as ultimately unifying and friendship oriented, productively competitive like team sports:

> We created a kind of confrontation. This or that neighborhood would go play in another neighborhood in order to see who played better, or show who played better. And then there was always a group of girls that would accompany us from their neighborhood to ours — and there was terrible [i.e., great] stuff! Sometimes we would get angry and end up in fights. That was terrible! [*laughs*] But in the end, it was healthy because we made great friends in that period. We ended up coming together at big parties where we would all play music. We even began to see that all of us were in favor of creating more happiness and animation in the culture of Luanda.[58]

Initially, bands were a form of recreation formed by groups of male schoolmates or friends from the same musseque. Rivalries between bands produced a sense of music as recreation, or music as a sports-like activity.⁵⁹ Indeed, bands are much like teams—a group of people must work together, each refining his or her talent and skill in the context of the whole. Rivalries between bands created an opportunity for young men to learn to interact with youths from other neighborhoods and schools, to defend themselves, and also to see conflict as resolvable.⁶⁰ Female friends and attention were associated with these struggles and were, indeed, a sort of prize or symbol of victory. As Pimentel noted, if band members played particularly well a group of girls might follow them home to their neighborhood.

Band nomenclature reflected and amplified rivalries. The musician Carlos Lamartine's first band, formed with his friends from the Marçal neighborhood where he lived, was called the Kissueias do Ritmo. Lamartine explained:

> *Kissueia* is a Kimbundu term that more or less means enemies, or bandits, vampires. But in the good sense. In that period the groups, because of their interaction with other groups, had this tendency to use these names that denoted competence. Some could have happier names while others would look for different designations in order to intimidate the others and say we are stronger.⁶¹

Similarly, Pimentel noted that bands often played a song with their name in it in order to fix themselves in the minds of their audiences.

As bands became increasingly oriented to an urban music circuit that included many different neighborhoods and performance sites, rivalries centered on offering something new to the audience. Bands competed for audience approval whether at a party, at a club, or in one of the musical talent shows of the mid-1960s. Matemona Sebastião, the guitarist for the band Ngoma Jazz who moved to Luanda in 1960, described the rivalry in terms of sportsmanship:

> In that period, we played as if there were a dispute. [MM: What do you mean?] A dispute, as if it were soccer—you go to the field and see who wins. At that time the dispute was about who had come out with a new song. There would be a party with lots of people and we would create something new to surprise the other groups. I remember one time there was a group that had come down from Cabinda for an appearance at Aguarela Angolana [Angolan Watercolor, a talent show at one of the big cinemas in the musseques]. And we thought, ha, let's go see who they are! Who'll play better? They played and everyone applauded—it was Cabinda Ritmo. Now, it

was Ngoma Jazz's turn and I remember that I got up and walked in with my guitar and everyone was all enthusiastic! We had followers just like in soccer.[62]

At other points in the interview Matemona stressed the significance of the audience to band success. A good band and a good musician knew how to read their audience and play to them. Yet Matemona's description also shows how bands directed themselves to one another, composing new material to surprise the other bands as much as the audience.

The sports analogy that Matemona used elucidates the male culture of bands that emphasized an explicit competitive component as fundamental to this new musical form of artistic expression. But Matemona also employed the sports analogy to say that musicians were important, that they mattered, because athletics was a realm already associated with fame and popularity. The 1950s witnessed a proliferation of soccer clubs in the musseques and at least two of the multinationals with factories in the city sponsored soccer teams.[63] In fact, some of the earliest clubs were founded on soccer teams. Even before 1961, Angolan athletes received scholarships to study and play in Portugal and Angolan athletes were lauded both in the metropole and in Angola, thus enjoying a visibility unusual for Africans in colonial society.[64]

Musicians offered the sports analogy to describe musical life, and in fact some musicians played soccer as well as music.[65] As soccer became increasingly popular in the musseques it was available as a symbolic resource used to give meaning to other activities like music. Unlike the war for independence going on at the same time, these were disputes that produced a greater sense of connection, of "we-ness" among the competitors.

The phenomenon of rivalry and dispute resonated with another local cultural practice—carnival (tracks 13 and 14 on the CD). Every year, in accordance with the church calendar, carnival groups would perform in the streets of the musseques and in the avenues of the baixa. Rivalries between different groups fueled song compositions and dance choreography as much as did the parody of royal and bureaucratic power.[66] Song lyrics often ridiculed rival groups and the dynamics of insult and riposte might be drawn out over several carnival seasons.[67] In his discussion of carnival and soccer groups in the 1980s, Ruy Duarte de Carvalho notes that the development of song repertoires took many years. Carnival groups included both men and women, young and old, though dance sections were often subdivided by gender and/or age. Many women participated, and indeed many male cultural producers (musicians as well as emcees, club owners, and so on) remembered attending carnival practice with their mothers, aunts, or grandmothers.[68]

Carnival was banned from 1961 to 1968, and the local press and people I interviewed depicted the post-1968 carnivals as struggling to attain their former glory but consistently falling short. Carnival had given way to the urban music scene. The music scene was more youth-centered and more cosmopolitan and had greater range throughout Angola, thanks to the spread of radio and the fact that bands traveled to perform in other cities. But the role of women as cultural producers was eclipsed in this process as music moved out of backyards and carnival groups to become professionalized and centered in clubs. Youth and gender, more than neighborhood, now shaped the content of the rivalry.

Playing in bands taught young men something about social interactions between neighborhoods, between male peers, and between young men and women. But learning to play, that is, musical education, was an intergenerational male experience.[69] Pimentel, for example, remembered frequenting the Clube Atlético de Luanda, where he would sit by the table where the members of the band Ngola Ritmos were seated in order to listen to them play and learn what he could through observation. All of the musicians interviewed recounted similar experiences of learning to play, compose, and sing at the feet of their *mais velhos*. Luanda's Music Academy offered a program in classical music but admitted few Africans. Guilhermo Assis, an African civil servant, opened a music school in the city neighborhood of Ingombotas that some, although not many, musicians frequented.[70] By far the most common form of musical education consisted of watching others play and begging a try from a *mais velho* when he took a rest. In this context, informal musical apprenticeships with older musicians marked the generational transmission of particular styles.[71]

Male friendships, both within and across generations, shaped musical study and production. Musseque residents typically spent Saturdays with family and neighbors at late afternoon lunches in the backyard. A circle of *mais velhos* in conversation, some with instruments in hand, would form and an impromptu jam session would begin. At such family gatherings, it was not unusual for women to sing or even play an instrument. Given the division of domestic labor by gender and generation, however, it is perhaps not surprising that the musician Rui Mingas remembers his grandmother participating by singing and playing *dikanza*, but not his sisters (even though one of his sisters later went on to become a singer).[72] The *hungu* player Kituxi learned by watching a cousin of his who played this instrument.[73] Kituxi would go to his cousin's house in Rangel with a jug of wine in hand in order to persuade his cousin to teach him.

The music scene moved from backyards in the late 1950s and early 1960s to clubs and street festivals by the late 1960s. Part of this transition was the emergence of groups called *turmas*.⁷⁴ They played a significant part in the development of later bands and the creation of new urban popular music like semba beginning in the 1950s. Mateus Valódia defines a *turma* as "a group composed of a collection of friends of music, that get together to sing and dance and produce other cultural activities," and he notes that a number formed in Bairro Indígena, Marçal, and Rangel.⁷⁵ Alongside *turmas* from Bota Fogo and the others mentioned in chapter 2 (Escola do Samba, Xenda, Hala, and Ngongo) emerged others like the Turma do Babaxi, Turma do Rico, and the Turma dos Caboverdianos. Members of these groups then moved on to form the earliest bands, which began to consolidate the new sound of semba and the new club scene.

In the 1960s the number of bands grew, many without any roots in the *turmas*. Many musicians, though not yet professionals who could earn a living playing music, concentrated on improving their technique, rehearsing for hours and playing regularly at the new clubs and festivals. The increasing importance of fame and popularity accompanied this transition.⁷⁶ Musicians garnered admiration and respect and made a decent amount of money, at least enough to cover expenses of the trade—instrument maintenance, clothing, shoes, and nightly food and drink.⁷⁷ When I asked the composer Xabanu what the scene in the clubs was like, he said, "It was very hot! The scene was really hot because if you didn't go to the clubs you were a nobody, you weren't known." For many young Angolan men and women, the clubs were the place to be. Club owners pointed out that people came from other provinces to visit Luanda's clubs and that by the early 1970s Portuguese tourists and residents began to frequent the musseque-based clubs as well.⁷⁸ Being seen at these clubs was important, and particularly so for musicians. I asked Xabanu, "If you were to go to Maxinde [one of the most popular clubs] on a Friday night, would there be a lot of people you knew?" He replied,

> No, no. There would be a lot of people I didn't know. But the majority of people were known—or what I mean is that we were known to everyone but we couldn't possibly know everyone because we were the *expoentes maximos* [illustrious representatives, famous ones], you know? When we hung out in an area chatting, people would gather around us to look and see what we were doing and try to be friendly with us. The only thing is that in that period no one asked for autographs because they didn't know to!⁷⁹

Many musicians contrasted the respect and attention they received back in the 1960s with the ignominy and poverty they experience today. Chico Coio remembered that when a particularly renowned artist would enter a club people would stand up and clap before he had even begun playing.

Audiences demonstrated their respect for artists by showing up on time to see the bands and artists perform. Coio echoed Xabanu's sense that music made you somebody:

> Everyone sang. Many of our leaders that are out there played guitar and, in those days, were musicians. What I mean is that there was an expression like they had in Brazil at that time—to be someone you have to play soccer or you have to sing—in order to be known, in order to be on top. So many of our leaders, I am not going to cite names, also dedicated themselves to music. Even people with medical degrees left medicine to go into music because music gave you more: it gave you fame and it gave you money. So therefore people abandoned other arts and in that period everyone was a musician. Today no, now everyone wants to be a politician, a deputy in parliament, and I don't know what else. Why? Because music has no expression.[80]

Coio mentions that music was the predominant arena of artistic expression. Though he has a critical view of people wanting to do what will make them famous and earn them money (being a musician in the 1960s and being a politician in the 1990s), his comments also point to the lack of space for African politicians in the colonial system and the fact that music came to represent respectable male labor. The music scene thus developed into a unique realm where African men could create a public profile among the urban population. Bands and individual artists attracted fans that would follow them from club to club, event to event. Musicians expressed common experiences of life in the musseques and made people dance. For this, they gained the respect and often the adoration of their listeners. Unlike sports stars (Diniz, Rui Mingas, Barceló de Carvalho) who moved to Portugal to play on the metropole's teams, musicians continued to live in the same neighborhoods where they had always lived, went to their day jobs, and experienced day-to-day conflicts with the colonial system just like everyone else. If the clubs produced a kind of "provisional nation," or a proxy for nation, popular musicians functioned as metaphorical representatives and representers of that nation, as firsts among equals.

Although musicians lived in conditions similar to those of audience members, being well known did have its perks. Whereas the attention of groups of young women had been the prize in neighborhood band rivalries, girlfriends were a measure of notoriety on the club scene. Girlfriend, in this context, meant something more than just a fan or friend but something less than a

The band Os Kiezos at a musseque club, early 1970s. *Courtesy of Cirilo Metodio Lopes and Rosa Alberto dos Santos Lopes*

committed relationship: a love interest perhaps. Male musicians would invite their girlfriends to the clubs for their performances. By inviting many girlfriends on the same night musicians could demonstrate their popularity, often at the expense of the young women's emotions. This situation, Lamartine explains, caused some consternation for families preoccupied with their daughters' well-being and reputations, not to mention for the young women themselves:

> We started to become famous and with this fame the artists would influence the behavior of young people who went to the clubs and were fans of Carlos Lamartine, of Urbano de Castro, etc. On a single night an individual [artist] might have four, five, six, ten girlfriends attending the show and he wouldn't know which one he was going to leave with! And if I brought ten girlfriends to the center, Artur Adriano would bring so many others, and the band members would bring along so many more. And Os Kiezos, for example, was a band with at least eight to ten members, and each of them invited two or three girlfriends to the club, so you can imagine what the place was like. They would enter the club as the girlfriends of the band, but this didn't mean that they wouldn't drag in behind them a pile of men

that were interested in them. Naturally, there were some altercations, some battles between the diverse attendees of the club. If this, on the one hand, created a certain insecurity for some families, you know, respected ones that went to the centers but didn't want their daughters involved in such conflicts, on the other hand it gave us a certain pleasure to see lots of women crying because in the end they discover that their boyfriend has a bunch of girlfriends![81]

Lamartine notes that such situations worried the parents of young women who were keen to protect their daughters' honor. Clubs were potentially dangerous places for young women's reputations. They might be duped by some young musician or rub shoulders with prostitutes.[82] Clubs in Marçal and Bairro Operário were located near zones notorious for prostitution, and prostitutes who earned a decent living could easily buy a ticket and enter the club. A clear double standard regarding male and female sexuality existed: young men could frequent the clubs without parental concern and they could even patronize prostitutes (seen as part of becoming a man) as long as they eventually found the right girl and married her. The different stakes for young men and young women are underscored by Lamartine's comments that seeing young women upset and lost in the game of love was entertaining, a sort of sideshow to the performance.[83]

Women in the clubs helped define masculinity. Men outnumbered women in the musseques, thus bolstering the symbolic capital of the female attention lavished on musicians. Song lyrics often centered on women—in either praise or condemnation—and figured men as victims of heartbreak or of scheming women. The musician Chico Coio offered one compelling interpretation for the thematic prominence of women in song:

> Our music from that other time spoke more about day-to-day relations—love songs, popular songs, songs for or against women. The music used to be like it was in Brazil or in other places and here it wasn't so different—some in favor of women, but mostly it was speaking badly about women . . . songs that criticized women, that women are this or that . . . The world only talks, it doesn't provide [it is just idle gossip]. Even today they talk about women, talk about men, talk about people. As my father said, "When someone is spoken about, he is spoken about because he did something good, or because he possesses some good." No one talks about someone who is in the garbage, right? Lots of people today talk about women—that they are like this or like that. Because they are good, who doesn't

like women? It is because of this that they are discussed . . . Because they are valuable.[84]

Women matter. According to Coio, women were and are the subject of so much discussion and reflection in song, and in conversation, because they are important to men and because they are socially valuable, particularly so when they are few in number. Didier Gondola argued for the significance of women in 1950s Congolese popular urban music: "Although women were not composing or performing, all musical creation, diffusion, and performance revolved around them. Woman was a powerful source of inspiration for the musicians."[85] Likewise, in Angola, while women were not the main producers of music they were nevertheless productive of it.

Band organized, club-based music was male-dominated and generated a novel, urban masculinity. Young men learned to play instruments from *mais velho* male musicians and relatives, honed their skills in all-male, generally neighborhood-based bands, and counted on women to demonstrate their success, parade their sexuality, and quantify their notoriety. Songs about women included both social critique, aimed at defining women's behavior in particular ways, and romantic praise that idealized women and showcased the power they had to break men's hearts.[86]

"GOOD GIRLS"

I had difficulty finding women who attended clubs as audience members whom I could interview. Hence, the picture offered in this section is based on the recollections of men, of female musicians, of women who chose not to attend the clubs, and on speculation. If male behavior and participation in the music scene was in part characterized and transformed by "dueling bands," female behavior and participation was supposed to follow social norms that constructed them as "good girls." Most male musicians had sisters and female cousins who attended shows, and some were looking for marriageable (that is, respectable) young women. Thus they too sought to uphold patriarchal norms of female behavior—conservative dress, going out in groups, dating only with parental permission and the intention to marry. Dishonoring a young woman by taking her virginity not only was considered socially reprehensible but was legally reproachable, just as a young woman's lack of virginity could constitute grounds for canceling an engagement.[87]

While female musicians distanced themselves from the scene beyond the stage, young female audience members were critical to the scene. Although we do not hear their own voices on the matter, we can get at some of their actions and thoughts indirectly. As Lamartine's comments about the sideshow of upset young women indicate, some young women did not find it entertaining that their hearts were broken, that they had been betrayed, and that their boyfriends had shown a lack of respect for them in a very public way. But clubs also offered a novel form of entertainment and a degree of independence from the kind of family oversight that reigned at parties in the homes of friends and family. For young women proactive in their sexuality, clubs were spaces where they could maneuver more freely. Finally, women who engaged in prostitution also likely looked to clubs as places where they could establish a social profile and connections in urban African society.[88] The clubs where musicians played embodied contradictions for women: they required women's presence to make them viable and yet they were also potentially dangerous spaces for women. Consequently, female presence in clubs was the subject of class, generational, and gender contestation.

The double standard was most exaggerated for artists. If male artists could flaunt their popularity by having many girlfriends (that is, their sexualization followed their fame), female artists had to struggle against the image of the female singer as prostitute (that is, they were assumed to be already oversexualized). Lamartine explains:

> Our parents . . . thought that the artistic life was the lumpen life, the life of a bandit, one without a future, and for this reason singers were not considered to be responsible, not even for marriage. And therefore the girl that sang, or hung out with bands, or participated in theater could be taken as someone lacking judgment, a prostitute, or just irresponsible—these were the most pejorative terms used to characterize people that participated.[89]

Despite the fact that most of these young people would have known or at least known of female cultural producers who performed publicly (in carnival and in the politico-cultural groups of the 1950s), women who performed in clubs had to combat the notion that they were morally besmirched.[90]

Male musicians, on the other hand, were seen as merely irresponsible. Luanda in 1960 was a predominantly young and male city in which women had fewer economic opportunities than men.[91] Since no one could live solely off music, male artists all had other jobs. In general, musicians were civil servants or practicing mechanics, painters, tailors, and so on, part of the emerging petty bourgeoisie, and they could therefore more readily combat their depiction as irresponsible. For male musicians, music was recreation. As it became increasingly professionalized in the late 1960s and more lucrative with the growth of a recording industry in the early 1970s, music became a respectable male occupation. For female musicians, on the other hand, who had less access to education and to employment, and whose reputations were more dependent on their family name and their behavior, music had a more ambivalent meaning.

Dina Santos and Lourdes Van Dunem, two of the best-known female vocalists in the late 1960s and early 1970s, both emphasized that they were not interested in the club scene beyond the opportunity it offered them to perform. They did not, for the most part, hang around the clubs before or after performances and they had little to say about club ambiance. Van Dunem was born in 1935 and perhaps the crowd was a bit young for her, but this was not the case for Santos. Most of the other artists and those attending the clubs were her age and some were her friends. Her husband was the lead singer of the band Os Kiezos, which was a staple of the club scene.[92] Yet for Santos the clubs held little charm: "I have a failure, a defect—I don't drink, I don't smoke and the artists that don't know me don't believe it."[93] Santos associated the clubs with the stereotype of the artist dependent on drink or drugs for inspiration. For her, clubs were not a place where she was going to learn anything new about music, meet her friends, or improve her social profile. If male musicians could, in part, measure their success by number of girlfriends and by the musicians' social attractiveness as participants in club audiences, female musicians had to distance themselves from the interactions of the club party scene and focus their attention on their stage performance.

The song "Semba Kassequel" by Dina Santos (track 3) demonstrates some of the tensions women experienced in the urban environment, as well as some earlier characteristics of the Luanda music scene. In the song she sings about how the young women in the musseque Kassequel want to put a curse on her. Here we see the territorialism of urban neighborhoods also present in the rivalry of different bands. The lyrics do not explain why the young women want to put a curse on the song's narrator, but given what we know about the context, we can guess that it has something to do with men or, if it is autobiographical, with Santos's success as a singer.

Mana, yalongwe o divwa dyami	Sister, just look at my disgrace
Ilumba ya Kassequel	The girls from Kassequel
Andala ngo kungilowa	Want to put a curse on me
Kizuwa kina ngasengwele ka kassequel	That day when I went to Kassequel
Mana Rosita wamugikola aiué	Sister Rosita called to me

Aiué mama ué	Aiué mama ué [wailing sound]
O ilumba ya kassequel	The girls from Kassequel
Andala ngo kungilowa	Want to put a curse on me
Aiué mama ué	Aiué mama ué
O ilumba ya kassequel	The girls from Kassequel
Andala ngo kungilowa	Want to put a curse on me
Andala ngo kungijiba[94]	They want to kill me

The lyrics focus on the narrator's disgrace, her worry, and her shame. From the lyrics we can see that women, as well as men, policed female behavior and engaged in their own kinds of rivalries. The instrumentation, fast paced

Belita Palma (dressed as a *bessangana*), album cover, early 1970s, produced in Angola on the Rebita label. *Courtesy Radio Nacional de Angola (RNA) and Sociedade Angolana do Direito do Autor (SADIA)*

Urbano de Castro, photograph from the early 1970s, reproduced on an album cover by Teta Lando Produções, Luanda, 1998. *Courtesy SADIA*

and edgy, makes the narrator's grief danceable. By transforming this scene into danceable music, Santos transforms her personal disgrace into her public success. Yet the very public nature of musical performance opens her to the charge of moral turpitude. Literally in the limelight, and limited in number, female singers found their activities open to public censure and public comment. Given the attention to their public visibility, female performers also more often dressed "typically" while male musicians could highlight the new urban style, as the album covers of Belita Palma and Urbano de Castro illustrate. Female performers also spoke negatively about other female performers in order to construct foils for themselves. Both Santos and Van Dunem mentioned that they were not like some of the other women performers out there, thus advancing the stereotype of the dissolute female singer while distancing themselves from it. Conscious of the stereotype, these female performers guarded their own behavior while policing that of other women, who always remained nameless.[95]

Tia Lourdes, as Van Dunem is affectionately known, told a journalist that her parents defended her choice of a musical career against the censure of her neighbors.[96] She also proclaimed to the same journalist, "I am the personification of contradiction," a phrase he used as the title of his interview with her. Van Dunem's self-description succinctly sums up the difficult position in which female musicians found themselves. In order to protect her good name, her father's cousin, "Liceu" Vieira Dias, one of the founders of Ngola Ritmos, had to pick her up before their rehearsals and drop her off afterward.[97] Like Santos, Tia Lourdes emphasized that she does not drink or smoke and would much rather go to bed early than stay out all night in the clubs, in part to preserve her youthful looks—a concern tied to her sense of what it means to be a woman and to her role as a female performer. While Santos and Van Dunem privatize, as individual taste, their decisions to not participate in nightlife beyond performance, these seemingly personal predilections are nonetheless strategically chosen positions in a field of limited and loaded options for female performers.[98] Their lack of desire to maneuver in the proxy nation of the club scene exposes its gendered bases and the different opportunities male and female performers encountered for participating in it.

The club scene was not completely off limits to young women even if it was an ambivalent space. If, as Lamartine mentioned, clubs generated a certain anxiety for young women's parents, some young women probably attended clubs as an escape from parental control. Lamartine consolidated his relationship with the woman who would later become his wife at Club Maxinde, even though she was from a "good" family. Young women could attend events with siblings, girlfriends, and cousins or might attend a particular dance with their boyfriends. After all, one of the signs of audience approval was dancing, so women were a required presence in the clubs. Clubs therefore struggled to control prostitution in their environs and to promote a "family" atmosphere.[99] Young couples would attend club parties in groups so that they could dance with one another's girlfriends and boyfriends without worry. An unaccompanied male might end up in a fisticuffs if he was too audacious in inviting other young men's dates to dance, so it was wise to bring one's own date. When I, a bit puzzled, naively asked if there were women at the clubs, three different interviewees affirmed: if there was music then there was dancing and if there was dancing then there had to be women!

Women were likewise involved at the organizational level in the clubs. Maxinde's longtime president, Alberto Jaime, recounted that the club had female members and therefore women were involved in the administration as well.[100] Olga Baltazar participated in Maxinde's party commission that was responsible for organizing dances, hiring bands, doing publicity, organizing dress competitions (dresses made from local magazines), and holding children's matinees. Jaime deliberately promoted the club as a family environment. To that end, the distribution of activities followed gendered lines. For example, Jaime's wife, Cipriana Jaime, was in charge of the kitchen and cooking while other female members decorated the club for parties. Events often found the directors seated at tables with their wives and other adult family members. Yet not everyone agreed that the clubs offered a family environment. Albina Assis and Efigénia Mangueira mentioned that they had attended the clubs at one time or another but that during the period in which the clubs flourished, they were married and the clubs did not hold much interest for them. They also suggested that the cultural scene in the clubs did not possess the same political tenor as the politico-cultural groups they had been involved in and were therefore not as appealing to them. Neither one condemned the clubs, but they both demonstrated a certain reserve in discussing them, with Assis mentioning that clubs were more appropriate for her "bohemian" brother (the highly regarded musician Manuel Assis "Manec" Faria) and his ilk. While Jaime defended the clubs as spaces where the family of Angolan men and women built the new nation, Assis and Mangueira looked back to the earlier politico-cultural groups as associations that offered a more authentic nationalism, greater cultural integrity, and opportunities for legitimate female activism.[101]

As these contrasting interpretations show, clubs were a site of struggle in this period of social upheaval, and battles over changing class lines played themselves out in gendered terms. The old-line Luanda families had been marginalized economically and socially by increased white migration to the capital. Many had been forced out of their homes in urban neighborhoods and into the musseques. Changes instituted by the colonial government after 1961, which granted access to education and jobs in the civil service to a larger group of people, further eroded the old elite's hold on precious social and cultural capital. Some families that were not of the old guard had garnered a name in the urban social scene for being families that educated their children and exhibited respectable behavior. As the club scene became the centerpiece of urban entertainment, it further challenged the older generation's cultural hegemony. Clubs opened to whoever could pay the entrance fee and for certain dances and parties women got in free while men had to purchase tickets. Lamartine remembers that the tickets cost 100–200 escudos in the late 1960s, a price he said would have been accessible to civil servants, to mechanics, painters, tailors, and their ilk, and to students whose parents had some means. Others described the price as modest without giving exact figures. Unlike the earlier neighborhood-based "contribution parties," where each person would bring something, bands played for free, and everyone just made do with what was there, the clubs depended on ticket sales to pay the bands and other costs associated with the parties. The more tickets sold, the better the take for everyone.

Since entrance depended primarily on the purchase of a ticket, Lamartine remembered that prostitutes, often thanks to Portuguese soldier johns, could sometimes afford to dress well and buy a ticket to enter a party at Maxinde. Prostitutes could thus try to negotiate a better position in the urban African social milieu. At the same time, the stigma of prostitution haunted female performers. Some, who hailed primarily from the urban elite, therefore used the label of "prostitute" to dismiss other women involved in the cultural scene who they felt did not meet their own standards for high-class womanhood. Meanwhile, the clubs maintained a dress code and guidelines for behavior—patrons should not get drunk and should treat others at the club respectfully—in order to set a standard for club attendance that cut across moral and social divisions of class. As the people I interviewed reminded me, someone with a history of poor behavior would not be allowed to enter, no matter what his or her social class or position.[102] In this way, clubs produced Anderson's sense of "horizontal comradeship" by replacing older criteria of family and origin with a set of rules about conduct and dress; while still prohibitive, these standards were nonetheless attainable by a broader slice of urban society.

⁓

Once in the club, gendered relations and hierarchies troubled any facile sense of "horizontal comradeship" that cut across class lines. If the term *patrício* came to signify a leveling of class relations, a kind of citizenship based on the idea that all were equal, such interchangeability was belied by the fact that no one ever used the female form of the word, *patrícia*. Clubs intimated the nation, but what kind of nation was it? It was musseque-based, urban, youth-oriented, "hot" according to some, urbane, and gendered. On the one hand, the gendered interactions and processes that played out in the clubs give us some clues about the fissures and fractures and fragments of the nation, its potential future fault lines. On the other hand, these fragments also constituted a productive tension that helped create the nation. It took both men and women, as I was reminded, to create a meaningful audience, to sing along and dance to these new Angolan intonations. In other words, gendered difference did not rend the "we" of nation; rather, it helped render it, even while drawing distinctions between male and female participation in clubs.

While the guerrillas struggled in the forests against the colonial power in the name of political independence, urban-based audiences and performers manifested a cultural sovereignty that moved them into nation and toward nationalism. They created adjacent temporalities and alternative spaces that if not beyond the gaze of the state, have remained largely outside the ken of scholars. In the spatio-temporal realm of urban culture, Angolan men and women created the social and cultural stuff of nation. It was fundamentally distinct from the social and cultural world of the guerrilla struggle.

The urban cultural world of musseque residents would inform their political involvement in independent Angola in particular ways. Urban residents created a cultural sovereignty for themselves that shaped their political conviction that independence should be popularly based and self-run. The spontaneous neighborhood committees and political cells that appeared in late 1974 sprang from this urban milieu.[103] The MPLA tried to harness this energy as *poder popular* (people's power). But despite its roots in an earlier urban Luanda, the MPLA no longer understood urban political culture. This misunderstanding and the political differences it produced exploded in the attempted coup against the government in 1977. It was with reference to this world that Teta Lando mused that it was certainly no mistake that three of the most popular musicians from the period were killed by the MPLA in the crackdown on coup dissidents.[104]

Before turning to that story in chapter 6, let us look at the lyrics and the musical spaces and venues where music was performed to further texture our sense of how the nation was forged in the music scene. This is the time to listen to the CD and imagine that it is Saturday night in the musseque. The air smells of smoldering charcoal. The sounds of radios and muffled conversations hover over street corners; the giggles of children, tired adult voices, and bursts of laughter vie for the ear's attention. At one wooden home a group of young women and men greet the woman at the door with the honorifics *tia* and *dona* and then ask if her daughter may join them. Their newly sewn dresses and suits shine in a darkness otherwise lit only by small gas lights and candles. Nearby two young men in bell-bottoms, medallions bouncing off their lapels as they rush ahead, knock hurriedly on the door of a friend to borrow a guitar since one of theirs has broken . . .

4 ∽ "Ngongo Jami" (My Suffering)

Lyrics, Daily Life, and Musical Space, 1956–74

IN THE MID-1950S, the band Ngola Ritmos performed at the Teatro Nacional (National Theater) in Luanda's baixa. The venue's name referred, of course, to the Portuguese nation that embraced Angola as an overseas territory. This was no longer custodial colonialism but fierce possession dressed up in lusotropicalist discourse. Angolan "folklore," which Ngola Ritmos represented, served to encapsulate and perform difference, making quaint what was potentially explosive cultural difference. The Portuguese nation would thus subsume Angolan specificity in a demonstration of Portuguese skill at including its tropical territories within the nation. Yet when Ngola Ritmos sang that night at the Teatro Nacional the emcee reinscribed the divide between musseque and baixa, African and Portuguese, thus disrobing the lusotropicalist fantasy.

When the emcee presented the band he also announced the names of the songs they were going to sing and read their translations into Portuguese from Kimbundu.[1] Zé Maria of Ngola Ritmos recounted the event: "We had a song that was called 'Ngongo Jami.' At that time we called it 'Ngongo Jami'—my suffering. And the emcee said, 'Well, not my suffering, *theirs*,' when he presented us. But just like that: 'Not mine, *theirs*.'"[2] Zé Maria was obviously offended by the emcee's condescending attitude. At the same time, the emcee's gaffe baldly expressed the racism, economic deprivation, and absence of political representation or rights that most Angolans living in the musseques felt keenly. Musseque residents likely would have said, "My suffering, yes, but *ours* as well."

Music in late colonial Angola took private grief and by performing it publicly made it collective. The sound, and perhaps even the process, was attractive to whites as well, and in an ironic twist on the lusotropical narrative, by the early 1970s whites made their way to the musseques in sizeable numbers to hear Ngola Ritmos and other popular bands play.[3] In the end, it was Angolan music and Africans who succeeded in producing a culture, both cosmopolitan and African, that attracted European audiences.

This chapter offers a glimpse at the relationship between musical lyrics and the pleasures, pain, and preoccupations of daily life. It also looks briefly at the different spaces in which music was performed and made meaningful by audiences. As the anecdote above reveals, context and location shape the interpretation of music. Furthermore, musical lyrics were just one of the elements of music that Angolans living in the musseques and throughout the country found so compelling. By looking at the lyrics of seven songs that were popular between the mid-1950s and the early 1970s as emanations of life in the musseques and representations of that experience, we can see how song writers and musicians explored the limitations of life under colonial rule while making people dance.[4] By looking at the venues where music was performed we can get a sense of how music started in musseque backyards, took off in the club scene, and flourished and became more accessible through music festivals in Luanda's streets and cinemas.

In my interviews and conversations with Angolans, time and again I was told that day-to-day concerns occupied people's attentions in the late colonial period: social and familial relations, getting an education, making enough money to feed one's family, and maintaining one's dignity under difficult socioeconomic conditions. In music, musicians interpreted, re-created, and transformed that world. Carlos Pimentel remembered the lyrics:

> Our music was oriented to the troubles we had, to the suffering we had. But we didn't play music because we were political, no, but because we lived that reality and we saw that the rest of the people that lived in the musseques lived in bad and squalid conditions [*mal e porcamente.*] So we sang about our bitterness in Kimbundu and they didn't know [what we were saying]. We even talked badly about them [the Portuguese] and they didn't know it![5]

Pimentel emphasizes that politics was organic to the situation. For the most part, politically driven musicians did not decide to sing in order to send a message or make a political statement. Rather, they sang about what they knew and what they saw. Under conditions of colonial exploitation, however, that was political, because the impediments to people's aspirations and the hardships they suffered were often created by the colonial state and its lackeys.

Pimentel notes that by singing in Kimbundu and other local languages, musicians were able to criticize the Portuguese colonial system and its representatives. It was in this sense that music "passed a message" and figured as a site of resistance. But lyrics were not only a way of saying "no," as Amadeu Amorim, a band member of Ngola Ritmos, described it.[6] Lyrics and the music were also about saying "yes": affirming and producing *angolanidade* and, in the process, marking out a culturally autonomous space forged and expressed in African-owned and -operated clubs, in music festivals, in dress and dance and attitude. Lyrics did not simply mirror daily life or nationalist consciousness; they interpreted the former and created the latter. When Teta Lando intoned, "Um assobio meu é pra esquecer as minhas tristezas" ("My whistling is to forget my sadness"), he was echoing more traditional music in style and sound (slow laments that connote a kind of fatalism), commenting on colonialism (because the Portuguese language in which he sang was that of the colonizer), and inciting nationalist sentiments. As Albina Assis told me, "Everyone knew that the source of his sadness was the murder of his father by the Portuguese."[7]

Reflecting on daily life, musicians collectivized and transmuted individual suffering and disgrace into public entertainment: pathos became ethos. Songs that contained social critiques targeted both the colonial order and musseque society. Criticisms of drunkenness, indebtedness, and women with loose morals indirectly pointed the finger at colonialism but also denoted struggles over the moral contours of the nascent nation.[8] Since the majority of musicians and composers were young men, their relationships with women often featured in song. Indeed the gendered dynamics addressed in the previous chapter were in part constructed and negotiated in lyrics. By the late 1960s and early 1970s, audiences often heard lyrics that talked about women, whether in praise or in condemnation. Loves lost, found, frustrated, and sullied were the subject of hundreds of songs. As the song "Chofer de Praça" demonstrates, love stories could also contain political critiques. At the same time, the romantic genre was one of the elements of the music's cosmopolitanism, since much of the foreign music that was the fare at parties and on the radio consisted of love songs.[9]

Songs were sung in a variety of languages: in Kimbundu, Kikongo, or Umbundu (the languages of the three largest ethnic groups), in Portuguese, or in a mixture of Portuguese and Kimbundu. Occasionally words or lines in French or English or Spanish would appear. Many musicians remembered imitating foreign stars, from Otis Redding to James Brown to Charles Aznavour, as a part of their repertoire and musical education, a kind of stepping-stone on the way to creating a local sound with international resonance.[10] A few rock bands emerged in the late 1960s and early 1970s (Os Rocks, the 5 Kings, and Os Kriptons), but they did not garner the same degree of public acclaim as semba. While music was sung in almost all of the local Angolan languages, Kimbundu was the predominant one. Because Luanda was the colonial capital and the site of the longest and most intense colonial presence, by the early twentieth century the urban elites no longer spoke Kimbundu, by and large.[11] In fact, many musicians learned Kimbundu as adults and used it only in song and not in conversation. Therefore, in Luanda and indeed throughout Angola, Kimbundu, more than other languages, simultaneously symbolized life outside the city and the violent denial of African culture by colonial fiat. Kimbundu might have a regional specificity but its negation by the colonial authorities who denigrated it as the "language of dogs" resonated throughout the territory. The new urban Angolan music became a kind of lingua franca, its sung language less important than the fact that it spoke of a shared culture that was urban, African, cosmopolitan, and still vibrating with the rhythms of life and sounds of the rural world.

Singing in local languages created a new and different sound. Musicians drew upon a variety of resources in their compositions and performances: fables from different ethnic groups, songs sung in the contexts of wakes and carnival rivalries, Congolese guitar styles, Latin American dance beats, Angolan instruments like the *dikanza* and *kissange*,[12] foreign cinema, and European and American fashions, not to mention their own experiences.[13] This mixing, far from symbolizing a lusotropical creolization, actually stood that notion on its head. Things European (not just Portuguese) and Latin American—instruments, song length, romantic themes, fashions—were used to emphasize things African: local stories, flora and fauna, parables, dances, languages. The result was to create things uniquely Angolan.[14] As Jorge Macedo put it when describing the music of Ngola Ritmos and the ensuing style played in the musseques, "Latin American sounds, the twin of African rhythms, fed a climate of Africanization."[15] In this way, the divisions instituted through colonial rule between the traditional and the modern, the rural and the urban, the black and the white, the musseque and the baixa, were played on, broken down, and reorganized.

SOME NOTES ON READING AND LISTENING TO THE MUSIC IN THIS CHAPTER

Clubs and music shows attracted large crowds and this could not but attract the attention of the PIDE. Yet for the PIDE, culture was incidental to politics; the secret police did not concern themselves with form but merely with content. It was politically incendiary lyrics, by and large, that worried them. The

PIDE sent agents to clubs and hired informers who could translate lyrics sung in local languages into Portuguese. In contrast to this approach, I take live musical performance as a complex palimpsest of practice that functions at the level of verbal expression but also as performance, as sound, as a relationship between audience and artists. Following Askew, performance has real effects in that it

> does not merely offer occasion to reflect on and perhaps rehearse "real" life. Swahili women who comment on each other's behavior and socially reposition each other through allegations and counterallegations in *taarab* performance are not mirroring social reality or merely reflecting upon it but are *actively creating it*.[16]

Similarly, Angolan musicians and audiences rearranged social relations among themselves and with colonial rule and rulers through the production and consumption of music. As they did so, a sense of Angolan nation became a social reality binding musicians and audiences together.

Musicians did not compose in isolation. They reflected on and interpreted the world around them, and they wrote and rehearsed and performed their music with their audiences in mind. After the initial debacle at the Teatro Nacional, Ngola Ritmos conquered Portuguese audiences by playing typical Portuguese songs like "Maria Vai a Fonte" and "Timpanas" on Angolan instruments while dressed in European formal wear.[17] The duo Ouro Negro represented Angola in Portugal with music in Umbundu, Tchokwe, and Kimbundu; the two mixed-race young men wore a mix of African and hip European dress and played local instruments.[18] In Angola they sang songs like "Amanhã vou acender uma vela na Muxima" (tomorrow I am going to light a candle at Muxima), which was eventually banned by the PIDE for explicitly advocating independence. They brought the music of the south to the north and vice versa.[19]

The album covers of Angolan music produced in the late 1950s and early 1960s are particularly useful for demonstrating how Portuguese companies marketed Angolan music as folklore. Images of assimilado musicians like the three young men of Ngola Melodias—one black, one white, one mixed-race, holding acoustic guitars and a local drum, all shirtless in rolled-up khakis and bare feet—were meant to represent the truth of lusotropicalism. Ironically, some of these very musicians, like Mário de Souza Clington of Ngola Melodias, engaged in the nationalist politics and saw their cultural practice in very different terms. The cover photo of Alba Clyngton, Mário de Souza's sister, shows a woman standing outside a grass hut with a basket in her hand. She is

Alba Clyngton, "Embaixatriz do Folclore Angolano" (Ambassador of Angolan Folklore), album cover, early 1960s, produced in Portugal on the Alvorada label. *Courtesy RNA*

dressed in what the Portuguese understood to be traditional African garb—brightly printed fabric, beads, bare feet—while her hair and makeup suggest a more cosmopolitan sensibility. The Portuguese label Alvorada pitches her as the "ambassador of Angolan folklore," a cultural representative from the overseas territory.

When Angolan musicians played for Angolan audiences, they tried to make people dance. Matemona Sebastião discussed the importance of audiences: "Music has a secret. You can't bore people. You start with a slow music and go along with the tempo; you play danceable music and you watch what is happening in the club."[20] In other words, it is in part through the interactions of musicians and audiences that "good" music is produced.

Whereas bands playing for Portuguese or European audiences in or outside Angola preoccupied themselves with offering up "authentic folklore,"

Ngola Melodias album cover, early 1960s, produced in Portugal on the Alvorada label. *Courtesy RNA*

bands playing in clubs and at parties in Luanda and other Angolan cities strove first and foremost to make the audience dance. In a discussion of Yoruba popular theatre, Karin Barber describes a similar artistic process: "Your first thought might be 'I want to stage a play' rather than 'I want to demonstrate the consequences of treachery.'"[21] Likewise, in the clubs, backyards, and public venues where music was played in Luanda, the first order of business was making people dance. If they criticized colonialism in the process, so much the better, but that was rarely the purpose of music even if it was the basis of a particular song. Even Ngola Ritmos band members Amorim and dos Santos described their band's innovation as making traditional themes and music "danceable."[22] Elias dia Kimuezu, lauded as the "king of Angolan music" for his capacity to sing in Kimbundu and remind the older members of the musseques of nighttime gatherings in the rural areas, recounted that "if we went to play at a party, the people's objective was to dance—they couldn't care less about the lyrics."[23] Underscoring this, Maria Francisca Jacinta, who translated the lyrics of most of the songs in this chapter, commented, "It is only now that you are asking me about these songs and we are listening to the music that I am really thinking about what they mean."[24]

To put it another way, music's meaning was not first and foremost literal, but kinesthetic. Luandans went to clubs and parties to dance. And a band's virtuosity rested in part in the musicians' ability to make audiences dance by producing memorable rhythms. Jomo Fortunato recounts that the band Os Kiezos, which means brooms in Kimbundu, got its name when the band members crashed a party in the mid-1960s.[25] These party crashers played so compellingly and the partygoers danced so fervently that they raised the dust in the yard just as a good broom would. The band's name therefore underscored their expertise and served as a kind of calling card, announcing their prowess before they played a single note. In Angola, music and dance were, and are, intimately intertwined if not inseparable.[26]

Jacques dos Santos asserts that "the model of dancing that we adopted, that came from many years ago and overcame barriers from the north to the south of the country, that model that is today the pattern in the majority of dances that are held in Angola, from Cabinda to Cunene, has its origins in the parties of Luanda's suburbs [musseques]."[27] Dos Santos is speaking of semba, which refers to both the dance and the music and which derives its designation from the name of an older dance, *massemba*, common in early twentieth-century Luanda and its surrounding areas. Semba, dos Santos notes, the dance and music, came to represent a new urban lifestyle that was not limited to the musseques but took on a national character. Undeniably influenced by European salon dances, this dance was nonetheless a uniquely Angolan creation and form. It differed from *rebita*, an earlier urban dance, and from African dance used in the context of theatrical performances that sought to recover and represent "traditional" practices, or what Albina Assis referred to as "dancing like our grandparents."[28]

Semba as dance and music had *rebita* and carnival dance and music as antecedents. But its moment and constituency were different. As a dance, semba was danced by couples in clubs or in homes at backyard parties. Whereas *rebita* bands were associated with particular groups of dancers, this was not true of semba. Bands and musical artists occupied a stage close to but separate from the audience. Dancers danced with their dates, and with family members and friends. The dance evolved in part through the contribution parties and backyard parties of the 1950s in which Cuban music and Congolese rumbas predominated on the record players of the day. The majority of disks were

"Traditional" Angolan dance, undated photo. *Courtesy of Arquivo de Fotografia de Lisboa, Torre do Tombo*

recorded by the British label HMV (His Master's Voice). A set of numbers beginning with the letters GV identified each record, and this marking soon became the shorthand for this type of music and for the records themselves, which were called "gee vees."[29] Partygoers and dancers often remembered particularly popular songs by their number, not their title. Dancing to GVs, and not just moving along but masterfully executing steps, lateral moves, and twirls, was a means of garnering notoriety on the scene.

Two renowned dancers of the 1950 and 1960s earned their sobriquets on the dance floor. Jack Rumba developed his style and refined his skill dancing to GVs of Caribbean sounds (rumba, *son*, *conga*) and to the Congolese rumbas of the same period. Joana Pernambuco was another Luanda legend who could write her name in the sand as she danced.[30] Her name comes from the term *perna mbuka*, a mix of Portuguese and Kimbundu that means "limping leg." In dancing she transformed her physical liability into a boon.[31] Along with Rumba and Pernambuco, dancers of particular skill like Mateus Pelé do Zangado and João Cometa made their names dancing at the parties that preceded the heyday of the clubs. Dom Caetano's song entitled "Som Angolano" (Angolan Sound) remembers the glory days of these dancers while reiterating the tight relationship between music and dance in the refrain "Angolan sound, how rich its dance."

As local bands and the club scene grew, dancing developed along with them. Semba, the dance, was a partner dance in which the male led the female. The execution of lateral entrances and exits of varying complexity differentiates it from other dances and allows the dancer to showcase his or her skill, creativity, and experience. Two currently popular styles of music have eponymous styles of dance: *kisomba* and *kuduro*.[32] While some musicians from the golden age despair that these current genres of music offer nothing distinctively Angolan, they cannot say the same for the dances that carry the same names. Such a complex relationship between music and dance underscores the necessity of understanding music in context.

As you read this chapter and listen to the songs on the accompanying CD, remember that most of this music was made for dancing. If lyrics seem skeletal or incomplete, they were only one part of a larger whole. Indeed, in interviews musicians and others often only remembered the refrains or particular lines from songs rather than all the lyrics. While the passage of time may account for some attrition of memory regarding lyrics, it also seems to be the rule that people remember, and sometimes only ever knew, a beat, a few words or lines. Just that little bit often summons a richer and thicker world in imagination and memory.

SONGS FROM THE 1940S AND 1950S: PRIVATE BACKYARD LUNCHES AND PARTIES

The songs in this section are most typical of the early days of Angolan music—of the backyards and family gatherings and small politico-cultural groups highlighted in chapter 2. In the 1940s and 1950s entertainment and recreation revolved around gatherings of friends and families at lunches and parties to celebrate birthdays, baptisms, weddings, and anniversaries, as well as gatherings to mourn the death of loved ones. The most common such events were weekend lunches. Alberto Jaime returned to Bairro Indígena on Saturday after soccer matches in other neighborhoods to

> attend those afternoon sessions of *os mais velhos*. At that time we didn't have record players but gramophones that you wound up by hand, and vinyl records, and we would accompany the *mais velhos*. Sometimes there were people playing guitars, drumming, playing on cans or whatever—in the neighbor's yard.[33]

Young people often became interested in music and began their apprenticeships at such spontaneous jam sessions. These weekend afternoon sessions, as

Jaime noted, were central to the intergenerational transmission of knowledge, both musical and otherwise.

By the late 1940s some clubs had opened and had begun to attract a growing number of musseque residents for recreational and sports activities including theatrical, dance, and musical performances. Drama, dance, and music were not discrete practices but rather were presented together. On the other hand, parties, whether at these clubs or, more commonly, in houses or in the yards of friends and neighbors, focused specifically on music, dancing, and socializing. These *festas da contribuição* (contribution parties) in which everyone brought something—drinks, food, music, a turntable, electricity, gas lamps—gathered young people together by invitation only. Such parties differed from the get-togethers of family and friends (which continued throughout the late colonial period and indeed continue today) in that they were primarily for youth. By the late 1940s some people began to modify their homes and yards to allow them to host parties on a regular basis. In these new venues, hosts would charge an entrance fee and parties opened to that slice of musseque society willing and able to pay for entertainment. Of course, people known for their skill on the dance floor often entered parties for free, and lively *patos* ("ducks" or party crashers) always managed to find a way in. Events hosted by party organizers like Idalina Costa and Pedro Bonzela Franco and others were the precursors of the privately owned clubs of the 1960s.[34] Dos Santos suggests that government control, in the form of licensing, came after the fact and only required that the owner acquire the simplest kind of permit to allow the venue to operate legally after midnight.

Whereas people played instruments in their homes or at Saturday lunches, parties were dominated by disk jockeys or *discotequeiros*.[35] These deejays played their collections of music on gramophones hooked up to car batteries until those were replaced by stereos with speakers that ran on electric current. Brazilian, Congolese, French, and Portuguese music composed the typical aural fare. Congolese music had a large following in this period. Men and women who were young in this era remember the great Franco and his band Okay Jazz.

Despite the fact that some hosts began to charge entrance fees and to open to a "public," the partiers generally knew, or knew most of, the people in attendance.[36] Friends, friends of friends, cousins of friends, and familiars visiting from other towns and cities constituted the social horizon. Without being totally private, these parties encompassed a social world that was a known quantity. Such social intimacy allowed the elite to reproduce itself through friendships and marriages and by defining socially acceptable behavior. At the same time, as the last chapter made clear, new criteria were emerging. Idalina

Costa is a figure who embodies the changing racial norms. Her contemporaries both praised and criticized her: she was lauded by some as a cultural innovator and dismissed by others as a prostitute.[37]

All of this constituted the larger sociocultural context in which Ngola Ritmos began to produce their music. They did not, at least initially, play at these parties although they certainly attended them. Amorim is, aside from his renown as a musician, known for his finesse on the dance floor. Certainly these parties helped inspire musicians to make local sounds danceable. Parties offered up a mix of African and international sounds, giving Congolese and Latin American music local play while generating an Angolan style of dancing with an international sensibility.

Ngola Ritmos pioneered their new old sound in this ambiance and then brought it to Saturday afternoon lunches and to performances at the Liga with the theatrical group Gexto or even one time or another to the *quintal* (backyard) of Bota Fogo. Ngola Ritmos based some songs on popular tunes from different areas of Angola, including songs drawn from carnival, which they elaborated to make danceable or playable on the radio.[38] Many of these became the old standards of Angolan music. Indeed, one could argue that "Angola Avante Revolução" (Angola Forward the Revolution) is the national anthem but "Muxima" is the anthem of the nation (track 4).[39] This song conjures the cultural milieu of the 1950s from which it emerged while simultaneously evoking the nation as a cultural formation associated with it (as opposed to the national political state that arrived on the scene in 1975).[40]

"Muxima" summons pure nostalgia. Today, when a band plays this song, the entire audience sings and sways along and if they do not know all of the lyrics they at least know the refrain. More than any other song, "Muxima" has no single author, but it is associated with the work of Ngola Ritmos and is an example of the way they would take a local song and retool it. In this case, they did not aim to make it danceable but to make it audible in concert halls and on radios. Countless versions of the song exist and, as Zé Maria of Ngola Ritmos noted, "it has already gone around the world" because it is the song that musicians traveling overseas and representing the Angolan nation cannot fail to include in their repertoire.[41]

Muxima is a Kimbundu word that means "heart." It is also the name of a town built on the banks of the Kwanza River some sixty miles south of Luanda. The Portuguese constructed a fort there in 1599 and a Catholic church, Nossa Senhora de Muxima (Our Lady of Muxima), followed shortly thereafter.[42] The church is associated with spiritual beneficence. Pilgrims from throughout the country and particularly from Luanda travel to the church in search of blessings.[43] The church's patron saint is St. Anne or Santa Ana, the mother of the Virgin Mary and patron saint of women in labor (also of miners and of those with mental illness). Hence the name Santana in the lyrics, from Santa Ana. Anne allegedly remained childless until late in life and therefore the church at Muxima has become the destination of many women who have difficulty conceiving.[44] The song tells a story of a misunderstanding between two women in which one accuses the other of witchcraft. The accused then proposes that they travel to Santana (Muxima) to resolve the situation.

Muxima Oh! Oh! Muxima	Muxima Oh! Oh! Muxima
Oh! Oh! Muxima	Oh! Oh! Muxima,
Muxima Oh! Oh! Muxima	Muxima Oh! Oh! Muxima
Oh! Oh! Muxima	Oh! Oh! Muxima
Ki wangyambê wanga wami	If you think I am a witch
Ka ngibeke bhwa Santana	Take me to Santana
Ki wangyambê wanga wami	If you think I am a witch
Ka ngibeke bhwa Santana	Take me to Santana
Kwata o dilaji mujibê	Grab the crazy one and kill him
Kwata o dilaji mujibê	Grab the crazy one and kill him
Kwata o dilaji mujibê	Grab the crazy one and kill him
Laji ni laji k'azoka wa	Two crazy people don't argue
Kwata o dilaji mujibê	Grab the crazy one and kill him
Kwata o dilaji mujibê	Grab the crazy one and kill him
Kwata o dilaji mujibê	Grab the crazy one and kill him
Laji ni laji k'azoka wa	Two crazy people don't argue
Muxima Oh! Oh! Muxima	Muxima Oh! Oh! Muxima
Oh! Oh! Muxima	Oh! Oh! Muxima
Muxima Oh! Oh! Muxima	Muxima Oh! Oh! Muxima
Oh! Oh! Muxima[45]	Oh! Oh! Muxima

The song tells a common story: accusations of witchcraft were and are often at stake in disputes between neighbors, family members, or lovers. The church at Muxima was an institution of local lore, and despite the ties of the Catholic Church to the colonizing project of the colonial state, the church had a local meaning and series of uses much abstracted from the colonial project. The song, sung in Kimbundu and using a mix of local instruments and acoustic guitars, celebrates Angolan cultural practice and represents quotidian traumas.

One of the first songs that Angolan musicians identify as part of the new urban music dates to the late 1800s. But the version musicians recall is from the late 1940s and 1950s and is by a band called Garda e o Seu Conjunto (Garda and Her Band).[46] Garda was an Angolan woman who had studied classical music at the Music Academy in Luanda, but who subsequently departed from her classical training and the strictures of assimilado society at the time. Garda's decision to play and record the song "Madya Kandimba" (track 5) is indicative of the new ways in which assimilado elites began to identify themselves and define *angolanidade*. According to Mário Rui Silva, an Angolan musician and musicologist, "Madya Kandimba" is one of the earliest pieces transcribed by the Angolan ethnologist Oscar Ribas, who dates the song to 1875.[47] This song tells the story of a woman, Maria Kandimba, who works as a housekeeper for a Portuguese man in Luanda. They fall in love and have an affair. When the man's wife discovers their tryst, she goes after Maria (which in Kimbundu is pronounced Madya) with a pistol. Maria flees on a steamboat in the harbor

Madya Kandimba atrevida	Daring Madya Kandimba
Wasingile bumwelo ya sinhola	She offended at the woman's door
Sinhola wa kwata pixitola	The woman grabbed a gun
Kandimba walenge muvapolo	Kandimba fled on the vapor[48]
Malé, malé, malé, malé	Malé, malé, malé, malé
Jisonyi ngana ja kudiwana	She has no shame
Madya Kandimba atrevida	Daring Madya Kandimba
Wasingile bumwelo ya sinhola	She offended at the woman's door
Kandimba walami jisonyi	Kandimba has no shame
Wandala kunyana dyala da sinhola[49]	She wanted to steal the woman's husband

The lyrics, predominantly in Kimbundu, contain adaptations of Portuguese words. *Sinhola*, for example, means *senhora* or lady and in this case almost certainly refers to a Portuguese lady, since Kimbundu has a word for woman (*muhatu*) and a word for formally addressing an adult male or female (*ngana*). The word *pixitola* means *pistola* or pistol. Words adapted from Portuguese describe those things particularly associated with Portuguese culture and contact with it. The song does not criticize the colonial experience or the Portuguese settlers. Instead it censures Madya's shameless coveting of another woman's husband. It is nonetheless a story that is marked by colonial relations and local values that also points to a certain kind of trouble introduced by the Portuguese presence.

"João Dumingu" (track 6) is another song by Ngola Ritmos that people I interviewed often mentioned when asked about the connection between music and politics. "João Dumingu" has roots in a piece of music from the area around Luanda.[50] Because the only copy available at the national radio is on old magnetic tape, the song is rarely played anymore. Amorim, himself a band member, described this song as a call to consciousness: "It was necessary to understand Kimbundu in order to perceive where the song enters—so down underneath, the song says that it was necessary to prepare our people, our youth, professionally for tomorrow."[51] The song critiques people in the local society for the futility of a certain kind of resistance, of foot dragging, while it faults the colonial government indirectly for having created this situation and the problem of "contract" or forced labor in the first place.

"João Dumingu eu, João Dumingu eu"	"I, João Dumingu, I, João Dumingu"
Ambela gente ye	He says to his people
Ngwetu confiança mi mesene ja ufuno	That he doesn't want his master's trust
"João Dumingu eu, João Dumingu eu"	"I, João Dumingu, I, João Dumingu"
Ambela mesene	He says to his master
Ngwetu confiança mi mesene ja ufuno	That he doesn't want his master's trust
Ngibanza ange mungongo mwene mwala	I think that I am still in this world
Ngasumbo metulu	I bought a meter stick
Metulu waisunona	I lost it
Ngasumbo nivele	I bought a leveler
Nivele waisunona	I lost it
Tala dyala dyaiba kutoba	See how the stupid man will
Dya nda kufil kukimbangula[52]	End up dying in the contract

João, a sort of Portuguese "John" or everyman, begins by proclaiming that he wants nothing to do with his master (his boss in the type of master-apprentice relationship common in the carpentry profession at the time). While his defiance is understandable, the song ends by critiquing this short-sighted approach, calling João Dumingu a stupid man who will end up losing his job and having to return to forced labor. From Amorim's perspective, the song served to alert people to the fact that they had to negotiate the day-to-day struggle over labor in such a way that it could benefit the nascent nation. A new nation would need people trained in a variety of vocations and not just rebels. This vision had very clear class bases: the people who wrote and sang this song were civil servants, involved in anticolonial political organizing, and while they rebuked their parents' investment in moving up in the bureaucracy and protecting their gains, they also promoted education and hard work as tools required to build a new society and nation. In this sense, this song echoes the sensibilities about sovereignty expressed in the previous chapter.

Shortly after the band began playing this song, the PIDE detained and interrogated the band member Euclides de Fontes Pereira ("Fontinhas") for eight days. By this time, "Liceu" Vieira Dias and Amadeu were already imprisoned in the Tarrafal prison in Cape Verde and police agents closely followed the band members' activities. Asked about this song, Fontinhas told his interrogators that it was a traditional song to which Ngola Ritmos had only added a more elaborate musical arrangement. He went on to explain to the interviewer that he handily convinced the interrogators that the song

> was about a small story between a man and his wife: the husband was nothing but a poor contract worker, someone who transported concrete. His wife was anxious for him to be promoted to stone layer and she bought him a measure and a level so that the poor man could learn a trade. But the man, stupid as ever, lost the instruments. Disgusted, the wife condemns him, saying, "João Domingos, you will die under the contract."[53]

In this instance, a tale of gendered struggle covers for what might otherwise be interpreted as political or social commentary. Gender provided an explanation that was meant to depoliticize the music. In the period that followed (1961–74), it would be in part through gender that the political would be constructed as the nation was imagined in gendered club relations and lyrics commenting on women's behavior. Yet again, what passed for seemingly trivial quotidian struggles between men and women had a more complex meaning.

SONGS FROM THE "GOLDEN AGE"

Music from the so-called golden age of Angolan music, the late 1960s and early 1970s, often articulated social and political critiques in stories about day-to-day events in the musseques. Lyrics narrated tales of suffering—the loss of friends and family to forced labor, witchcraft, broken hearts, the disgraces of alcohol and of cheating spouses. The use of local languages in song lyrics, Kimbundu in particular, allowed for the subversion of meaning because, as the example that closed the last section demonstrates, state agents relied on Angolans for translation and interpretation. When PIDE officers asked for translations of songs they often received a literal translation of the lyrics. These skeletal translations generally omitted the shades of meaning that only context could illuminate. Or, as in the case of Fontinhas, translators offered alternative contexts in which to understand the lyrics. But singing in Kimbundu did more than provide safe cover for critique. It Africanized the music, valorizing local cultural expression that had been derided.

Ironically, two songs most remembered for criticizing the colonial regime were sung in Portuguese, albeit an Angolanized Portuguese. Luis Visconde's 1968 hit "Chofer de Praça" (track 7) tells the story of a young man whose attempts to visit his girlfriend are thwarted by an arrogant taxi driver from the baixa, who refers to himself as a "chauffeur" and who refuses to take the young man to the musseque:

Mandei parar um carro de praça	I hailed a car from the plaza [taxi]
Ancioso em ver meu amor	Anxious to see my love
Chofer de praça então reclamou	The chauffeur then complained
Quando eu lhe disse que meu bem morava no subúrbio	When I told him my honey lived in the suburbs
"Tempo chuvoso no subúrbio, não vou	"Rainy season in the suburbs, I won't go
Pois sou chofer de praça e não barqueiro"	I am a plaza chauffeur, not a boatman"
Então emplorei	So I implored
"Peço o senhor chofer leve-me por favor	"I am asking you, Mr. Chauffeur, please take me
Ela não tem culpa de morar no subúrbio	It's not her fault she lives in the suburbs
Enquanto a chuva é obra de natureza"	And rain is the work of nature"
Então chofer dominado por mim	Then the chauffeur, overcome by me,
Na boracha puxou atravesssando lagoa	Hit the gas, crossing the mud puddles
Quando olhei pra relógio e lhe pedindo	When I looked at my watch and asked him
Que colasse o acelerador ao tapete	To glue the accelerator to the floor
Então chofer trombudo respondeu	The chauffeur, annoyed, responded
"Se vôce quer ver seu amor	"If you want to see your love
Atravessa a lagoa a pé	Cross the mud puddles on foot

Não vou partir meu pôpô I won't ruin my wheels
Só porque vôce quer dar show!" Just so you can show off!"

The singer mocks the chauffeur's voice with nasal and mechanical tones that show the latter's indifference to the narrator's plight. It is probable that the chauffeur is Portuguese, since the influx of white population from the 1940s on meant that many Portuguese displaced Africans from what would have been deemed "African" jobs in other colonies.[54] Describing attempts to combat racism after 1961, Gervase Clarence-Smith noted that "the greatest difficulties were encountered in the self-employed sector of the towns, where the authorities found it extremely difficult to put an end to racial discrimination among groups such as taxi drivers."[55] The racial tension between taxi drivers and musseque residents exploded in 1972 when white taxi drivers attacked sixty residents of Cazenga in retaliation for the death of a fellow taxi driver found in his car in a nearby neighborhood. The drivers acted with impunity and in collaboration with the Public Security Police.[56] Although it postdates Visconde's song, this event illuminates the social and economic tensions that animated urban colonial society. The chauffeur in Visconde's song is an unsympathetic figure who stands in for the colonial bureaucracy and bureaucrats (whether Portuguese or African) who are only concerned with conserving their own socioeconomic positions. The cab driver's arrogant proclamation, "I am a plaza chauffeur, not a boatman," shows him identifying with the baixa's plazas and asphalt and distancing himself from the musseque, where in the rainy season the dusty streets flood and a boat would be better transport than a car.

The song's narrator makes a valiant attempt to reason with the driver and succeeds to a certain extent ("Then the chauffeur, overcome by me"). He addresses the driver politely as Mr. Chauffeur and eloquently argues that it is not his girlfriend's fault that she lives in the musseques, that she did not choose this, and that rain is a work of nature and not something under human control. Indeed, the narrator's use of proper Portuguese to argue rationally with the taxi driver contrasts with the driver's use of slang despite his sniffing sense of superiority. Ultimately, however, the narrator's impatience makes the driver reconsider and he opts not to risk damaging his car and imperiling his livelihood so that this young man can charm his girlfriend. Impugning the young man's frivolity, the driver takes a stab at the narrator's youthful folly and vanity. This song humorously depicts the daily struggles of young working men, presumably of club-going ilk, and their efforts to navigate the segregated urban geography. The colonial regime is never addressed directly, but it is implicit in the division between the musseque and the baixa, the former with its muddy streets and the latter with its fine plazas, and in the driver's struggle to keep his business in the baixa while the narrator strives to impress his intended by arriving in a taxi from the posh side of town.[57]

A more explicit critique of the colonial state appeared in the Os Kiezos performance of a song called "Milhorró" (track 8). The musician and radio announcer Murimba Show (who earned his moniker because "he himself was a show, he played lots of instruments!"[58]) and the composer Babaxi, both from Bairro Indígena, composed this song in 1960. Úbia, a sister-in-law of a Kiezos band member, is credited with bringing the song to the band's attention.[59] Os Kiezos made the song a big hit in the early 1970s, and stories attesting to the song's significance abound. For instance, Azevedo ties it to Bota Fogo, since Murimba Show was a member of that group. Azevedo thus projects the politics of an earlier moment and movement into this later period and onto this song. For him, this song represents the confrontational nationalist politics of Bota Fogo. The police imprisoned Vate Costa, the lead singer of Os Kiezos, for singing this song,[60] and the singer Dina Santos, then Costa's wife, remembered that this was the band's most requested tune.[61]

The song's title, "Milhorró," was local slang for the Portuguese word *melhoria* or "improvement." According to the Angolan musician and journalist Jomo Fortunato, the song was composed in 1958–59 "as a reaction to the arrival in Angola of the first Portuguese police who wore gray uniforms, the 'Araraquara' who, in their markedly repressive profile, provoked the indignation of many Angolans."[62] The music is fast paced and the lyrics are a mix of Portuguese and Kimbundu.

Oh, não quer bailar	Oh, he doesn't want to dance
Pala kubanga sokudye	To make friends
Pala kubanga milhorró	To improve
Pala kubanga milhorró	To improve
Pala kubanga mbibibibi	To "mbibibibi"
Pala kubanga milhorró	To improve
Chegando naquele dia	Arriving on that day
Chegando a melhoria	The improvement arriving
E vocês de fora	And you from outside
Aí, vocês não querem farrar	Aí, you don't want to party
Isso assim não pode ser	It can't be that way
Não tem mais sentido	It doesn't make any sense
E nós não queremos	And we don't want this

Vão, vão-se embora	Go, get out of here
Isso assim não pode ser	It can't be that way
Muxiyetu mwatuvalela até timbilangô[63]	In our land where we were born we only cry

The liner notes from a CD compilation of Angolan music from the 1970s relate that "when os Kiezos launched this song in '72, they were arrested in Batalha's club by the PIDE. Murimba Show had to invent an explanation: the invitation to leave was directed at [the band] Cabinda Ritmos that was encountering great success in Luanda, stealing audiences and girlfriends [from os Kiezos]."[64] Given the stories of band rivalries and of women as trophies of those battles, recounted in the previous chapter, this explanation would have rung true. However, because the song does not specifically name the "outsider" it is open to interpretation and indeed slippage from the band outsider to the colonial outsider. Thus it is not surprising that when people remember this song they remember the refrain "Vão, vão-se embora!" ("Go, get out of here!") and say that it was about the Portuguese. Here a local rivalry came to represent a national problem. If the story is true, Murimba Show was clever in suggesting that it was about Cabinda Ritmos, since not only were they not from the neighborhood (in this case Marçal, where Batalha's club was located and the band Os Kiezos was from), they were not even from Luanda. It could be read as an incarnation of the divide-and-rule narrative that would make any colonialist proud.

Yet the ambiguity around "outsider" or "you from outside" also evoked the colonial power. The song suggests that those who refuse the call of the music and its invitation to dance cannot be trusted. To rebuke them so forthrightly, to shoo them from the scene was daring. Yet the tone of the music is festive, lightheartedly mocking the outsiders who do not want to party or dance, make friends or improve the situation. You get the sense that the colonizers will be danced out of town, that a heartily felt cultural autonomy just may have political implications. The song asserts a kind of equality, reading the outsider in insider terms. These outsiders were not committed to the same program as the club goers. Indeed, *milhorró*, improvement, might be read as a local alternative to Portuguese development projects that the colonial administration vaunted as improvements in daily life.[65] Or perhaps it was another affirmation of expectations that exceeded the improvements actually being offered. Underscoring this sense of different projects and visions of improvement and of the dance party as a place where differences get worked out is a small piece of evidence from the PIDE archives: Bittencourt cites an MPLA radio directive inviting the PIDE to "a party on the 10th."[66]

By 1972, this was no longer just about the Araraquara, or police. Between 1960 and 1972 Luandans experienced an influx of immigrants, the imprisonment of many fellow urban residents, and the brutal Portuguese repression of rebellions in 1961, not only in Luanda but in the Baixa de Kassanje and in Uíge. The Portuguese military presence had increased substantially as a result. At the same time, by the early 1970s Portuguese were leaving the clubs in the baixa to attend clubs in the musseques, since that was where bands created and performed the hottest music. It could indeed have been the case that the song also took aim at those Portuguese soldiers on leave in the city who both recognized and partook of the musseque pleasures—prostitutes, drink, music—but who otherwise represented the attempted annihilation of independent Angola (in the form of the liberation movements) for which this urban culture longed.

The divisions of colonial society also played out among Angolans. Gendered struggles were common fare in song lyrics. Given that the majority of composers were male, it is not surprising that we find songs of women doing men wrong as well as songs praising the beauty of young women. As the last chapter argued, women may not have been the main producers of music but they were nevertheless productive of it. This was true both because women were often the subject of song and because many musicians cite their mothers, aunts, and grandmothers as figures critical to their musical inclinations if not educations.[67] Many of the social critiques in lyrics involved women as well. Urbano de Castro's "Semba Lekalo" is purportedly a criticism of young women who drink too much,[68] and África Show's "As Meninas de Hoje" ("Girls Today") has the narrator stalling a young woman's advances as he tells her that he does not want to get involved without her parents' permission, lest he bring problems on himself.[69] The implication is that "girls today" are bolder about their sexuality than girls used to be so the proper thing to do is to consult a girl's parents, whether she wants that or not.

Elias dia Kimuezo's "Diala Monzo" (track 9) recounts a tale of infidelity, of one woman (the narrator's wife) who had two men, "one inside, one outside" the house.

Ngamubanza o isunji y nga mumona	I am thinking about the situation I am in
Muhatu moxi, mala mayadi	One woman, two men
Tundeke nga mateka kingami monami kima	When I ask her what she is after
Kingimu budisa i mayahiywa musota	She says she isn't after anything

Mwene wamba kingimubanga kima	She said that I have done nothing
Tundi kingama teka nga mona kima	Since we've been together I don't see anything [she said]
Muhatu moxi, mala mayadi	One woman, two men
Diala monzo, diala bukanga	One inside, one outside
Kingima kwata wambi kiki kizangu	When I catch her she says it's a disgrace
Diala monzo, diala bukanga	One inside, one outside[70]

Given that the music scene is one of the sites where gender is produced and performed as new standards of classed behavior are defined and policed, it is perhaps no surprise that female behavior is so criticized and censured. On the other hand, "Madya Kandimba" and "Muxima" are evidence that commenting on women's behavior and struggles between women was not entirely new.

Songs about women were common in the romantic genre, along with songs about broken hearts and unattainable loves. Urbano de Castro's "Rosa Maria"[71] and Artur Adriano's "Belita" both lament the devastation experienced when the love of one's life is lost. Singing about women was part of what identified the music as cosmopolitan, as one of a number of international sounds. In this way, local music addressed what were deemed universal themes. But the music was Angolan, and therefore different. Part of that difference, that specificity, was the colonial experience of oppression. As Johannes Fabian points out in his discussion of gendered themes in Zairean popular painting: "The male-female imagery expresses wider societal ills in a metonymical fashion: personal trouble and colonial oppression are linked by external association."[72] But, at the same time, the gendered themes also allowed the music to look beyond such specificity to an imaginary where Angola was not so different from other nation-identified sounds.

Like "Diala Monzo," Prado Paim's "Bartolomeu" (track 10) got audiences dancing to tales of suffering. "Bartolomeu" was the first single to go gold, selling over twenty thousand copies.[73] It is a simple tale of a man longing for a friend who has just passed away. According to some, Bartolomeu was a well-known resident of the musseque Sambizanga.[74] Mourning his death in song not only relieves the narrator's grief but makes audiences dance to the song's upbeat tempo.

Usukuyimwana ki ngenda ubeka wami	Day and night I look
Kamba dyami dya muxima	For my soulmate
Kalunga wamambata	That death has taken away

Bartolomeu, Bartolomeu	Bartolomeu, Bartolomeu
Kingimusote jingongo jami jangitula	The more I look for you the more it hurts
Usukuyimwana nginanga ni	Day and night I cry
Kudingongwema	From thinking so much about my friend
Kamba dyami dya muxima	My soulmate
Kalunga wamambata	That death has taken away
Bartolomeu, Bartolomeu	Bartholomeo, Bartholomeo
Kingimusote jingongo jami jangitula	The more I look for you the more it hurts
Kamba dyami dya muxima	My soulmate
Ngibanga divoto ngimujingaleja	I am going to pray in the church
Ngibanga divoto musota kamba dyami	I am going to pray for my friend
Kalunga wamambata	That death has taken away
Kamba dyami dya muxima	My soulmate
Ngibanga wamusota[75]	I have looked for you

"Bartolomeu" is a perfect example of simple song lyrics combined with an infective and danceable beat that transforms one man's distress into a collective celebration. While lyrics in Kimbundu mark the song's narrator as coming from the central-northern region of the country, they would have resonated throughout the country, suggesting an Angolan articulation of the universal experience of loss while also potentially raising questions about who or what (perhaps the colonial system of contract labor) caused Bartolomeu's disappearance.

TAKING IT TO THE STREETS: FROM CLUBS TO *KUTONOCA* AND NGOLA CINE

The spaces in which Angolans listened and danced to music were critical to the music's meanings. Veit Erlmann discusses the important relationship between musical performance and space:

> Performance as a "signifying practice" mediates between heterogeneous worlds by constructing social spaces in which the coherence of the lived experience is reestablished. The notion of space is crucial here, because it denotes the existence of a sphere of human activity in which the reordering of social relations takes place in nonpragmatic ways.[76]

Clubs, as described in the last chapter, were just such spaces. And the club scene marked the music in important ways. But clubs were just one of a set of spaces that shaped the ways Angolans understood and used music and reimagined social relations. Others included family parties and street and cinema-based music festivals. If family parties promoted a sense of community, music played at clubs and festivals (as well as on radio) gathered people in such a way as to constitute a public and a nation.

Discussing the popular arts in Africa, Karin Barber argues:

> Music and drama can be performed in stadiums or even in open fields, as well as in halls and hotels: they can be said to attract a public rather than a community. Thus though the prevalent use of popular implies, in one sense, limits, in another sense it points to the rise of a populace of a different range altogether from what was known in the traditional world.[77]

Clubs ranged in size, but the largest could accommodate a few hundred people. If family and friends, friends of friends, and assorted other familiar faces constituted the limits of partygoers at backyard parties, club attendees and especially festival audiences were a less-known quantity. At the same time, one knew that other attendees in a club, even if one did not know them personally, had to have a certain income and manner of dress and behavior to get in (or stay in) the club. Perhaps more importantly, a shared taste in cultural performance joined any specific audience, whether in clubs or at music festivals. In fact, the musseque public began to demand that the music played in clubs and on the radios be accessible to them.

Clubs grew out of the associative practices detailed in chapter 2, but by the mid-1960s they were almost purely recreational and sports oriented. The recreation part was centered more on parties with live bands than on theater pieces or poetry recitations.[78] Clubs were subject to government oversight and had to be registered with the state.[79] Membership-based clubs were forbidden to enroll as a member anyone who had been jailed for subversive activity, but this did not preclude such individuals from attending events. The club section that organized musical performances had to work, initially, through the Angolan Center for Information and Tourism (Centro de Informação e Turismo de Angola, CITA) and later through the Concert Services office to receive authorization to book bands for parties and dances. On the one hand, this gave the government access to the clubs and what was going on there, but on the other hand, it served as a way to promote a variety of different artists who were registered at CITA and were listed on their performance roster. Artists remembered this way of organizing events and musicians in a positive light, often explicitly contrasting it to the poor conditions and support available for artists today.[80] And this despite the fact that it created a lot of running around, stamping, signing, and filing of papers.

The sports section and the clubs' soccer teams were part of the Provincial Association of Luanda. The Provincial Association provided them with a small subsidy to defray operating costs. Otherwise, the clubs were economically independent. Those clubs without a sports component tended to be privately owned, whereas those with sports teams, like Maxinde, were membership-based.[81] A group of founding members would invest their own money and the club then survived on the basis of membership dues and ticket sales for events like dances, parties, children's matinees, and dress-making competitions. The commercial exigencies of putting on shows and throwing parties meant that clubs sometimes sacrificed ideal social norms (for example, by admitting prostitutes) out of economic necessity.

All of the clubs were based in the city's musseques.[82] The baixa had some nightclubs that were largely for Portuguese and foreign businessmen, although they sometimes booked local acts.[83] All the musseques housed clubs but there was a certain concentration in Marçal, considered the birthplace of Angolan music, as well as in Sambizanga, Rangel, and São Paulo. Monteiro's study of the musseques lists twenty sports clubs registered with the government and thirty-eight unofficial clubs. He noted that the number had surged in the ten years prior to his study, from roughly 1961 to 1971.[84] Many of these clubs had a social and cultural section that promoted parties and events for children, and at least four of the fifty-eight were among the most frequented and frequently mentioned clubs among the people I interviewed.[85] Monteiro identified nine clubs as the "best known" for having dances popular with the city's youth and he asserted that the clubs explained "the proliferation of musical groups in the musseques."[86] Each weeknight a different club had live music and on weekends all clubs had live music shows.[87] In combination with the music shows *Dia do Trabalhador* (Worker's Day) and *Kutonoca*, this meant that by the late 1960s aspiring musicians had a variety of opportunities to perform and to hear other bands, and people had somewhere to go for recreation.

Monteiro emphasized that it was predominantly youths who visited the clubs. His surveys, completed by heads of households, inquired how people spent their free time. He reported that only 7.7 percent of heads of households frequented such clubs, mainly because this involved costs that a head of household could only occasionally afford. Given that Monteiro relied on the head of household in his assessment, and given that the average household also contained young folks who might have had some disposable income but would not have been surveyed, it seems plausible that the numbers might be slightly higher.

Nonetheless, clubs were just one facet of urban recreation. Musseque residents still attended parties and dances held in the homes of friends and family. Though clubs replaced these as the primary site of musical production and consumption, home-based entertainment, so central to the social fabric of the musseques, did not disappear. In fact, the vibrant live music scene in the clubs meant that families and groups of friends increasingly tried to have live music at family and neighborhood parties, and bands sometimes volunteered to play for free at parties hosted by people they knew. As Dionísio Rocha commented: "It became rooted in the whole population, as much in the baixa as in the musseque, that fundamentally the presence of Angolan music was absolutely necessary—if I am going to a party I am going to hear live music, I don't want to hear recorded music, I want live music!"[88] So while the clubs might have accounted for only a small percentage attendance-wise, they had a broader cultural impact.

In Monteiro's study the two most-cited uses of free time were "soccer and other sports" (30 percent) and "cinema" (44 percent). Interviews with participants in the musseque recreation scene of the period highlighted soccer games and championships as pretexts for celebrations. Matemona remembered that the place they rehearsed in Marçal also had a soccer team and that if the team had a party then his band would play.[89] Like soccer, cinema was not a discrete category of leisure. CITA sponsored *Dia do Trabalhador* (Workers Day), a music program pitched toward the musseques, at a local cinema. This weekly event convened at the cinema Ngola Cine, very accessible to Rangel and Marçal and other musseques. Monteiro surmised that Ngola Cine was the most popular cinema among survey respondents for both its accessibility and its low prices. While Monteiro neglected to mention the music show, the cinema's acclaim likely had something to do with the tremendous popularity of *Dia do Trabalhador* and its monthly "best of" show, *Aguarela Angolana* (Angolan Watercolor).

Kutonoca, a weekly variety show held in the street, also escaped Monteiro's attention but not that of many musseque residents. A Portuguese enthusiast of Angolan culture, Luiz Montez, developed and promoted this show which CITA eventually incorporated.[90] Again, the government came to culture belatedly and only after entrepreneurial and artistic initiative had opened the way. By all accounts these shows were hugely popular. *Kutonoca* was held every Saturday beginning in the mid-1960s in the different musseques of the city. It was open-air and entrance was free. In an interview in 1999 with the journal *Afro-Letras*, Luiz Montez recounted the history of the show. He said that the *Dia do Trabalhador* and *Aguarela Angolana* began to draw a big crowd, and

> several times we were approached by people who wanted a ticket to go to the show but who didn't have the economic conditions to satisfy this desire. This made me restless, because I wanted to offer some sort of contact with our artists for free, but I would have to bear all the costs. Obviously, this wasn't going to work. So it was then, when I was contacted by a beer company that wanted to launch its product among the masses, that I suggested the outlines of a show. And that is how *Kutonoca*, this interesting show, emerged with support from Nocal and Gás Flaga. It was so successful that later on the office of tourism at the Luanda City Hall, directed by Lemos Pereira, and CITA bought the publicity rights to it, maintaining the same model and schedule.[91]

Montez's memory reveals the clamor among the urban populations for access to this new music as motivating the creation of the street festival format. Despite the fact that the government eventually adopted sponsorship of the show, Dionísio Rocha, who had worked as an emcee for this and other programs and also performed there, said that the government never used *Kutonoca* for political announcements. But musicians sometimes took advantage of the gathering to present songs with a political message. Indeed, as the earlier part of this chapter shows, a simple depiction of daily life in the musseques could be a critique of the colonial situation and a form of political expression.

Kutonoca occurred every Saturday from 3:00 to 6:00 p.m. in different musseques. One Saturday it might be in Rangel and the next Saturday in Prenda, then Marçal or Sambizanga. And it was always packed. With a mobile stage they could take the same lineup to different neighborhoods on consecutive weekends, giving every neighborhood an opportunity to hear the music. Once one lineup had toured all the musseques a new one would begin the same circuit. The popularity of the show exceeded the organizers' expectations. In fact, it was such a hit that people would attend the same show more than once, first in their own neighborhood and then in a different one. This created a circulation of people between neighborhoods that would not have existed to the same extent in the absence of the show. Armando Correia de Azevedo, who served as the emcee for *Kutonoca, Dia do Trabalhador,* and *Aguarela Angolana*, reflected on *Kutonoca*:

> Beyond hearing the show in his neighborhood—because his neighborhood was also part of the program and the show had a schedule—

> he [the audience member] was so imbued with the desire to be present and to see the show that he would follow it. And there were many people who followed the show! They knew that on the next weekend it was in this neighborhood at such and such a place and they would get themselves together, catch the bus and [*he claps his hands together*] off they go to attend again. Each time the crowd got a bit bigger. It was very animated and people were very happy because people wanted to see . . . they would climb on top of the trees, cars, and houses.[92]

This gave artists and aspiring artists a tremendous amount of exposure and performance experience. Many of the best-known musicians debuted in these shows before moving into the club scene.

For folks in the audiences, *Kutonoca* offered a new form of entertainment and a new way of coming together. Like large sports events and carnival (banned between 1961 and 1968), *Kutonoca* brought huge numbers of people together to celebrate Angolan culture. Unlike in a more intimate club or family environment, a spectator might recognize many people but certainly did not know everyone. Here musicians valorized Kimbundu and other local languages in song, people's everyday experiences were represented back to them, and fellow Africans appeared as esteemed public figures on stage. While it would have been dangerous to sing about the guerrillas or the struggle, songs that dealt with daily life critiqued colonial oppression and took aim at antisocial behavior. In interviews and conversations, when I asked about why people liked the show, Angolans repeatedly told me "it was ours" and "it was fun." Despite the fact that everyone now theoretically enjoyed the rights and privileges of Portuguese citizenship, more than ever they felt Angolan. Correia de Azevedo explained the show's popularity and put it in the context of the experience of colonization:

> In the colonial period, people didn't know Angola well. They didn't know—not even the students—the rivers in Angola, the railroads, Angolan geography, Angolan history. But students had to learn the history of Portugal. So, when people start singing Angola this really creates a different sentiment, you know, in people's consciousness, and especially so when these songs are sung in national languages, that is, there is an even greater penetration. And it was really from there that many people gained a national consciousness.[93]

For the many Africans living in the musseques, music, and not political pamphlets, created a sense of nation and sparked a political consciousness.

But in what sense was this scene producing the nation? Clubs and festivals drew together people who were equals in their appreciation of the new urban music, if not in the production of it. In a sense, every performance invited people to the republic of semba, and audiences in their similarity of taste, often constructed through their difference, simulated and symbolized the nation.[94] As Barber argues, "Audiences themselves, by choosing to participate, constitute themselves as members of a collectivity."[95] Describing the music played at clubs and what the scene was like, the musician Santocas noted:

> When musical groups were invited to play at these sports and recreational clubs, it was unusual for people to leave before the band stopped playing. What I mean is that there was a certain interest, a certain connection, and it was in that way that we felt that national music had a certain following, a certain accreditation because it was national, played by nationals, and also put at the disposal of nationals.[96]

Santocas here highlights an interchange between Angolans. It was as if, in his reading, leaving before the band was over would have been unpatriotic.

∽

Semba spoke to life in the musseques, where the urban and rural met and transformed each other. As Jomo Fortunato put it: "Musseques . . . would be that transitional space between the rural universe and the city, a textual laboratory of songs that would absorb the expectations of the urban cultural environment."[97] Song lyrics represented quotidian experiences—the loss of loved ones, heartbreak, work troubles—translating urban life into the language of the rural areas and thus also making rural lifeways present in the urban space. When musicalized and performed, these songs intervened in daily life by giving people a reason to come together in new ways in clubs, backyards, and streets. In exchanges between musicians and audiences, and between different social and performance spaces, Angolans created semba and danced their cultural nation into existence.

The new form of music became a kind of common language that linked the world of the musseques with the worlds outside the city. On the one hand, it looked to rural areas and practices, specifically the use of Kimbundu, to articulate urban woes and aspirations in a local language; at the same time it quite literally dressed those desires in cosmopolitan chic. The music oriented itself to an urban audience that forged its *angolanidade* with sounds and symbols drawn from rural Angola, from transnational musical practices (rock, rumbas, and Rio samba) and from European couture. Finally, semba attracted a public that cut across differences of gender, ethnicity, neighborhood, class, and location even as those differences were the very stuff that marked the music as local and Angolan. Cultural innovators, audiences, and technological innovations would take semba from its origins as a musseque novelty to cities and towns throughout the territory and back again.

5 ⮑ Radios, Turntables, and Vinyl

Technology and the Imagined Community, 1961–75

THE MUSIC OF Luanda's musseques produced meaning through sound, dance, space, and story. It symbolized the world of cultural sovereignty, of African-owned and -run clubs, and of African-produced music that drew on rural and cosmopolitan resources to express an urban Angolan experience. In the production and consumption of this music, people created a sense of nation—of Angolan specificity and self-sufficiency. For all its pretenses to being representative, and even at its most popularly accessible in the street festivals, the musseque music scene was, arguably, a circumscribed phenomenon limited to Luanda's African neighborhoods. It required the development of a local recording industry and the spread of radio broadcasting to overcome physical and social distance and elaborate an ethos of nation that was also national in terms of its territorial presence.[1] The aim of this chapter is twofold. First, it explores to what extent the local phenomenon of the "nation" established in musseque clubs and festivals became "national." Was it just something produced and consumed in Luanda musseques or did it have a greater range? Second, it looks at the ways in which the cultural technology of radio was critical to producing a sense of nation in Luanda by linking the capital with other cities and with the guerrilla struggle (a process that was paralleled in other cities and towns).

Building on Benedict Anderson's concept of print capitalism as the techno-material engine that drives the imagination of nation through novels and newspapers, I argue that "sonorous capitalism," in the form of radio and the recording industry, was the motor that drove the development and spread of music as a medium for imagining the nation in late colonial Angola. The music of Luanda's musseques took on national significance when the technology of the radio and the establishment of a small recording industry made the music reproducible and thus mobile. Even before the advent of local record production, radio broadcast the sounds of musseque music recorded at Luanda stations throughout the territory and beyond. The local recording industry further enabled the spread of the sounds and styles produced in Luanda by putting records into people's hands and homes and into the collections of stations based outside Luanda. People moving back and forth between various Angolan cities and towns and between Angola and other countries could take the music and its images (on album covers) with them. In this sense, radio and the recording industry reterritorialized the music produced in the musseques, giving it a national presence and meaning.

Thus radio disseminated a new sound over a larger geographic area and connected the guerrilla struggle with those who stayed behind. But the link between radio and nation was not limited to this. Radio also helped produce a sense of nation within Luanda and other places. Radio serialized music: it was one reality among, but attached to, many. Radio connected people in the musseques to people in other parts of the country and people at various places throughout Angola to the "world outside": to the guerrilla struggle, to the international media, and to independent African countries. These different sites constituted the various "meanwhiles" that radio concatenated and through which Angolans realized the imagined community of nation. Political repression may have been great in the late 1960s and early 1970s, but Angolans sought connection to the outside world and to the guerrilla struggle, even if only for a few minutes a day and at great risk. Tuning in to various worlds, they imagined their own world in different terms.

RADIO AS A CULTURAL TECHNOLOGY: SOUNDING OUT THE NATION

Central to Anderson's analysis of the nation as imagined community is the concept of print capitalism. In *Imagined Communities* he links cultural processes with technological innovation and economic dynamics. In this account, print capitalism does not create the nation but rather fuels it with mass-produced novels and newspapers. Music, I have argued, is the cultural practice through which Angolans imagine the nation. But the music of Luanda's clubs in and of itself would have only a limited impact were it not for the technologies that record and reproduce sound and the radios and turntables that transmit it. In proposing the concept of "sonorous capitalism" I want to shift attention from the novels, newspapers, and printing presses Anderson highlights to vinyl records, radio, and recorded sound.[2] These latter cultural technologies massified music and thereby helped make it the most salient cultural practice in the 1961–74 period, both in and outside Luanda.

Anderson argues that novels offered Latin American creoles a way to imagine a community beyond the local by signaling homogeneous empty time (linking events that occur simultaneously but in different places). He encapsulated this concept in the word "meanwhile." Radio broadcasting performed this same function in late colonial Angola, opening up a variety of meanwhiles: different Angolan anticolonial movements, Luanda clubs, other cities and towns in Angola, the international arena. I use the plural "meanwhiles" in place of Anderson's singular to signal the complex context and outcome of Angola's nationalisms and anticolonial nationalisms more generally. I do so in order to underscore how simultaneity is structured as much from spaces outside as inside. Some of those spaces later come to form an independent Angola— guerrillas and political movements that return even if not as victors. Others do not and cannot: solidarity groups and other nations, with or without interests in Angola, whose broadcasts locals found important, including the BBC, Radio Netherlands, Radio Brazzaville, and radio from Zaire. All of these spaces offered exterior coordinates (other than Portuguese ones) with which Angolans imagined their nation.

Radio provided news through the MPLA's program *Angola Combatente*, broadcast from Congo-Brazzaville, Tanzania, and Egypt; the FNLA's *Angola Libre*, broadcast from Kinshasa; and other foreign news services such as Voice of America and Radio Moscow.[3] It connected those within the country to those fighting from outside the country and to those in solidarity with the anticolonial struggle. Radio clubs and stations existed throughout the colonial territory, linking various localities, while access to international radio framed the territory from without, placing it within the international sphere of relations between nations that the Portuguese colonial regime so doggedly denied.

Radio, like books or film, is a cultural technology whose specific mode of communication gives it a particular relation to the production of nation. Joy Elizabeth Hayes argues that the development of the radio medium has two important social implications: "the creation of a new mode of mass-mediated intimacy and the formation of a new kind of collective space."[4] Intimacy and collectivity are elemental to nation. Radio produces a sense of intimacy as the voice of the broadcaster enters the ear and home or space of the listener. Like the newspaper and the novel, radio also creates intimacy through temporal leveling—one has access to other "meanwhiles." Hayes argues that "radio's fleeting presence mimics the modern experience of reality as ephemeral and forward moving. This constant movement, or 'flow,' contributes to a sense of the immediacy, realism, and timeliness of radio content."[5] Radio in this sense may in fact trump novels, and maybe even newspapers, in giving us a sense of being able to participate, even if only as aural witness, in a spatially different "now."

At the same time, one tunes in with the knowledge that others in a vast space can do the same. In her study of radio in Zambia in the colonial period, Debra Spitulnik notes that "with radio, places were experienced as closer together and places that were minimally connected before became strongly linked . . . while the horizons of people's worlds expanded. . . . It also appears that distances overall became shorter and even more tangible."[6] In other words, radio pulled people and places closer together while also pushing out the limits of their worlds. Radio listening often unites people in a collective experience: people gather around a radio to listen. In this way, radio can produce a sense of collectivity that is at once local—those of us here around the radio—and more dispersed, linking local listeners to a larger listening "we," or in Hayes's words, a "virtual commons" where an intimate anonymity reigns. In the case of music, radio broadens geographically and socially, the public that it attracts and the nation it produces.

A BRIEF HISTORY OF RADIO IN ANGOLA AND THE MASS-MEDIATED URBAN SOUNDSCAPE

Radio broadcasting in Angola began as the activity of amateurs and hobbyists. As with other cultural practices in this period, the state arrived belatedly. Of the twenty-six radio stations that existed in nineteen different cities and towns at the end of the colonial period, nineteen were commercial stations and only seven were government-run.[7] The first radio transmission occurred in 1933 in Benguela from the private transmitter of a Portuguese man named Álvaro de Carvalho.[8] Carvalho later established the country's first station. This was followed by a series of radio clubs that gathered amateur broadcasters who pursued radio out of interest and not for financial gain: beginning in 1938, clubs formed first in Lobito, then in Luanda, and finally in Benguela. By the late 1940s, all the major cities in each province had their own radio clubs and the move toward professionalization began. Sebastião Coelho, involved in Angolan radio for many years, identifies as pivotal the moment in 1948 when the Huambo Radio Club, in the country's central plateau region, began competitions for staff admission and hired two well-known Lisbon radio journalists.[9]

Despite the Huambo club's slogan and self-description as a "Portuguese voice in Africa,"[10] this club, and others like it, had a distinctly local character and focus. Radios featured local news and events in their broadcasts, even as the stations maintained "the pretense of covering all of Angola and even the world."[11] While the Portuguese radio hobbyists, and eventually the state, intended to strengthen the ties between the metropole and this bit of "overseas territory" under the wing of the Portuguese nation, the results could often differ from the intentions. The radio clubs' primary activities included news and entertainment, often broadcast live from their studios. Since radio broadcasting was done on shortwave, a radio club, no matter where it was located, could broadcast throughout the country. To a certain degree, programs and personnel also circulated among various cities and stations. For many of those moving from city to city or to other towns this generated a stronger sense of *angolanidade* as they came to know different parts of the country and brought their knowledge, experiences, and hometown practices with them.[12] The first radio stations opened outside Luanda, and though not beyond the reach of colonial law, they did not belong to the state. The Emissora Oficial de Angola (Official Broadcasting Station of Angola, EOA) began broadcasting daily only in the mid-1950s.[13]

Radio produced in Angola was not, however, the only radio that Angolans received and tuned in to. Albina Assis remembered that as schoolgirls in the mid-to-late 1950s, she and her friends listened to foreign radio stations in order to hear news about Portugal that government censors red-lined from broadcasts on local radio. She recalled, in particular, listening to Radio Moscow and to Danish radio.[14] Once the war started in 1961 Luandans began to tune in to radio broadcasts from other African countries. Listeners procured news programs in Portuguese and local languages prepared by the MPLA and the FNLA, in particular, and broadcast from Congo-Brazzaville, Egypt, Tanzania, Zaire, Zambia, and Ghana.[15] PIDE documents note that agents followed Radio Cairo broadcasts in Portuguese (1964) and Radio Tanzania broadcasts of twenty minutes' duration that encouraged support for independence movements in Namibia (Southwest Africa), Angola, and Mozambique (1965).[16]

People also tuned in to foreign stations to listen to music. Brazzaville's transmitter was strong enough that Angolans throughout the territory could pick it up[17] (see the map based on one from the PIDE archives). Angolan listeners were keenly aware that both Congos had attained independence in 1960 and that the Congolese music on the airwaves was being broadcast by newly independent African nations. Knowledge of independent neighbor states and Angolans' desire for their own political sovereignty deepened their appreciation of the music itself.

The availability of programming was only part of the picture. For radio music to have a presence and an audience, people had to own radios or have access to them. So how present were radios in the musseques and throughout Angola? According to a study done in the late 1950s, of 344 families surveyed

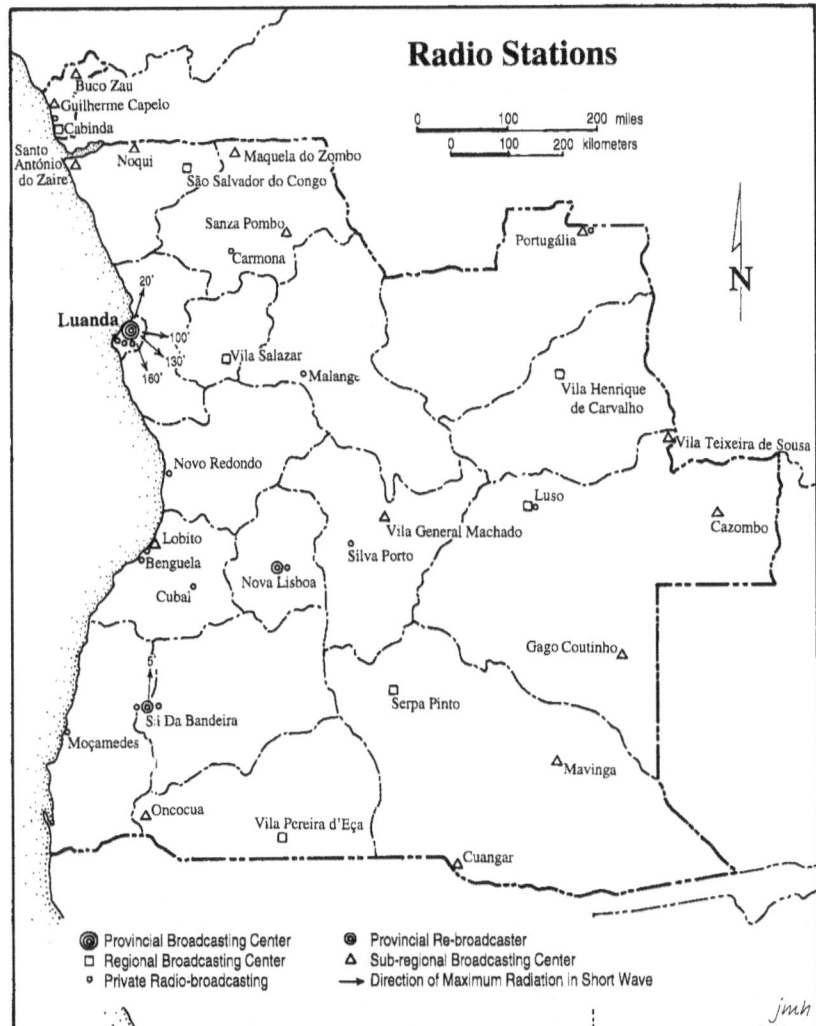

Radio stations in Angola, 1975

only four owned radios.[18] Here, as in other parts of the continent, radios, like gramophones and later turntables, symbolized if not elite status at the very least a desire for modernity and an "upward mobility and urbanity."[19] In one of the photos of the interior of a musseque home shown in Monteiro's study (discussed in chapter 1), the family poses around a radio and tape recorder prominently displayed on the table in their living room.[20] As Debra Spitulnik argues, "the social place of radio as a technology depends upon ways in which the technology itself embodies ideologies of status and modernity."[21] Thus it is no surprise that the economic changes of the late 1960s found Angolans investing in such technology. By the early 1970s radio ownership had increased significantly: Monteiro found that about 43 percent of heads of households in the musseques reported listening to radio at home, meaning that they owned radio sets. Transistors were even more popular: Monteiro claimed that individuals would often forgo other necessities to purchase a transistor. Elaborating on the desire for this technology he opined that "the great love that they have for music constitutes one of the principal motivations."[22] Despite his paternalistic and racist tone, music certainly was one of the reasons Angolans wanted radios. The desire to tune in, or at least to capture the value of the radio, also led to an increase in radio thefts, which doubled between 1968 and 1970.[23]

Radio listening was not a pastime limited to Luanda or even to urban areas, wrote Monteiro:

> This is a phenomenon that is not exclusive to urban or suburban zones, but is also felt in the rural areas where he who owns a radio is surrounded by a certain social prestige and where his friends and family members get closer to him in order to enjoy the opportunity of listening to music or news in which they are interested. In Angola, actually, those villages that do not yet possess one or more radio sets can be considered in the minority and in some of the more economically developed areas the number of families that owns a set is more than 10 percent.[24]

As this quote suggests, radio listening was not a solitary activity. One radio served many sets of ears and as a consequence survey material certainly underreported the scale of audition. By the mid-1960s PIDE documents suggest that radios were common, although they do not give exact numbers. Reporting from the town of Pereira d'Eça (today Ondjiva), in the southernmost region of the country, a PIDE agent worried about broadcasts from Radio Tanzania heard locally and remarked that "there are numerous radios in existence among the locals."[25] Likewise, reporting on Malanje province, another agent recommended that "due to the elevated number of radios owned by natives of this area, it would be wise to efficaciously interfere with the above mentioned broadcasts," in this case from Radio Brazzaville.[26] I will return to the practice of interfering with nationalist broadcasting shortly.

Radio listening and radio ownership often had transborder and international dimensions. In 1970 the Angolan Broadcasting Plan's Coordinating Committee proposed placing FM receptors in all imported radios and in all radios made or assembled in Angola while simultaneously disabling their shortwave receptors. Thirteen Luanda businesses, all vendors of radios, responded negatively to the proposal and enumerated their reasons in a six-page letter to the governor general. After noting the economic disincentives to the proposed measure, they argued that the move would not end shortwave listening

> because [the proposal] does not propose apprehending the thousands of radios owned by the province's population; because, in the face of this measure, they will continue to tune in with radios that are entering the country illegally.... Starting from the premise that one-tenth of the population possess radios, that would mean there are 500,000 units throughout the province and that at least half of those would have shortwave reception. It is worth noting that the numbers cited fall significantly short of the reality.[27]

A short message in 1968 on the audition of Voz de Angola in Maquela (in northern Angola) from the local PIDE post noted that the great majority of radio receivers in the area were of poor quality. The agent surmised that these radios were made and purchased in Congo-Kinshasa.[28] Commercial and social exchange with both Congos was nothing new. But radios also arrived by extralegal means, namely via the FNLA. Holden Roberto recalled that the movement purchased and distributed transistors and batteries to run them in the Angolan provinces of Zaire, Uige, Bengo, Luanda, Malanje, Kwanza Norte, Kwanza Sul, Lunda Norte, and Lunda Sul. He surmised that more than a thousand radios arrived in this manner over a fourteen-year period and that one radio might serve three hundred to four hundred listeners.[29]

In Luanda, the association between musseques, music, and radio was particularly strong.[30] PIDE preoccupations, and those of some Luanda-based Portuguese, centered on radio programs beamed from neighboring countries. By mid-1968, according to one letter to the editor in the local popular press, foreign broadcasts formed part of Luanda's urban soundscape. Much to the chagrin of the letter's author, these programs were more popular among the urban "masses" than were the many shows broadcast by the twenty local stations available at the time, shows closely watched by government censors:

> It is of this mass, connected to other traditions, educated in other environments that I am going to speak. Now, it doesn't go unnoticed by anyone when we are walking in the street, or on the beaches or when we enter into bars and cross paths with individuals carrying transistor radios, their gullets open, with their *banga* [vanity], showing that that is what is good. Ninety percent, approximately, of these individuals

have their radios tuned in to broadcasts from Brazzaville, the Republic of the Congo, and Zambia. This is not news to anyone and I even like to hear those rhythms. What I don't like is the news that they broadcast in Portuguese and in almost all the languages of Angola. We all know the politics that these countries practice against us . . . Out of curiosity, I asked some individuals why they listened to those stations and undervalued ours and the responses were variable and I note them here: "because it is hot music," "it is our music and our friends," "they also speak our language," "they play music that the people like." Mr. Director, why don't we combat this Congomania because this is not the Congo, it is Angola, for all of us. Why not create a program that broadcasts consecutively music in the same melodic line. Our folklore, which all of us like to hear and that unfortunately we have few opportunities to applaud, would then have greater projection.[31]

The letter writer's concerns demonstrate the intimate link between politics and urban culture. The author, António José Garcia da Silva, describes the swagger and pride of young urban males who use transistor radios like political fashion accessories. And he decries the fact that Angolans listen to Congolese news broadcasts that he deems sympathetic to the nationalist/anticolonial cause. Finally he proposes a solution: the promotion of Angolan music, "our folklore," is required to combat "Congomania." Local music, da Silva suggests, can remedy the subversive news and potentially subversive music from the Congo. Popular practices, in his view, could be co-opted and rechanneled to support Portugal's pluri-continental nationalist project. Local music, in this reading, was not innocuous but prophylactic: it offered protection against the insidious effects of Congomania, against the craze of anticolonial nationalism.[32]

For Angolan musicians, by contrast, Congolese music seemed less like an infectious disease and more like a spark of inspiration that returned them to their roots, linked them to other cosmopolitan musical practitioners, and reminded them of the armed struggle being waged for Angolan independence. Xabanu recalled that "those of us here, Angolans in the musseques, tuned into Congolese radio—from the Congo, which played lots of Latin American and Congolese music."[33] Jorge Macedo said that people listened to Congolese and Latin American music broadcast by Belgian radio from the then capital Leopoldville, today Kinshasa, as early as the mid-1950s. But radio was not the sole vector of Congolese music. It also arrived in Luanda on vinyl: records from Kinshasa and Brazzaville were played at parties in the musseques in the 1950s and 1960s, as described in the preceding chapter. In particular, Angolans clamored for Franco, Dr. Nico, and Wendo, in part because they sang in Lingala and created an urban African sound: a sound that Macedo also described as "ours," that he said "inflamed our nationalist spirit."[34]

When Angolans claimed that the Congolese musicians played "our" music and "spoke our language" (in the metaphoric sense, since most Angolans did not speak Lingala), they made a rhetorical move identifying themselves with an independent African nation instead of with Portugal. Asserting a pan-Africanist "we," these Angolans claimed a cosmopolitan nationalism that did not have Portugal or even Europe as its template.[35] If the Huambo radio club presented itself as "a Portuguese voice in Africa," then Congolese radio projected an African voice in Africa. Sometimes Congolese music could even symbolize an Angolan voice. Santocas recalled the association of Congolese music with the Angolan struggle for independence. He said that listening to Congolese music intensified the feeling of connection to the nationalist movements, colloquially referred to as the *irmãos kambutas* (short brothers), because "there existed the complete consciousness that the liberation movements were headquartered in both the Republics of Congo Brazzaville and of Congo Kinshasa. So whenever the music of Franco or [Tabu Ley] Rochereau, those amazing stars, was played, the sentiment was greater."[36] Finally, the fact that Congolese radio from both Brazzaville and Kinshasa intercalated news broadcasts with music—whether the MPLA's *Angola Combatente*, the FNLA's *Angola Libre*, or local Congolese news—identified Congolese music with the nationalist struggle by simple association.

ANGOLA COMBATENTE

I gained insights into radio broadcasting and reception through interviews in 2005 with the MPLA's secretary of international affairs, Paulo Jorge, and with Adolfo Maria, a member of the Revolta Activa and an early nationalist militant. However, I was unable to locate any documentation regarding *Angola Combatente*.[37] Documents from the PIDE archives at the Torre do Tombo in Lisbon reveal the concerns and perspectives of the colonial regime. But, again, it is the memories of those who listened to radio that anchor this section.

The risks of listening and the hour that the radio program aired, 7:00 p.m., consistently and prominently marked the memories of Angolans who spoke to me about *Angola Combatente*. Because of the highly politicized nature of the broadcasts it was dangerous to be seen or heard listening to them. So people would gather with select, trustworthy friends and family to hear the broadcasts. Others tuned in alone. Those without radios or the possibility of hearing it received the news secondhand. Many Luanda residents recounted listening to

Angola Combatente with their heads under pillows, or even under the bed. Some went further. Manuel Faria sought the cover of night and a remote listening spot: "I would put my car in the soccer field, because I lived just near there, and you know, there in the soccer field it is dark and so on and I could listen to that little bit of radio at 19h00."[38] Outside Luanda people took similar precautions before tuning in: former mineworkers at Diamang in eastern Angola recounted memories of hidden listening to the researcher Todd Cleveland.[39] Both inside and outside the capital, the specter of the PIDE, notorious for terrorizing musseque residents, induced fear and inspired creative listening strategies.

Like other listeners, Alberto Jaime remembered the role the program played in rousing consciousness as well as the caution listeners took when tuning in:

> *Angola Combatente* woke us up. They would come with a message saying that those of us in Luanda shouldn't be intimidated [by the colonial authorities]. But you had to be careful. I would listen with my neighbor but it was difficult, it was difficult. You had to know with which neighbors you could hear *Angola Combatente* because that was a death certificate! If the police caught you listening to it at night they would confiscate your radio and take you in for interrogation. And no one wanted to end up in jail. This Pacavira of Kwanza Norte was left without the ability to have children because of the prisons.[40]

But despite the fear of violence associated with being caught, people did listen to *Angola Combatente*. They listened to hear what was going on with the guerrilla struggle in its own terms and to hear the words of encouragement that Jaime so clearly recalled. The EOA, on its program *Voz de Angola* (Voice of Angola), played good music but the station's news broadcasts consisted only of propaganda and highly censored reports of local and international events.[41] *Angola Combatente* was therefore an alternative source of news about international events in general and about the Angolan liberation struggle in particular.[42] Foreign stations and *Angola Combatente* reported on United Nations resolutions and debates that related to Angola or other Portuguese colonies; these events never made the local news.

Although only fifteen to twenty minutes in duration,[43] the program also managed to communicate, in code, news of those who had fled to join the fight. One PIDE report recorded such transmissions on May 16, 1970: "Attention papa! Mama had twins!" And then another message minutes later: "Attention Muigi in Matadi! Your messages have been received with regularity." The PIDE officer writing the report concluded that this "leads us to believe that the MPLA has, at least, one agent in Matadi."[44]

For those involved in the clandestine political struggle in Luanda after the war broke out in 1961, *Angola Combatente* gave them a way to stay in touch with what was happening in the guerrilla fronts in the north and east of the country and with exiled political leaders in Brazzaville and Dar es Salaam. News about who had arrived, like the message about the twins (which perhaps announced the arrival of two new nationalists), and the silence about those who had not, provided information anxiously awaited by Luanda's political activists.

Code allowed politically engaged Angolans in the country to communicate with one another as well as with those outside the territory. Albina Assis recounted how she and others involved in clandestine political groups used the radio and employed their own codes to talk about what they were doing.

> By the time the MPLA started broadcasting, via *Angola Combatente*, we already knew and we would say . . . since no one would say what they were actually going to do. . . . So we [a group of school friends] would say "We're going to bençon. What is bençon? A bençon was a kind of mass that was held during the month of May for the whole month, which is the month in the Catholic Church—the month of Maria—in which the people would go to the church at 7:00 p.m. and stay there for about an hour. . . . So we would say this when someone was around in order to be able to leave where we were. We all had an obligation to hear *Angola Combatente* so that the next day we could report on what was happening and how the war was developing, who had left for there and who had arrived. We were young girls but we already knew all those codes of the messages—so and so left, because they wouldn't give someone's name, and "Andorinhas" arrived. Since we knew of the movement and who was leaving, we were able to say who had made it and who had not.[45]

Assis and her colleagues used the trappings of piety to cover up what would have been considered subversive activities by the PIDE and dangerous engagements by parents and friends. Who would dare question young folks going off to church in the evening? Indeed, it must have seemed like a real blessing that *Angola Combatente* broadcast at the same hour as church services. The use of this particular code, of a religious practice, underscored the sense of devotion to and sanctity of the cause. As Assis herself noted, political involvement also entailed obligation and devotion. One did what was required: in this case that included listening to the broadcast, understanding the various levels of the messages communicated, and then sharing that information the following day with others in the group who had not heard it, or comparing notes with those who had.[46]

Others remembered listening to *Angola Combatente* with members of their political cells. Xabanu was part of a political cell formed in 1962–63 with other students from the Rangel neighborhood. He recalled that each person had a friend or small cell with whom they would listen to *Angola Combatente*, and groups even got as large as ten people. In fact, *Angola Combatente* often broadcast instructions on how to organize political cells, hide arms, and make bombs.[47] Although he had to leave the group when he went off to do military service in the local contingent of the Portuguese army, Xabanu said, "We never stopped listening to our *Angola Combatente* even as the soldiers that we were. We always had the nucleus of a group that would say—*eh, pá*, it is 19h00, let's go listen to *Angola Combatente!* And we would listen . . . but if they caught you, look out!"[48] The risks were substantial. Other soldiers might turn them in to the PIM (Polícia de Informação Militar or Military Information Police), who would likely deem them traitors and send them off to military prison. As soldiers in the Portuguese army they were listening to the "enemy," betraying the flag they bore on their uniforms. Angolans could be compelled to perform military service, but many Angolan soldiers were still nationalists. A PIDE agent posted in Maquela found that MPLA broadcasts were easily audible in the area and that soldiers in the local battalions and those stationed in surrounding areas "frequently listened to these broadcasts," which often addressed soldiers directly and encouraged them to give up the fight.[49] Finally, a police officer caught a small group of *cipaios* (African policeman) in the town of Chiumbo near Huambo in central Angola listening to *Angola Combatente*. The *cipaios* claimed they were merely listening to the music, not the talk, but the reporting police officer concluded that local staff could not be trusted.[50]

According to one 1968 note in the PIDE files, musseque residents commonly listened to *Angola Combatente* on the airwaves of Radio Brazzaville. The note from a police brigade chief to his senior officer related the following message from a study done by a business associated with the Coordinating Commission: "The commission received a bit of information that held that many radio owners actually have two radios. One is located in the entrance and tuned to a Luanda station and a second is placed in a compartment in the back of the home and tuned in to Brazzaville." To this he added his own experience: "African owners of transistor radios generally listen to Radio Brazzaville. And I can guarantee that they don't even take the precautions that this report mentions. They listen, comment and discuss only because the responsible services have not yet put the expensive apparatus to work yet."[51] While this contrasts with the memories of individuals who recall listening while hiding, it may have to do with the difference between listening to music and Congolese news (the usual fare on transistors) and listening specifically to *Angola Combatente*, which would have been done "in the back of the house" or even more clandestinely.

Angola Combatente often opened its news shows with music, usually music produced by bands composed of Angolan MPLA soldiers with musical inclinations. Most mentioned was the group N'zaji, which included the man who would later become Angola's president, José Eduardo dos Santos.[52] Bands like N'zaji played the kind of music that soldiers in the struggle often sang to keep their spirits up and pass the time. It included some older, "typical" Angolan songs, popular songs already transformed by Ngola Ritmos, which were indirect critiques of colonialism. Examples include "Kaputu" (track 11) and "Monetu ua Kassule," in which the narrator tells of a young son who was found without documents and sent off to São Tomé.[53] But the bands also played newer songs that spoke directly of the struggle and the MPLA, like "Dr. Neto," named after the MPLA's president. These were played with a typical Angolan beat and sung in Kimbundu.[54]

This genre of music also represented the MPLA's struggle internationally. The LP *Victory Is Certain!* (one of the MPLA slogans), produced by Parendon Press in New York in 1970, educated an international audience about the MPLA's politics. Liner notes in English indicate that it aimed to reach a foreign audience.[55] This music was a more politicized and polished version of what went on in the guerrilla camps, where people gathered around a bonfire at night to sing. Luzia "Inga" Van Dunem, who served as a communications expert for many years in the guerrilla struggle, remembered: "The person would sing, manifest, reflect on what they were living—the suffering, the rains, the lack of food, the deaths. Everything was expressed in the songs and it became a revolutionary music. Music that talked about what we went through in that sacrifice for independence."[56] *Angola Combatente* did not typically broadcast this type of spontaneous music but these groups of guerrillas were avid listeners of *Angola Combatente*. Gathering around a bonfire and singing or listening to radio connected them with others in the struggle as well as with a potential audience of sympathetic listeners, including family and friends, in the urban areas. Guerrillas also used music to educate and motivate local populations and those same populations shaped those musical forms and practices.[57] Soldiers on the other side, that is in the Portuguese military, also used music to punctuate their days. Mixed groups of Angolan and Portuguese soldiers would drink beer and play music, both Angolan and Portuguese songs, to pass the time.[58]

In the early 1970s companies in Angola produced records of local music that often found their way across borders. This allowed *Angola Combatente* to play the music popular in Luanda. Innovative radio operators took advantage of this to hoodwink authorities and transmit *Angola Combatente* semi-surreptitiously. Roldão Ferreira, whose Kimbundu-language radio show *Kussunguila* played popular urban Angolan music, remembered listening to *Angola Combatente* in public and with the volume at normal levels.

> At the National African League [the Liga] . . . every Thursday we already had the program schedule for *Angola Combatente*. And I managed to play the music almost simultaneously. The songs were placed, via the guide of *Angola Combatente* in Brazzaville, and we would put them on here as well on the program *Kussunguila*. [João das Chagas: This didn't cause you problems?] No, no it didn't. Because we, I and some others, were normally in the São João bar with a number of whites on the other side, listening, attentive, wanting to hear either *Kussunguila* or *Angola Combatente* to know what it was they were saying. And there was such a complication of music that those who were nearby couldn't tell if it was *Angola Combatente* or *Kussunguila* . . . because the songs coincided. . . . We listened to *Angola Combatente* even with the enemies right next to us![59]

Ferreira spoke with pleasure at being able to slip one by whites who were curious to know what *Angola Combatente* was saying. For Ferreira and his friends, this act of defiance took advantage of the fact that censorship and PIDE repression kept even local whites from listening to *Angola Combatente*. In playing the music from *Angola Combatente* simultaneously with his own *Kussunguila* show (whose name refers to the nightly gathering of elders and youth where stories and fables are recounted), Ferreira amplified the music's subversive potential. The same music that would have aired on *Voz de Angola* and been considered anodyne by the authorities suddenly acquired a direct nationalist resonance when played on local radio in synchronization with *Angola Combatente*.

A local administrator in Mungo town in Huambo province reported a similar incident in 1967. He happened upon a group of ten to fifteen African men listening to *Angola Combatente* in a bar. They used the telephone as a radio receptor and switched back and forth between stations.[60] The desire of populations throughout the Angolan territory to listen to *Angola Combatente* and their ingenuity in finding ways to do so demonstrates a widespread interest in the activities of the nationalists. When Angolans synchronized news from *Angola Combatente* with broadcasts of popular urban music they intensified the kinship between the two. The fact that records produced in Angola made it to Brazzaville showed that movement and communication between Luanda and Brazzaville, and many towns in between, continued to elude Portuguese authorities and that cultural news and objects traveled routes similar to those of political news and materials.

RADIO, COUNTERINSURGENCY, AND MUSIC

Until the 1950s, radio was the bailiwick of small groups of hobbyists and enthusiasts, mainly organized in radio clubs spread throughout the country.[61] According to Sebastião Coelho, a couple of Portuguese radio enthusiasts who had spent some time at the Benguela Radio Club proposed the idea of a national radio station to the provincial governor in Luanda and convinced the head of the Post, Telegraph and Telephone system to adopt the project of creating the Official Broadcasting Station of Angola, or EOA. Despite its territorial name, the EOA primarily focused on Luanda. It therefore encountered serious competition from the radio clubs in other urban areas and from Rádio Ecclésia, the Catholic radio station already established in Luanda.[62] The state radio station did not have a strong presence until the mid-1960s, when it put to work 100-kilowatt transmitters that allowed it to reach almost all of Angola with shortwave broadcasts.[63] Nonetheless, while almost every city in the province of Angola had a commercial radio station, not every city had an official radio station, although the local commercial station was linked with the EOA and broadcast the official news reports throughout the day.[64] The colonial state piggybacked on local initiative just as it did with local music clubs.

Furthermore, the nationalist guerrillas had set the communications agenda. In the late 1960s the military's countersubversion efforts began to use radio to broadcast the administration's propaganda. The colonial state found itself forced to respond to rebel broadcasts that were accessible to anyone with a shortwave radio.[65] The most direct and obvious state response was to jam the foreign-based transmissions,[66] but perhaps the more effective response was to develop a radio network throughout Angola. On March 27, 1961, on the heels of the uprisings in February and March of that year, the overseas minister created a Coordinating Commission for a Radio Broadcasting Plan for the Province of Angola.[67] This plan provided for an increase in broadcasting and for a newly coordinated broadcasting system throughout the province that would link local clubs and commercial stations to the EOA. But it was not until

1967, after many years of liberation movement broadcasting, that CITA convened the first Colloquium on Radio Broadcasting to evaluate the success of the prior plan and to discuss radio in frankly political and propagandistic terms. In an unpublished article on the history of radio in Angola, Júlio Mendes Lopes argues that

> the participants introduced the concept of "radio broadcasting as a national force" in the debates, and they committed themselves to making a contribution to "the high mission of the Armed Forces" (i.e., the colonial war). Here it can be inferred that radio in Angola was an integral and important part of the system of colonial administration, a privileged instrument in the fight against all the nationalist movements.[68]

This colloquium was part of a larger effort by the colonial government to win the war of ideas. In the same year, 1967, the Portuguese government established the General Council for Countersubversion.[69] From November 1968 to March 1969 they held a Symposium on Countersubversion where they discussed the problem of "enemy" radio (i.e., that of the nationalist movements) and the usefulness of radio to their own campaign, already underway at *Voz de Angola*.[70]

Documents from the symposium state that *Voz de Angola* was already an effective means of "electronic warfare." They report that the radio program was widely heard throughout Angola as well as outside it. Countersubversion experts attributed much of the program's success to its use of "native tongues."[71] *Voz de Angola* employed Angolans who spoke local languages in order to broadcast news and information that would reach the widest possible audience. Lourdes Van Dunem worked as an announcer on *Voz de Angola* and it was there that she learned to speak Kimbundu, though she had been singing in Kimbundu for years.[72] Roldão Ferreira, who had worked as an announcer on Coelho's *Tondoya Mukina o Kizomba*, was recruited by the EOA for his Kimbundu language skills.[73] Local-language news broadcasts on *Voz* commonly included interviews with real and imagined deserters from the guerrilla troops, speeches praising public institutions that provided social assistance to the population, and conversations with "African heroes" who were loyal to the Portuguese.[74] Ferreira described this as the government's attempt to "unite the useful with the pleasant."[75] Most Angolans had no trouble seeing this for the propaganda it was, but they tuned in just the same, in order to hear the local music that accompanied the news. The bands and artists that had established themselves on the club scene and via the music festivals also took advantage of the potential publicity that radio afforded them. One musician referred to the station as "our publicity agent."[76]

However, *Voz de Angola* was not the only game in town. Rádio Ecclésia broadcast popular urban music as well. It was here that Sebastião Coelho made his name with the programs *Café da Noite: Boa música em boa companhia* (Nighttime Coffee: Good Music in Good Company), beginning in 1963, and *Tondoya Mukina o Kizomba* (There Is a Party in Our House), which started in 1964.[77] *Café da Noite* played Angolan music but not exclusively. It did, however, express a certain *angolanidade* in its focus on local issues, and Coelho closed each show with the Kimbundu word *mungweno* ("until tomorrow").[78] *Tondoya*, on the other hand, dedicated its programming to the promotion of Angolan music and employed announcers who broadcast in both Kimbundu and Portuguese.[79]

Coelho broadcast his first radio show with an entirely Angolan format in 1960 from the Huambo Radio Club. This show was completely in Umbundu, the language predominant in that area. CUCA, a foreign-owned but locally operating beer company, sponsored both the Luanda and Huambo shows. These radio shows highlighted music by local artists recorded in their studios.[80] The fact that the first radio show oriented to an African audience, playing Angolan music and communicating in a local language, was broadcast from Huambo helps decenter, ever so slightly, Luanda's role in the history of popular Angolan music. Radio, as Coelho argues, was critical to the massification of popular Angolan music. He contends that the "great turn" in the history of Angolan music happened from the moment at which music from Angola was heard daily on the radio, starting its diffusion on a grand scale.[81] It happened first in Huambo, giving impetus to young folks who decided to form bands and small theater groups.[82] Yet only when programs of a similar nature, with a range extending to various areas of the country, began to air did the music have anything like a national reach. This only happened with the inauguration of *Voz de Angola* and with Rádio Ecclésia, which the radio clubs of all the other major urban centers and provinces then rebroadcast.[83] Independent producers and radio enthusiasts working with local musicians initiated this move and the government and EOA adopted what was already popular.

From his studio in Luanda, Estúdios Norte, Coelho produced programs that aired both on the Angolan Radio Club (based in Luanda) and on Rádio Ecclésia. Perhaps most importantly, his studio recorded a tremendous amount of local music. *Voz de Angola* also recorded music at the EOA's studios in order to be able to play Angolan music on the radio before the local recording industry took off. Prior to this the only Angolan music available was recorded and produced in Portugal. It made its way back to Angola with travelers from

Ngola Ritmos album cover, early 1960s, produced in Portugal on the Alvorada label. *Courtesy RNA*

the metropole. Among the singles produced in Portugal were those by Ngola Ritmos, on the Portuguese label Alvorada, in 1960; Trio Assis and Garda e o Seu Conjunto on the English label Parlophone (the album is undated, but Dionísio Rocha thinks it was recorded in the mid-to-late 1940s, and a handwritten note on the album indicates it was played on air in 1961); and Ngoleiros do Ritmo, on Alvorada in 1960.[84] These Portuguese-made album covers convey Angolan culture as folkloric, as the quaint, caricatured local color of empire. This image appealed to a lusotropicalist sensibility in the Portuguese market. In contrast, albums produced slightly later and by companies in Angola (see images in chapters 3 and 4) offered up the local in a cosmopolitan form, an image that catered to the Angolan market. Regardless of the market destination, the possibility of playing and/or recording at the various radio stations added to the growing professionalization of urban musicians. Likewise,

Garda and Her Band album cover, circa 1950s, produced in Portugal on the Parlophone label. *Courtesy RNA*

music festivals and song competitions sponsored by local businesses and radio shows provided other opportunities for perfecting one's technique and honing one's performance style.

THE RECORDING INDUSTRY

For the new urban popular music to circulate as it did required a conjunction of different processes. In *Imagined Communities*, Anderson asserts: "What, in the positive sense, made the new communities imaginable was a half-fortuitous, but explosive, interaction between a system of production and productive relations (capitalism), a technology of communications (print), and the fatality of human linguistic diversity."[85] In Anderson's account, it was neither simply capitalism nor just printing, but their concurrence and interaction

Ngoleiros do Ritmo album cover, early 1960s, produced in Portugal on the Alvorada label. *Courtesy RNA*

with emerging vernaculars in the context of waning dynasties and the decreasing religious domination of society. So too in Angola, it was the confluence together of technological, cultural, social, and political dynamics that made imagining nation possible. Sonorous capitalism issued from the coincidence of radio broadcasting, the availability of inexpensive radios, and the arrival of a recording industry. Together these elements nourished a new form of music, semba, and within it the imagination of nation.

While radio stations often broadcast live recordings, for music to really spread and to have a continuous presence it had to be recorded. Indeed, as mentioned above, both Coelho's Estúdios Norte and the EOA recorded music in order to more easily play, and in Coelho's case, commercialize it. Recording technologies made music reproducible and more accessible. Both radio stations and individuals could buy vinyl LPs and, more typically, singles and could thereby repeatedly broadcast and listen to the music played live in clubs.

The production of singles of local music facilitated the professional development of musical practice. It offered recording opportunities in which playing had to be repeated and refined, and it created the possibility of living off one's art. The recording industry catalyzed the spread of music by making the same music played in clubs available to various stations and listeners at the same time.[86] Listeners separated by physical distance were united by sharing an experience of music.

Before the local record industry started up in the years 1968–74, one could purchase records in Angola but not of Angolan music. The first records and gramophones entered the country in the 1920s in the hands of sailors who crewed on ships traveling between Lisbon, Angola, and Mozambique (this route included a stop in Cape Town, where they had access to a world of goods).[87] Records arrived in a similar way in Lobito and Benguela, and no doubt further afield, thanks to the deepwater port in Lobito and the Benguela railway system that moved goods and people from the coast to the interior and vice versa.[88] Manuel Faria, who was a prominent *discotequeiro* or disk jockey for parties in the 1950s and 1960s (by day he worked as a welder), remembered purchasing GVs from truck drivers who had traveled to Brazzaville and Leopoldville and other vinyl records from sailors passing through or returning to Luanda. In the late 1960s and early 1970s he bought records from the Fadiang company in Bié, which imported vinyl from Europe and from the Congos before starting its own label. Faria said that he had a contract with them and they would send along the music they knew he wanted: Latin American music (plenas, rumbas, merengues, Brazilian sambas and bossa novas) and Congolese music. In the 1950s, Faria played at contribution parties where he would show up with his records, someone else would bring a gramophone, and still others would supply a radio with speakers and a car battery to power the system. Both difficult to come by and expensive, gramophones and records signified an elevated social status in Luanda society.[89] But by the late 1960s, turntables were available at various shops throughout the baixa, the area near the São Paulo neighborhood, and along the main road that connected the baixa to the mussuques.[90] By the early 1970s, Faria owned three complete stereo systems, and given the new availability of records this meant that he could play music at three parties simultaneously.[91]

I was unable to locate any documents regarding the five companies that produced records from the late 1960s on.[92] The owners of the record companies abandoned their businesses at independence and the state then nationalized them in 1978–79, according to António Fonseca, who at the time I interviewed him was director of ENDIPU, the parastatal in charge of the national production of recordings.[93] Documents were lost or destroyed in the process of nationalization. The three main companies were Rádio Reparadora do Bié, known as Fadiang; Valentim de Carvalho, a Portuguese company linked to Britain's EMI; and Fonográfica, which with Estúdios Norte and Companhia de Discos de Angola (CDA) was part of Sebastião Coelho's business. These companies worked in conjunction with publishing/editing houses—until 1973, Estúdios Norte functioned as such—and sold the records they produced in a variety of stores. Some stores, like the Discoteca de Angola, were linked directly with Fadiang or another company and sold only their records, while other shops had a section that sold records made by these three companies but produced by a larger number of publishers.[94] Coelho estimated that by the mid-1970s, Angolan-owned companies produced three of every five records sold in the country.[95]

Despite the concentration of production in Luanda (with the exception of Fadiang in Bié), records were sold throughout the Angolan territory, and it is likely that businesses that sold records continued to draw from vendors across colonial borders. Xabanu remembered expanding his record collection as he traveled throughout the country to fulfill his obligatory military service. In particular, he recalled well-stocked stores in the north of the country.[96] Maria Luisa Fançony, who worked at the Lobito Radio Club, remembered that records were sold at a number of stores in Lobito. And a 1974 article in the local magazine *Notícia* noted that even in little Pereira d'Eça (today Ondjiva) in the far southern province of Cunene, where not even daily papers and magazines were available, a bookstore and a record store sold music to the local community.[97] According to the same article, records were not cheap, especially relative to prices in neighboring Zaire and South Africa, but they sold nonetheless.[98] Even in this small town, where the print capital of daily papers had not yet taken hold, sonorous capital had.

It is difficult to understand the growth of the recording industry without placing it in the context of prevailing economic conditions. As noted in chapter 3, after the revolts in 1961 the colonial government enacted economic and social policies intended to improve the lives of average Angolans, which succeeded to a degree. While extractive industries like oil production, mining, and cash crop agriculture were dominated by foreign (non-Portuguese) capital, Portugal did in fact have large amounts of capital involved in all sectors of the economy.[99] In the case of the recording industry, Portuguese capital was paramount.

According to Coelho, Rádio Reparadora do Bié, or Fadiang, was the oldest of the companies and it continued to produce records even after independence. A Portuguese family associated with a label produced in Porto, Portugal, owned this business. Fadiang had the capacity to produce 78s and singles, and though initially they only produced international music they eventually turned out numerous works by Angolan artists on the Rebita label. Valentim de Carvalho opened up shop in Luanda in 1968. They were responsible for printing the first record entirely produced in Angola, the song "Brinca na Areia" by the Dikanzas do Prenda.[100] They had a shop that sold records, a recording studio, and a factory that produced the vinyl discs on the labels Decca (for rock music) and Ngola (for local tunes). Sebastião Coelho opened Fonográfica and the Companhia de Discos de Angola in 1973 in part out of dissatisfaction with his attempts to record music at Valentim de Carvalho. Estúdios Norte, linked as it was with Coelho's radio programs *Tondoya Mukina o Kisomba* and *Café da Noite*, had a rich archive of music by various Angolan musicians and, according to Coelho, good relations with local artists. Although the factory did not open until 1974 or 1975, it produced a number of singles on the Merengue label through 1978. Fonográfica/CDA had its own studio band, the Merengues, led and formed by Carlitos Vieira Dias. The band started by accompanying the vocalists recording at the studio but became so popular that its members managed to develop professional lives as musicians apart from the studio as well.[101]

If radio contributed to the massification of Angolan music, the recording industry propelled its commodification. The industry produced the most music in the early 1970s. Santocas recalled that "every week in Luanda, at least two new singles, two new records, came out." By this time many Angolans owned turntables and purchased records. "They had turntables that met everyone's capacities . . . and you could buy based on your financial ability."[102] According to the radio journalist Gilberto Júnior, between 1969 and 1978 these companies produced 750–800 records, predominantly singles, with 1973 being the most productive year.[103] Generally companies produced two thousand to three thousand copies of each record but in 1973–74 Prado Paim and Teta Lando both launched albums that went gold. This gives some indication that the market was growing.[104]

Dionísio Rocha recalled that, along with radio, the local production of records gave a boost to local sounds:

> Pop music or what was known as modern music, like the band the Jovens [youth] or the band the Rocks, although they had also recorded, they began to lose acceptance if we compare them with popular Angolan music. Because while you could hear pop music from all over the world, Angolan music was only produced in Angola.[105]

As a result, even the rock bands tried to Angolanize their music with local themes. The names of the labels themselves—Rebita, Merengue, Ngola, Batuque, Dikanza, and Semba[106]—locate the music in Angola and within cosmopolitan circuits that include Latin America (via Zaire, with merengue) and other African countries (*batuque* means drum and was seen as characteristic of African music in general). Consumers purchased local records but bought into an idea of Angola situated internationally. If all that was available for purchase before had been international rock, Brazilian music, French music, Cuban music, and Congolese music, having Angolan music for sale meant that Angola was on a par with these other countries. That there was now something that one could refer to as "Angolan music," produced locally and on labels with Angolan names and symbols, reinforced the idea not just of *angolanidade* but of the Angolan nation.

The music produced in urban clubs symbolized the very sovereignty that Angolans experienced in the music scene. But the music's meaning and impact were not contained by the site of its enunciation. Radio and recording technologies made music mobile. They reterritorialized the musseque sound and gave it national range just as bands from other cities came to record and play in Luanda and diversified its sound. Sonorous capitalism was manifest in the fact that one could buy and listen to Angolan music throughout the country. A local recording industry producing Angolan music reconfirmed and spread the sense of self-sufficiency and cultural sovereignty created in the musseque clubs. But radio also provided a network for the circulation of music, ideas, and news and creative ways of linking those three that produced a sense of nation. The specificity of radio as a cultural technology helped actualize the nation, linking various "meanwhiles" within Angola to one another and to those of the international press and the liberation struggles outside the country. With bits of news, words of encouragement from nationalist leaders, and refrains of song in their heads, Angolans went about their daily business with a sense that they were living and creating their own Angola.

6 ～ The Hiatus

Music, Dissent, and Nation Building after Independence, 1975–90s

> The involvement of politics in music and of music in politics ended up being translated into political conflicts, which later came to reflect themselves in the area of music.
>
> —Mário Rui Silva, on music after independence

GIVEN THE VIBRANCY of the music scene and its relationship to the battle *for* the nation, it is perhaps no surprise that music came to play an important role in the battle *over* the new nation. A military coup in Portugal in April 1974, announced when the radio station played Zeca Afonso's "Grândola, Vila Morena," set the stage for Angolan independence and, simultaneously, for civil war.[1] By late 1975 the MPLA controlled the state, UNITA took on the role of rebel opposition, and the FNLA was effectively neutralized both politically and militarily. Despite the political and military organization and unity required to take over the state and control the capital, relations within the MPLA and between the MPLA and urban populations, particularly in Luanda, were fraught with tension.

Following the military coup in Portugal, most of the musicians popular in the heyday of Angolan music supported or joined the MPLA, whose cosmopolitan nationalist message resonated with their own imaginations of themselves and their nation.[2] Three or four bands from the central highlands joined UNITA and played music, initially music from the late colonial period, and later propagandistic music through the 1980s.[3]

By all accounts, music suddenly became a partisan and highly politicized affair. Part of what made the earlier period a golden age was the sense that people were united in their desire for independence. As Armando Correia de Azevedo put it: "Everyone was united, the sentiment was the same: to one day see your country free. The people had one voice. And later the contradictions established themselves here with the politicians. The politicians were the ones that came with contradictions."[4] He asserts that those who returned from exile and became the political elite disrupted and disarticulated a unity that Angolans who had stayed behind had established for themselves. Adolfo Maria echoed this sentiment when discussing a later moment, the Bicesse Accord, that led to elections in 1992: "[It] consecrated the division of power between two parts and left no space for the Angolan nation to declare itself."[5] Independence and civil war ushered in a politics that was a rarefied field of activity, increasingly distant from the desires and expectations of most Angolans.

Not only differences between the three parties but differences within the MPLA took on new meaning after independence. An alleged attempted coup in 1977 led to a purge in the party and a narrowing of political debate: "In the aftermath of the coup, MPLA became a more exclusive, secretive and less accountable organization."[6] Meanwhile, the civil war had begun in earnest, further raising the stakes over who got to define the nation and nationalism and how it would be done. Under these conditions, the independent state used music as a nation-building tool and actively promoted music production from 1978 until the early 1990s. Musicians continued to produce music but under very different conditions than before. In the early 1990s the state introduced economic and political reforms: the economy was unfettered and opened to the market and in 1992 the first elections were held. At the same time, the then minister of culture informed musicians it was time to fend for themselves.[7]

This chapter analyzes the relationship of music to independent Angola and, in particular, to the internal politics of the MPLA. Musicians claim that this period initiated a "hiatus" in music, as the historical narrative of Angolan music parted ways with the official historical narrative of Angolan nationalism. At the same time, some musicians remember this period with nostalgia: it was a time when the state supported and respected musicians, when everybody got something to eat even if it meant standing in line—a time contrasted with today's feral capitalism unleashed in the early 1990s.[8] Thus this chapter underscores the contingent relationship between politics and music. It is here where musicians pull the narrative of nation away from that of nationalism. They point to the establishment of a new political elite and identify themselves as typical or average Angolans, the *povo* or people.[9] Despite having been part of an emerging petty bourgeois class, their sense of having done for themselves, of having created a degree of cultural and economic sovereignty in the late colonial period in and around the production of music, translated politically, in many cases, into what Assis Malaquias has termed "people-centered" politics.[10] This marked their difference from, and often defined their conflicts with, party elites.

MUSIC AND THE TRANSITION:
APRIL 25, 1974, TO NOVEMBER 11, 1975

On April 25, 1974, in Portugal a peaceful military coup known as the Revolução dos Cravos (Revolution of the Carnations) overthrew Salazar's fascist state. This coup resulted in part from the pressures that the wars in Angola, Mozambique, and Guinea-Bissau placed on the Portuguese society and polity, coming on top of more than thirty years of life under fascist rule. In Angola this coup caused a rapid and unexpected shift in the struggle, ushering in a period of transition to elections and then independence.[11] This shift required that the three liberation movements reinvent themselves as political parties.

These were heady and confusing times. In Luanda, the musseques were the site of fighting between FNLA and MPLA partisans, and to a lesser extent UNITA, with propaganda campaigns by all three parties. The staccato of gunshots interrupted the diurnal sounds of the urban dawn. Whites attacked Africans, and some whites packed up and set off for Portugal or South Africa.[12] As food shortages squeezed daily routines, people turned their attention to securing food and engaging in political and self-defense activities through locally based committees, party cells, and neighborhood organized militias. The clubs that had animated the musseques on nights and weekends closed, opening only sporadically.

In the nineteen months between April 25, 1974, and independence day on November 11, 1975, the MPLA did not hesitate to make good use of the musicians who joined the party. Music's capacity for gathering an audience was useful for political leaders who wanted to address the urban masses. Correia de Azevedo remembered the last *Kutonoca*:

> I was hosting the show in Sambizanga in the Mario Santiago soccer field. By the middle of the show the place was totally full. I gave the microphone—as a sign that the *Kutonocas* were over, at least for me— I gave the microphone to a member of the Central Committee of the MPLA, who then turned the *Kutonoca* into a political rally. And that was the end of *Kutonoca*. It was Zé Van Dunem, he has already passed away, who was the member of the Central Committee of the MPLA. So I gave him the microphone and then since there was an enormous mass of people that filled the whole area, that *Kutonoca* was transformed into a rally of a political nature. It was, in essence, the first MPLA rally with the masses inside the city of Luanda, because at this time the MPLA had not yet officially entered Luanda.[13]

By stepping into the *Kutonoca* emcee's position, the MPLA assumed the helm of the "provisional nation." The MPLA intended to host the national show. But they would first have to translate that sense of commonality, that unity of sentiment, and that cultural sovereignty into an explicitly political project, and audiences were perhaps not as pliable as the MPLA had hoped.

Given the repression of information during the fourteen years of the liberation struggle, the MPLA had much work to do throughout Angola to make their political project known. But the limits on communication imposed by the war also affected the guerrillas' and exiled leaders' access to information about what life was like inside the colonial territory. The guerrillas and exiled leadership were, to some extent, more cut off from what was going on inside the country than those who stayed behind were from what was going on with the liberation movements.[14]

In the violence and confusion that erupted in Luanda and other urban centers with the April 25 coup, a number of local groups—neighborhood commissions, action committees, student associations, unions, worker commissions, self-defense militias, and unarmed political parties—emerged more or less spontaneously in the musseques.[15] Some of these groups had strong links to the MPLA while others had none at all. Referring specifically to the Commissões Populares de Bairro (Popular Neighborhood Commissions), Tali says: "At their origin was the necessity of organizing the populations of the African neighborhoods for their self-defense and self-management in an environment of extreme violence, but even more the necessity of taking hold of the political space left empty by the fall of the colonial regime."[16] Many musicians became involved in these groups, which mushroomed prior to the MPLA's official arrival in Luanda in November 1974. Given the cultural sovereignty that musicians and cultural producers experienced in the musseque cultural scene of the late colonial period, and given the generalized sense of revolt in the musseques captured in the PIDE documents, it should be no surprise that they quickly engaged in these forms of self-organization. These groups, Tali argues, "decided the destiny of the MPLA in urban centers" throughout the country and in Luanda.[17]

Musicians like Chico Coio got involved in the spontaneously formed self-defense militias in the musseques. Such militias defended against attacks from Portuguese merchants, Cape Verdean volunteer forces working for the Portuguese police, and FNLA militants. Other musicians participated in groups that were explicitly aligned with the MPLA. The composer Xabanu, for example, was part of an MPLA cell led by two other musicians and based in the musseque Rangel.[18] Cell members helped prepare for the arrival of the MPLA delegation from Brazzaville. Xabanu also spent time on the party's behalf recording incidents of violence by white shop owners against Africans.

Carlos Lamartine began work in an MPLA cell based in the musseque Marçal in June 1974. Unlike most musicians, he had worked since 1969 in various clandestine activities including collecting medical supplies for the first Politico-Military Region of the MPLA guerrilla struggle (in the Dembos and Nambuangongo in the region north of Luanda), as well as printing and distributing pamphlets and writing songs with a political character. Carlitos Vieira Dias also worked in this cell. Together Lamartine and Vieira Dias worked to integrate local musicians into the party and particularly into its youth wing, the JMPLA (Juventude do Movimento Popular de Libertação de Angola), known as *jota*. By October 1974, according to Lamartine, he had left his position in the Department of Geology and Mines to work full time in the party organizing and heading up the music section of the JMPLA. In 1975, with the musicians Artur Nunes and Urbano de Castro, Lamartine accompanied the then party president and soon to be first Angolan president, Agostinho Neto, on his first trip throughout Angola.[19]

As artists integrated themselves into the formal MPLA structures they lent their popularity in the musseques, indeed their notoriety throughout the country, to the party's nationalist message. The MPLA was competing with the FNLA and UNITA for popular support throughout the territory, and this lineup traveling with Neto (Lamartine, Nunes, and de Castro) deftly aligned three extraordinarily popular and well-known musicians with the MPLA, whose profile and political program were less understood.[20] Fola Soremekun, an analyst and observer of the decolonization process, noted that the party took advantage of and further developed an information media structure to spread its message. Print and radio "were buttressed at the level of common people by various popular singers like David Zé, Urbano de Castro, Artur Nunes and others like them who composed and sang songs that told the people what all the problems of the country were all about, and where the nation was heading to."[21] Communications media, of which music was one component, proved central to the MPLA's ability to establish its presence throughout the Angolan territory. Thanks to these media and to its military, the party controlled Luanda and twelve of the country's sixteen provinces by November 1975.[22]

On November 11, 1975, the MPLA unilaterally declared independence. The attempted transition had largely failed: elections were foregone for military engagement between the three parties, each emboldened by Cold War resources and rhetoric.[23] With the help of Cuban troops, the FAPLA (Forças Armadas Populares de Libertação de Angola or Popular Armed Forces for the

Liberation of Angola) routed South African forces just south of the city of Luanda and defeated FNLA troops to the near north at Kifangondo just hours before the declaration. The new flag was hoisted to the intonations of the new national anthem, "Angola Avante Revolução" (Angola Forward the Revolution). Written by Lamartine, Carlitos Vieira Dias, Rui Mingas, and the poet and jurist Manuel Rui Monteiro, it had a sonic sensibility and lyrical content more rooted in the Communist International than in local musical practices.

FROM CULTURAL SOVEREIGNTY TO *PODER POPULAR*

Large-scale popular mobilization occurred in the musseques of Luanda and the neighborhoods of other cities.[24] Musicians, and their audiences, actively took part in the self-organizing commissions and cells that pioneered this mobilization. During the transition period of 1974–75, the MPLA both benefited from and struggled with these groups that had sprung up to respond to the violence and mayhem occasioned by the April 25 coup in Portugal. Alliances with these groups allowed the MPLA to control Luanda—the capital and key to control of the state—both militarily and politically against FNLA and UNITA forces in a short time.[25] While these Angolan groups were pivotal to the MPLA's success in Luanda at the neighborhood level, the party relied on non-Angolan forces to secure its position in Luanda from the outside. To the north Cuban and FAPLA forces held back Congolese mercenaries, the Congolese army, and FNLA troops, while to the south they stalled South African mercenaries who pressed well ahead of UNITA. But military integration of Cuban troops proved easier than politically integrating neighborhood committees and militias into the party's organizational structure.[26] Much to the MPLA leadership's chagrin, a number of these groups resisted such a move and demonstrated their desire to "conserve their autonomy."[27] Labor unions likewise refused absorption into the party and reserved the right to organize workers on their own terms.[28] While some of these groups eventually cast their lot with the party leadership, others continued to manifest divisions and differences with that leadership in terms of both ideology and political action.[29]

Poder popular (people's power) emerged as a critical point of contention. For the spontaneously formed neighborhood commissions and political committees—Comités Amilcar Cabral, Comités Henda, and Grupo de Reflexão de Sita Valles (Sita Valles reflection group)—*poder popular* provided a check on the party and its control of the state.[30] Some historians regard this as a manifestation of a far leftist ideology in the *comités*. The committees' members, they argue, hoped for a Bolshevik revolution rooted in the alliance of peasants and workers and had become disillusioned with what they saw as the elitism of the MPLA leadership.[31] The party consolidated this elitism after the alleged coup in 1977. As Assis Malaquias argues:

> The hunt for the coup organizers provided an ideal opportunity for the governing post-colonial elite to rid itself of those MPLA members who—whether sympathetic to the coup plotters or not—defended a people-centered approach to post-colonial politics.[32]

A "people-centered approach" may have been precisely the kind of *poder popular* that most musicians and club-attending musseque residents expected.

It remains exceedingly difficult to know what was going on in the minds of ordinary musseque inhabitants and of those who formed or joined the popular neighborhood commissions for self-defense and self-management.[33] Despite the leftist ring of the phrase *poder popular* and despite the petty bourgeois background of many musicians and their audiences, the appeal of self-rule on a local level, of people-centered politics, may have had little to do with left ideologies or rational class interests. Instead, it may have reflected the experience of cultural sovereignty and the self-organization associated with the musseque club scene. In those clubs, struggles over budgets and house rules gave members a sense of self-rule. Audiences contributed to this when they spent their hard-earned money on entertainment, dress, and victuals performed and prepared by and for Angolans in the new social spaces of musical production. It seems plausible that the experience of autonomy in the musseque clubs also informed some activists' notion of *poder popular*.

MAY 27, 1977

If April 25, 1974, is still remembered as a day inaugurating hope, then May 27, 1977, marks one of Angola's darkest hours.[34] The oft-heard moniker "the 27th of May" condenses complex processes into the events of a single day. It refers to what the state calls the *tentado de golpe* (attempted coup) by an alleged splinter group within the MPLA just a year and a half after independence had been declared. While May 27 is little known internationally, within Angola its interpretation is hotly disputed. Its origins can be located as early as the 1960s, in the first years of the liberation movements, or even earlier, in the social cleavages spawned by colonial rule. The detentions and intimidation that followed from that day continued for three years or longer, until the last detainees were released, and their effects are still palpable both personally and politically.[35]

Conceptualizing May 27 as an event discursively contains a more unwieldy dynamic to a discrete, if nasty, episode. But in the minds of many, particularly of the survivors and the descendants and relatives of those killed, it is shorthand for unimaginable terror and thirty years of governmental denial and society's silence.[36] Many of those involved in or touched by the incidents still prefer not to speak about them.[37] Most families who lost loved ones never received death certificates for those killed and were never able to bury them. For such people this is not a small political insult but a moral and cultural affront. Luís dos Passos, a survivor of the events and the founder of an opposition political party, frames the larger issues: "Questions like national reconciliation and the pacification of spirits will have to be resolved."[37] The absence of death certificates also compromises citizenship by raising numerous bureaucratic hurdles in the lives of descendants, survivors, and relatives, who often cannot remarry or obtain various official documents without a certificate of death.

Aside from the human costs, social and political effects were, and are, tangible and widespread. Self-censorship, as one journalist notes, has been one of the most deleterious effects.[39] Not only do survivors and relatives of those killed remain reluctant to speak out or act politically, but an ongoing and generalized fear of openly criticizing the government and the party permeates Angolan society. When the party leadership sanctioned the killing and torture of a good number of its own militants it created a disincentive to political engagement among youth that continues today.[40]

In the last ten to fifteen years, some survivors and victims' family members have become more vocal.[41] These voices have not altered the basic chronology of events, although they do offer different interpretations of them. Before the party leadership arrived in Luanda in February 1975, Nito Alves (one of the people most associated with the factionalism) and other guerrillas and militants, who had come from the nearby First Politico-Military Region, were organizing in Luanda. They found support among the local cells, self-defense initiatives, and neighborhood committees taking shape at the time and they inspired the formation of others. In particular, Alves and other guerrillas newly returned from the bush resonated with the ideas of student-organized groups. Students, no longer stymied by the PIDE, channeled their political militancy into ideological discussions in groups formed around political prisoners released in the early 1970s and figures associated with the Portuguese Communist Party. José "Zé" Van Dunem was one such political prisoner. Like Alves, he had been elected to the MPLA Central Committee in 1974 (this is the same Zé Van Dunem who turned the last *Kutonoca* into a political meeting, as Correia de Azevedo mentions). The eventual success of the MPLA in taking Luanda and unilaterally declaring independence depended upon all of these groups.

During the transition period from April 1974 until November 11, 1975, the party leadership accommodated these various groups and the variety of opinions and political debate they represented. But once the MPLA declared independence and assumed state power in the context of a civil war, ideological differences were redefined as dissent and met with hostility. Class and racial prejudices generated by the colonial system accompanied and compounded ideological differences. By 1976, these differences had solidified around the question of *poder popular*. Some groups of party militants who saw *poder popular* as a check on elitism and as the basis of the revolution had coalesced around Alves. And Alves and this line of thinking found sympathies in some of the party-run and local media throughout the country.[42] The party leadership, aware of the debt they owed to urban activists for mobilizing the musseque masses, could not simply dismiss *poder popular* but hoped, instead, to harness it to their own state-driven project.[43] As a result, tensions flourished within the party and its ranks.

In October 1976 the party's Central Committee met. Based on material collected by DISA, the political police (Direcção de Informação e Segurança de Angola or Angolan Directorate for Information and Security), the committee formally accused Nito Alves and Zé Van Dunem of factionalism.[44] The committee removed Alves from his post as minister of internal administration and appointed a commission of inquiry into the factionalism with José Eduardo dos Santos as its chair. Between this meeting in October 1976 and the next Central Committee meeting on May 20, 1977, DISA stepped up its raids on suspected adherents of the splinter group in the musseques. This witch hunt aggravated an already tense situation, within Luanda and throughout the country, created by the food shortage and economic crisis.[45]

At the May 20 meeting the commission of inquiry stated its conclusions: Nito Alves and Zé Van Dunem were the leaders of a faction that had infiltrated various party organs. They were summarily expelled from the Central Committee. On the afternoon of the next day President Neto held a political meeting in the capital's stadium to publicly announce the inquiry's results and the Central Committee's decisions. Rumors of a coup started to circulate in the capital's neighborhoods. The MPLA's Political Bureau, its most powerful governing body, published its analysis of the factionalism on May 26 and on the morning of the 27th the city awoke to the sound of gunshots.[46] Nito Alves and his supporters (referred to as Nitistas and hailing mainly from the musseques and the military) occupied the radio station and the main prison in the São Paulo neighborhood.

The Nitistas called for popular mobilization in the streets to demand that the president root out the corruption and elitism they claimed was gripping the party's upper echelons. Hours later, the MPLA, with the support of Cuban forces, retook the radio station and imprisoned those involved. Nito Alves, Zé

Van Dunem, and others went into hiding. State troops and DISA forces encircled the neighborhoods where they believed the coup plotters had the most support, particularly Sambizanga, Rangel, and Prenda—some of the most important musseques in Angola's music history, which had active neighborhood commissions. They raided homes in search of those associated with Alves and Van Dunem and with the neighborhood committees. Alves and Van Dunem were eventually captured and killed, as were thousands of others in various cities throughout the country. None of those killed or detained had cases filed against them or court hearings.[47] Killings and persecution continued until at least 1979, but by the beginning of 1978, according to Adolfo Maria, "the country was finally (or apparently) at peace: it was the peace of cemeteries and collective fear!"[48]

ALTERNATIVE READINGS OF MAY 27

Fighting a civil war, the MPLA was unprepared to deal with internal strife. As Tali and other scholars argue, May 27 was the last, and most critical, in a series of "dissidences" that had occurred between the party's founding in 1960 and its consolidation as a "workers' party" in late 1977.[49] Following this line of thinking, it was not solely the civil war but a culture internal to the MPLA that caused the party, over time, to define disagreement as dissent.

It is difficult to delineate with certainty what relationship, if any, existed between music, musicians, the golden age music scene, and the small committees and groups that organized spontaneously around the MPLA in the period between the April 25 revolution in Portugal and the return of the party leadership to the country in early 1975. At the very least and by their own account, many musicians and others who had created the vibrant cultural scene of the late 1960s and early 1970s got involved in these groups.

Urbano de Castro, David Zé, and Artur Nunes were killed in the purge, although there are no published accounts of their deaths. This book opened with Teta Lando suggesting that their power and popularity with "the people" in the musseques was part of the reason they became targets of political violence. In this articulation, their association with the coup plotters mattered less than the fact that their musical notoriety accorded them visibility and popular support. Other musicians and cultural producers that I interviewed took a different view, suggesting that these three musicians were killed not because they were musicians or because of their music but simply because they had joined the coup plotters. In other words, it was their politics and not their music that landed them in the line of fire. But such a supposition creates a false dichotomy between music and politics. The question remains: did their experience as musicians, their experience of cultural sovereignty, in the late colonial period shape their politics?

The desire for autonomy from a centralizing party leadership that the various committees, neighborhood associations, militias, and unions manifested resonated with the sense of cultural sovereignty and of being able to do for oneself that many Angolans associated with the clubs and club scene. Many who suffered political repression following the attempted coup possessed the same social profile as those who forged the culturally autonomous world of the music scene in Luanda's musseques. One survivor of the witch hunt that followed the stymied coup remembered that the state security services would "enter into houses to get young intellectuals, artists, athletes and small businessmen," the same groups that tended to be club goers.[50] In fact, Nito Alves was closely associated with the Progresso soccer club in Sambizanga,[51] where he was idolized and remembered for hanging out, talking politics, and playing checkers, chess, and cards with youths on Saturday afternoons.[52] Another survivor, interviewed recently by Lara Pawson, remembered that the soccer club met nightly at 6:00 p.m. in Salão Faria, where the size of the meetings grew and the topic quickly turned to politics.[53]

The starlike status and visibility of musicians like Urbano de Castro both in the musseques and throughout the country helped garner support for the MPLA, but it may also have worried the party leadership. Before the MPLA arrived in Luanda, Agostinho Neto had a mythical aura in the minds of many.[54] But it was not long before problems within the party, and the distance of its leaders from the reality that had developed within the country, became apparent. A sense of disillusionment set in, exacerbated by a growing food crisis that threatened the rhythms of daily life throughout the country.[55] The situation was desperate enough that, as musician Filipe Zau remembered, he fished in the bay with a flashlight in order to be able to eat.[56]

Under such circumstances, the party needed charismatic spokespeople who could reassure the people and redirect their concerns. Nito Alves fit the bill: "In an organization—the MPLA—which did not have a reputation for possessing great orators among its leaders, Nito Alves was an exception: he knew how to find the right tone—vigorous and daring—to speak to the populace."[57] Musicians allegedly involved with Nito Alves, notably Urbano de Castro, David Zé, and Artur Nunes, likewise stood out in the popular imagination because of their stage presence and recognizable voices. Audiences respected them for their ability to represent the troubles and joys of daily life, troubles and joys that these musicians, unlike the recently returned political leaders, knew firsthand. Musicians are communicators and, as Askew asserts in her ethnography of music in Tanzania, "communicative potency draws its effectiveness largely from the intimacies of social knowledge that accompany life in local communities."[58] The most popular musicians were skilled alchemists who transmuted individual suffering under colonial rule into a collective will and sensibility. They symbolized the cultural sovereignty of the music scene: they were trendsetters in dress and individuals who proclaimed and strutted their *angolanidade* in a mix of local street smarts, international savvy, and African roots. When they traded in their stage duds for fatigues and lent their voices to the MPLA's cause, their fans paid attention. But perhaps it was not just their fans but the party leadership as well who saw their notoriety and sensed in it a threat to their own public image and their ability to control the urban populace.

IN THE WAKE OF MAY 27

Animated political debate both between the three major liberation movements and within the MPLA characterized the period between the Revolução dos Cravos and May 27, 1977, in Angola.[59] But the failed transition that resulted in civil war meant that political debate became increasingly polarized and restricted in independent Angola. The events of May 27 only worsened this situation. The violence and repression visited upon the MPLA's own members and, by all accounts, a number of people not involved in the party inevitably damaged both the general political atmosphere and that within the party. Tali argues that Angola's youth, in particular, retreated from politics or carefully toed the party line. He describes the movement's cells as "resonance boxes" for the decisions made in the party's upper echelons. The party shifted from a moderate socialist ideology to an explicit and more doctrinal Marxist-Leninist stance when it declared itself a workers' party in late 1977.[60] Politics became the bailiwick of the party elite and the party faithful who turned *poder popular* into a top-down party tactic.

What happened to music and the music scene? Musicians describe the period from 1974, when the movements first returned to Angola, until the early 1990s as a hiatus in the history of Angolan music. As a character in José Eduardo Agualusa's recent novel commented, "The revolution did not benefit music."[61] The music that bespoke the nation, that represented *angolanidade*, stopped at independence. This is not to say that music was banned or that no one played music. To the contrary, music continued to be important to the MPLA, and to UNITA, but it was music with a different tone and with a distinctly different mode of production.

From roughly 1978 to 1989, the independent government undertook a variety of initiatives in the cultural arena and relative to music in particular. In this period, civil war shaped and limited daily life and political expression.

The FNLA forces had been effectively neutralized, and UNITA, backed by the United States and South Africa, rivaled the MPLA-controlled state. After the MPLA proclaimed itself a workers' party in 1977 all state-sponsored cultural practices (writing, music, theater, dance) took on an explicitly revolutionary cast. Music was no exception, and given the upheaval of 1977 and the need to look consistently forward instead of asking too many questions about the past, this meant that the music needed to be new. The party used music to engage the country's youth in a nation-building project and to mobilize the *povo* (people) against UNITA. Outside the country, artists performed in a circuit of leftist cultural festivals (in Cuba and Russia for example) representing a national revolutionary culture on the socialist cosmopolitan scene.[62]

Several musicians made a name for themselves in this period: Mito Gaspar, Santos Júnior, Moises and José Kafala, André Mingas, Filipe Mukenga, Pedrito, Santocas, and Filipe Zau, among others. The greatest bands of the golden age, like Os Kiezos and Jovens do Prenda, continued to play but they were no longer center stage. Whereas bands in the late 1960s and early 1970s were either self-run or organized by independent managers, after independence particular state institutions took on this function, putting bands at the disposal of a variety of state offices. Such was the case, for example, with the bands Primeiro de Maio, associated with UNTA (União Nacional dos Trabalhadores de Angola or National Union of Angolan Workers); Semba Tropical, associated with SECULT, the Secretary of State for Culture; and the Merengues, sponsored by the JMPLA.

RECREATION CENTERS AND MUSIC FESTIVALS: BUILDING THE MUSICAL NATION

Bands performed music at recreation centers, traveling music festivals, and institutional celebrations. The music produced was meant to "consolidate independence," as the singer Santocas noted, "to do what arms cannot" by serving as a postindependence nation-building tool.[63] Lamartine went further to describe the music as "revolutionary," its job being "to mobilize the popular masses, to contribute to the education of young people in confronting the problems of war and of illiteracy, and to help motivate the youth toward production goals."[64] Furthermore, the MPLA's conversion to a workers' party in late 1977 required a redefinition of musical practice as the provenance of the working classes and not the product of petty bourgeois venues and class interests.

According to Santocas, to play music you had to have an argument for doing so and it had to be politically relevant.[65] In other words, songs that

Paulo Pinheiro and the band Os Kiezos, *Ho MPLA Nkango Angola* album cover, produced in Angola by Valentim de Carvalho on the Ngola label, undated but after 1974. *Courtesy RNA*

praised heroes from the struggle or promoted party policy were the order of the day. One such album was Paulo Pinheiro's *Ho MPLA Nkango Angola*. According to Jean-Michel Tali, this title corresponded to the MPLA slogan "The MPLA is the *povo*! And the *povo* is the MPLA" and asserted the MPLA's exclusive right to represent the Angolan people.[66] Santocas's "Valódia" (track 12) is another example of such music.[67]

Bem longe	Far away
Ouví aquele nome	I heard that name
Inesquecível dos filhos de Angola	Unforgettable to Angola's children

Valódia	Valódia
Valódia	Valódia
Valódia tombou em defesa do povo Angolano	Valódia fell in defense of the Angolan people
Valódia	Valódia
Valódia	Valódia
Valódia tombou na mão dos imperialistas	Valódia fell at the hands of the imperialists
Que pretendem impor-nos o neo-colonialismo	That want to impose neocolonialism on us
Povo angolano, todos bem vigilantes	Angolan people, be very vigilant
Que no neocolonialismo a repressão é pior	Because under neocolonialism the repression is worse
A miséria é um martírio	Misery is a martyr
A pobreza também	Poverty as well
E o neocolonialismo não tem cor	And neocolonialism has no color
Valódia, o filho bem amado do povo Angolano	Valódia, well-loved by the Angolan people
Valódia deu a sua vida por uma causa justa	Valódia gave his life for a just cause
Valódia morreu	Valódia died
mas o seu nome ficou cá com o povo	But his name stayed here with the people
Abaixo capitalismo	Down with capitalism
Abaixo imperialismo	Down with imperialism
Abaixo neocolonialismo	Down with neocolonialism
Avante socialismo	Forward with socialism
A reacção não passará	The reaction will end
A opressão não passará	The oppression will end
A luta continua	The struggle continues
Até a vitória final	Until the final victory
A luta continua	The struggle continues
Até a vitória final	Until the final victory

A reacção não passará	The reaction will end
A opressão não passará	The oppression will end
A reaccão não passará	The reaction will end
A opressão não passará[68]	The oppression will end

Once described as the "flag bearer for the MPLA's ideology," Santocas, like many other musicians, embraced and promoted the party's philosophy.[69] The MPLA's Department of Information and Propaganda (DIP) produced "Valódia" in 1975. Santocas sings the praises of an MPLA commander who was killed in the bush in the early 1970s. As the lyrics insist, Valódia was killed by the imperialists but his defiant spirit remains: "His name stayed here with the people" to invigorate their continued struggle against oppressive forces, whether military (i.e., South Africa and the United States supporting UNITA troops) or more strictly capitalist (the variety of countries interested in Angola's resources). This music is slower paced than the music of the golden age. It is not music for dancing but a solemn tune with a slightly rousing tone meant to recognize the loss of a great leader while redirecting that regret into resolve. And fighting what was referred to as the Second Independence Struggle—the struggle against the imperialism that fueled the Angolan civil war—required resolve.

After suspected Nitistas de Castro, Zé, and Nunes were killed in the repression following the failed coup, their music was marginalized. And eventually, most of the music of the late colonial period met the same fate. This is a sore point for many musicians. Rui Mingas remembered that the music up to 1975 "was of good quality but it lost much after independence. It is one thing to have politically interventionist music in an exploited society and quite another to have propagandistic music that has something negative to it . . . it is music with conditions."[70] In Mingas's reading, music had lost its political spontaneity. No longer a response to daily life and an attempt to transform it, music seemed more like a straightjacket. However, spontaneity did continue at the level of production. Santocas remembered tremendous enthusiasm for getting things done without thinking about remuneration or quotidian concerns: "Music in that period wasn't commercialized and there was that feeling that, hey, we are all politically involved and what matters is attaining independence."[71] At least in the very heady days around independence, young people directed their energies to helping the party build the new nation, and both music and venues found a new purpose.

In his capacity as adjunct coordinator for the Directing Commission of the JMPLA, Lamartine oversaw the inauguration of the first recreation center.

Located in Bairro Popular, the center was named after Saydi Mingas, the first minister of finance, who had been killed by Nitistas in the attempted coup. This was a center, like others to follow, built from what had been a club in the late colonial period.[72] The state symbolically reclaimed music, musicians, and entertainment for its nation-building project. What had been sovereign centers of cultural production and a sense of nation became state-supported centers of national cultural values. Most recreation centers were individually owned but they also received substantial support through the Ministry of Culture's policy of cultural promotion. Manuel Faria, who owned Kudissanga KwaMakamba and later Kianda Kianazanga, remembered that the club scene stopped in 1974 with the arrival of the three parties in Luanda and the violence that ensued. According to Faria, activity did not pick up again until the late 1970s and early 1980s when the second president, José Eduardo dos Santos, launched the slogan: "Work with happy faces, not sad faces." The Ministry of Culture's authorization and promotion of recreation centers followed soon after this announcement.[73]

Despite the critiques of the new sound and role of music, some musicians and center owners remember this period with tremendous affection. Unlike at present, in this era the state acknowledged and supported the work of musicians and cultural producers. Ticket sales at the recreation centers provided cash payment for artists while the state ensured a supply of food and beer to these venues. Center owners went directly to state-owned businesses to receive foodstuffs, and beer company trucks delivered crates of bottles and kegs to the centers.[74] The state set ticket prices to keep them accessible, but artists remember earning well in this period.[75] The symbols of organization and respectability established in the late colonial period, "a well-set table with a nice tablecloth," continued. Such details linger in the memories of artists and others who frequented the centers. And there was always the possibility that one would share the audience space with the president, prime minister, or other leader.[76]

Renowned recreation centers from the period included Maxinde, Mãe Preta, Cubata, Kudissanga KwaMakamba, Kizomba, Giro-Giro, Centro Recreativo de União de São Paulo, and Gagajeira. Some of these were built on the basis of former clubs and involved former club members or owners, like Maxinde and Kudissanga KwaMakamba respectively. The Ministry of Culture booked musical acts. Lineups included some popular bands from the golden age, like the Jovens do Prenda and Os Kiezos, as well as new bands like the Merengues (formed just before independence), associated with the JMPLA, and individual artists like Santocas, Dina Santos, and Santos Júnior.

Music festivals and competitions mobilized young artists. The JMPLA, for example, organized three *festivais de canção política* (festivals of political song) in the 1980s in Huambo, Benguela, and Luanda as the civil war with UNITA was going on all around.[77] Unlike in the late colonial period, when music was commercialized and professionally driven, music in independent Angola was meant to be an amateur affair based on a sense of collective endeavor. Festivals drew young men and women from the various towns surrounding these cities to sing and demonstrate their own musical practices as well as receive instruction from established artists like Elias dia Kimuezu, Lourdes Van Dunem, and Dina Santos. Lamartine remembered the festival ambiance:

> The environment was the healthiest possible. We had the participation of all the provinces. Each person would come with his/her intrinsic cultural forms: Umbundus, Kimbundus, Tchokwes, Mumuilas, Luchazes, and there was understanding. . . . relationships and marriages even emerged. There was a festive environment and a conscious one in which some great artists developed.[78]

In particular, Lamartine noted that festivals emphasized the inclusion of female performers and consciously worked to dispel the preconceptions of earlier generations that regarded male artists as irresponsible and female artists as prostitutes. This position issued from government policy that promoted female emancipation more generally. The policy had an impact on musical performance at festivals, and the Ministry of Culture also used music to promote it. The album cover and song "Emancipação da Mulher Angolana" (Emancipation of the Angolan Woman) reflect this. Music was presented as a respectable activity so long as it helped build the new nation and its component parts.

Other state institutions like the UNTA, the Forças Armadas Angolanas (Angolan Armed Forces), and the Ministry of Culture also hosted music festivals for their members and the public and certain targeted constituencies (for example, the Ministry of Culture convened a festival specifically for female singers).[79] UNTA produced an album from its first festival and promoted it with the slogan "We will make art and sports a right for all people." The album offered the following explanation of the union's intentions:

> The festival aims to give to all WORKERS the possibility of an elevated moral appreciation of OUR CULTURAL VALUES and, overall, to awaken in them the feeling of COLLECTIVISM and other deontological behaviors essential to a harmonious life, to HUMAN RELATIONS and between the INDIVIDUAL and SOCIETY.[80]

Emancipation of the Angolan Woman album cover. Nino and the band Os Merengues, produced in Angola by Companhia de Discos de Angola on the Merengue label, 1975. The text on the back cover describes the song as "a meeting with the Hour of Liberty. The time of 'only preparing funge' is over, and women must cooperate side by side with men in the work of reconstruction." *Courtesy RNA*

Abstruse language may or may not have appealed to the workers involved, but this quote does demonstrate how the union put itself at the service of the state in furthering national culture and the state-centered socialist ideal of collective production over individual action. The incentives to participate in such festivals were not commercial. Instead, state institutions appealed to a sense of solidarity and offered aspiring and accomplished musicians the possibility of participating in national and international festivals in place of money.

António "Tó" Manjenje, an artist from Lobito, who was ten years old at the time of independence, traveled to Sweden, England, North Korea, and the Soviet Union by winning and advancing through the state-organized music festivals of the 1980s playing trova. If semba predominated in the 1960s and 1970s, trova characterized the 1980s and, in particular, music festivals. It is the form most closely associated with postindependence socialist politics. Unlike semba, which had incorporated electrical instruments, trova was based on simple arrangements played on acoustic guitar accompanied by local instruments like the *kissanje* and a variety of flutes (at least in the central region from which Manjenje hails). Its most well-known exponents are the Irmãos Kafala (Kafala Brothers), with whom Manjenje got his start, and Mito Gaspar, who emerged in music festivals organized by the armed forces. Manjenje described trova as "political songs, pamphletary songs."[81] As the secretary for the MPLA's Brigada de Manguxi (Manguxi Brigade, Manguxi being Agostinho Neto's nickname), Manjenje helped organize singers of political music. The Manguxi Brigade acclaimed the "defense of the Fatherland, the unity of the Angolan people and international solidarity."[82] Such institutions promoted a very different sense of nation and a different kind of nationalism than the clubs had represented.

What musicians of the golden age defined as the hiatus in Angolan music opened up space for a new kind of music that did not symbolize the nation in terms of autonomy but rather harmonized a patchwork of different ethnic and regional sounds and linked it to a patriotic sentiment that orbited the state and party. This musical mosaic was intended to mobilize people to meet economic production goals, to forge new social relations, and to fight. UNITA and the imperialist forces of apartheid South Africa and the United States were the foil. An LP entitled *Angola: A Luta Continua* (Angola: The Struggle Continues), produced in Mozambique by the MPLA's DIP, defines the stakes in no uncertain terms. The album is undated but quoted President Agostinho Neto in the early days of independence:

> Angolans will resist. We the MPLA, we the people, are not afraid. Angolans will resist all and any imperialist invasions. The enemy can come from Europe with its airplanes. It can come from South Africa. It can drop bombs over our country. But this enemy should not think that we, Angolans, will submit. Angolans will resist.[83]

This album includes such songs as "Savimbi's Treason," "The Worker," and others that refer to historical events and figures. Thus the album locates the nation on a trajectory from past to future with the worker and party at the center in the present but still engaged in a struggle against imperialism's forces within and without the country.

Music had gone from being a political realm where the nation was manifest in a shared musical sensibility, in African and cosmopolitan sound, dance, and dress, to one in which the nation was mandated in a revolutionary cast around a one-party state. The ethnomusicologist Jorge Macedo, while recognizing the importance and quality of some of the music and musicians from this period, had this to say: "If the nationalist and partisan intervention, or nationalist partisan, made the music, the urban music, markedly more Angolan, it also made music lose much of its quality of *angolanidade*."[84] In other words, music may have become more territorially representative and more explicitly nationalist (even if partisan), but it no longer expressed Angolanness to the same degree.

RADIO AND THE RESURGENCE

The state ran the music industry in postindependence Angola. State institutions promoted music consonant with policies issued by the Ministry of Culture. The state sponsored production either at Rádio Nacional de Angola (Angolan National Radio, RNA) or through the national record company, ENDIPU. DIP, the party's propaganda arm, also produced some music. Companhia de Discos de Angola continued to record music and produce records, often on government contract. And the RNA established a Department for the Collection of Music that sent sound technicians and musicians on junkets around the country to record folkloric music.[85]

All this state involvement and intervention in music did not mean an absence of creativity or imply that the state directly determined musical sound and content. Rather, a number of musicians from the earlier generation, like Lamartine and Santocas, willingly embraced the challenge of nation building through music. Others engaged for reasons of survival, and still others opted out when they could not abide the politicization and partisanship.

Musicians of a younger generation, the one that came of age during the 1980s, got their start at state-organized music festivals in the period. The creativity of these talented young artists produced the musical genre that came to dominate the late 1980s and 1990s, *kisomba*. It drew on international sounds like Caribbean zouk and responded to the ever-prevalent desire for music that was danceable, something that trova was not. The well-known Antillean band Kassav played in Angola in the 1980s, and musicians claim that its sound had a lasting impact on the youth of that decade, who knew little of the music of the golden age.

It was not that no one ever played semba. Youth born in the 1970s who came of age in the 1980s certainly heard their parents talk about or remember hearing the Kiezos and the Jovens do Prenda, if not live then on television. In this sense, Fernando Martins's evocation of Os Kiezos as a cornerstone of patriotic knowledge was not off the mark. But by and large, festivals and recreation centers and radio broadcasts all highlighted trova. Semba, which had so indelibly marked the earlier period, stagnated or became impoverished.[86] Lamartine, despite his position as a promoter of new styles and organizer of new music venues, notes that semba was actively sidelined: "The political process we lived through in the country during the time of the centralized economy negated, to a certain degree, listening to older music in order to produce music of the moment." One result was that the practice of semba was not passed on to the younger generation as it might have been under different conditions.[87] The national radio station, RNA, often opted to play foreign music rather than older music. The Ministry of Culture brought foreign artists, including Kassav and Silvio Rodríguez, a Cuban singer/songwriter, to perform in Angola. Indeed, some musicians fault the radio station for broadcasting too much foreign music in these years. Ironically, some are slow to remember their consumption of foreign music in their youth, when it functioned as a springboard for Angolan sounds.

The national radio station, RNA, played a decisive role in the production and dissemination of music after independence.[88] Not only was music produced and promoted through recording and broadcasting, but unofficial censorship also set limits on what disc jockeys played and on how people thought about music. Censorship never came in the form of an official decree and yet musicians and music enthusiasts alike were unanimous in saying that the music of Urbano de Castro, David Zé, and Artur Nunes was simply not played on the radio after the attempted coup in 1977. Auto-censorship and individual acts of censorship accomplished what the state would not do explicitly. Individual disc jockeys and managers of the record collection at the RNA internalized the intimidation around them. Maria Luisa Fançony, the director of programs at RNA from the early 1980s to 1992, remembered a May Day celebration covered by reporters who spontaneously burst into a eulogy of party leaders. She reminded them that they were not obliged to do so and that they should remember they were doing so of their own volition. On the other hand, she also recalled having the unfortunate responsibility of "having a word" with reporters about the language they used. She remembered coaching them: "If you would just take out this word here . . . Why do you have to put in adjectives? Because if you put in an adjective you will immediately elicit a reaction, but if you leave it open then there is more room to negotiate."[89] Lamartine suggested that the process was done elliptically rather than through edicts or direct proclamations. Referring to de Castro, Zé, and Nunes, he noted, "Their music was not prohibited but it was not played as a matter of the political influence that was exercised at the time. It was more like a psychological action, an informal conversation, that influenced the youth."[90]

This silent pressure had material effects. In the time I spent looking at records in the RNA collection, still actively used by disc jockeys and radio journalists, I encountered numerous vinyl discs with deliberate scratches and X's through particular songs or with writing on the label that said *não tocar* (do not play). I found only one single by Urbano de Castro in the stacks. When I asked whether they had any music by de Castro, Zé, and Nunes, the head of the department delivered a small stack of 45 rpms to me personally and asked me to return them directly to him when I was finished reviewing them.[91] It may be that playing their music is still a sensitive issue or it may be that these records came from someone's personal collection, to fill in a purposeful if past lacuna, and needed to be protected. Whatever the case, that tidy stack and the intentionally scratched vinyl discs refer back to an earlier moment when certain records were deemed dangerous.

Changes in music and information broadcasting began at the RNA before the party officially introduced changes. But they were part of a broader trend toward economic and political liberalization that occurred from 1985 to 1991.[92] These changes were the result of radio journalists who wanted to play and preserve music from the golden age as well as open up news programming. Fançony remembered that Carlos "Cassé" Ferreira petitioned the party's Political Bureau to open up news broadcasting in the mid-1980s and finally got limited approval in 1986. But she also recalled that not all radio journalists were so successful. Some new programming was quickly deemed too politically edgy and met an early fate.

In the area of music programming, a group of young journalists[93] took the lead in initiating *Os Tops dos Mais Queridos*, a greatest-hits show in which listeners would call in and vote for their favorite current music, and *Quintal do Ritmo* (Rhythm Patio), which played the hits from the late colonial period and featured those artists on the program. In 1987 the journalists João das Chagas, Gilberto Júnior, and Amadeu Pimental, who were music enthusiasts, opened a competition for the largest record collection in Angola on their show *Quintal do Ritmo*. Over the course of the year, and with the involvement of their listeners, they were able to develop a list of the music produced by local record companies between 1969 and 1978. Given the ways in which the RNA's collection had been marked by the vicissitudes of time and history and the fact that record company archives no longer existed or could not be located, this was a particularly ingenious way of restoring the RNA's music collection and of doing history. *Quintal do Ritmo* and *Caldo de Poeira* (Dust Soup), a more recent addition to RNA programming that also plays music from the golden age, have found an enduring appeal among an older generation of listeners and some younger ones as well. Since Urbano de Castro was the artist who produced the most records from 1969 to 1978, playing his music was unavoidable, although it may also have been a conscious act on the part of disc jockeys. De Castro looms large in the memory of this period and the reinauguration of his music on the radio marked a change in political culture as well as in cultural politics.

In 1990 the party shed the titular appendage "PT" (*partido de trabalho* or workers' party) and opened the economy to private investment. The state signed the Bicesse Accords with UNITA the next year, opening the way for a multiparty system and the first multiparty elections in the country in 1992.[94] Around this time, the Ministry of Culture withdrew its support of artistic production. To fill in the production gap, some musicians and businessmen have opened recording studios and production companies, but artists still struggle to come up with the money needed to produce CDs and even buy instruments. Nonetheless, music from the late colonial period is beginning to make a reappearance. In 1997–98 Teta Lando, the musician and producer, launched a collection of CDs called *Ritmos Angolanos* (Angolan Rhythms) that was to include twenty volumes.[95] Among those already released in 1998 were CD collections of various artists and CDs by single artists that included Teta Lando, David Zé, Artur Nunes, and Urbano de Castro.

Today, when musicians reflect on the period of time around independence they consistently say that the party forgot the contribution that musicians made to the MPLA's ascendancy. Some musicians involved in nationalist politics, both before and especially after independence, formed a group called Artistas de Primeira Grandeza to advocate on their behalf. The group petitions the government for material help and works for recognition of artists' contributions to the pacification, defense, and mobilization of the Angolan nation.[96] In general, musicians and cultural producers, whether self-proclaimed party militants, activists, members, or sympathizers, note a certain lack of gratitude by the party for the work they did. But while they disparage the elitism of party politics and the arrogance of those who think they made independence with a "handful of exiles,"[97] musicians also emphasize their links with individuals in positions of power. More than a few times I heard people proclaim their proximity to power: "Zé Du [the president] slept on my floor when he escaped to the guerrilla [combat]," "Lopo was always at a table at Maxinde," "Nandó [the current prime minister] was our neighbor in Bairro Indígena," and so on.

The narrowing and repression of politics caused by the response to May 27 and the prolonged civil war, sharpened by the paroxysms of the Cold War in the region and in the country, created what musicians refer to as a hiatus in the history of Angolan music. In using this term, musicians and cultural producers suggest that politics in independent Angola has betrayed music. They pull the narrative of Angolan music away from the narrative of Angolan nationalism at the moment of independence. When they do this they make claims about the relationship between culture and politics both before and after independence. Describing the period after independence as a hiatus in the history of Angolan music, musicians and cultural producers can then intervene in the narrative of Angolan nationalism to locate a different kind of politics in the cultural world of the late 1960s and early 1970s.

Through the music scene Angolans declared a cultural sovereignty that did not simply lead them to politics but was political in its own right. Cultural sovereignty shaped their expectations about independence and nationalism. Their experience in the clubs and around the production and consumption of music had taught them that they could run things by and for themselves. *Poder popular* would certainly have made sense to them, but not in the form that the government would later render it. They did not expect a one-party state where decisions were made at the top and handed down, where political police followed and intimidated citizens, and where consumption was circumscribed by a centralized economy or accessible only to the already rich. The last century of colonial rule, and particularly the period from the 1930s on, had made clear the limitations of such a system. Thus nostalgia for the golden age of Angolan music is not nostalgia for the late colonial period as such but nostalgia for a lost milieu. Independence, Angolans say, is always preferable but "we gained *and* we lost."

Epilogue

> Everyone played. Many of our leaders out there, the majority of them, played guitar and, in that other time, were musicians. What I mean is that we had an attitude like they have in Brazil: to be someone you have to play soccer or you have to sing—to be known, to be on top. So, many of our leaders out there, I won't cite names, also dedicated themselves to music. Even people with degrees left medicine to go play music, meaning that music gave you much more, it brought you fame and it brought you money. So they abandoned other arts and in that period everyone was a musician. Today no. They want to be politicians, ministers in parliament, and I don't know what. And why? Because music has no expression . . . Today music has lost its expression, the politicians muffled music and we want to reactivate the situation. Because music is a part of what's good. It is a nutrient for any people, from any society.
> —*Chico Coio, February 15, 2002*

I DON'T COMPLETELY agree with Chico Coio on the state of Angolan music. Young Angolan musicians have produced some mordant lyrics that punctuate infectious if not necessarily complex beats. And some young artists, in particular Paulo Flores, have gone acoustic and reinvigorated the semba of yesteryear. But while Coio says Angolan music has, in his words, "no expression," he also says much more than that, pointing to a connection between music and politics. If in the late 1960s and early 1970s it was both financially and socially lucrative to be a musician, today financial and social lucre is reserved for political elites and those connected to them. Indeed, the penury in which some of the best musicians of the late colonial period now find themselves often gave me pause. Their economic conditions are related to the change from a centralized economy to a market-driven one in the early 1990s.

Coio bemoans not only the economic frailty and low social standing of many musicians but the poverty of today's musical content. When he says that "the politicians muffled music," Coio refers to the time in the postindependence period when the state created a politicized environment in which expression was constrained, musicians censored themselves, and trova was promoted over semba. By 1992 the state had stopped supporting music altogether. As Carlos Lamartine put it: "Hoje cada um puxa a brasa para a sua sardinha" (today each person grabs charcoal for his sardine—in other words—today each person fights to cook his own fish). In this way, an opening of the economic market and, to a more limited degree, a relaxation on the limits of what can be said has been accompanied by a restriction on *who* can speak, since access to the public sphere is largely a function of liquidity.

If Angolan music today has "no expression," that deficiency has less to do with content, with lyrics and instrumentation, than it has to do with context. In the late colonial period what made music vital to nation was the conjuncture: the combination of content, venues, people, the broader political climate (anticolonial war and the euphoria of independence), economic changes, and the technological and commercial development of communications. This is not to say that music is no longer important or interesting. Trenchant social critiques still predominate in lyrics, but the music scene has changed and its dynamism has waned because the elements that created the former context have fallen away.

One symptom of that disarticulation is the change in venues and the kinds of music played there. When I arrived for the first time in Luanda in November 1997, the city offered a plethora of discos but only one pricey venue, Xavarotti, had live music. Disc jockeys dominated the discos and parties of the city, playing a mix of music as cosmopolitan as it was in the 1960s and 1970s. Discos and parties were always packed with young and old alike as people danced into the wee hours. But otherwise, these discos had little to do with the clubs of yesteryear, which were just that: a thing of the past.

Although I did not know it at the time, the absence of live music at discos and *festas dos quintais* (backyard parties) marked a radical departure from the 1960s, 1970s, and even 1980s. Even the recreation centers of the 1980s have all closed since 1992, although they are occasionally rented out for parties and weddings. Most have been converted into warehouses, bread shops, or evangelical churches. The spaces where people gathered to hear live music have been invaded by the necessities imposed by the new economy and evacuated by a change in the government's cultural policy.

But contemporary urban Angolan culture is not just reflective of changes in politics or economics; it is not just a realm where political processes are evident or play themselves out. Music in urban Angola has, for at least half a century, been a transformative activity. It has transformed men and women, though mostly men, from regular folks into public figures and it has transformed quotidian dramas into expressions of discontent and acts of solidarity. It has given some musicians access to travel and given politicians a way to speak to the *povo*—the people. It was in and through music that Angolans found their nation and put their stakes on nationalism.

Today, music's capacity to transform is constrained, but not stymied, by economic conditions and by the desire of political elites (mostly still MPLA) to harness music's mobilizing pulse. Angolan politicians strategically use music at political inaugurations and parties, and bankroll the production of CDs, because they know that music still moves people. Musical production itself is bound up in the patronage system that some scholars argue is the modus operandi of contemporary Angolan politics.[1] For example, the minister of public works (then governor of Kwanza Sul province), Higino Carneiro, paid for the production of Carlos Lamartine's CD *Memórias* in 1998. A powerful general from the Angolan military allegedly sponsored the production of *kuduro* star Dog Murras's last two CDs.

The older generation of musicians and cultural promoters who rubbed shoulders with some of today's top brass and politicians in the musseque clubs, but who are largely outside or on the fringes of political power, alternate between recounting the social and cultural genealogies that connect them to political leaders and critiquing these same figures. By doing so, they sketch the connections of patrimonial relations that are operative and show how their failure to yield benefits in a particular moment can result in riposte. In the two meetings I had with Chico Coio, his critical tone waxed and waned relative to his fortune in getting his connections to work for him. In saying that he "won't cite names," at a moment when he had no shows on the horizon, he claimed a kind of moral power for himself relative to those musicians turned politicians whom he sees as opportunists. Coio's comment threatened to bring memory and history to bear on the present but it was a threat that rang fairly hollow because doing so would mean severing the reciprocity that promised some possibility, if no guarantees.

Even as these patron-client relations may evoke precolonial social practices and values, they do so in a new environment and in new ways. They did not pertain, at least in the realm of music, to the golden age. In that era, musicians' reciprocal relations were with neighbors, audiences, and club members, and eventually with CITA, the tourism office, which helped get them gigs. That reciprocity was lived and breathed in the clubs, backyard parties, streets, and cinemas. Gathering in large groups where one certainly did not know everyone in the audience, where performers moved in and out of the audience, and where the audience represented a cross section of Angolan society, instantiated the nation. Perhaps Angola's current regime understands this fact and that is why the only clubs that play live music today are reserved for the elite, those who can fork out anywhere from $35–$100 for the entrance fee, and those musicians with connections that can get them a gig. But ultimately, it is audiences that make musicians successful and popular.

Young Angolan musicians such as Euclides da Lomba, Angelo Boss, Eduardo Paim, Betinho Feijó, and Paulo Flores are reworking old rhythms, to the delight of an older generation of artists and their young listeners as well. Flores's 2002 album *Recompasso* (*compasso* means a step, time, or beat, and *recompasso* is to revisit or repeat it, in this case, with a difference) includes a song called *Anos Depois* (Years Later). This song takes a critique of the colonial regime (Rui Mingas's musicalization of a poem about contract labor called "Monangambe," written by António Jacinto) and redeploys it against the current regime. Other songs on this album rediscover an old musical path and take it in new directions. The song "Poema do Semba" (Semba Poem) tweaks the language of patriotism in the service of music when it proclaims that "semba is our flag" and "semba is the sound that helps me bear my pride in being Angolan." In other words, semba brought us together and symbolizes the nation, and it is the sound, the rhythm, and the soul that allows one to be proud of being Angolan in an era when civil war and corruption dominate the country's image both at home and abroad.

The struggles of daily life have crept back into the instrumentation and lyrics of new musical styles. We can hear the results of economic constraints as keyboards and mixing tables have replaced bands outfitted with instruments. One style that has developed in the last ten to fifteen years and has enlivened street corners, backyards, and discos throughout the country is known simply as *kuduro* (hard ass). At their best, *kuduro* lyrics hark back to those of an earlier period, representing the quotidian struggles of the urban poor. As with most music in Angola, *kuduro* has an eponymous dance style, one of whose adepts is a young man missing a leg, symbolic of the enormous destruction of the war, the tens of thousands who wear that loss, and their tremendous resilience. Murras's 2002 hit "Aqui'tas" (You're Here) summed it up: "Sofrimento na cidade aumentou criatividade" (suffering in the city has increased creativity). In other words, music in Angola is not immune to the difficult economic and social conditions, but by presenting them in new and different terms, music allows people to engage these conditions critically and mockingly and to celebrate their own survival.

Even while initially being bankrolled by a politically influential general, Dog Murras's music and presentation is a complicated mix of out-and-out jingoism and grassroots solidarity. A quick glance at Murras's CD covers, where he is adorned in flag wear, might make you think he is in the party's pocket.

Arguably, he made the Angolan flag from the socialist period chic at a moment when a competition was underway to redesign the flag to better represent the new Angola. But this may have nettled the party as much as it pleased them; they issued a statement at the end of 2005 encouraging citizens to treat the nation's symbols with respect, a move widely seen as an attempt to reassert control over the personal appropriation of the flag as style. Murras's music, as much as the images, offer a fascinating array of political jabs and dodges. The beats are energizing, almost ecstatic. The lyrics critique antisocial behaviors (lying, vanity, intrigue, gossip) as much in the musseques as in the halls of power, while also implicating social relations.

In "Filhos Querem Pão" (Children Want Bread), he assumes the voice of a desperate father talking to someone whom he refers to as "brother," but who won't give him respect or roll down his window. For me, this immediately calls to mind the image of a one-legged veteran in dusty fatigues I saw swing himself over to a general's glistening SUV to knock on the window and ask for help.[2] The military man, clad in beret and dark sunglasses, gunned the engine and sped off, "puxando a brasa" (going for his charcoal) while leaving his "brother" to "puxar a sua" (get his own). The person Murras is addressing remains nameless and faceless but most Angolans have some experience to fill it in and make the story their own. In this way, this musical content is not too far from the critiques proffered in the music of the late colonial period.

I have sometimes wondered how this music (and there are many other examples by Murras, Flores, and others) gets played on the radio and how these artists find themselves invited to perform at events sponsored by the president or other political figures.[3] I think there are two reasons. The first has to do with the disarticulation of the conjuncture: times have changed, the venues for live music no longer serve the subaltern sector of the population, and most musicians need rich benefactors (members of the political elite or individuals connected closely to them) or a base outside Angola to become professionally successful. The second reason has to do with the existence of another, more radical vein of music. It is one that circulates from hand to hand and by word of mouth and often blares from the speakers of *candongueiros*, the blue-and-white Hiluxs and VWs that serve as collective transport. It is played in the cramped backyards and still-dusty streets of the musseques by musicians who live there. This music's more trenchant critiques make the more polished sounds of elliptical critiques by Flores, Murras, and others palatable to politicians and radio programmers.

The musseques have changed tremendously since the 1970s. Luanda has grown from a population of half a million at independence to an estimated three to four million, in large part thanks to the civil war that displaced millions of people from other parts of the country, rich and poor alike. Still home to the urban poor, most of whom have recently arrived from rural areas, the musseques have swelled and spread with the arrival of various waves of people fleeing the twenty-seven-year civil war. Some former residents have moved out and up, into high-rises in the baixa or to neighborhoods with cement houses. But many remain. The musseques continue to struggle with the problems of yore—sporadic or no electricity, poor water supply, no garbage collection service—but these problems now loom on a larger scale.[4]

Arsénio Sebastião, known as "Cherokee," was a young man hailing from the musseque Marçal (the musseque that Angolans refer to as the cradle of Angolan music). He worked as a car washer at the docks of Mussulo, an island just off Luanda's southern coast that has beautiful beaches and has become a vacation spot for those who can afford it. The docks from which boats depart to Mussulo were a bustling place in the late 1990s. By 2005, when my family and I returned to Angola, I was shocked to see that the docks area was empty save for the fishermen selling boat rides to the island and a few straggling vendors of soda, beer, and ice cream. The place had been razed by the government, purportedly because it presented a danger to public health. More likely, it was an eyesore to Exxon's foreign employees who live in a compound overlooking it, or to the owner of that compound, a close friend of the president's. Or perhaps the government was trying to erase memories of Cherokee and his demise.

On November 22, 2003, Cherokee was washing cars and was singing a song to pass the time between jobs.[5] He sang the lyrics of a rap song by the singer MCK, from the Chaba neighborhood, called "The Technique, the Causes and the Consequences." This song exhorts its listeners to "clean the dust out of your eyes / open your eyes brother / switch off TPA [public television] / tear up the newspapers and analyze daily realities."[6] It critiques the state of affairs in which "we have more firearms than dolls, fewer universities than discos, and more bars than libraries."[7] A group of presidential guards who happened to be at the docks overheard Cherokee singing and they began to beat him. People at the scene tried to intervene but were threatened with the same treatment. Guard reinforcements arrived and carried Cherokee off a few meters to the ocean's shore where they beat him repeatedly, tied his hands and legs with one of the guard's bootlaces, and dunked his head in and out of the water for several minutes at a time until he drowned. Divers were sent to retrieve his body but it was not found until the following day when it washed ashore bloated, limbs still bound with bootlaces. The presidential guard reportedly sent Cherokee's family a coffin, trucks so that mourners could attend his burial, ten armed soldiers, and some sacks of food.[8]

Perhaps the moral of the story is that explicit political critique can get you or your audiences killed. MCK's music has been banned from radio and television but still circulates informally. More important, I think, is another consequence of this heinous murder, one probably little considered in the halls of power. MCK has become involved in the life of Cherokee's neighborhood and family. He and other like-minded rappers raised $1,000 to contribute to the family. And MCK, a university student of philosophy, has assumed the costs of educating Cherokee's two children.[9] This incident, then, has both inflamed and mobilized at least one small corner of the musseques. Like the music of the 1960s and 1970s, this new music produces a kind of sovereignty in the maws of repression and a sense that democracy comes from taking the initiative, from doing for oneself and one's neighbors. If there are no clubs in which this sentiment can cohere, perhaps the streets are the next venue. And perhaps this music is the social, if not the instrumental, heir to the music of the golden age.

Notes

All interviews were conducted by the author unless otherwise noted.
All translations from the Portuguese, unless otherwise noted, are by the author.

INTRODUCTION

Epigraph: Christine Messiant, "'Em Angola, até o passado é imprevisível': A experiência de uma investigação sobre o nacionalismo angolano e, em particular, o MPLA: Fontes, crítica, necessidade actuais de investigação," in *Actas do II Seminário Internacional Sobre a História de Angola: Construindo o passado angolano: As fontes e a sua interpretação, Luanda 4 a 9 de Agosto de 1997* (Lisbon: Commissão Nacional para as Comemorações dos Descobrimentos Portugueses, 2000).

1. Interview with Alberto Teta Lando, May 7, 1998, Luanda. These three musicians were David Zé, Urbano de Castro, and Artur Nunes. Their music was unofficially banned from the airwaves and was not played for over a decade.

2. The alleged coup attempt, known in Angola as 27 de Maio, and the state's repressive response are discussed in more detail in chapter 6 of this book. See David Birmingham, "The Twenty-seventh of May: An Historical Note on the Abortive 1977 Coup in Angola," *African Affairs* 77, no. 309 (October 1978): 554–64, and Jean-Michel Mabeko Tali, *Dissidências e poder de estado: O MPLA perante si próprio (1962–1977)* (Luanda: Editorial Nzila, 2001), vol. 2. The particulars of these events and their effects are only beginning to come to light. A series of articles in the independent press in 1998 was one of the first signs that this issue was reopening to public debate. See, for example, *Folha 8*, no. 312 (May 26, 1998), which had a series of articles on various aspects of the alleged coup attempt and its effects. The headline was "Era preciso o Holocausto?" ("Was the Holocaust Necessary?").

3. Fernando Martins, "Os Kiezos: Do Bairro Marçal para a eternidade," *Agora*, August 1998, 10.

4. Unlike studies of the Mau Mau or of the guerrilla fighters in Zimbabwe, the literature on Angolan nationalism by and large does not include accounts by combatants or by those involved in the struggle at the guerrilla bases. Inge Brinkman's work has begun to address this lacuna. According to Maria Conceição Neto, there was a project in the 1980s, in which she was involved, that interviewed women who

had been involved in the struggle. However, nothing was ever done with the interviews and they were not made available to the public. The earliest material comes from journalists who traveled with the guerrillas and published accounts of camp life. See for example Don Barnett, *With the Guerrillas in Angola* (Seattle: Liberation Support Movement Information Center, 1970) and *Liberation Support Movement Interview: Sixth Region Commander Seta Likambuila, MPLA* (Seattle: Liberation Support Movement Information Center, 1974); Don Barnett and Roy Harvey, *The Revolution in Angola: MPLA, Life Histories and Documents* (New York: Bobbs Merrill, 1972); and Caetano Pagano, "Visit to MPLA and Their Liberated Areas," May–September 1974 (International University Exchange Fund, 1974). Brinkman, "A canção política, as religiões e o conceito de 'cultura popular,'" unpublished paper presented in Luanda and Mbanza Kongo, December 2003 (draft from author cited with permission). Also see Brinkman, ed., *Singing in the Bush: MPLA Songs during the War for Independence in South-east Angola (1966–1975)* (Köln: Rüdiger Köppe Verlag, 2001), and "War, Witches and Traitors: Cases from the MPLA's Eastern Front in Angola (1966–1975)," *Journal of African History* 44, no. 2 (July 2003): 303–26. A famous fictional account of life in the armed struggle is Pepetela's *Mayombe*, 5th ed. (Lisbon: Publicações Dom Quixote, 1993). Some first-person accounts and memoirs have been published recently: Paulo M. Júnior, *Lembranças da vida* (Luanda: INALD, 1998); Michel Laban, *Viriato da Cruz: Cartas de Pequim* (Luanda: Edições Chá de Caxinde, 2003); Dino Matrosse, *Memórias (1961–1971)* (Luanda: Editoral Nzila, 2005); Fernando Tavares Pimenta, *Angola no percurso de um nacionalista: Conversas com Adolfo Coelho* (Porto, Portugal: Edições Afrontamento, 2006); Deolinda Rodrigues, *Diário de um exílio sem regresso* (Luanda: Editorial Nzila, 2003) and *Cartas de Langidila e outros documentos* (Luanda: Editorial Nzila, 2004); and Adriano Sebastião, *Dos campos de algodão aos dias de hoje* (Luanda, 1993).

5. There is a growing body of literature on the role of music and musical performance spaces in creating new connections across class and ethnicity. See, for example, David Coplan, *In Township Tonight! South Africa's Black City Music and Theatre* (Johannesburg: Raven Press, 1985), esp. chap. 6 on Sophiatown; Laura Fair, *Pastimes and Politics: Culture, Community, and Identity in Post-Abolition Zanzibar, 1890–1945* (Athens: Ohio University Press, 2001); Ch. Didier Gondola, "*Bisengo ya la joie*: Fête, sociabilité et politique dans les capitales congolaises," in *Fêtes urbaines en Afrique: Espaces, identités et pouvoirs*, ed. Odile Goerg (Paris: Karthala, 1999), 87–111 and "*Ô Kisasa makambo!* Métamorphoses et représentations urbaines de Kinshasa à travers le discours musical des années 1950–1960," *Le Mouvement Social*, no. 204 (July–September 2003): 109–29; Phyllis Martin, *Leisure and Society in Colonial Brazzaville* (Cambridge: Cambridge University Press, 1995), especially chap. 5; and Richard Shain, "Roots in Reverse: Cubanismo in Twentieth-Century Senegalese Music," in "Special Issue on Leisure in African History," *International Journal of African Historical Studies*, 35, no. 1 (2002): 83–101.

6. For example, see the following trial records at the Instituto dos Arquivos Nacionais, Torre do Tombo, Lisbon, Polícia Internacional e de Defesa do Estado/

Direcção Geral de Segurança, Delegação de Angola, Divisão de Informação–1a Secção (hereafter cited as IANTT-PIDE/DGS, DInf./1A): Processo no. 15.12.D/1 Muçeque Prenda, nt 2086, pp. 207, 226; Processo no. 15.12.D Muçeque Rangel, nt 2086, pp. 56–65; and Processo no. 15.12.E/5 Muçeque Marçal, nt 2086, pp. 98–102.

7. IANTT-PIDE/DGS, DInf./1A, Processo no. 15.12.D Muçeque Rangel, nt 2086, pp. 330–33; Processo no. 15.12.D/1 Muçeque Prenda, nt 2086, p. 216; and Processo no. 15.12.B/5 Muçeque Caputo, nt 2085, p. 9.

8. IANTT-PIDE/DGS, DInf./1A, Processo no. 15.12.D Muçeque Rangel, nt 2086, p. 80.

9. IANTT-PIDE/DGS, DInf./1A, Processo no. 15.12.D Muçeque Rangel, nt 2086, pp. 47–48, 55, and Processo no. 15.12.B/6 Sambizanga, nt 2085, p. 79.

10. IANTT-PIDE/DGS, DInf./1A, Processo no. 15.12.E/5 Muçeque Marçal, nt 2086, pp. 21–22.

11. This government of the Republic was overthrown in 1926. In 1932, António Salazar, an economist, became the prime minister. He died suddenly in 1968 and Marcello Caetano, former minister of overseas affairs, took the helm of the fascist state until 1974, when a military coup ushered in a transition to democracy.

12. Among the groups that formed between about 1953 and 1960 were the Angolan Communist Party (PCA); the Party of United Struggle for Africans in Angola (PLUA); the Union of Angolan Populations (UPA), which later became the National Front for the Liberation of Angola (FNLA); and the Popular Movement for the Liberation of Angola (MPLA).

13. On the Casa dos Estudantes de Império, O Clube Marítimo Africano, and O Centro de Estudos Africanos, see Edmundo Rocha, *O Clube Marítimo Africano: Uma contribuição para a luta e independência nacional dos países sob domínio colonial português* (Lisbon: Biblioteca Museu República e Resistência, 1998) and *Angola: Contribuição ao estudo da génese do nacionalismo moderno angolano (período de 1950–1964): Testemunho e estudo documental* (Lisbon: Kilombelombe, 2003), 78–98. Also see Filipe Zau, *Marítimos africanos e um clube com história* (Lisbon: Embaixada de República de Angola em Portugal, 2005), chap. 2.

14. "Pronunuciados por actividades contra a segurança do Estado mais trinta e dois indivíduos na Comarca de Luanda," *Jornal ABC: Diário de Luanda*, December 18, 1959.

15. For example, Mário Pinto de Andrade and others went to Paris and Lúcio Lara went to Germany.

16. These three rebellions included a revolt in the cotton-growing area of Baixa de Cassange in January, an attack on the main prison and police headquarters in Luanda on February 4, 1961, and an uprising in the coffee-growing areas of Uíge in northern Angola beginning on March 15, 1961.

17. The founding dates of these parties, and in particular of the MPLA, are the subject of much debate. The official MPLA founding is 1956, but historians and other scholars generally agree that this date has no historical evidence to support it. The party was more likely founded in January 1960 during the Second

Pan-African Conference in Tunis, where Angolan members of a pan-luso-African front, MAC, needed to present themselves as a specifically Angolan movement and prove that they had contacts in the Angolan interior in order to receive external support. See Marcelo Bittencourt, *Dos jornais às armas: Trajectórias da contestação angolana* (Lisbon: Vega, 1999), 176–203; Michel Laban, *Mário Pinto de Andrade: Uma entrevista* (Lisbon: Edições Sá da Costa, 1997); Messiant, "'Em Angola, até o passado é imprevisível,'" 808–11; Carlos Pacheco, *MPLA: Um nascimento polémico* (Lisbon: Vega, 1997); Rocha, *Angola*, 135–37; Tali, *Dissidências*, 1:52–68. All of these scholars also contest the MPLA's claim to have instigated the February 4, 1961, attacks on the prison and police station in Luanda, organized to some degree by people linked to the FNLA, which was founded in 1957.

18. This is an argument presented initially by John Marcum in *The Angolan Revolution*, vols. 1 and 2 (Cambridge, MA: MIT Press, 1969 and 1978). It has been debated and refined by other scholars although his book is still largely seen as the definitive work on the history of nationalism. See David Birmingham, *Frontline Nationalism in Angola and Mozambique* (Trenton, NJ: Africa World Press, 1992); W. G. Clarence-Smith, "Review Article: Class Structure and Class Struggles in Angola in the 1970s," in "Special Issue on Contemporary Politics," *Journal of Southern African Studies* 7, no. 1 (October 1980): 109–26; Douglas Wheeler and Réne Pélissier, *Angola* (New York: Praeger, 1971).

19. For more on the MPLA's different politico-military regions see Jean-Michel Mabeko Tali, *Dissisdências e poder de estado: O MPLA perante si próprio (1966–1977)*, (Luanda: Editorial Nzila, 2001) and for UNITA's secret agreement with the Portuguese see William Minter, *Operation Timber: Pages from the Savimbi Dossier* (Trenton, NJ: Africa World Press, 1988).

20. Bittencourt, *Dos jornais às armas*; Marcelo Bittencourt, *Estamos juntos* (Lisbon: Kilombelombe, 2008); Drumond Jaime and Helder Barber, *Angola: Depoimentos para a história recente, 1950–76*, vol. 1 (Lisbon: privately published, 1999); Pacheco, *MPLA*; Rocha, *Angola*; Tali, *Dissidências*, vol. 1.

21. Messiant, "'Em Angola, até o passado é imprevisível'"; Didier Péclard, "Religion and Politics in Angola: The Church, the Colonial State and the Emergence of Angolan Nationalism, 1940–1961," *Journal of Religion in Africa* 28, Fasc. 2 (May 1998): 160–86; Didier Péclard, "Etat coloniale, missions chrétiennes et nationalisme en Angola, 1920–1975: Aux racines sociales de l'UNITA" (PhD diss., Institut d'Etudes Politiques de Paris, 2005).

22. Messiant, "'Em Angola, até o passado é imprevisível,'" 815.

23. Inge Brinkman, *A War for the People: Civilians, Mobility, and Legitimacy in South-East Angola during the MPLA's War for Independence* (Cologne: Rüdiger Köppe Verlag, 2005), 17. See also Brinkman, *Singing in the Bush* and "War, Witches and Traitors."

24. See Robin D. G. Kelley, *Race Rebels: Culture, Politics, and the Black Working Class* (New York: Free Press, 1996).

25. Gage Averill, *A Day for the Hunter, a Day for the Prey: Popular Music and Power in Haiti* (Chicago: University of Chicago Press, 1997), xi.

26. James C. Scott, *Domination and the Arts of Resistance: Hidden Transcripts* (New Haven, CT: Yale University Press, 1990), 199.

27. Johannes Fabian and Karin Barber make similar arguments. See, for example, Fabian, "Popular Culture: Findings and Conjectures," *Africa* 48, no. 4 (1978): 315–34, and *Remembering the Present: Painting and Popular History in Zaire* (Berkeley: University of California, 1996), and Barber, "Popular Arts in Africa," *African Studies Review* 30, no. 3 (1987): 1–78 and *The Generation of Plays* (Bloomington: Indiana University Press, 2000). See also Kelly M. Askew, *Performing the Nation: Swahili Music and Cultural Politics in Tanzania* (Chicago: University of Chicago Press, 2002), 23. For work on this question in a diasporic context, see George Lipsitz, *Dangerous Crossroads: Popular Music, Postmodernism and the Poetics of Place* (New York: Verso, 1994), 137.

28. Fair, *Pastimes and Politics*, 9.

29. My thinking on this is informed in a very general way by C. L .R. James's notion of self-activity and his argument that workers were already producing and living socialism on shop floors and around production processes. See for example, C. L. R. James, Grace Lee, and Pierre Chaulieu, *Facing Reality* (Detroit: Bewick Editions, 1974, orig. pub. 1958).

30. My analysis somewhat echoes that of Partha Chatterjee, who argues that anticolonial nationalism in India creates the material and spiritual as separate domains of social institutions and seeks out sovereignty in the latter before making a claim to political power in the former. I differ from Chatterjee in that I see the spiritual, what I call the cultural space, as an area created by common folk and not by the intelligentsia. Furthermore, it is simultaneous with the contest for political power and not prior to it. See Partha Chatterjee, *The Nation and Its Fragments: Colonial and Postcolonial Histories* (Princeton, NJ: Princeton University Press, 1993).

31. António Venâncio, "O 'semba' em discussão: Subsídios para a sua compreensão," *Angolense*, March 18–25, 2000, 16.

32. Paulo Flores, *Recompasso* (Lisbon: N'jila Produções and Ruben Produções, 2001, compact disc).

33. From the *Oxford English Dictionary* online.

34. Ibid.

35. Robin D. G. Kelley, *Yo' Mama's DisFUNKtional! Fighting the Culture Wars in Urban America* (Boston: Beacon Press, 1997).

36. Tali makes this point in volume 2 of his work, where he shows that in the initial period of transition the MPLA was still not forcefully present in Luanda and that the fact of local urban support had more to do with urban youth who took the initiative. He also notes that contact with the population was limited to radio broadcasts after the dismantling of clandestine cells in urban areas, namely Luanda, in 1969. See Tali, *Dissidências*, vol. 2, chap. 10.

37. PIDE files on the musseques reporting on incidents in which police intervened show the great geographic and ethnic diversity of Luanda because they include for each individual the name, birth date, place of birth, and name and

residence of parents. See, for example, IANTT-PIDE/DGS, DInf./1A, Processo no. 15.12.A Muçeque Lixeira, nt 2084; Processo no. 15.12.A/1 Muçeque Calemba, nt 2084; Processo no. 15.12.B/1 Muçeque Zangado, nt 2085; Processo no. 15.12.B/2 Muçeque Catambor, nt 2085; Processo no. 15.12.B/3 Muçeque Mulemba N'gola, nt 2085; Processo no. 15.12.B/4 Muçeque Ilha do Cabo, nt 2085; Processo no. 15.12.B/5 Muçeque Caputo, nt 2085; Processo no. 15.12.B/6 Sambizanga, nt 2085; Processo no. 15.12.D Muçeque Rangel, nt 2086; Processo no. 15.12.D/1 Muçeque Prenda, nt 2086; Processo no. 15.12.E/4 Muçeque Moto, nt 2086; and 15.12.E/5 Muçeque Marçal, nt 2086.

38. Eric Hobsbawm, *Nations and Nationalisms since 1780* (Cambridge: Cambridge University Press, 1990), 10. Anthony Smith's ethno-symbolic approach takes issue with this conceptualization and Ernest Gellner is overwhelmingly concerned with the modernity of this process. While in the overall discussion on nationalism these are debate marking positions they are less germane to my concerns here. See Ernest Gellner, *Nations and Nationalism* (Ithaca, NY: Cornell University Press, 1983) and Anthony Smith, *Ethnicity and Nationalism* (New York: E. J. Brill, 1992).

39. Benedict Anderson, *Imagined Communities* (London: Verso, 1996). Pheng Cheah, in his introduction to Pheng Cheah and Jonathan Culler, eds., *Grounds of Comparison: Around the Work of Benedict Anderson* (New York: Routledge, 2003), 5, makes the point that Anderson is often misread in this sense. While many scholars take off from Anderson to analyze how states produce nations, I follow Anderson's focus on the prior moment and on form more than on content.

40. See Partha Chatterjee's critique of Anderson's model as suggesting there is nothing left to be imagined by nations emerging from the colonial yoke. Chatterjee, *Nation and Its Fragments*, 5.

41. See Partha Chatterjee, *Nationalist Thought and the Colonial World: A Derivative Discourse* (Minneapolis: University of Minnesota Press, 1993) and *Nation and Its Fragments*. Work by the subaltern studies collective has also been pivotal in this case, in particular, Ranajit Guha's *Dominance Without Hegemony: History and Power in Colonial India* (Cambridge, MA: Harvard University, 1997). See also Frederick Cooper and Ann Laura Stoler, eds., *Tensions of Empire: Colonial Cultures in a Bourgeois World* (Berkeley: University of California Press, 1997), and Anne McClintock, *Imperial Leather: Race, Gender and Sexuality in the Colonial Contest* (New York: Routledge, 1995).

42. For a good example see Homi Bhabha, ed., *Nation and Narration* (New York: Routledge, 1990).

43. Susan Geiger, *TANU Women: Gender and Culture in the Making of Tanganyikan Nationalism, 1955–65* (Portsmouth, NH: Heinemann, 1997); Askew, *Performing the Nation*; and Thomas Turino, *Nationalists, Cosmopolitans, and Popular Music in Zimbabwe* (Chicago: University of Chicago Press, 2000). Luise White's *The Assassination of Herbert Chitepo* (Bloomington: Indiana University Press, 2003) takes a different tack on nation, opting for a cultural historical analysis

of nation rather than looking at cultural practices and their relationship to nation and nationalism. Although it does not deal directly with nationalism, Laura Fair's *Pastimes and Politics* shows the interplay between the cultural and political in the everyday leisure activities of the Zanzibari underclass.

44. Coplan, *In Township Tonight!* and *In the Time of Cannibals: The Word Music of South Africa's Basotho Migrants* (Chicago: University of Chicago, 1994); Veit Erlmann, *Nightsong: Performance, Power and Practice in South Africa* (Chicago: University of Chicago, 1996); Alec J. Pongweni, "The Chimurenga Songs of the Zimbabwean War of Liberation," in *Readings in African Popular Culture*, ed. Karin Barber (Bloomington: Indiana University Press, 1997), 63–72; Leroy Vail and Landeg White, *Power and the Praise Poem: Southern African Voices in History* (Charlottesville: University Press of Virginia, 1991).

45. The works of Askew, Geiger, and Turino are obviously exceptions, as is Gregory H. Maddox and James L. Giblin, eds., *In Search of a Nation: Histories of Authority and Dissidence in Tanzania* (Athens: Ohio University Press, 2005).

46. In the case of Africa generally, Basil Davidson is perhaps the best example, but Terence Ranger's relationship to the Zimbabwean nationalist struggle is also well known.

47. For Angola, Marcum's *Angolan Revolution* is still seen by Angolan and foreign scholars alike as the definitive work.

48. While South Africa (and Namibia) and Zimbabwe were under the yoke of white settler rule in the form of apartheid and UDI (Unilateral Declaration of Independence), the Portuguese fascist state maintained rule from the metropole and hobbled attempts at white rule in its colonies while supporting it regionally. On lusotropicalism see Cláudia Castelo, *"O modo português de estar no mundo": O luso-tropicalismo e a ideologia colonial portuguesa (1933–61)* (Porto, Portugal: Edições Afrontamento, 1998).

49. Castelo, "O modo Português," 50–51.

50. Castelo, "O modo Português."

51. For a discussion of this see Jeremy Ball, "Colonial Labor in Twentieth Century Angola," *History Compass* 3, no. 1 (2005), AF 168, as well as his "'Colossal Lie': The Sociedade Agrícola do Cassequel and Portuguese Colonial Labor Policy in Angola, 1890–1977" (PhD diss., University of California, Los Angeles, 2003). Examples of this include Gerald Bender, *Angola under the Portuguese: The Myth and the Reality* (Berkeley: University of California Press, 1978); Charles R. Boxer, *Race Relations in the Portuguese Colonial Empire 1415–1825* (Westport, CT: Greenwood Press, 1963); James Duffy, *Portuguese Africa* (Cambridge, MA: Harvard University Press, 1961); and Thomas Okuma, *Angola in Ferment: The Background and Prospects of Angolan Nationalism* (Boston: Beacon Press, 1962).

52. Basil Davidson, *In the Eye of the Storm: Angola's People* (Garden City, NJ: Doubleday, 1972), and Marcum, *Angolan Revolution*, vols. 1 and 2.

53. See for example, Russell Hamilton, *Voices from an Empire* (Minneapolis: University of Minnesota Press, 1975) and *Literatura africana, literatura necessária*

(Lisbon: Edições 70, 1984); Jorge Macedo, *Literatura angolana e texto literário* (Lisbon: Edições ASA for União de Escritores Angolanos, 1989); Ana Mafalda Leite, "Angola," in *The Postcolonial Literature of Lusophone Africa*, ed. Patrick Chabal (Evanston, IL: Northwestern University, 1996), 103–64; Alfredo Margarido, "The Social and Economic Background of Portuguese Negro Poetry," *Diogenes* 37 (1962): 50–74; and Phyllis Reisman Peres, *Transculturation and Resistance in Lusophone African Narrative* (Gainesville: University Press of Florida, 1997).

54. For example, see Mário António Fernandes de Oliveira, *A formação da literatura angolana (1851–1950)* (Lisbon: Imprensa Nacional–Casa de Moeda, 1997), and Douglas Wheeler, "Origins of African Nationalism in Angola: Assimilado Protest Writings, 1859–1929," in *Protest and Resistance in Angola and Brazil*, ed. Ronald Chilcote (Berkeley: University of California Press, 1972).

55. Marcum, *Angolan Revolution*, 1:231, and Tali, *Dissidências*, 1,:224.

56. Bittencourt, *Dos jornais às armas*, 115–16.

57. Bittencourt, *Dos jornais às armas*, 121–22.

58. Messiant, "'Em Angola, até o passado é imprevisível,'" 846–47.

59. Mário de Souza Clington [Ary Kemitow Zirka], *Angola Libre?* (Paris: Éditions Gallimard, 1975), 167–70. In an interview with Jomo Fortunato, José Oliveira de Fontes Pereira said that he, Clington, and José Rodrigues formed this group in 1958. It also included a women's section. The group's philosophy was to promote Angolan music and dance. See Jomo Fortunato, "José de Oliveira de Fontes Pereira: A alma da dikanza," *Jornal de Angola*, June 4, 2000, 1–3.

60. Lúcio Lara, *Um amplo movimento . . . : Itinerário do MPLA através de documentos e anotações*, vol. 1, *Até fevreiro 1961* (Luanda: LitoTipo, 1998), 13, 41. See also Jacques Arlindo dos Santos, *ABC do Bê Ó* (Luanda: Edições Chá de Caxinde, 1999), 217.

61. Prasenjit Duara, *Rescuing History from the Nation: Questioning Narratives of Modern China* (Chicago: University of Chicago Press, 1995), 10.

62. For example, see Basil Davidson, *The People's Cause: A History of Guerrillas in Africa* (London: Longman, 1981); Allen Isaacman and Barbara Isaacman, *Mozambique from Colonialism to Revolution, 1900–1982* (Boulder, CO: Westview, 1983); David Lan, *Guns and Rain: Guerrillas and Spirit Mediums in Zimbabwe* (Berkeley: University of California Press, 1985); David Martin and Phyllis Johnson, *The Struggle for Zimbabwe* (New York: Monthly Review Press, 1981); and Terence Ranger, *Peasant Consciousness and Guerrilla War in Zimbabwe* (Berkeley: University of California Press, 1985).

63. Martin J. Murray and Garth A. Myers, eds., *Cities in Contemporary Africa* (New York: Palgrave Macmillan, 2006), 27.

64. See, for example, Belinda Bozzoli, *Theatres of Struggle and the End of Apartheid* (Athens: Ohio University Press, 2004); Coplan, *In Township Tonight*; Filip de Boeck and Marie Françoise Plissart, *Kinshasa: Tales of the Invisible City* (Tervuren, Belgium: Royal Museum for Central Africa, 2004); Fair, *Pastimes and*

Politics; James Ferguson, *Expectations of Modernity: Myths and Meanings of Urban Life on the Zambia Copperbelt* (Berkeley: University of California Press, 1999); Tom Lodge et al., *All, Here, and Now: Black Politics in South Africa in the 1980s* (New York: Ford Foundation and Foreign Policy Association, 1991); Martin, *Leisure and Society*; Don Mattera, *Gone with the Twilight: A Story of Sophiatown* (London: Zed Books, 1987); Murray and Myers, *Cities in Contemporary Africa*; Garth Andrew Myers, *Verandahs of Power: Colonialism and Space in Urban Africa* (Syracuse, NY: Syracuse University Press, 2003); Richard Rive, *Buckingham Palace, District Six* (London: Heinemann, 1987); Allen F. Roberts and Mary Nooter Roberts, *A Saint in the City: Sufi Art in Urban Senegal* (Los Angeles: UCLA Fowler Museum of Cultural History, 2003); and A. M. Simone, *For the City Yet to Come: Changing African Life in Four Cities* (Durham, NC: Duke University Press, 2004).

65. I discuss this band in greater detail in chapter 2.

66. Band members "Liceu" Vieira Dias, Amadeu Amorim, and José Maria dos Santos, as well as their dramatist colleague Gabriel Leitão, were all arrested and jailed in the political crackdown known as the Processo de 50. Dos Santos was not part of the original fifty-nine accused but was picked up in a later sweep in 1960 around the time that Agostinho Neto, who would become Angola's first president, was also arrested. Other band members like Euclides Oliveira de Fontes Pereira were transferred to jobs outside the colonial capital of Luanda in retaliation for their politics.

67. José Junior, "Liceu faleceu há quatro anos," *Jornal de Angola*, August 19, 1998, 13. This article is part of a larger attempt, though I do not know that it is an organized attempt, to rehabilitate Vieira Dias's place in Angolan history. His second wife was Portuguese and some say he was dismissed from the party or distanced himself. The filmmaker Ole told me an interesting story when we met in 1997. He said that when his film came out it had to pass the censorship board and they decided not to let it run. He took the issue to the president, who viewed the film and said it should be shown. However, President Neto died before an official order was drafted and Ole's film was not shown in the country until the late 1980s. Conversation with António Ole, July 9, 1998, Luanda.

68. Popular Memory Group, "Popular Memory: Theory, Politics, Method," in *Making Histories: Studies in History Writing and Politics*, ed. Richard Johnson et al. (Minneapolis: University of Minnesota Press, 1982), 207.

69. Popular Memory Group, "Popular Memory," 207.

70. Jomo Fortunato, "Música popular angolana: A música tradicional na consolidação do semba," *Jornal de Angola*, February 14, 1999, 1–2.

71. Messiant also makes this point in "'Em Angola, até o passado é imprevisível,'" 814.

72. Interviews with Dionísio Rocha, May 15, 1998; Jorge Macedo, May 11, 2001; and Rui Mingas, January 13, 2002, all in Luanda. See also Jomo Fortunato, "Entrevista com Carlitos Vieira Dias: Carlitos, da lírica dos Gingas à Banda

Xangola," *Jornal de Angola*, August 8, 1999, 1–4. All of these sources use the word "hiatus."

73. Record albums from the immediate postindependence period often included party slogans and practical information such as how to identify traffic signs.

74. For work on African music and cosmopolitanism see Shain, "Roots in Reverse"; Turino, *Nationalists*; and Bob W. White, "Congolese Rumba and Other Cosmopolitanisms," in "Musique, joie et crise dans le cosmotropole Africain," ed. Bob W. White, special issue, *Cahiers d'Etudes Africaines* 168, XLII, no. 4 (2002): 663–86.

75. In saying this I do not mean, following Benedict Anderson, that nationalism was a modular Euro-American Creole creation that was then transported to Third World countries. Rather, I follow Turino, who argues that nationalism is a cosmopolitan doctrine "emanating from and being shaped in multiple locales," including places like China, Russia, Tanzania, and Ghana. Turino, *Nationalists*, 13.

76. Current scholarship emphasizes the varieties of cosmopolitanisms and their particularities. See, for example, Pheng Cheah and Bruce Robbins, eds., *Cosmopolitics: Thinking and Feeling beyond the Nation* (Minneapolis: University of Minnesota Press, 1998), and Timothy Brennan, *At Home in the World: Cosmopolitanism Now* (Cambridge, MA: Harvard University Press, 1997).

77. Turino, *Nationalists*, 9.

78. White, "Congolese Rumba," 681.

79. Ferguson, *Expectations of Modernity*, 99.

80. On the difficulties of working with the PIDE archives in particular, see Messiant, "'Em Angola, até o passado é imprevisível,'" 848–55. For an example of the way these archives are used to pursue personal and political acrimony, see Severino Carlos, "'Eu vi as fichas do Pacavira e do Norberto na Torre do Tombo': Alberto Neto abre o dossier PIDE/DGS," *Angolense*, February 9–16, 2002, 6–7, 24.

81. Teta Lando Produções has a series called Ritmos Angolanos through which Lando has issued both collections of various musicians and reissues of albums by particular musicians and bands, including the president's former band Nzaji. The French researcher Ariel de Bigault, with the help of local musicians, ethnomusicologists, and print and radio journalists (whom I also consulted), has produced a set of five CDs of Angolan music: *Angola 60's, Angola 70's* (two disks), *Angola 80's*, and *Angola 90's*.

82. Jorge Macedo—musician, writer, literary critic, and ethnomusicologist—is working on two manuscripts as of this writing in 2008. One is on semba music. The book will be a formal musicological analysis of the style and its antecedents. His second manuscript is on marimbas and the various schools of playing that exist throughout Angola. Jomo Fortunato—musician, journalist, and literary and music critic—is writing a book about the popular urban form of music. In a series of interviews with various artists that have been published in *Jornal de Angola*, the local daily, he has laid out a sketch of musical practice that

focuses on the development of style and the generation of a uniquely popular form of music.

83. Judging from the rows of shelves holding boxes, there exists an as-yet untapped wealth of material having to do with the late colonial period and with Luanda. Because this material is not catalogued it is unavailable to researchers. Archivists have begun a survey of the material that indicates the basic document titles of the holdings.

84. Laura Fair has made great use of the archives of record companies in her work on music and politics in postabolition Zanzibar. See *Pastimes and Politics*, chap. 4, and Fair, "Music, Memory and Meaning: The Kiswahili Recordings of Siti Binti Saad," *Swahili Forum*, September 1998, 1–16. In Angola, most record companies were abandoned and then nationalized. Company archives or records were likely destroyed, taken from the country, or ruined by neglect. I was unable to locate any such material, though it may exist in Portugal in personal archives or in Angola with individuals I do not know.

85. Maria da Conceição Neto alerted me to the paper *Tribuna dos Muçeques*, which though ostensibly produced by the PIDE (Portuguese secret police) would have material related to daily life in the musseques. It was apparently distributed throughout the country. While the paper is listed in the holdings of the Luanda Municipal Library, I was informed in 1998 that it was out for binding. When I returned to the library in 2000 in search of it, I was told that it had disappeared. Library employees had not been paid in many months and the director despaired that books and papers sometimes went missing as workers compensated themselves. The National Library in Lisbon, Portugal, likewise does not hold this paper.

86. Like the *Tribuna dos Muçeques*, CITA was said to be infiltrated by PIDE agents. According to the director of the library, after independence the party confiscated the collection of magazines produced by CITA because they feared that it contained security sensitive information. The magazines have never been returned. The director told me this story in a tone and with a phrase—"they came from outside"—that I heard from many others as well and that points up the dichotomy between those who went off to join the armed struggle or went into exile and those who remained in the country.

87. Bittencourt, *Dos jornais às armas*; Messiant, "'Em Angola, até o passado é imprevisível'"; Péclard, "Etat coloniale"; Rocha, *Angola*; Tali, *Dissidências*, vol. 1.

88. Only nine of the total are women. I went to Angola with the intention of interviewing an equal number of women and men. But I also went without knowing exactly how women or gender would figure in my argument, in part because the fragmentary nature of social historical work on Angola made it difficult to even conceptualize. Chapter 3 offers an analysis of the relation between gender and nation as it played out in Angola's music scene.

89. Otto Roesch cited in Allen Isaacman, *Cotton Is the Mother of Poverty: Peasants, Work, and Rural Struggle in Colonial Mozambique, 1938–1961* (Portsmouth, NH: Heinemann, 1996), 16.

90. Geiger, *TANU Women*, 14.

91. James Ferguson notes a similar sense of loss among Zambians with respect to the early days of independence: "And what had been lost with the passing of this era, it seemed, was not simply the material comforts and satisfactions that it provided but the sense of legitimate expectation that had come with them." Ferguson, *Expectations of Modernity*, 12.

92. Clarence-Smith, "Review Article," 109–26, and *The Third Portuguese Empire 1825–1975: A Study in Economic Imperialism* (Manchester, UK: Manchester University Press, 1985), and M. Anne Pitcher, *Politics in the Portuguese Empire: The State, Industry and Cotton, 1926–1974* (New York: Oxford University Press, 1993).

93. While it was of course true that the completion of my dissertation and book, and by implication the research connected to these projects, promised to improve my financial situation in the long term, most people were only concerned with more straightforward kinds of exploitation and profit. I was constantly told that a certain French researcher doing work on Angolan music had profited by producing a collection of Angolan music that included, for example, photographs she allegedly used without permission.

94. Interview with Alberto Teta Lando, May 7, 1998, Luanda. One musical example of this was a recording I found in which the singer and composer Elias dia Kimuezu was accompanied by Rui Mingas, Teta Lando, and Bonga (later identified respectively with the MPLA, the FNLA, and UNITA). The record was a single, "Muenha ua Muto," that came out on the Ngola label produced by the Portuguese company Valentim de Carvalho.

95. This was the sound of Cuba transported and transposed by Zairean musicians in the production of their own form of urban popular music that preceded and influenced Angolan music.

96. Scholars Christine Messiant and Tony Hodges, making an implicit parallel to the Soviet Union, have called Angola's state and party elites a *nomenklatura*. See Tony Hodges, *Angola: Anatomy of An Oil State* (Bloomington: Indiana University Press; Oxford: James Currey, in association with the Fridtjof Nansen Institute, 2004).

CHAPTER 1 ⇁ MUSSEQUES AND URBAN CULTURE

1. Interviews with Amadeu Amorim and José Maria dos Santos, April 4, 2001; Carlos Lamartine, August 9, 2001; António Sebastião Vicente "Santocas," November 22, 2001; Alberto Jaime, December 4, 2001; and Chico Coio, February 15, 2002, all in Luanda.

2. On a visit to Lisbon with my parents in early 2000, we ducked into a bar in Bairro Alto to escape a sudden downpour. The bar was fairly full but I immediately noticed two young men seated at the bar who seemed to me to be Angolan (dress, demeanor, manner of speaking, or just plain intuition). As we were leaving

I greeted them and they asked, "But where are you from?" I responded that I was from the United States but presently living in Luanda. They said that they were both from Luanda and immediately wanted to know where I lived in the city. I then asked them the same thing. One was from São Paulo and the other from Bairro Azul and they were both shocked and overjoyed that I knew their neighborhoods. That I had been in Luanda was interesting but that I was familiar with their neighborhoods meant that I somehow knew Luanda and knew something about them.

3. Murray and Myers, *Cities in Contemporary Africa*, 2–3.

4. Ilídio do Amaral, *Luanda: Estudo de geográfia urbana* (Lisbon: Junta de Investigações do Ultramar, 1968), 13–14.

5. See Joseph C. Miller, *Way of Death: Merchant Capitalism and the Angolan Slave Trade, 1730–1830* (Madison: University of Wisconsin Press, 1988).

6. Amaral, *Luanda*, 55.

7. "Creole" is a much-debated term. Mário António in *Luanda, ilha crioula* (Lisbon: Agência Geral do Ultramar, 1968) used the term to describe Luanda's specificity, and the book and term were quickly adopted as part of lusotropicalism's creed. A lively debate over the usefulness of the concept "creole" in defining Angolan literature began in the late 1980s, most publicly between the Portuguese literary critic José Carlos Venâncio and the Angolan literary critic Luís Kandjimbo. I am partial to Kandjimbo's position that *angolanidade* as a literary manifestation has a multiplicity of bases and that the African ones always get underplayed. However, Marcelo Bittencourt, a historian, makes a compelling case for using "creole" in historical circumstances because it avoids colonial state categories of assimilado and indígena and is better at getting at a particular sociohistorical reality. I use the word here in this more historically specific sense. I would not, for example, use it to describe Luanda today or *angolanidade* in general.

8. See Fernandes de Oliveira, *A formação da literatura angolana*, and Wheeler, "Origins of African Nationalism."

9. See "Variações da população em relação ao censo de 1950," *Actividade Económica de Angola: Revista de Estudos Económicos* 69 (May–August 1964): 206. An example of this policy was the appropriation of lands in Ndalatando and Lucala belonging to African owners whom the government accused of preparing a revolt. See António de Assis Júnior's *Relato dos acontecimentos de Dala Tando e Lucala*, 2d ed. (Luanda: União dos Escritores Angolanos, 1980). For an analysis of the *colonatos* and the project of white occupation see Bender, *Angola under the Portuguese*.

10. Amaral, *Luanda*, 26–27.

11. Fernando Mourão, "Configurações dos núcleos humanos de Luanda, do século xvi ao século xx," in *Actas do Seminário: Encontro de Povos e Culturas em Angola*, vol. 1 (Lisbon: Comissão Nacional para as Comemorações dos Descobrimentos Portugueses, 1997), 126.

12. Ramiro Ladeiro Monteiro, *A família nos musseques de Luanda (Subsídios para o seu estudo)* (Luanda: Fundação de Acção Social no Trabalho em Angola,

1973); Óscar Ribas, *Ilundu: Espíritos e ritos angolanos* (Porto, Portugal: Edições ASA para União de Escritores Angolanos, 1989).

13. I know of no research on the history of the word *musseque* as used by musseque residents themselves.

14. Ilídio do Amaral, "Contribuição para o conhecimento do fenómeno de urbanização em Angola," *Finisterra: Revista Portuguesa de Geografia* 13, no. 25 (1978): 67; Monteiro, A *família nos musseques*, 54, 56, 62; Mourão, "Configurações dos núcleos humaos," 122. Monteiro concurs with and cites Amaral but adds that the early groupings of huts were likely referred to as *sanzalas*. A 1966 article discusses the musseque Katambore as a "concentration of poor people in the middle of so many riches surrounding it on all sides" and as "a bit of the rural life in the middle of Luanda," suggesting that a few such musseques in the middle of the city remained. See Lourenço Mendes da Conceição, "Katambore, lago seco da capital angolana," *Angola: Revista de Doutrina e Estudo*, 1966, 37.

15. Mourão, "Configurações dos núcleos humanos," 122.

16. Amaral, "Contribuição," 65; Amaral, *Luanda*, 28; Monteiro, A *família nos musseques*, 61. The writer José Luandino Vieira's earlier work *A cidade e a infância: Estórias*, 3d ed. (Luanda: União de Escritores Angolanos, 1977) depicts a world where multiracial friendships and a blurring of the border between musseque and baixa stand in stark contrast to the racial tensions and de facto segregation that dominated urban society and geography in the 1960s and 1970s.

17. See, for example, Amaral, "Contribuição," 58; José de Sousa Bettencourt, "Subsídio para o estudo sociológico da população de Luanda," *Boletim do Instituto de Investigação Científica de Angola* 2, no. 1 (1965): 91. Bettencourt cites writers from the eighteenth and nineteenth centuries who, in describing the city and its population, referred to huts as a part of it without using the term musseques. Bettencourt does not use the term musseque until talking about the city "today" (i.e., in the mid-1960s).

18. These numbers are based on the censuses for the years noted and are found in Bettencourt, "Subsídio para o estudo sociológico," 95, and Mourão, "Configurações dos núcleos humaos," 206.

19. Amaral, *Luanda*, 70, and Amaral, "Contribuição," 67.

20. For examples, interviews with Albina Assis, January 17, 2002; Chico Coio, February 15, 2002; Alberto Jaime, December 4, 2001; and Efigénia Barroso Mangueira Van Dunem, February 2, 2002, all in Luanda.

21. Renee Gagnon, who was working at the Film Institute in Lisbon when I met her in 1997, shared with me articles from the popular press in Quebec about the photos she took of musseque architecture and the exhibit she had in Luanda in 1975 that demonstrated this eclectic construction. The articles are "Mon Angola," *Le Maclean*, March 1976, 43–45, and "Les musseques de Luanda ou la civilisation du déchet version africaine," *Colóquio: Artes* (Fundação Calouste Gulbenkian, Lisbon), February 1976, 43–51. See also Monteiro, A *família nos musseques*, 261; José Redinha, "A habitação tradicional em Angola: As-

pectos da sua evolução," *Revista do Centro de Informação e Turismo de Angola*, 1964, 21.

22. Interview with Efigénia Barroso Mangueira Van Dunem, February 2, 2002, Luanda.

23. For a complete analysis and lyrics see chapter 4.

24. See Amaral, *Luanda*, 68. According to Amaral, in 1970 approximately 55 percent of the total population of Luanda was born outside the city (this included the categories black, white, *mestiço*, and other).

25. Monteiro, *A família nos musseques*, 96. For the overall population that proportion was in the 50 percent range because many were first-generation Luandans, the children of more recently arrived immigrants.

26. Monteiro, *A família nos musseques*, 96. See also Bettencourt, "Subsídio para o estudo sociológico," 106–7. The statistics presented do not list ethnicity but rather the district and sometimes village of origin. However, both authors also included a breakdown of each musseque by ethnic group.

27. Christine Messiant, "Luanda (1945–61): Colonisés, société coloniale et engagement nationaliste," in *"Vilas" et "cidades": Bourgs et villes en Afrique lusophone*, ed. Michel Cahen (Paris: L'Harmattan, 1989), 127.

28. For 1960 numbers see Bettencourt, "Subsídio para o estudo sociológico," 106–7. For 1970 numbers see Monteiro, *A família nos musseques*, 102–28.

29. Monteiro, *A família nos musseques*, 87.

30. According to Mourão, in 1845 Luanda had a total population of 5,605, of whom 3,513 were black (1,408 men, 2,105 women), 1,601 were white (1,466 men, 135 women), and 491 were *mestiço* (230 men, 261 women). Mourão, "Configurações dos núcleos humanos," 205.

31. Mourão, "Configurações dos núcleos humanos," 205–6, table 1.

32. Amaral, "Contribuição," 57.

33. Messiant, "Luanda," 137.

34. That said, the Portuguese were also notorious for putting to work the wives and children of those who had fled contract labor, so women might have had similar incentives to leave. But at the same time, the central role of women in agricultural production might have put a brake on this.

35. Messiant, "Luanda," 139.

36. Monteiro, *A família nos musseques*, 214; José António Pereira Nunes, "Inquéritos socio-económicos dos muçeques de Luanda: Salários, alimentação, habitação, mobiliário e baixelas," *Mensário Administrativo Portugal*, no. 14 (1961): 161–66. The change is explained in part by the fact that Monteiro separated male from females, so his 90 percent is 90 percent of males, whereas Nunes Pereira offered his percentage based on a combination of male and female workers. Given the large number of female *quintandeiras* or produce vendors who were self-employed, this would have affected the overall tabulation.

37. Monteiro, *A família nos musseques*, 227.

38. Monteiro, *A família nos musseques*, 232.

39. Monteiro notes this tendency in A *família nos musseques*, 225. See Michael A. Samuels and Norman A. Bailey, "Education, Health, and Social Welfare," in *Portuguese Africa: A Handbook*, ed. David M. Abshire and Michael A. Samuels (New York: Praeger, 1969), and Elisete Marques da Silva, "Social Conditions of School Attendance and Achievement of Minors in Suburban Luanda: A Preliminary Test of Some Hypotheses," in *Social Change in Angola*, ed. Franz-Wilhelm Heimer (Munich: Weltforum Vertag, 1973), 194–210, on education after 1961.

40. Marques da Silva, "Social Conditions of School Attendance." For a criticism of this supposed improvement, see Bender, *Angola under the Portuguese*, 173, 213.

41. The language of enframing and reframing comes from Myers, *Verandahs of Power*, 17, riffing on Timothy Mitchell.

42. In the introduction to his thesis Monteiro notes that he chose his research subject (families in the musseques) for its utility to the administration. He is cited as the head of the SCCIA secret service in Caroline Reuver-Cohen and William Jerman, eds., *Angola: Secret Government Documents on Counter-Subversion* (New York: IDOC, 1974), 63. And he signed off on a document about the broadcasting strength of the MPLA's radio program in various provinces throughout the country, which confirms his central position. See Instituto dos Arquivos Nacionais, Torre do Tombo, Lisbon, Serviços de Centralização e Coordenação de Informações de Angola (hereafter cited as IANTT-SCCIA), Processo no. 190, U.I. caixa 260, pp. 29–35, signature on p. 35.

43. Instituto dos Arquivos Nacionais/Torre do Tombo, *Inventário* (Lisbon: IANTT, n.d.), 1–2.

44. In particular the Junta de Investigação do Ultramar (Overseas Provinces' Commission for Research) and the Instituto de Investigação Cientifica de Angola (Scientific Research Institute of Angola).

45. Frederick Cooper, *Africa since 1940: The Past of the Present* (Cambridge: Cambridge University Press, 2002), 134. On the development projects of the British and French colonial states in the postwar period more generally, see Frederick Cooper's *Decolonization and African Society: The Labor Question in French and British Africa* (Cambridge: Cambridge University Press, 1996).

46. Pitcher, *Politics in the Portuguese Empire*, 249.

47. For a comprehensive treatment of this see Castelo, "O modo português." Castelo details the reception of lusotropicalism in Portugal from the early 1930s to the early 1960s and examines the changes in that reception over time and by cultural and political figures and institutions. She also shows that only certain aspects of the theory became state ideology while other aspects were rejected. Bender, in *Angola under the Portuguese*, systematically and carefully refutes the lusotropicalist argument proffered by the Portuguese state with an analysis of demographic material from Angola, Brazil, and other comparative historical situations of colonization in Africa, the Caribbean, and South America (see chaps. 1 and 2). Both

Bender and Castelo point out the selective use of Freyre's theory by the Estado Novo as well as Freyre's complicity with the state when he accepted an official invitation to travel to the various "overseas territories" on a research trip in 1951. That trip resulted in the works *Aventura e rotina: Sugestões de uma viagem à procura das constantes portuguesas de caráter e ação* (Lisbon: Edições Livros do Brasil, 1954) and *Um brasileiro em terras portuguesas: Introdução a uma possível luso-tropicalogia, acompanhada de conferências e discursos proferidos em Portugal e em terras lusitanas e ex-lusitanas da Ásia, África e do Atlântico* (Lisbon: Edições Livros do Brasil, 1954). One of the earliest refutations of lusotropicalism as a cogent and accurate defense of Portuguese colonial relations is found in Boxer, *Race Relations in the Portuguese Colonial Empire*. Clarence-Smith, in *The Third Portuguese Empire*, and Pitcher, in *Politics in the Portuguese Empire*, debunk Portuguese culturalist arguments with analyses of the economic relations created and preserved in the late colonial period.

48. Criticisms of lusotropicalism by nationalist leaders from the Portuguese colonies can be found in Mário Pinto de Andrade [Buanga Fele], "Qu'est-ce que le 'luso tropicalism'?" *Présence Africaine* 4 (October/November 1955): 24–35, and Amilcar Cabral, foreword to *The Liberation of Guiné*, by Basil Davidson (Baltimore: Penguin Books, 1969).

49. Bender, *Angola under the Portuguese*, xx–xxi.

50. Castelo, "O modo português," 100.

51. Castelo, "O modo português," 99, and J. D. Sidaway and Marcus Power, "'The Tears of Portugal': Empire, Identity, 'Race,' and Destiny in Portuguese Geopolitical Narratives," *Environment and Planning D: Society and Space* 23, no. 4 (2005): 542.

52. Sidaway and Power, "Tears of Portugal," 543.

53. Mária da Conceição Neto, "Ideologias, contradições e mistificações da colonização de Angola no século XX," *Lusotopie* 1997 (Paris): 348.

54. This was in opposition to Freyre's argument that the crux of lusotropicalism was cultural exchange and the Portuguese talent for symbiosis. Castelo argues that this was a common example of how Freyre's theory was not adopted *tout court* but rather was used instrumentally to support colonial policy. See Castelo, "O modo português," 84–87.

55. Bender, *Angola under the Portuguese*, 207.

56. An example of this can be found in Basil Davidson's *Eye of the Storm*, 145–46.

57. I am referring to Bender's *Angola under the Portuguese: The Myth and the Reality*. Okuma's *Angola in Ferment* has a brief section entitled "The Myth of a Multiracial Society," 96–98.

58. Ronald Chilcote, ed., *Emerging Nationalism in Portuguese Africa: Documents* (Stanford, CA: Hoover Institution Press, 1972), xxx. This collection of documents contains a number of pieces that directly refute lusotropicalism and, in particular, multiracialism.

59. Américo Boavida, *Angola: Cinco séculos de exploração portuguesa* (Rio de Janeiro: Civilização Brasileira S.A., 1967).

60. Bender, *Angola under the Portuguese*, xxiv.

61. Davidson, *Eye of the Storm*, 148.

62. This trend continued after independence, especially in the work of Jofre Rocha and Boaventura Cardoso. See Luís Kandjimbo, *Apologia de Kalitangi: Ensaio e crítica* (Luanda: INALD, 1997), 113–20, and Macedo, *Literatura angolana*, 46–48, 55–59.

63. See Hamilton, *Voices from an Empire*; Leite, "Angola," 142–43; and Macedo, *Literatura angolana*, 31–74.

64. From Monteiro, *A família nos musseques*, 86. The numbers of musseque inhabitants is derived from data in the police files for the musseques.

65. Mourão, "Configurações dos núcleos humanos," 206, table 1.

66. Bettencourt, "Subsídio para o estudo sociológico," 88.

67. Amaral, *Luanda*, 14.

68. See Amaral, *Luanda*, 72, for an example. Also Monteiro, *A família nos musseques*, 25–26.

69. Ilído do Amaral, "Aspectos do povoamento branco de Angola," *Junto de Investigaçáo do Ultramar: Estudos, Ensaios e Documentos* 74 (1960): 54.

70. Bettencourt, "Subsídio para o estudo sociológico," 93. Bettencourt adds, "The socio-cultural [language, religion, citizenship] dominates, completely and absolutely, the bio-social" realities, which Bettencourt claims are not manifest in statistics (103).

71. Messiant, "Luanda," 137.

72. Amaral, "Aspectos do povoamento branco," 54, and *Luanda*, 74.

73. Bender, *Angola under the Portuguese*, 223.

74. Amaral, *Luanda*, 118.

75. *Noite e Dia*, November 2, 1968, 72–77; May 16, 1970, 44–51; September 5, 1970, 24–25; June 5, 1971, 70–75; and March 4, 1972, 30–33. See also *Semana Ilustrada*, March 15, 1969, 15, and especially June 13, 1970, 7, and August 8, 1970, 14–17. These were popular urban magazines produced by and for a primarily white Angolan population but they were widely known, read, and recognized by the urban African population as well. As such, they offer an indication of tensions between local and metropolitan whites, as well as the ways in which young white urban dwellers took an interest in local cultural practices like music and carnaval.

76. Amaral, *Luanda*, 118–19.

77. Bender, *Angola under the Portuguese*, 223. Unlike Bettencourt and Amaral, who were writing for Portuguese institutes and were required (or chose) to toe the line, Bender was initially doing research for his dissertation and was set on overturning what he considered the "myth" of Portuguese colonialism as being kinder and gentler, that is, lusotropicalism.

78. For an example see Monteiro, *A família nos musseques*, 408.

79. Amaral, *Luanda*, 75.
80. Amaral, "Contribuição," 68.
81. Bettencourt, "Subsídio para o estudo sociológico," 118.
82. Anangola is a kind of acronym for Associação dos Naturais de Angola, in Portuguese, but it is also a Kimbundu word that means children of Angola. For a history of these organizations in the 1920s and 1930s, see Eugénia Rodrigues, *A geração silenciada: A Liga Nacional Africana e a representação do branco em Angola na década de 30* (Lisbon: Edições Afrontamento, 2003).
83. According to Mário Pinto de Andrade, houses in Ingombotas were leveled to make way for apartment buildings to accommodate Portuguese immigrants. See Laban, *Mário Pinto de Andrade*, 10, 13, 55. Also see José Luandino Vieira, *O nosso musseque* (Luanda: Editorial Nzila, 2003), 147–48. On racism, see Messiant, "Luanda," 155.
84. Mourão criticizes the way in which the urban elite is made to appear as a coherent category and points to his work "Continuidades e descontinuidades de um processo colonial através de uma leitura de Luanda" (thesis, Faculdade de Filosofia, Letras e Ciências Humanas, Universidade de São Paulo, 1988). See Fernando Mourão, "O contexto histórico-cultural da criação literária em Agostinho Neto: Memória dos anos cinquenta," *Africa: Revista do Centro de Estudos Africanos* 14–15, no. 1 (1991/92). See also Messiant, "Luanda," 157–61.
85. Laban, *Mário Pinto de Andrade*, 35–37. See also Maria da Conceição Neto, "Ideologias," 347, especially n. 31.
86. Messiant, "Luanda," 171–76.
87. Messiant, "Luanda," 173.
88. Pepetela, *Luandando* (Porto: Elf Aquitaine, Angola, 1990), 108.
89. This was significant given the Portuguese attempts to define ethnic groups against one another, denying any precolonial plasticity that existed. One oft-cited example of this was the use of Ovimbundu workers from the central plateau region to work on coffee plantations in the north in predominantly Bakongo areas. See Maria da Conceição Neto, "Entre a tradição e a modernidade: Os Ovimbundu do Planalto Central à luz da história," in *Ngola: Revista de Estudos Sociais* 1, no. 1 (January–December 1997): 193–216.
90. Bettencourt, "Subsídio para o estudo sociológico," 118.
91. Bettencourt, "Subsídio para o estudo sociológico," 122.
92. Bettencourt, "Subsídio para o estudo sociológico," 119.
93. Instituto António Houaiss, *Dicionário Houaiss da língua portuguesa* (Rio de Janeiro: Editora Objectiva, 2001), 1091.
94. Monteiro, *A família nos musseques*, 316.
95. Monteiro, *A família nos musseques*, 317.
96. Amadeu Amorim, interview by Drumond Jaime and Helder Barber for the Rádio Nacional de Angola program *Foi Há Vinte Anos*, commemorating the twentieth anniversary of independence in 1995.

97. Bettencourt, "Subsídio para o estudo sociológico," 108, 18.

98. For example, in 1846, of 1,830 whites only 156 were women. Bender, *Angola under the Portuguese*, 65.

99. Júlio de Castro Lopo, *Alguns aspectos dos musseques de Luanda* (Angola: Editorial Angola, 1948), 5–6.

100. Amaral, *Luanda*, 75.

101. Amaral, *Luanda*, 119.

102. Amaral, "Aspectos do povoamento branco," 22.

103. Monteiro, *A família nos musseques*, 394.

104. Monteiro, *A família nos musseques*, 398.

105. Duffy, *Portuguese Africa*.

106. This is evidenced in the greater numbers of African women than men in Luanda in the mid-1800s (see Mourão, "Configurações dos núcleos humanos," 205, table 1; for a literary treatment see Alfredo Troni, *Nga Mutúri* (Lisbon: Edições 70, 1991).

107. Vieira, *O nosso musseque* 168–69.

108. Dos Santos, *ABC do Bê Ó*, 395. Linda Heywood reports the same thing for Angolan cities in the central highlands in the 1950s, noting that establishments were often owned by Portuguese women who employed Afro-Portuguese and Ovimbundu women as prostitutes. See Heywood, *Contested Power in Angola: 1840s to the Present* (Rochester: University of Rochester Press, 2000), 149.

109. This scene is also evoked in dos Santos, *ABC do Bê Ó*, 179, 185.

110. Interview with Carlos Lamartine, September 4, 2002, Luanda.

111. Monteiro, *A família nos musseques*, 395–96, and interviews with Olga Baltazar, November 22, 2001, and Lourdes Van Dunem, April 9, 2002, both in Luanda.

112. Bettencourt, "Subsídio para o estudo sociológico," 119.

113. Bettencourt, "Subsídio para o estudo sociológico," 119.

114. Bettencourt, "Subsídio para o estudo sociológico," 120.

115. Monteiro, *A família nos musseques*, 359, 61, 63.

116. Monteiro, *A família nos musseques*, 360.

117. For a detailed study of soccer (football) and its role in the development of an African consciousness and politics, see Peter Alegi, *Laduma! Soccer, Politics and Society in South Africa* (Scottsville, South Africa: University of KwaZulu-Natal Press, 2004), and Fair, *Pastimes and Politics*, chap. 5 in particular.

118. See, for example, António Cardoso, *Baixa e musseques*, 2d ed. (Havana: Ediciones Cubanas for the União de Escritores Angolanos, 1985); Jorge Macedo, *Gente do meu bairro, enas e contos*, 2d ed. (Havana: Ediciones Cubanas for União de Escritores Angolanos, 1985); and Luandino Vieira, *A cidade e a infância*.

119. Amadeu Amorim, interview by Drumond Jaime and Helder Barber, *Foi Há Vinte Anos*, Rádio Nacional de Angola, 1995.

120. For a more developed argument about fashion and nation see Marissa Moorman, "Putting on a *Pano* and Dancing Like Our Grandparents: Dress and

Nation in Late Colonial Luanda," in *Fashioning Africa: Power and the Politics of Dress*, ed. Jean Allman (Bloomington: University of Indiana Press, 2004), 84–103.

121. Interview with Alberto Jaime, December 12, 2001, Luanda.

122. Mourão, "Configurações dos núcleos humanos," 111.

123. Mourão, "Configurações dos núcleos humanos," 112.

124. Jorge Macedo, *Ngola Ritmos: Obreiros do nacionalismo angolano* (Luanda: União de Escritores Angolanos, 1989), 17–18.

125. Fortunato, "A música tradicional," 1–2; interviews with Carlos Lamartine on August 3, 1998, August 4, 1998, August 14, 1998, September 3, 2001, September 4, 2001, September 9, 2001, and September 11, 2001, all in Luanda; Macedo, *Ngola Ritmos* and *Literatura angolana* and interviews with Macedo on May 11, 2001 and June 27, 2001, Luanda; Mário Rui Silva, "Estórias da música em Angola," part 3, "A geração dos anos 1940/50. Luanda e as suas figuras mais marcantes," *Austral* (TAAG Angolan Airlines in-flight magazine), April–June 1996, 33–40, and part 4, "A música suburbana luandense das suas origens até aos fins dos anos 50," *Austral*, October–December 1996, 49–57.

126. Maria Eduarda, "O musseque e as suas gentes," *Boletim Cultural: Repartição de Cultura e Turismo*, 1973, 18.

127. Interview with Alberto Jaime, December 12, 2001, Luanda.

128. See, for example, Macedo, *Gente do meu bairro*; José Luandino Vieira, *Luuanda: Short Stories of Angola*, trans. Tamara Bender (London: Heinemann, 1980); and José Luandino Vieira, *A vida verdadeira de Domingos Xavier* (Lisbon: Edições 70, 1974).

CHAPTER 2 IN THE DAYS OF BOTA FOGO: CULTURE AND THE EARLY NATIONALIST STRUGGLE, 1947–61

1. Women appear in this narrative but their contributions are generally interpreted and contained within the dominant narrative. For example, in José Fortunato's *Angola: Documentos do MPLA*, Deolinda Rodrigues is pictured as a heroine who founded the OMA (Organização das Mulheres de Angola) and was later killed by imperialist forces. In this way her story is subsumed in that of the party or liberation movement, in this case the MPLA. See José Fortunato, *Angola: Documentos do MPLA*, vol. 1 (Lisbon: Ulmeira, 1977), 91–92.

2. Susan Geiger, "Tanganyikan Nationalism as 'Women's Work': Life Histories, Collective Biography and Changing Historiography," *Journal of African History* 37, no. 3 (1996): 468.

3. See, for example, Birmingham, *Frontline Nationalism*, 16, 79; Bittencourt, *Dos jornais às armas*, 114–26; Fernandes de Oliveira, *A formação da literatura angolana*, 266–67; Marcum, *Angolan Revolution*, 1:22–27; Messiant "Luanda," 162, 167; Mário Pinto de Andrade, "O protonacionalismo: Ideaias e práticas políticas," chap. 3 in *Origens do nacionalismo africano* (Lisbon: Publicações Dom

Quixote, 1997), 75–178; Rocha, *Angola*, 99–113; Wheeler and Pélissier, *Angola*, 147–49.

4. Bittencourt, *Dos jornais às armas*, 30, 116 n. 8 (on Bota Fogo and Ferroviário soccer clubs); Michel Cahen, "Syndicalisme urbain, luttes ouvrières et questions ethniques à Luanda: 1974/1981," in Cahen,*"Vilas" et "cidades,"* 216; Messiant, "Luanda," 147–48; Rocha, *Angola*, 76–77.

5. Lara, *Um amplo movimento*, 1:41. Messiant notes that the relation of such groups, including Bota Fogo and Ngola Ritmos, to the MPLA needs to be clarified. See Messiant, "'Em Angola, até o passado é imprevisível,'" 803–59, esp. 846–47.

6. Rocha, *Angola*, 76–77; Messiant, "Luanda," 147–48.

7. Rocha, *Angola*, 113.

8. For work on Angolan literature in the colonial and postcolonial periods see Patrick Chabal, *The Postcolonial Literature of Lusophone Africa* (Evanston, IL: Northwestern University Press, 1996), specifically the chapter on Angola by Ana Mafalda Leite, 103–64; Fernandes de Oliveira, *A formação da literatura angolana*; Hamilton, *Voices from an Empire* and *Literatura africana*; Margarido, "Portuguese Negro Poetry"; Peres, *Transculturation and Resistance*; Michael Wolfers, ed., *Poems from Angola* (London: Heinemann, 1979).

9. Leite, "Angola," 142–43.

10. Recent work on nationalism and culture in African societies by Askew, Geiger, and Turino (cited in the introduction) makes this argument. Askew's use of performance theory, Geiger's notion of TANU women's "culture of politics," and Turino's engagement of theories of cosmopolitanism complicate the relationship of culture and politics in the history of nationalist politics.

11. Bender, *Angola under the Portuguese*; Heimer, *Social Change in Angola*; and Franz-Wilhelm Heimer, *Decolonization Conflict in Angola, 1974–76: An Essay in Political Sociology* (Geneva: Institut Universitaire de Hautes Études Internationales, 1979). For works that focus on economic growth and development and its complex relationship to politics, primarily in order to deepen our understanding of the Portuguese colonial state in relation to the colonies, see Clarence-Smith, *Third Portuguese Empire*, chap. 7, "Late Colonialism, 1961–1975," and Pitcher, *Politics in the Portuguese Empire*, chap. 10, "The Decline of the Authoritarian Regime, 1958–1974," and chap. 12, "The Collapse of Portuguese Colonialism." For a more strictly economic perspective, see Maria da Luz Ferreira de Barros, "Alguns aspectos da situação socioeconómico em Angola (1961–1974)," *Africana*, no. 14 (September 11, 1994): 41–62, and Ana Maria Neto, *Industrialização de Angola: Reflexão sobre a experiência da administração portuguesa, 1961–1975* (Lisbon: Escher, 1991).

12. The exception to this is Ball, "'The Colossal Lie.'"

13. See Clarence-Smith, *Third Portuguese Empire*; Carlos Rocha Dilolwa, *Contribuição à história económica de Angola*, 2d. ed. (Luanda: Editorial Nzila, 2000); and Pitcher, *Politics in the Portuguese Empire*.

14. Michael O. West, *The Rise of an African Middle Class: Colonial Zimbabwe, 1898–1965* (Bloomington: Indiana University Press, 2000), 1–2.

15. Recent feminist work has focused increasingly on the category of gender instead of women. This shift in focus is also true in the literature on African history: for example, see Nancy Rose Hunt, Tessie Liu, and Jean Quataert, eds., *Gendered Colonialisms in African History* (Malden, MA: Blackwell, 1997), and Lisa A. Lindsay and Stephan F. Miescher, eds., *Men and Masculinities in Modern Africa* (Portsmouth, NH: Heinemann, 2003). Other feminist scholars have insisted that the category of women and research agendas that look at women's history, actions, and experiences are still relevant and constitutive of the study of gender. See, for example, the introduction to Jean Allman, Susan Geiger, and Nakanyike Musisi, eds., *Women in African Colonial Histories* (Bloomington: Indiana University Press, 2002), 3–4.

16. On the effects of the glorification of women in the nationalist historical narrative in Zimbabwe, see Tanya Lyons, "Guerrilla Girls and the Zimbabwean National Liberation Struggle," in Allman, Geiger, and Musisi, *Women in African Colonial Histories*, 305–26.

17. For other work on gender and nationalism in Africa see, among others, Judith Byfield, "'Unwrapping' Nationalism: Dress, Gender, and Nationalist Discourse in Colonial Lagos" (Discussion Papers in the African Humanities, AH no. 30, African Studies Center, Boston University, 2000); LaRay Denzer, "Towards a Study of the History of West African Women's Participation in Nationalist Politics: The Early Phase, 1935–50," *Africana Research Bulletin* 6, no. 4 (1976): 65–85; Susan Geiger, "Women and African Nationalism," *Journal of Women's History* 2, no. 1 (1990): 227–44, and "Tanganyikan Nationalism as 'Women's Work,'" and *TANU Women*; Cora Ann Presley, *Kikuyu Women, the Mau Mau Rebellion and Social Change in Kenya* (Boulder: University of Colorado Press, 1992); Elizabeth Schmidt, *Mobilizing the Masses: Gender, Ethnicity, and Class in the Nationalist Movement in Guinea, 1939–1958* (Portsmouth, NH: Heinemann, 2005).

18. For example, Jorge Macedo, "Fontinhas, compositor, tocador de reco-reco, cantor: O semba é uma criação de Ngola Ritmos," *Angolense*, March 9–19, 2002, 20–21.

19. Conversation with Jacques Arlindo dos Santos, January 8, 2001, Luanda.

20. See Laban, *Mário Pinto de Andrade*, 8, and dos Santos, *ABC do Bê Ó*, 10. In my interview with Amélia Mingas she mentioned the financial difficulties her family encountered when her father was jailed since her mother had not been working. The Grupo Feminino Santa Cecília raised money for the families of political prisoners, which suggests that this problem was more generalized.

21. Interview with Amadeu Amorim and José Maria dos Santos, April 4, 2001, Luanda.

22. On pamphlets, see Rocha, *Angola*, 340–42, where he summarizes the pamphlets he found in the PIDE documents archived at the Arquivo Nacional da

Torre do Tombo, Lisbon. Rocha refers to this early period of nationalist agitation in Luanda as the "pamphlet phase" (113).

23. Rocha, *Angola*; Bittencourt, *Dos jornais às armas*, 124 n. 33.

24. Mateus Valódia, "Das turmas aos conjuntos musicais," *Angolense*, August 3–10, 2002, 21.

25. Dos Santos, *ABC do Bê Ó*, 253–55.

26. Interview with Dionísio Rocha, May 15, 1998, Luanda.

27. José Redinha, "Angola terra de folclore," *Boletim Cultural: Repartição Estatística, Cultura, Propaganda e Turismo*, July–September 11, 1967, 57.

28. Ana de Sousa Santos, "Aspectos de alguns costumes da população Luandense," *Boletim do Instituto de Investigação Científica de Angola* 7, no. 2 (1970): 55–71.

29. Bettencourt, "Subsídio para o estudo sociológico," 127; Monteiro, *A família nos musseques*, 363.

30. While the nature of their artistic activity, that is, valorizing Angolan cultural practices, seems to confront colonial cultural policy head on, at least a couple of people involved in these groups mentioned that it was not until well into the 1960s that they became politically conscious and pro-independence. Both Dionísio Rocha and Olga Baltazar mentioned that nationalist politics did not really enter their minds until after they had been in Portugal on tour in 1964 with Ngoleiros do Ritmo and Fogo Negro respectively.

31. See, for example, Bettencourt, "Subsídio para o estudo sociológico," 119–20.

32. Dos Santos, *ABC do Bê Ó*, 204.

33. "Liceu" Vieira Dias quoted in Silva, "Estórias da música em angola," part 3, 37.

34. Silva, "Estórias da música em angola," part 3, 38.

35. Fortunato, "A música tradicional," 1; Mário Rui Silva, "Estórias da música em Angola," part 1, "A história, os instrumentos e a influência da música angolana na América Latina e Caraíbas," *Austral* (TAAG Angolan airlines in-flight magazine), August–September 11, 1995, 15–20; also Silva, "Estórias de música em Angola," parts 3 and 4.

36. Jomo Fortunato, "A magnitude simbólica dos 'Kiezos,'" *Jornal de Angola*, July 29, 2001, 4.

37. Interview with Dionísio Rocha, June 2, 1998, Luanda.

38. Interview with Amadeu Amorim and José Maria dos Santos, April 4, 2001, Luanda.

39. António Ole, *O Ritmo de N'gola Ritmos* (Luanda: Instituto Angolano de Cinema, 1978). Both Franciso Xavier Hernandez and Gabriel Leitão were arrested in the Processo de 50. Marcum refers to Hernandez as a Cuban sailor. See Marcum, *Angolan Revolution*, 1:33n63.

40. See Ole, *O Ritmo de N'gola Ritmos*.

41. In particular, a good number of Ovimbundu from central Angola lived in this neighborhood and worked at the port.

42. Interview with Elias dia Kimuezu, May 11, 2001, Luanda.

43. Interview with Elias dia Kimuezu, May 11, 2001, Luanda.

44. According to Kimuezu, the other members included "Guanga" Barduino, Brito Sozinho, and Pedro de Castro "Loy" Van Dunem.

45. Angolans, and Luandans in particular, also refer to *kotas*, which is a word that comes from Kimbundu and means someone who is older and wiser.

46. Interview with Dionísio Rocha, May 18, 1998, Luanda.

47. Interview with Amadeu Amorim and José Maria dos Santos, April 4, 2001, Luanda.

48. Interview with Amadeu Amorim and José Maria dos Santos, April 4, 2001, Luanda.

49. Interview with Miguel Frances Santos Rodolfo "Kituxi," April 17, 2002, Luanda. The *hungu* is an Angolan instrument that is related to the Brazilian *berimbau*. The musicological term is "gourd-resonated musical bow." It is monochordic and composed of a thin bowlike piece of wood that has one string of soft metal running from top to bottom and across a hollowed-out gourd that is placed against the belly and used as a resonance box. The metal string is plucked or struck with a small stick in one hand while the other hand holds a piece of dull glass or a stone between the string and the gourd and moves the gourd on and off the belly to create different sounds. See Silva, "Estórias da música em Angola," part 1, 15–20.

50. According to Mário Rui Silva, Bota Fogo was founded in 1951 and closed in 1953 to reopen again in 1956, "housing many Angolan revolutionaries." Silva, "Estórias da música em angola," part 4, 53.

51. According to Bittencourt, the name comes from the Brazilian club of the same name. *Estamos juntos*, 331.

52. Bettencourt, "Subsídio para o estudo sociológico," 119–21; Monteiro, *A família nos musseques*, 359–61.

53. Interviews with Albina Assis, January 17, 2002; Armando Correia de Azevedo, January 25, 2001 and September 11, 11, 2001; Barceló de Carvalho "Bonga," January 28, 2001; Alberto Jaime, December 4, 2001; and Efigénia Barros Mangueira Van Dunem, February 2, 2002, all in Luanda. See also pieces of Bittencourt's interviews with Adriano dos Santos in *Estamos juntos*, 330–32.

54. Tali, *Dissidências*, 1:219.

55. Messiant disaggregates the small (in numbers) but politically important colonial social category of assimilado in "Luanda," 171–76. She argues that the "new" assimilados are more identified with the rural areas and have a different social trajectory, generally though not always via the Protestant churches, than the "old" assimilados, who are descended from the nineteenth-century Luanda elites. Messiant argues that both were critical to nationalist organizing and politics.

56. Bettencourt, "Subsídio para o estudo sociológico," 95, and Mourão, "Configurações dos núcleos humanos," 206.

57. This was the language Mangueira and others used. It defines the middle class not in strict economic terms but in terms of a kind of consciousness. For a similar definition see West, *Rise of an African Middle Class*, 2. As Mangueira noted, many homes were occupied by single women with children who washed

clothes for a living so they could send their children to school. Alberto Jaime, who was raised by his mother, a market woman, also lived in Bairro Indigena and, like Efigénia, attended the São Paulo mission school.

58. Interview with Efigénia Barroso Mangueira Van Dunem, February 20, 2002, Luanda. A Register of Correspondence received at the Administrative Commission for Native Neighborhoods in Luanda, April 2, 1948–April 9, 1957, shows that of sixteen pieces of correspondence entered, all of which were requests for homes in "native neighborhoods," ten were made in general by the LNA and by Anangola for its members. Of the ten, six were made for women and four for men. Arquivo Histórico de Angola (Luanda), codice 5268, 16–4–6.

59. This is an instance of colonial architecture attempting to reshape African practices and of urbanized Africans resisting this attempt to Europeanize them while still taking advantage of opportunities like education.

60. See also Sebastião, *Dos campos*, 65. Sebastião's sisters-in-law lived with him and his wife in the musseque Rangel so that they could continue their education. They had trouble getting the coveted ID cards that would allow them access to the *liceu*, despite the fact that their father was a nurse who worked in the colonial system.

61. Bittencourt, *Estamos juntos*, 331. He mentions Catete, Golungo Alto, and Malanje.

62. Monteiro, *A família nos musseques*, 69.

63. *Fubeiros* comes from the word *fuba*, which is the milled corn or cassava used to make *funji*, a staple of the Angolan diet. *Fubeiros* were often lower-class Portuguese immigrants in Angola who lived in the musseques where they owned some of the few commercial establishments. They often exploited local populations with exorbitant prices, predatory lending schemes, and the sale of alcohol. *Fubeiros* often appear in literature about the musseques. At least one white nationalist, António Cardoso, was the son of a *fubeiro*. See Michel Laban, *Angola: Encontro com escritores* (Porto, Portugal: Fundação Eng. António de Almeida, 1991), 1:335.

64. "Trincheira firme" was a phrase popularized by President Agostinho Neto after independence. It was used in the slogan "Angola, Trincheira Firme da Revolução em África" to proclaim Angola as site of resistance to imperialism. Personal communication from Domingos Coelho, April 28, 2008.

65. Interview with Alberto Jaime, December 4, 2001, Luanda.

66. Amaral, *Luanda*, 100, 106–7.

67. Amaral, *Luanda*, 64.

68. Laban, *Mário Pinto de Andrade*, 32; Sebastião, *Dos campos*, 61; interviews with Rui Mingas, January 13, 2002, Luanda, and Carlos Alberto Pimentel, October 3, 2001, Benguela.

69. See Laban, *Mário Pinto de Andrade*, 55–56, and interview with Armando Correia de Azevedo, January 25, 2001, Luanda. Ingombotas was considered a historically Angolan neighborhood because it was here that some distinguished assimilado families (the Vieira Diases and the Van Dunems among others) lived until the mid-twentieth century. At that time, following the boom in coffee production and

profits, Portuguese purchased and/or repossessed the homes and lands occupied by Africans, razed them, and erected multistory buildings in their place.

70. Interview with Armando Correia de Azevedo, January 25, 2001, Luanda.

71. See Bittencourt on Bota Fogo in *Estamos juntos*, 330–32.

72. It is of more than just passing interest that women—grandmothers, aunts, and so forth, who were also Ribas's primary informants—were critical to the reproduction of cultural knowledge and the possibility of recuperating African cultural practices in urban areas in this period. Vieira Dias also noted several times that he learned "traditional" songs from his mother, aunts, sister, and grandmother. And José Oliveira de Fontes Pereira remembered that his mother served as master of the salon at *rebita* gatherings. See Fortunato, "José Oliveira de Fontes Pereira," 2.

73. Interview with Albina Assis, January 17, 2002, Luanda.

74. Interview with Dionísio Rocha, May 18, 1998, Luanda.

75. Valódia, "Das turmas," *Angolense*, August 10–17, 2002, 20.

76. Interview with Albina Assis, January 17, 2002, Luanda.

77. Interview with Albina Assis, January 17, 2002, Luanda. However, dances were different. Whether at Bota Fogo or the Liga, women could only attend when accompanied by brothers or cousins.

78. Both Assis and Mangueira, as well as Lourdes Van Dunem, who is a musician, recalled the restrictions and limitations placed on young women in the 1950s in terms of attending dances and parties. This issue is taken up in the next chapter.

79. Interview with Alberto Jaime, December 4, 2001, Luanda.

80. This was Anibel Melo, a highly regarded Angolan journalist and writer who was initially involved with the FNLA and later a member of the MPLA. Other staff members were likely imprisoned for being against the fascist Portuguese state. This did not necessarily make them anticolonialists, but they were nonetheless persecuted by the PIDE.

81. Referring to an earlier period, Mário Pinto de Andrade noted the important role that contact with newspapers had in politicizing some civil servants. This was the case for his uncles, who were typographers, and this gave his family access to news not available to others. See Laban, *Mário Pinto de Andrade*.

82. The palace was the seat of the colonial government.

83. This individual was Aristides Van Dunem, who was a childhood friend of Jaime's from the neighborhood. Van Dunem was consequently arrested and jailed for many years.

84. Interview with Alberto Jaime, December 12, 2001, Luanda.

85. Tereza, Engracia, and Lucrecia Cohen, Maria Mambo Café, Maria do Carmo, Maria Gama, Manuela da Palma, Elsa Almeida e Sousa, Emerciana Machado, and Nair Cruz were some of the other participants remembered by Assis, Mangueira, Padre Vicente, and Azevedo. PIDE reports from November 1963 include the following names: Silvia Maria Octário Belo, Manuele Maria Elsa de

Fátima Alouso de Palma, Judite Cirilo de Sá, Margarida Maria Lourenço, Efigénia Barros Magueira, Albina Faria de Assis, Graciete Bessa Victor, and Georgina Octávio Xavier Belo. IANTT-PIDE/DGS, DInf./1A, Processo no. 13.20.A/5 Grupo Feminino de Sta. Cecília, nt 1989, ff. 15, 16, 19–20. Gendered racial tension over the groups' constitution and direction is discussed in ff. 2, 7, 8, and 13–14.

86. Interview with Padre Vicente José Rafael, March 4, 2002, Luanda.

87. Many of these ex-seminary students were later members and leaders in all three independence movements and later political parties — FNLA, MPLA, and UNITA — and included members of Bota Fogo as well. Padre Vicente remembered men like N'zau Puna, Zé Belo, Paulo Tchipilica, Manuel Miranda, Tony Fernandes, and Rosário Neto.

88. See Didier Péclard's dissertation "État coloniale, missions chrétiennes et nationalisme en Angola" for a study of the relationship between religion and politics focused on the central plateau region.

89. Their forced exile followed the arrest of several other Catholic priests, including Conêgo Manuel Joaquim Mendes das Neves, a mixed-race from Golungo Alto who was the second in command in the Catholic Church in Angola, following the bishop. He was seen as an instigator of the February 4 attack on the prisons. He was highly respected in Luanda, where he had been president of the Liga and was a prominent cultural figure. See Laban, *Mário Pinto de Andrade*, 54–55, and interview with Carlos Alberto Pimentel, October 3, 2001, Luanda. See also Carlos Pacheco, *Repensar Angola* (Lisbon: Vega, 2000), 88–97. According to Padre Vicente, the following priests were also jailed shortly after the events in February 1961: Martin Samba, Lino Alves de Guimarães, Alfredo Osório Gaspar, and António Domingos Gaspar. Alexandre do Nascimento would later become the bishop of Luanda in independent Angola.

90. St. Cecilia is the patron saint of church music and musicians. See the New Advent Catholic Encyclopedia, http://www.newadvent.org/cathen/03471b.htm.

91. Interview with Efigénia Barroso Mangueira Van Dunem, February 20, 2002, Luanda.

92. Interview with Albina Assis, January 17, 2002, Luanda.

93. Deolinda Rodrigues, *Diário de um exílio sem regresso* and *Cartas de Langidila*.

94. Bittencourt's *Dos jornais às armas*, Pacheco's *MPLA*, Péclard's "État coloniale," Rocha's *Angola*, and Tali's *Dissidências*, among other works, have significantly complicated the MPLA's originary status in the history of nationalism in Angola.

CHAPTER 3 ⟿ DUELING BANDS AND GOOD GIRLS: GENDER AND MUSIC IN LUANDA'S MUSSEQUES, 1961–75

1. See, for example, Marcum, *Angolan Revolution*, 1:23: "Condemned to slum living, Luanda's Africans developed into a volatile black proletariat whose simmering discontent needed only organization and leadership to become a strong

political force." Also see Wheeler and Pélissier, Angola, 164. For a characterization of the masses and the distance of their experience from that of the MPLA leadership, see Birmingham, Frontline Nationalism, 36–37. For two notable exceptions see Messiant, "Luanda," 125–99, and Cahen, "Syndicalisme urbain," 200–79.

2. It is as incorrect to homogenize guerrilla experience as it is to homogenize the experience of Angolans who did not go off to fight. On different experiences of what constituted the *guerrilla*, even within the MPLA, see Messiant, "'Em Angola, até o passado é imprevisível,'" 803–59 (on the question at hand see 840). On the distinct sociological situations of the struggle in different MPLA military regions see Tali, *Dissidências*, vol. 1, chap. 5. On the differences between guerrilla fighters and people living in camps, see Brinkman, "War, Witches and Traitors."

3. Jean-Michel Mabeko Tali notes that the support of people from the musseques for the MPLA was decisive in allowing the movement to take control of Luanda against the forces of the FNLA and UNITA. See Tali, *Dissidências*, vol. 2, chaps. 9 and 10. On the semi-autonomous nature of the groups that arose to support the MPLA, see Heimer, *Decolonization Conflict in Angola*, 50–51, 58. Edmundo Rocha, following Christine Messiant, suggests that it was the tailors, catechists, nurses, pastors, drivers, and workers of the musseques who were critical to nationalist mobilization, both within the city and in the rural areas. Rocha, *Angola*, 76.

4. Ch. Didier Gondola analyzes a similar set of processes at work in colonial Leopoldville. He treats music as a political discourse and shows how an anticolonial stance was already present in the city's music well before political leaders began demanding political changes. Gondola, "Ata ndele . . . et l'independence vint: Musique, jeunes et contestation politique dans les capitales congolaises," in *Les jeunes en Afrique: La politique et la ville*, vol. 2, ed. Catherine Coquery-Vidrovitch et al. (Paris: L'Harmattan, 1992), 463–87.

5. Aside from changes in citizenship, access to school, and jobs, the people I spoke with noted such things as access to bank loans, which allowed them to purchase their homes, cars, and furniture. Interviews with Abelino "Manuel" Faria, March 19, 2002, and Carlos Lamartine, September 11, 4, 2001, both in Luanda.

6. Patrick Chabal points out that political representation was, even in this period, notoriously lacking in Portugal's African colonies. See Chabal et al., *A History of Postcolonial Lusophone Africa* (Bloomington: Indiana University Press, 2002), 31, 42–43.

7. Phyllis Martin's work on Brazzaville and Ch. Didier Gondola's work on Brazzaville and Kinshasa look at the same phenomenon. Martin follows the development of Congolese music in the interwar period in the African-owned clubs in Brazzaville's African neighborhoods and Gondola's work looks at the music, parties, and bar dancing of the two cities in the same period. See Gondola, "*Bisengo ya la joie*" and "*Ô Kisasa makambo!*" and Phyllis Martin, *Leisure and Society*.

8. Interview with Armando Correia de Azevedo, September 11, 2001, Luanda. "Confusion," in this context, had a positive spin. It was a sign of the fact that the music and the scene were extremely popular and exciting.

9. UNITA (União Nacional para a Independência Total de Angola) was formed in 1966 when Jonas Savimbi broke ranks with the FNLA. Its forces entered the guerrilla war and fought the Portuguese colonial troops in eastern Angola until they forged a secret alliance with those troops at some point in the early 1970s. See William Minter, *Operation Timber*. MacQueen describes UNITA as having had a "limited investment in the liberation war." Norrie MacQueen, *The Decolonization of Portuguese Africa*, 159.

10. Interview with Olga Baltazar, November 22, 2001, Luanda.

11. Interviews with Chico Coio, February 15, 2002, and Luís "Xabanu" Martins, November 21, 2001, both in Luanda.

12. Anderson, *Imagined Communities*, 24–25.

13. I am using "alternative" in contrast to "oppositional" following Robin D. G. Kelley, who borrows the term from Raymond Williams. See Kelley, *Race Rebels*, 47. See also Veit Erlmann on the creation of an alternative space by South African performers, who, he argues "created alternative worlds and cultural spaces in which blacks could rightfully reflect upon and direct their own destiny, free of white control." Erlmann, *African Stars: Studies in Black South African Performance* (Chicago: University of Chicago Press, 1991), 18. David Coplan discusses, in the context of urban South Africa and Sophiatown specifically, the development of African cultural autonomy in clubs and through music. This is eventually eroded, he argues, by increasingly strident apartheid policies that defined urban space as white and by white predatory capital in the form of producers and the recording industry, which both aided and constrained the production of African urban music from the 1950s on. See Coplan, *In Township Tonight!* I opt for the term "cultural sovereignty" because I find that it resonates with the explicitly political idea of "sovereignty," in which there is more obviously an implication of nation and state than with "autonomy."

14. Kelley, *Race Rebels*, 44.

15. For literature looking at the relationship between music and dance and nation, see Geiger, *TANU Women*; Macedo, *Ngola Ritmos*; Turino, *Nationalists*; and Askew, *Performing the Nation*. For earlier related work see Terence Ranger, *Dance and Society in Eastern Africa* (Berkeley: University of California, 1975), and Margaret Strobel, *Muslim Women in Mombasa, 1890–1975* (New Haven: Yale University Press, 1979). For work outside the African continent, see Hermano Vianna, *The Mystery of Samba: Popular Music and National Identity in Brazil* (Chapel Hill: University of North Carolina Press, 1999); Robin D. Moore, *Nationalizing Blackness: Afrocubanismo and Artistic Revolution in Havana, 1920–1940* (Pittsburgh: University of Pittsburgh Press, 1997); and Peter Wade, *Music, Race and Nation: Música Tropical in Colombia* (Chicago: University of Chicago Press, 2000).

16. Interview with Matemona Sebastião, February 27, 2002, Luanda.

17. Interview with Jorge Macedo, May 5, 2001, Luanda.

18. Interviews with Alberto Jaime, December 12, 2001, and Chico Coio, February 15, 2002, both in Luanda.

19. The musician Xabanu said that people went out to clubs to "forget" the ups and downs of day-to-day life and the violence of the colonial police that terrorized the musseques. Interview with Luís "Xabanu" Martins, November 21, 2001, Luanda. Armando Correia de Azevedo described culture in the period as an "escape tube." Interview with Armando Correia de Azevedo, January 25, 2001, Luanda.

20. McClintock, *Imperial Leather*, 353.

21. Ella Shohat and Robert Stam, *Unthinking Eurocentrism: Multiculturalism and the Media* (New York: Routledge, 1994), 103.

22. Aside from the formal interviews I conducted, I spoke informally with many women about the music of this period. All of them, from the receptionist at the Arquivo Histórico de Angola in Luanda, to the women who work in the music collection of the Rádio Nacional de Angola, to the president of the Republic's special advisor, Albina Assis, told me that the music from the late 1960s and early 1970s was authentically Angolan and linked to the struggle for independence.

23. In *Leisure and Society*, 135, Martin notes marked class differences in the club and music scene in Brazzaville in the interwar period. Ch. Didier Gondola looks at music in Kinshasa as a terrain of gendered struggle in which women are able to reshape power relations. See Gondola, "Popular Music, Urban Society, and Changing Gender Relations in Kinshasa, Zaire (1950–1990)," in *Gendered Encounters*, ed. Maria Grosz-Ngate and Omari H. Kokole (New York: Routledge, 1997), 65–85.

24. Bender, *Angola under the Portuguese*, chap. 6; Davidson, *Eye of the Storm*, 305–21; Dilolwa, *Contribuição à história económica*, 215, 218, 222; Franz-Wilhelm Heimer, "Education, Economics and Social Change in Rural Angola: The Case of the Cuima Region," in Heimer, *Social Change in Angola*, 111–44.

25. Benedict Schubert asserts that "members of the majority black population (not just those that were never touched by the war) said and say that they never got along as well as they did in that period [the 1960s]. It is a profound contradiction of the Angolan war whereby the colonial system, just as it was being attacked, got stronger in such a way that it corrected certain injustices and hardships and it transmitted to many—not just whites and *mestiços*—the impression that in Angola they were making a step towards progress." Benedict Schubert, *A guerra e as igrejas: Angola 1961–1991* (Lucerne: P. Schlettwein, 2000), 82.

26. Scholars of popular culture and African music, notably Karin Barber and Christopher Alan Waterman, have identified such an intermediate class as critical to the emergence of popular urban styles. See Barber, "Popular Arts in Africa," 14–15 and 29–30 and *Generation of Plays*, 2–3, and Waterman, *Jùjú: A Social History and Ethnography of an African Popular Music* (Chicago: University of Chicago Press, 1990), 9, 87.

27. Clarence-Smith, *Third Portuguese Empire*, 194.

28. Clarence-Smith, *Third Portuguese Empire*, 204–14, 217–18. The Portuguese oligopolies he singles out are Companhia União Fabril, Champalimaud, and Grupo Espírito Santo.

29. Pitcher, *Politics in the Portuguese Empire*, 253–57.
30. Pitcher, *Politics in the Portuguese Empire*, 203–4.
31. Clarence-Smith, *Third Portuguese Empire*, 216–18, and Heimer, *Decolonization Conflict in Angola*, 12–14.
32. This program was instituted in 1967. For details on this program see Reuver-Cohen and Jerman, *Secret Government Documents*, 21.
33. Schubert, *A guerra e as igrejas*, 81.
34. Bender, *Angola under the Portuguese*, 156–57.
35. Bender, *Angola under the Portuguese*, 194.
36. Clarence-Smith, *Third Portuguese Empire*, 218.
37. Heimer, *Decolonization Conflict in Angola*, 12–13, 21. Barros makes this claim in "Alguns aspectos da situação," though her work is based solely on colonial decrees.
38. Interview with Abelino "Manuel" Faria, March 19, 2002, Luanda.
39. Barros, "Alguns aspectos da situação," 50–60 and, from a critical perspective, Henrique Guerra, *Angola: Estrutura económica e classes sociais: Os últimos anos do colonialismo português em Angola* (Lisbon: Edições 70, 1979), 127, and Pitcher, *Politics in the Portuguese Empire*, 257.
40. Dilolwa put the number employed in industry throughout the territory in 1970 at 59,000. *Contribuição à história económica*, 297.
41. Clarence-Smith, "Review Article," 113–15; Guerra, *Angola*; Monteiro, *A família nos musseques*, 227; Heimer, *Decolonization Conflict in Angola*, 14.
42. Interview with Carlos Lamartine, September 11, 4, 2001, Luanda.
43. Guerra refers to this group as the African semi-bourgeoisie. In contrast to the petty bourgeoisie, who possess some capital and some means of production, the semi-bourgeois have only their salaries and their "culture." He puts their numbers at around 20,000 in 1970 for the country as a whole, although the majority would have lived in Luanda. Guerra, *Angola*, 122–23, 109–12, 158–59.
44. Clarence-Smith, *Third Portuguese Empire*, 216–17.
45. Cited in Mário António Fernandes de Oliveira, "Problemas essenciais do urbanismo no ultramar, estruturas urbanas de integração e convívio," *Boletim Geral do Ultramar* (Agência Geral do Ultramar, Lisbon), 1962, 14.
46. Interview with Correia de Azevedo, January 25, 2001, Luanda.
47. Ramiro Ladeiro Monteiro, "From Extended to Residual Family: Aspects of Social Change in the Musseques of Luanda," in Heimer, *Social Change in Angola*, 211–33.
48. Interviews with Chico Coio, February 15, 2002, Luanda; Carlos Lamartine, September 11, 4, 2001, Luanda; Carlos Alberto Pimentel, October 3, 2001, Benguela; Matemona Sebastião, February 27, 2002, Luanda; and Luís "Xabanu" Martins, November 21, 2001, Luanda.
49. Chico Coio said that after many years in a band he had to leave and go solo when he started a family because the band rehearsals took up too much time.

50. Matemona Sebastião remembered splitting up his band over an argument with their manager, who was not accepting gigs for them outside Luanda. He stopped playing for three months. The other band members begged him to rejoin them and they then set out on their own. Matemona opened a bank account for each band member and helped them manage their earnings. He also said that more than once he helped other band members pay the rent when they were without work outside of the band. Interview with Matemona Sebastião, February 27, 2002, Luanda. Lamartine also referred to bands that were managed by non-musicians and remembered that disagreements over management often led to changes in these frontmen.

51. Interviews with Chico Coio, February 15, 2002; Abelino "Manuel" Faria, March 19, 2002; Carlos Lamartine, September 11, 4, 2001; and Luís "Xabanu" Martins, November 21, 2001, all in Luanda.

52. Monteiro, A família nos musseques, 359.

53. Interview with Alberto Jaime, December 12, 2001, Luanda.

54. Interviews with Alberto Jaime, December 4 and 12, 2001, Luanda.

55. Interviews with Alberto Jaime, December 4 and 12, 2001, Luanda. Interviews with Armando Correia de Azevedo and Carlos Lamartine also confirmed this.

56. Tali, Dissidências, 2:30.

57. For other work on masculinities in Africa see Lindsay and Miescher, Men and Masculinities in Modern Africa. Particularly in relation to music and culture, see Gondola, "Popular Music," where he discusses Congolese music of the 1950s and 1960s as a male culture, and Mwenda Ntarangwi, Gender, Identity, and Performance: Understanding Swahili Cultural Realities through Song (Trenton, NJ: Africa World Press, 2003), chap. 6.

58. Interview with Carlos Alberto Pimentel, October 3, 2001, Benguela. See also Martins, "Os Kiezos."

59. For related work on rivalry or competition between bands and musicians, see Waterman, Jùjú, 22, and Erlmann, African Stars, 169.

60. See Laura Fair on a similar dynamic that moves in the other direction (from ngoma to soccer) in Zanzibar. Fair, Pastimes and Politics, 227, 239, 263.

61. Interview with Carlos Lamartine, August 9, 2001, Luanda.

62. Interview with Matumona Sebastião, February 27, 2002, Luanda.

63. The two companies were Cuca, the Belgian-owned beer company, and Textang, a textile factory. I was unsuccessful in my many attempts to reach Cuca to see whether they had any archives or information relating to recreational activities. Elias dia Kimueza mentioned musical and sports events at Textang, where he was briefly employed. Interview with Elias dia Kimuezu, May 11, 2001, Luanda.

64. Interestingly, two Angolans who benefited from such scholarships were Rui Mingas and Barceló de Carvalho "Bonga." Once in Portugal, both distinguished themselves as musicians as well as athletes.

65. Phyllis Martin mentions soccer player, musician, and politician Emmanuel Dadet and soccer player–musician Paul Kamba. Martin, *Leisure and Society*, 119, 143–45.

66. See Ruy Duarte de Carvalho, *Ana a Manda: Os filhos da rede* (Lisbon: Instituto de Investigação Científica Tropical, 1989), chap. 10, and David Birmingham, "Carnival at Luanda," *Journal of African History* 29 (1988): 93–103.

67. Interview with Alberto Jaime, December 12, 2001, Luanda.

68. For example, Armando Correia de Azevedo, Alberto Jaime, and "Santocas" all remembered that their parents or grandparents participated in carnival. Azevedo and Jaime participated or attended with their parents.

69. Fair talks about how soccer marked the life cycles of men in the interwar period in Zanzibar, and I would argue that music functioned in a similar way in Luanda. See Fair, *Pastimes and Politics*, 228.

70. The musician Carlitos Vieira Dias remembers learning how to read music there as a boy, and Matemona attended the school as a young man in the 1960s in order to refine his guitar playing. Jorge Macedo, a musician and ethnomusicologist, credits Assis with transferring Angolan rhythms to the guitar as early as the 1950s. Interviews with Alberto Teta Lando, May 15, 1998; Carlitos Vieira Dias, March 28, 2002; Matemona Sebastião, February 27, 2002; and Jorge Macedo, May 11, 2001, all in Luanda.

71. Xabanu learned to play and compose with Catarino Barber; Pimentel remembers seeking out Manuel Faria; and the guitarist "Duia," who is credited with having studied and taken up Congolese guitar styles, particularly the emphasis on the solo, trained Marito Arcanjo, who later became known for his skill at playing Franco-like guitar solos for the band Os Kiezos. See Fortunato, "A magnitude simbólica dos 'Kiezos.'"

72. Interview with Rui Mingas, January 13, 2002, Luanda. See too Ole's film *O Ritmo de N'gola Ritmos*, where such a Saturday afternoon lunch is recreated. The gendered division of the inner circle of musicians (all male) and outer circle of spectators (male and female, young and old) is marked. The film also has scenes where we see female singers like Belita Palma and Lourdes Van Dunem singing with the band.

73. Interview with Miguel Frances "Kituxi" Santos Rodolfo, April 17, 2002, Luanda.

74. Jomo Fortunato, in "A música tradicional," 1, associates the *turmas* with carnival. "Liceu" Vieira Dias also referred to the *turmas* but suggested that they were groups of men who gathered at night after work to play.

75. Valódia, "Das turmas," 21.

76. Martin also notes the importance of notoriety for musicians, as remuneration was often negligible. Martin, *Leisure and Society*, 145, 147.

77. Interviews with Carlos Alberto Pimentel, October 3, 2001, Benguela; Matemona Sebastião, February 27, 2002, Luanda; Chico Coio, February 15, 2002, Luanda; and Luís "Xabanu" Martins, November 21, 2001, Luanda.

78. Interviews with Alberto Jaime, December 12, 2001, and Abelino "Manuel" Faria, March 19, 2002, both in Luanda.

79. Interview with Luís "Xabanu" Martins, November 21, 2001, Luanda.

80. Interview with Chico Coio, February 15, 2002, Luanda. An extended analysis of this quote opens the epilogue.

81. Interview with Carlos Lamartine, September 4, 2001, Luanda.

82. Monteiro commented on changing mores. We must keep in mind, however, that male heads of households were his primary informants. "It used to be that a young woman would not dare to go out at night and dating was undertaken with the knowledge and oversight of parents. Today, they go to parties at night with the greatest naturalness and 'secret dating' is the current practice." Monteiro, A família nos musseques, 182.

83. I do not want to create the impression that these young men were overly cruel and insensitive. It is important to remember that, for the most part, club attendees and the musicians themselves were quite young (late teens and early twenties), and love was largely still an experimental and gamelike affair.

84. Interview with Chico Coio, February 15, 2002, Luanda.

85. Gondola, "Popular Music," 72.

86. See chapter 4 for a more detailed discussion of how women figure in song lyrics.

87. Interviews with Carlos Lamartine, September 11, 4, 2001, Luanda; Carlos Alberto Pimentel, October 3, 2001, Benguela; and Luís "Xabanu" Martins, November 21, 2001, Luanda.

88. Interview with Luís "Xabanu" Martins, November 21, 2001, Luanda. The lyrics to the band Africa Show's song "As Meninas de Hoje" are one indication that young women were sexually proactive. Jose Luandino Vieira's book Nosso musseque presents a female character, Toneta, who makes and breaks sexual unions as she pleases, and Jacques dos Santos's book ABC do Bê Ó, includes both the fictional depiction of young prostitutes and stories of some of Bairro Operário's famed madames. On prostitution as a way of establishing oneself socially and financially, see Luise White, The Comforts of Home: Prostitution in Colonial Nairobi (Chicago: University of Chicago Press, 1990).

89. Interview with Carlos Lamartine, September 3, 2001, Luanda. Coplan notes a similar sentiment in urban South Africa and attributes the association of music and social deviance to the emergence of a Christian social morality among mission-schooled Africans. See Coplan, In Township Tonight, 175–76.

90. This may have had to do in part with the fact that several Portuguese-owned clubs in the city had dancing girls that did striptease or cabaret shows. Pimentel told me this and then noted that "at our parties the girls just sang and danced." The musseques, particularly Bairro Operário and Marçal, which were also the site of numerous clubs, were known for prostitution. See dos Santos, ABC do Bê Ó, especially 243–46, and Monteiro, A família nos musseques, 393–98. When the main site of musical production and consumption in the musseque moved

from backyard parties to more public clubs this caused some tension for women. Interview with Carlos Alberto Pimentel, October 3, 2001, Benguela.

91. Monteiro, A família nos musseques, 87, and Monteiro, "From Extended to Residual Family," 216.

92. Santos noted that her family was not at all pleased when she planned to marry a musician, but they eventually acquiesced. While this seems to contradict my argument I think it is a result of the very complex and agitated social scene of mid-twentieth-century Luanda, where the old-line *mestiço* aristocracy was displaced from the power center as they lost their jobs and neighborhoods to Portuguese immigrants and where a new generation of African families was able to establish itself. Santos's parents lived in the musseque Marçal but she grew up in her godparents' home in the baixa of the city; her godmother's sister was the highly regarded singer Belita Palma. Santos's ex-husband (who is a half-brother of Lamartine) came from a family of civil servants and his father was one of the founders of the Liga Nacional Africana. Nonetheless, his father was also a man with many wives, and Santos's family may have feared that, as Angolans like to say, "the son of a fish is a fish." On the other hand, his family was well established and musicians were earning a degree of respect for themselves, as Coio's comments suggest.

93. Interview with Ricardina "Dina" Carvalho Santos, April 6, 2001, Luanda.

94. Translated from Kimbundu to Portuguese by Maria Francisca Jacinta of RNA.

95. Olga Baltazar engaged in a similar discourse in a casual conversation we had before our interview when I asked her about a woman associated with carnival and backyard parties. She dismissed the woman's importance and called her a prostitute.

96. Advayo Vunge, "Lourdes Van Dúnem: Sou a personificação da contradição," *Figuras & Negócios*, September 30, 2000. *Tia* means aunt and is used here in the honorific sense to suggest she is the elder female of Angolan music. But given the fact that some women cast aspersions on her character, I wonder to what extent the honorific is also a domesticating or taming strategy.

97. The Van Dunem family is one of the largest and most well known of the old Luanda aristocracy. Many family members still exercise economic, political, and cultural power in present-day Angolan society.

98. My husband recalls his mother and her friends referring to Tia Lourdes as a *gaiteira*, a woman who speaks her mind freely and does what she wants. The term has a negative charge to it, however. A woman with a public presence is open to commentary on her behavior in a way that men are not.

99. Interview with Alberto Jaime, December 12, 2001, Luanda.

100. Interview with Alberto Jaime, December 12, 2001, Luanda.

101. Interviews with Albina Assis, January 17, 2002, and Efigénia Barroso Mangueira Van Dunem, February 2, 2002, both in Luanda.

102. Interviews with Olga Baltazar, November 22, 2001, and Carlos Lamartine, September 4, 2001, both in Luanda.

103. See Tali, *Dissidências*, vol. 2.

104. Interview with Alberto Teta Lando, May 15, 1998, Luanda.

CHAPTER 4 ⇝ "NGONGO JAMI" (MY SUFFERING):
LYRICS, DAILY LIFE, AND SOCIAL SPACE, 1956–74

1. An article in Anangola's *Jornal de Angola* (June 19, 1958, 7) notes that this was the band's common practice: "Vieira Dias, before each performance by his group, would explain the story of each composition so that everyone would integrate and understand perfectly the melody and the rhythm."

2. Interview with Amadeu Amorim and José Maria dos Santos, April 4, 2001, Luanda. Another similar story also circulates in popular memory and symbolizes the utter emptiness of lusotropicalist claims and the small-mindedness of Portuguese settlers. In this story the members of Ngola Ritmos are literally booed off the stage when they sing and are told to "go back to the bush." This story appears in dos Santos, *ABC do Bê Ó*, 226, and Silva, "Estórias da música em Angola," part 4, 52, and was repeated by many, many people. Amorim remembered a similar reception among the African elite at the Liga, who looked down on the use of Kimbundu. When the band sang there in the mid-1950s, Amorim remembered, members of the audience bowed their heads in disapproval. See Amadeu Amorim, interview by Drumond Jaime and Helder Barber, *Foi Há Vinte Anos*, Rádio Nacional de Angola, 1995.

3. Interviews with Abelino "Manuel" Faria, March 19, 2002; Alberto Jaime, December 12, 2001; Carlos Lamartine, September 4, 2001; and António Sebastião Vicente "Santocas," November 26, 2001, all in Luanda.

4. Five of these seven songs were translated from Kimbundu to Portuguese by Maria Francisca Jacinta of Rádio Nacional de Angola in Luanda in April 2002.

5. Interview with Carlos Pimentel, October 3, 2001, Benguela.

6. Interview with Amadeu Amorim and José Maria dos Santos, April 4, 2001, Luanda.

7. Interview with Albina Assis, January 17, 2002, Luanda.

8. Coplan also notes this kind of social critique and solidarity in the music of urban South Africa in the 1950s. See Coplan, *In Township Tonight*, 165.

9. Bob White likewise argues that romantic songs, in the Zairean repertoire of the same period, are a demonstration of cosmopolitanism or "worldliness." See White, "Congolese Rumba," 674.

10. On at least two occasions I attended musical events where figures from this generation played and where the main musical fare was European and American music from the 1960s and 1970s. At one of Luanda's most elite clubs, Xavarotti (which was the only place to hear live music when I first went to Angola in 1997), the mike was passed around to various musicians in attendance in the audience. They sang music by Frank Sinatra, Nat King Cole, and Roberto Carlos, a famous Brazilian singer, while audience members sang along. The club's owner, Mello Xavier, had been in a rock band in the 1960s. Today he is one of Angola's wealthiest entrepreneurs. Likewise, when Sinatra passed away in 1998, Dionísio Rocha dedicated one of his radio broadcasts to Sinatra's music and legacy. Many of these

folks are the same ones who pioneered and championed semba and its distinctively Angolan sound.

11. In earlier periods Kimbundu had actually been the lingua franca of the city, spoken by African, Portuguese, and Brazilian residents alike. Many musicians and cultural producers heard Kimbundu around them though they did not grow up speaking it. And Kimbundu was certainly spoken in the city, just not by the elites from the 1940s on.

12. The *kissange* is a thumb piano typically constructed with metal strips on a wooden box or base. In Zimbabwe it is called the *mbira*.

13. See Erlmann, *African Stars:* "The presence of diverse and sometimes heterogeneous symbolic levels through the use of several communicative channels such as dress, choreography, melodic and harmonic structure, and principles of internal group structure enabled migrants to metaphorically define a space in which their survival could best be organized" (174).

14. In this way, Angolan musicians created a cosmopolitan sound. As Turino defines it, cosmopolitan refers to "objects, ideas, and cultural positions that are widely diffused throughout the world and yet are specific only to certain portions of the populations within given countries. . . . [Cosmopolitanism] has to be realized in specific locations and in the lives of actual people. It is thus always localized, and will be shaped by and somewhat distinct in each locale. Cosmopolitan cultural formations are therefore always simultaneously local and translocal." Turino, *Nationalists*, 7.

15. Macedo, *Ngola Ritmos*, 17.

16. Askew, *Performing the Nation*, 23.

17. Interview with Amadeu Amorim and José Maria dos Santos, April 4, 2001, Luanda. See Silva, "Estórias da música em Angola," part 4, 52, and photos in dos Santos, *ABC do Bê Ó*, 226–27.

18. Interview with Raul Indipwo, August 10, 2001, Luanda. See also the album covers for *Hino à Paz* and *Pata Pata*.

19. Interview with Raul Indipwo, August 10, 2001, Luanda.

20. Interview with Matemona Sebastião, February 27, 2002, Luanda.

21. Barber, *Generation of Plays*, 11.

22. Interview with Amadeu Amorim and José Maria dos Santos, April 4, 2001, Luanda.

23. Interview with Elias dia Kimuezu, May 11, 2001, Luanda.

24. Conversation with Maria Francisca Jacinta, April 16, 2002, Luanda.

25. Fortunato, "A magnitude simbólica dos 'Kiezos.'" The same story is also recounted in "Os Kiezos: Um agrupamento emblemático no panorama musical nacional," *Angolense*, March 9–16, 2002, 23.

26. In discussing "traditional" music, Nlandu Mila Sebastião asserts that dance and music are closely integrated both in ritual performances and in more quotidian forms of performance. See Nlandu Mila Sebastião, "Música angolana de tradição oral," *Jornal de Angola*, January 6, 2002, 5.

27. Dos Santos, *ABC do Bê Ó*, 27.
28. Interview with Albina Assis, January 17, 2002, Luanda.
29. Dos Santos, *ABC do Bê Ó*, 167.
30. This testifies to the fact that this was preclub dancing in sandy backyards.
31. I am grateful to Augusto Cesar Wilson de Carvalho for this translation.
32. *Kisomba* is a Kimbundu word meaning party. Luandans told me that the style of dance and the music evolved in the 1980s and was influenced by the sound of zouk music from the Caribbean, and particularly by the band Kassav. During this period in the civil war curfews were common and so *farristas* (partiers) adapted by beginning parties later at night and remaining there until the wee hours. *Kuduro* is a combination—*ku* comes from the Portuguese word *cú* for ass and *duro* is Portuguese for hard, hence "hard ass." Insofar as *kuduro* has emerged from the musseques and chronicles daily life, seeks out "traditional" sounds, and is produced using the most accessible means (you can no longer buy instruments in Angola and so turntables and mixing boards have taken over), it is heir to semba. Both *kisomba* and *kuduro* continue the practice of making disgrace danceable.
33. Interview with Alberto Jaime, December 4, 2001, Luanda.
34. Dos Santos, *ABC do Bê Ó*, 265–70.
35. Abelino "Manuel" Faria remembered that by the early 1960s he could purchase Japanese stereos. He had three of them, plus speakers, an amplifier, and a huge collection of music, and could play at two parties at once. Interview with Abelino "Manuel" Faria, March 19, 2002, Luanda.
36. It is worth remembering here Xabanu's comment about the club scene (chapter 3), in which he indicated that everyone at the club "knew" him because he was a musician but that he did not know everyone at the club.
37. Jacques dos Santos includes Costa in his book and has made her a part of his cultural organization Chá de Caxinde. A woman I interviewed who was prominent in the 1950s cultural scene referred to Costa as a prostitute when I asked whether she knew her.
38. Interview with Amadeu Amorim and José Maria dos Santos, April 4, 2001. See also Macedo, "Fontinhas," 20–21.
39. "Angola Avante Revolução" was written just after independence by the writer and jurist Rui Monteiro and the musicians Carlos Lamartine and Rui Mingas.
40. Marcelo Bittencourt notes that "Muxima" was initially the opening song for the radio show *Angola Combatente* but it was replaced by the MPLA's anthem. Bittencourt, *Estamos juntos*, 309.
41. Interview with Amadeu Amorim and José Maria dos Santos, April 4, 2001, Luanda.
42. René Pélissier, *História das campanhas de Angola: Resistência e revoltas 1845–1941* (Lisbon: Editorial Estampa, 1997), 51.
43. Mário Rui Silva, *Chants d'Angola: "Pour Demain . . .,"* compact disc (Paris: Alliance Française, 1994), liner notes, 5.

44. See the Patron Saints Index, http://www.catholic-forum.com/saints/sainta03.htm.

45. Lyrics from Silva, *Chants d'Angola*," liner notes, 5. Translated into Portuguese by Madalena Afonso and then into English by the author.

46. A slightly different version of this song was also part of Ngola Ritmos's repertoire.

47. See Silva, *Chants d'Angola*, liner notes, 3. See also Sebastião Coelho, *Angola: História e estórias da informação* (Luanda: Executive Center, 1999), 152.

48. "Vapor" here refers to the steamboats used at the time. According to Mário Rui Silva, in the 1850s there were steamboats that traveled between Luanda and Dondo, in the immediate interior. They were owned by an Angolan business and run by an American captain.

49. Translated from Kimbundu to Portuguese by Maria Francisca Jacinta of RNA. 15–17 April 2002, Luanda.

50. See Macedo, "Fontinhas," 20–21.

51. Interview with Amadeu Amorim and José Maria dos Santos, April 4, 2001, Luanda.

52. Translated from Kimbundu to Portuguese by Maria Francisca Jacinta of RNA. "Contract" in this song refers to "contract labor," which was actually forced labor for the government or was "contracted" by the government for foreign companies working in Angola. In the early years of colonization many Angolans were sent to São Tomé to work on the farms there. Later on, forced labor was used to produce cotton in the colony or to build roads. This labor was not remunerated and workers were poorly fed, overworked, and often separated from their families for months at a time.

53. Macedo, "Fontinhas," 20.

54. Domingos Coelho did not remember Luanda having Angolan taxi drivers in this period but thought it might have been different in Benguela and Lobito. E-mail message to author, September 13, 2007.

55. Clarence-Smith, *Third Portuguese Empire*, 216.

56. Movimento Democrático de Angola, *Massacres em Luanda* (Lisbon: África Editora, 1974), 43–49. A radio listener sent a letter to the station Voz de Angola complaining that had it been black taxi drivers they would have been rounded up and jailed immediately. See IANTT-PIDE/DGS, DInf./1A, Processo no. 15.33.A/1, p. 26.

57. In the March 27, 1971, issue of *Notícia* there was a brief letter to the editor from a man who was traveling with his wife and son to the Dona Amália warehouse in Rangel to shop. The taxi driver refused to enter Rangel on a street that wasn't paved, claiming that he had once had a tire explode when he drove in the musseque.

58. Interview with Armando Correia de Azevedo, September 11, 2001, Luanda.

59. See Martins, "Os Kiezos"; Fortunato, "A magnitude simbólica dos 'Kiezos'"; Altino Matos, "Adolfo Coelho ainda tem voz para cantar," *Jornal de Angola*,

March 26, 2001, 17. Matos, based on a conversation with Adolfo Coelho, one of the band's vocalists and their *dikanza* player, says that it was Úbia who wrote the music.

60. Interview with Carlos Lamartine, September 4, 2001, Luanda. See also Martins, "Os Kiezos."

61. Interview with Ricardina "Dina" Carvalho Santos, April 6, 2002, Luanda.

62. Fortunato, "A magnitude simbólica dos 'Kiezos.'"

63. Translated from Kimbundu to Portuguese by Maria Francisca Jacinta of RNA. The transcription of this last line is cited in "Os Kiezos" by Martins, who got the lyrics from the band. It is slightly different than the spelling of the line by Maria Francisca Jacinta, but when read while listening to the song it sounds correct.

64. From the compact disc *Angola 70's: 1972–1973*, compiled by Ariel de Bigault (Paris: Budamusique, 1999), liner notes, 19.

65. Many thanks to Derek Peterson, who suggested such an interpretation.

66. Bittencourt, *Estamos juntos*, 318.

67. Interviews with Alberto Teta Lando, May 7, 1998; Armando Correia de Azevedo, January 25, 2001; Jorge Macedo, May 11, 2001; Raul Indipwo, August 10, 2001; Alberto Jaime, December 4, 2001; and Rui Mingas, January 13, 2002, all in Luanda. "Liceu" Vieira Dias is also said to have learned to love music at the feet of his aunt and his mother. See also Fortunato, "José de Oliveira Fontes Pereira," and "Joãozinho Morgado: A melódia dos tambores," *Jornal de Angola*, April 7, 2002, 4–5.

68. *Angola 70's: 1972–1973*, liner notes, 24.

69. *Angola 70's: 1972–1973*, liner notes, 24.

70. Translated from Kimbundu to Portuguese by Maria Francisca Jacinta of RNA.

71. Although Urbano de Castro is one of the figures most associated with this period, his music is technically not semba but rumba. See Venâncio, "O 'semba' em discussão," 16.

72. Fabian, "Popular Culture in Africa," 327.

73. *Angola 70's: 1974–1978*, compiled by Ariel de Bigault (Paris: Budamusique, 1999), liner notes, 18.

74. *Angola 70's: 1974–1978*, liner notes, 18.

75. Translated from Kimbundu to Portuguese by Maria Francisca Jacinta of RNA.

76. Erlmann, *African Stars*, 5.

77. Barber, "Popular Arts in Africa," 15.

78. Both Efigénia Mangueira and Albina Assis, who had been involved in Bota Fogo and Santa Cecília, emphasized the "recreational" aspect of Maxinde, which they set in opposition to the "political" nature of Bota Fogo.

79. The *Boletim Oficial* contains requests by individuals and associations for the license required to open an establishment. Many clubs also had a bar and

small restaurant, which meant they required a license from the Hotels and Tourism Board.

80. Interviews with Chico Coio, February 15, 2002, and Luís "Xabanu" Martins, November 21, 2001, both in Luanda.

81. The privately owned clubs most often mentioned were Manuel Faria's Kudissanga Kwamakamba, Lomilhão Batalha's Giro Giro, and Faria's Salão dos Anjos.

82. The only exception was Marítimo da Ilha, which was on the island. But this was probably a result of the fact that island's population was always considered by the colonial government and its ethnologists as "different." Even if neighborhoods on the island had conditions similar to those in the musseques, with little or no sanitation, electricity, and running water, they were somehow seen as not quite so urban since the island's fishing villages had existed since before the Portuguese arrived there.

83. These included Boate Tamar on the Island, the Cine Nacional, Cine de Restauração, Miramar, Cine Tropical, and o Avis.

84. Monteiro, A família nos musseques, 357–60. Specifically, the clubs were registered with the office of Provincial Inspection for Physical Education.

85. Of the four, three were official clubs: Sporting Club do Rangel, Sporting Club de Maxinde, and Marítimo da Ilha. The one nonofficial club that was frequently mentioned in the interviews was Las Palmas do Prenda. All were described as clubs with a vital role in the club scene.

86. Monteiro, A família nos musseques, 361. The men and women I interviewed mentioned the following clubs as places they attended or that were popular for music and dancing: in B.O., Ambrizetes, Ginásio Futebol Clube, and Grupo Baião; in Sambizanga, o Bragues, Kudissanga Kwamakamba, and Salão dos Anjos; in São Paulo, Centro Social de São Paulo and União Desportivo de São Paulo; in Rangel, Sporting do Rangel and Salão Vermelho; in Marçal, Bom Jesus, Giro Giro, Luar das Rosas, Salão Caravana, and Sporting Club de Maxinde; on the Island, Marítimo da Ilha; in Prenda, Las Palmas; in Bairro Cemetério, later Bairro Popular, Os Perdidos; in Samba, Onze Bravos; in Bairro Correia, Salão Azul, Maria Esquerquenhas, Calão da Xica, and Salão de Feira de Catetão.

87. Interviews with Abelino "Manuel" Faria, March 19, 2002; Dionísio Rocha, May 18, 1998; and Carlos Lamartine, September 4, 2001, all in Luanda.

88. Interview with Dionísio Rocha, May 18, 1998, Luanda. This was in distinct contrast to the situation in Luanda in 1997 when I arrived. All parties and discos had DJs and played recorded music. Live music was rare and difficult to find.

89. Interview with Matemona Sebastião, February 27, 2002, Luanda.

90. A note in the PIDE file on the musseque Prenda notes one such show and Montez's popularity with the local community. See IANTT-PIDE/DGS, DInf./1A, Processo 15.12.D/1 Muçeque Prenda, nt 2086; PIDE, inf. no. 1032/64 BIR, 7/6/65 Ass: exibição folclorico realizada no MP em 6/6/65, p. 211.

91. "Música: Luiz Montez," Afro-Letras: Revista de Artes, Letras e Ideias 1, no. 1 (March 1999): 18.

92. Interview with Armando Correia de Azevedo, September 11, 2001, Luanda.

93. Interview with Armando Correia de Azevedo, September 11, 2001, Luanda.

94. I am drawing here on Shohat and Stam, *Unthinking Eurocentrism*, in their discussion of film viewing: "The cinema's institutional ritual of gathering a community—spectators who share a region, language, and culture—homologizes, in a sense, the symbolic gathering of the nation. Anderson's sense of the nation as 'horizontal comradeship' evokes the movie audience as a provisional 'nation' forged by spectatorship" (103).

95. Karin Barber, "Preliminary Notes on Audiences in Africa," *Africa* 76, no. 3 (1997): 355.

96. Interview with António Sebastião Vicente "Santocas," November 26, 2001, Luanda.

97. Fortunato, "A música tradicional," 1.

CHAPTER 5: RADIOS, TURNTABLES, AND VINYL:
TECHNOLOGY AND THE IMAGINED COMMUNITY, 1961–75

1. Waterman notes a similar process at work in the spread of jùjú music throughout Nigeria and the development of a pan-Yoruba identity. Waterman, *Jùjú*, 12, 92–93.

2. The destruction of the documentation of all the record companies formerly in Angola has made it difficult to establish how successful they were as businesses or how many records they produced in the period under study. Thus far, my attempts to contact former owners and employees have not been successful. Marcus Power has argued that in Mozambique "broadcasting became central to the capitalist development of the colony." See Power, "*Aqui Lourenço Marques!!* Radio Colonization and Cultural Identity in Colonial Mozambique, 1932–74," *Journal of Historical Geography* 26, no. 4 (2000): 605. Writing on the history of radio in Angola, Júlio Mendes Lopes states: "Two aspects would mark the origin of radio broadcasting in Angola: in the first place, the improvement in the colony's economic situation, with positive entries in its balance of payments situation that was reflected in commercial activities, and in the second instance, the influx of Portuguese. This allowed for the consolidation of the economic, political, military, and administrative structures existing in the territory." Lopes, "Contribuição à história de radiodifusão em Angola" (Luanda: Rádio Nacional de Angola, 2000), 5. As I mention, state use of the radio followed local entrepreneurial initiative, and Diamang, the diamond concession, had its own radio transmitter and station. Certainly the development of radio was linked to capitalist development in the late colonial period but how, to what extent, and what the effects were remains to be investigated.

3. On *Angola Combatente*, see Lopes, "Contribuição." According to Jean-Michel Mabeko Tali, the broadcasts from Brazzaville and Dar were the most consistent and enduring. E-mail message to author, December 25, 2002. *Angola Libre* was discussed in my interview with Dionísio Rocha, June 12, 1998, Luanda.

4. Joy Elizabeth Hayes, *Radio Nation: Communication, Popular Culture, and Nationalism in Mexico 1920–1950* (Tucson: University of Arizona Press, 2000), 23.

5. Hayes, *Radio Nation*, 20.

6. Debra Spitulnik, "Mediated Modernities: Encounters with the Electronic in Zambia," *Visual Anthropology Review* 14, no. 2 (Fall/Winter 1998): 68.

7. S. Coelho, *Angola*, 240–41. See figure 5.1 in this volume for the dispersal of stations throughout the country.

8. Lopes, "Contribuição," 3.

9. D. P. Monteiro also points to this as a significant moment in radio's history in Angola in "Apontamentos para a história de radiodifusão de Angola," http://www.geocities.com/dpmonteiro/radioangolahistoria.htm (see the subsection on Radio Clube de Huambo).

10. S. Coelho, *Angola*, 124.

11. D. P. Monteiro, "Apontamentos," subsection on Voz de Luanda.

12. Carlos Alberto Pimentel, for example, was offered a job in the early 1970s at the Benguela Radio Club because local listeners were fans of his radio programs broadcast from the Kwanza Sul Radio Club. Though from Huambo, Sebastião Coelho was hired in 1951 as chief of production services and principal announcer for the Moçamedes Radio Club, making him the first white Angolan to hold such a position. He also established a studio in Luanda after being released from prison for activities in Huambo and prohibited from living there. See S. Coelho, *Angola*. Shows produced at the studio Voz de Luanda (Voice of Luanda) were broadcast throughout the country via the Commercial Radio of Lubango. Interview with Maria Luisa Fançony, October 16, 2001, Luanda.

13. Lopes, in "Contribuição," 4, says it was 1955, while Monteiro claims it was 1953.

14. Interview with Albina Assis, January 17, 2002, Luanda. Jorge Macedo also mentions the importance of Radio Moscow as an alternative news source. See *Ngola Ritmos*, 9.

15. Interview with Carlitos Vieira Dias, March 18, 2002, Luanda.

16. IANTT-PIDE/DGS, DInf./1A, Processo no. 14.26.A Postos Emissores Clandestinos, f91 and f12 respectively.

17. Phyllis Martin notes that this transmitter was the most powerful on the continent and was established by General de Gaulle during World War II. See Martin, *Leisure and Society*, 148. Christopher Waterman notes the popularity of Congolese music played on the radio in urban Nigeria: "By the late 1950s, Congolese guitar-band music, strongly influenced by the Cuban rumba and mambo, had become the craze in Lagos, its popularity sustained in part by the clear broadcasts from Brazzaville." Waterman, *Jùjú*, 93.

18. Pereira Nunes, "Inquéritos socio-económicos," 22.

19. Waterman, *Jùjú*, 93. See also interviews with Abelino "Manuel" Faria, March 19, 2002; António Sebastião Vicente "Santocas," November 22, 2001; and Luís "Xabanu" Martins, November 21, 2001, all in Luanda.

20. Monteiro, A família nos musseques, 277.

21. Debra Spitulnik, "Mobile Machines and Fluid Audiences: Rethinking Reception through Zambian Radio Culture," in *Media Worlds: Anthropology on New Terrain*, ed. Faye D. Ginsburg, Lila Abu-Lughod, and Brian Larkin (Berkeley: University of California Press, 2002), 339.

22. Monteiro, A família nos musseques, 368–71.

23. Monteiro, A família nos musseques, 379–80.

24. Monteiro, A família nos musseques, 371.

25. IANTT-PIDE/DGS, DInf./1A, Processo no. 14.26.A Postos Emissores Clandestinos, f12.

26. IANTT-PIDE/DGS, DInf./1A, Processo no. 14.26.A Postos Emissores Clandestinos, f22.

27. IANTT-PIDE/DGS, DInf./1A, Processo no. 15.33.A1 Emissora Oficial de Angola, f231–32.

28. IANTT-PIDE/DGS, DInf./1A, Processo no. 15.33.A1 Emissora Oficial de Angola, f318–19.

29. Interview with Holden Roberto, August 9, 2005, Luanda.

30. For another example see Eduarda, "O musseque e as suas gentes": "In the musseques life is lived on the basis of happiness. Radios are turned on from 6 in the morning until midnight! And on the weekends the music never stops" (18).

31. António José Garcia da Silva, "Dedo na Ferida," *Notícia*, June 22, 1968.

32. This sentiment was echoed in a PIDE note that likewise referred to "Congomania" but noted its decline in the wake of successful programming by the Voz de Angola. See IANTT-PIDE/DGS, DInf./1A, Processo no. 15.33.A1 Emissora Oficial de Angola, f465.

33. Interview with Luís "Xabanu" Martins, November 21, 2001, Luanda.

34. Interview with Jorge Macedo, May 11, 2001, Luanda.

35. Bob W. White argues similarly for Congo-Leopoldville relative to Afro-Cuban music: "It provided urban Congolese with an alternative to a particular form of cosmpolitanism—Belgian colonialism—that was strict and stoic if not cruel and in many ways anti-cosmopolitan." See White, "Congolese Rumba," 678. Meredith Terretta points to the ways in which nationalism and Pan-Africanism are not mutually exclusive but, rather, mutually reinforcing. See Terretta, "Nationalists Go Global: From Cameroonian (UPC) Village *Maquisards* to Pan-African Freedom Fighters" (paper presented at the Equatorial African Workshop, University of Wisconsin-Madison, October 14, 2006).

36. Interview with António Sebastião Vicente "Santocas," November 22, 2001, Luanda.

37. Conversation with António Adão Paulo, Division Head, Center for Historical Documentation and Investigation, MPLA National Headquarters, Luanda, April 2001.

38. Interview with Abelino "Manuel" Faria, March 19, 2002, Luanda.

39. Many thanks to Todd Cleveland for sharing his interview material and an article from Diamang's former employees magazine with me. His interviews

were conducted with former mineworkers in late 2004 and 2005 in Dundo, Lunda Norte.

40. Interview with Alberto Jaime, December 4, 2001, Luanda. Manuel Pedro Pacaviva was an MPLA activist and Governor of Kwanza Norte Province in 2001.

41. Reuver-Cohen and Jerman, *Secret Government Documents*, 95–96, 99.

42. Transcriptions of broadcasts on Radio Tanzania criticize U.S. and South African involvement with the Portuguese, talk about liberated zones administered by the MPLA, and encourage Portuguese soldiers to desert and fight fascism. IANTT-PIDE/DGS, DInf./1A, Processo no. 15.29/B Radio Tanzania, ff10–11, 28–30, 34–36, 38–41.

43. Marga Holness, who has a small collection of transcribed radio programs broadcast from Tanzania between 1968 and 1970, said that the programs were generally only fifteen minutes long. E-mail message to author, October 23, 2003.

44. IANTT-SCCIA, PdI #190, U.I. cx. 260, f. 62.

45. Interview with Albina Assis, January 17, 2002, Luanda.

46. In *A Dying Colonialism*, Frantz Fanon discusses the radical role of radio in the Algerian anticolonial struggle. As in Angola, it was not just the news being broadcast by the nationalist movements that was interesting, but the ways in which people listened and how they used radio. See Fanon, *A Dying Colonialism* (New York: Monthly Review Press, 1965), chap. 2, "This Is the Voice of Algeria."

47. IANTT-PIDE/DGS/Del. de Angola, Proc. 14.19.A/1, NT 2045, f55. Bittencourt argues that instructions on how to construct bombs and conduct insurrection had little effect. Bittencourt, *Estamos juntos*, 345.

48. Interview with Luís "Xabanu" Martins, November 21, 2001, Luanda.

49. IANTT-PIDE/DGS, DInf./1A, Proc. 14.19.A/1: Emissoras Estrangeiras, nt 2045, f3.

50. IANTT-SCCIA, PdI #190, U.I. cx. 260, p. 30.

51. IANTT-PIDE/DGS, DInf./1A, Processo no. 15.33.A/1 Emissora Oficial de Angola, f272–73.

52. Interviews with "Kituxi," April 17, 2002, Luanda, and António Sebastião Vicente "Santocas," November 22, 2001, Luanda. Teta Lando Produções recently released a CD of this band's reedited music entitled *Destinos* (Luanda: Teta Lando Produções, 1998).

53. Thanks to Dona Madalena Afonso for her translation.

54. Interview with Adolfo Maria, June 22, 2005, Lisbon.

55. SCCIA, the local investigative unit of the PIDE, had the album and liner notes translated. See IANTT-SCCIA, PdI #190, U.I. cx. 260, pp. 71–79. Another album with the same name was produced by the Angola Committee in Amsterdam with recordings made at RNA by the JMPLA. While the album had no date on it, this information indicates that it was made after April 25, 1974. There was also an album produced by a group of Italians in 1970 called *Guerra do Popoli MPLA: Angola Chiama (Documenti e Canti dale Zone Liberate)* (War of the People MPLA: Angola Calls: Documents and Songs from the Liberated Zone). UPA,

later to be called the FNLA, also had such an album: *Angola Freedom Songs—Recorded by the UPA Fighters in Angola*, produced by Folkways Records in New York City in 1962.

56. Interview with Luzia "Inga" Van Dunem, April 1, 2002, Luanda. Van Dunem remembered Florinda Joaquim Pedro, who would later be known as the artist "Mura," as being a particularly good lyricist and singer. Sometimes there were even acoustic guitars or improvised ones made out of wooden boxes and wires.

57. Brinkman, *Singing in the Bush*. The liner notes from the 1970 Parendon Press album show images of local people singing some of the songs that were on the record. This phenomenon was a keystone in the Zimbabwean *chimurenga*, or liberation struggle, and is documented by Alec J. C. Pongweni in *Songs that Won the Liberation War* (Harare: College Press, 1982).

58. Interview with Luís "Xabanu" Martins, November 21, 2001, Luanda.

59. Roldão Ferreira, interview by João das Chagas on the program *Música Angolana na Rádio* (Angolan Music on the Radio), Rádio Nacional de Angola, February 28, 2002.

60. IANTT-SCCIA, PdI #190, U.I. cx. 260, p. 8.

61. Sebastião Coelho offers 1952 as year when state radio began broadcasting as "Rádio Angola" from the Post, Telegraph and Telephone offices in the baixa of Luanda. But Júlio Mendes Lopes puts the date as 1955. In 1964, the Official Broadcasting Station of Angola came under the aegis of CITA, the Center for Information and Tourism. For more complete histories of radio in Angola, see S. Coelho, *Angola*, and Lopes, "Contribuição."

62. S. Coelho, *Angola*, 126. Mário Gama, a well-known singer, remembered that the two most dynamic shows were Coelho's and José Maria's *Program Luanda 72/73*. See *Música Angolana na Rádio*, Rádio Nacional de Angola, February 28, 2002.

63. Lopes, "Contribuição," 7.

64. *Música Angolana na Rádio*, Rádio Nacional de Angola, February 28, 2002. See also "Centro Emissor de Mulenvos" (Luanda: Centro Informação e Turismo de Angola, 1964), 4.

65. The colonial government, as part of its countersubversion program, encouraged the sale of radios and was developing television communications: "The sale of radios should not be restricted; that should be a solution only in extreme necessity. But only radios which can receive exclusively middle-wave should be sold." In Reuver-Cohen and Jerman, *Secret Government Documents*, 95.

66. S. Coelho, *Angola*, 137 n. 18. IANTT-PIDE/DGS, DInf./1A, Processo no. 14.19.A/1 Emissoras Estrangeiras, nt 2045, pp. 3, 4, 6–8, 47, 48, 61.

67. *Boletim Oficial de Angola*, 1 serie no. 15, April 12, 1961, 535, cited in Lopes, "Contribuição," 9.

68. Lopes, "Contribuição," 9.

69. See Reuver-Cohen and Jerman, *Secret Government Documents*, 10.

70. Reuver-Cohen and Jerman, *Secret Government Documents*, 11.

71. Reuver-Cohen and Jerman, *Secret Government Documents*, 99.

72. Interview with Lourdes Van Dunem, April 9, 2002, Luanda. She remembered the other announcers she worked with: José da Silva (who spoke Umbundu), Roldão Ferreira (Kimbundu), and Batista de Sousa. Roldão Ferreira mentioned Zé Viola as having been recruited because he spoke Umbundu, and Jacinto Timor because of his command of Kikongo. *Música Angolana na Rádio*, Rádio Nacional de Angola, February 28, 2002.

73. *Música Angolana na Rádio*, Rádio Nacional de Angola, February 28, 2002.

74. Reuver-Cohen and Jerman, *Secret Government Documents*, 95–96. This sort of propaganda was also prevalent in the local press. The popular magazine *Notícia* covered the war with a series of articles over several years entitled "On the front, with our troops." Many articles focused on Angolans who were fighting with the Portuguese troops and interviews with those who had abandoned the "enemy" to come and fight on the side of the Portuguese. See, for example, *Notícia*, November 16, 1968, 21–29.

75. *Música Angolana na Rádio*, Rádio Nacional de Angola, February 28, 2002.

76. Interview with Dionísio Rocha, May 18, 1998, Luanda.

77. On *Café da Noite*, Domingos Coelho remembered that it was typical in that period to have a cup of coffee at night, and the show's title referenced that ritual. Coelho also recalled that the show was enormously popular. E-mail message to author, August 29, 2007. On *Tondoya*'s title, see S. Coelho, *Angola*, 203 n. 18.

78. Interview with Arturo Neves, September 8, 2001, Luanda.

79. This program also included Norberto de Castro, Alves Neto Próprio Nini, and Maria Victória Lourenço. See S. Coelho, *Angola*, 203 n. 18, and *Música Angolana na Rádio*, Rádio Nacional de Angola, February 28, 2002.

80. S. Coelho, *Angola*, 202 n. 12.

81. S. Coelho, *Angola*, 194.

82. S. Coelho, *Angola*, 195–96.

83. S. Coelho, *Angola*, 204 n. 21.

84. Also Lilly Tchiumba, Alba Clyngton (Alvorada 1960), Ngoleiros do Ritmo—"Dionízio—Joãozinho—Nando—Jajão" (Alvorada 1960) and Ngola Melodias—Rui Legot, Joaquim Pataca, and Henrique Lopes—(Alvorada 1960). Duo Ouro Negro had tremendous success both within and without Angola. It represented Portugal in international music competitions. They were important in spreading a variety of styles of Angolan music, although Albina Assis remembered that those involved in the nationalist movement held them in some contempt for playing the music of Ngola Ritmos and not properly recognizing them. While not a part of the Luanda music scene, they did play there occasionally and they always sought out what was played locally. Raul Indipwo remembered Elias dia Kimuezu as a singer of particular talent.

85. Anderson, *Imagined Communities*, 42–43.

86. This was also an important component in the development of notoreity discussed in chapter 3.

87. S. Coelho, *Angola*, 187.

88. I am grateful to Maria Conceição Neto, who brought these lines of transportation and communication to my attention. Maria Luisa Fançony, who lived in Lobito in the late 1950s and 1960s, remembered that her uncle, who worked for a shipping company, had a record of Italian music that a sailor passing through had left for him. Interview with Maria Luisa Fançony, October 16, 2001, Luanda.

89. Xabanu remembered listening to music on the gramophone at a neighbor's house before he could afford to buy a turntable later in the 1960s. Olga Baltazar's father (who was Portuguese) owned a gramophone and she recalled listening to waltzes, tangos, and other Latin American music.

90. Conversation with Gilberto Júnior, November 5, 2001, Luanda.

91. Interview with Abelino "Manuel" Faria, March 19, 2002, Luanda.

92. According to ENDIPU and Fonseca these were Fonográfica-Companhia Fonográfica, S.A.R.L.; Companhia de Discos de Angola (CDA), S.A.R.L., Lda.; Valentim de Carvalho, Angola Lda.; Fonola-Empresa Discográfica de Angola, Lda.; and Fadiang–Fábrica de Discos de Angola, Lda. According to Sebastião Coelho, CDA is a publisher and not a record company per se. António Fonseca, *Untitled Report* (Luanda: ENDIPU, 2000).

93. *Diário da República: Orgão Oficial da República Popular de Angola*, July 17, 1992, I Serio no. 38 and September 9, 1992, I Serie no. 36; and interview with António Fonseca, September 11, 2000, Luanda. Sebastião Coelho claims that these actions were undertaken illegally. In particular, he accuses Fonseca of taking over Coelho's former company and of treating poorly the workers who remained, who were themselves shareholders in the company. Furthermore, he claims that in the confusion of transfer of ownership to the state, at Fonseca's behest, the archives for Estúdios Norte, which contained years of the programs *Tondoya Mukina o Kizomba* and *Café da Noite*, were destroyed. S. Coelho, *Angola*, 213–16.

94. According to the radio journalist Gilberto Júnior, these included Lusolanda, Mussangola, Telectra, Estúdios Norte, and, after independence, the party's Department of Information and Propaganda (DIP). Conversation with Gilberto Júnior, November 5, 2001.

95. S. Coelho, *Angola*, 209.

96. Interview with Luís "Xabanu" Martins, November 21, 2001, Luanda. Stores in the north would certainly have stocked a good collection of Congolese music as well as music from Europe and South America that passed through the port city of Matadi.

97. Jaime Moreira, "Como vai o mercado do disco?" *Notícia*, March 23, 1974, 23.

98. Moreira, "Como vai o mercado do disco?" 23.

99. Guerra, *Angola: Estrutura económica e classes sociais*.

100. Conversation with Gilberto Júnior, November 5, 2001, and interview with Carlos Lamartine, September 4, 2001, both in Luanda.

101. S. Coelho, *Angola*, 217 n. 3, and interview with "Liceu" Vieira Dias, March 18, 2002, Luanda.

102. Interview with António Sebastião Vicente "Santocas," November 22 and 26, 2001, Luanda.

103. Conversation with Gilberto Júnior, November 5, 2001. These numbers are based on innovative research by the radio journalists Gilberto Júnior, João das Chagas, and Amadeu Pimentel, who held a competition for the largest record collection in Angola on their radio show *Quintal do Ritmo* in 1987. The motivation was not to find out who had the largest collection but to try to get an idea of how many records were out there and to get a complete set of the Angolan music produced in this period recorded and in the archives at RNA, where they all worked.

104. Conversation with Gilberto Júnior, November 5, 2001, and interview with Dionísio Rocha, June 12, 1998, both in Luanda.

105. Interview with Dionísio Rocha, June 12, 1998, Luanda.

106. The Semba label belonged to Lusolanda, which functioned as an editorial house, and semba is the most distinctive style of the urban music played. In the RNA music collection I also ran across some records on the label Dikanza but I was unable to get more information about who owned the label.

CHAPTER 6 ↪ THE HIATUS: MUSIC, DISSENT, AND NATION BUILDING AFTER INDEPENDENCE, 1975–1990S

Epigraph: Mário Rui Silva, *O ensino da música* (Luanda: LitoTipo, 2003), 56.

1. Pitcher, *Politics in the Portuguese Empire*, 249–50. For lyrics and for more about this famous folk singer involved in the popular movements in Portugal, see the Web site of the Associação José Afonso (Zeca Afonso), http://www.aja.pt. See also the May 18, 2007 program on Portuguese music on National Public Radio's *All Songs Considered*, http://www.npr.org/programs/asc/archives/20070518/. My thanks to Konstantin Dierks for bringing this program to my attention.

2. Some prominent musicians were associated with the FNLA, including Teta Lando, who went into exile in Zaire and then Europe because he feared for his safety. Matemona Sebastião reported that he himself stopped playing publicly except in church. Hailing from the north and being a member of the persecuted Tokoist Church, he may have decided that opting out was the safest route.

3. Interview with Aurélio João Evangelista "Zito Calhas," August 13, 2005, Luanda. Zito Calhas, who was the director of UNITA's Vorgan radio station through the 1980s, remembered the following bands: Negros Oprimidos (Oppressed Blacks), Resistência Negra (Black Resistance), and Havemos de Voltar (We Will Return). This last band, interestingly, has the same name as the title of a famous and oft cited poem by Agostinho Neto that talks about returning to a land under colonial/foreign rule. Zito Calhas's background and experiences overturn many of the stereotypes of UNITA members as Protestant and provincial. His parents were assimilados, he went to Catholic seminary in Robert Williams (today Cahala)

in Huambo province, he listened to Os Kiezos, and he was an avid soccer player. He initially was an FNLA supporter in 1975 and only later joined UNITA from a refugee camp in Namibia.

4. Interview with Armando Correia de Azevedo, September 11, 2001, Luanda.

5. Pimenta, *Angola no percurso de um nacionalista*, 169.

6. Assis Malaquias, *Rebels and Robbers: Post-Colonial Violence in Angola* (Uppsala, Sweden: Nordiska Afrikainstitutet, 2007), 127.

7. The minister of culture at the time of this transition to a market economy was Ana Maria de Oliveira. Carlos Lamartine, "Caderno auto-biográfico: Sobre a sua vida profissional, política e sócio-cultural na sociedade angolana desde o periódo colonial (1943) ao pós-independência até (1999)" (Luanda, 1999/2000), 26. This is an unpublished manuscript provided to this author by Lamartine in 2002.

8. For a discussion of this more recent political economic history, see Hodges, *Angola*.

9. On the new political elite, see Hodges, *Angola*, 40–46, 130–40, 201–4.

10. Malaquias, *Rebels and Robbers*, 127.

11. See Norrie MacQueen, *Decolonization of Portuguese Africa: Metropolitan Revolution and the Dissolution of Empire* (New York: Longman, 1997), for a full and detailed discussion of decolonization in Angola and in particular the role of the Portuguese Armed Forces Movement.

12. For an account of the withdrawal of Portuguese settlers and the fighting between the three parties in September of 1975, see Ryszard Kapuściński, *Another Day of Life* (New York: Penguin Books, 1987). Kapuściński's is an impressionistic account. The best scientific study is Franz Heimer's *Decolonization Conflict in Angola*.

13. Interview with Armando Correia de Azevedo, September 11, 2001, Luanda. José (Zé) Van Dunem, along with Nito Alves, was the presumed architect of the May 27, 1977 attempted coup.

14. See Tali, *Dissidências*, 2:30, where he says that party leaders returned to a city they barely recognized.

15. See Tali, *Dissidências*, vol. 2, chaps. 10 and 11, especially 50–55. See also Cahen, "Syndicalisme urbain." On groups formed by members of the Revolta Activa, another faction attempting to challenge the MPLA from within, see also Pimenta, *Angola no percurso de um nacionalista*,125.

16. Tali, *Dissidências*, 2:54. See also Cahen, "Syndicalisme urbain," 218–19.

17. Tali, *Dissidências*, 2:67. See also Malaquias, *Rebels and Robbers*, 63–64.

18. Interview with Luís "Xabanu" Martins, November 21, 2001, Luanda. Xabanu also recounted an episode that caused his disenchantment with the MPLA and withdrawal from party-oriented politics in this same period.

19. Lamartine, "Caderno auto-biográfico," 7–8. These three musicians were arrested and detained by the Portuguese military police in Benguela for allegedly "inciting the popular masses."

20. Heimer, *Decolonization Conflict in Angola*, 74–76.

21. Fola Soremekun, *Angola: The Road to Independence* (Ile-Ife, Nigeria: University of Ile-Ife Press, 1983), 159.

22. Soremekun, *Angola*, 168.

23. For detailed analyses of this period and of international involvement, see Gerald Bender, "Angola, the Cubans, and American Anxieties," *Foreign Policy*, no. 31 (1978): 3–30, and "Angola: Left, Right and Wrong," *Foreign Policy*, no. 43 (1981): 53–69; Piero Gleijeses, *Conflicting Missions: Havana, Washington & Africa, 1959–1976* (Chapel Hill: University of North Carolina Press, 2002); William Minter, *Apartheid's Contras: An Inquiry into the Roots of War in Angola and Mozambique* (London: Zed Books, 1994); and Soremekun, *Angola*.

24. Tali, *Dissidências*, 2:243.

25. Malaquias, *Rebels and Robbers*, 63–64; Tali, *Dissidências*, 2:48–49.

26. William Minter, *Apartheid's Contras: An Inquiry into the Roots of War in Angola and Mozambique* (London: Zed Books, 1994), 21, 28.

27. Tali, *Dissidências*, 2:82.

28. Birmingham, "Twenty-seventh of May," 559.

29. In particular this was the case of the Comités Amilcar Cabral, which eventually broke with the MPLA and formed the OCA or Communist Organization of Angola. For details and primary source material see Tali, *Dissidências*, 2:67–71, 82–88, and annex 22.

30. Tali, *Dissidências*, 2:57. See also Cahen, "Syndicalisme urbain," 218–19. The Amilcar Cabral committees were associated with the Portuguese Communist Party and with leftist elements of the Portuguese Armed Forces Movement, but they also had ideological allies among the MPLA leadership, according to Tali. These committees were ostensibly named after the nationalist leader and thinker Amilcar Cabral of the PAIGC in Cape Verde and Guinea-Bissau. His well-defined nationalist-socialist theories that saw the dynamism of nationalism in the peasantry and working classes and his keen analysis of Portuguese colonialism appealed to these groups, which critiqued the MPLA leadership as elitist and petty bourgeois. See *Unity and Struggle: Speeches and Writings of Amilcar Cabral* (New York: Monthly Review Press, 1979), and Patrick Chabal, *Amilcar Cabral: Revolutionary Leadership and People's War* (Trenton, NJ: Africa World Press, 2003). The Henda committees were named after Hoji Ya Henda, born José Agostinho Mendes de Carvalho, an MPLA guerrilla hero who was killed in 1968.

31. Tali, *Dissidências*, vol. 2; Cahen, "Syndicalisme urbain"; and Birmingham, "Twenty-seventh of May."

32. Malaquias, *Rebels and Robbers*, 127.

33. A point made by Birmingham in 1978 in "Twenty-seventh of May."

34. Lara Pawson, "The 27 May in Angola: A View from Below," in *Instituto Português de Relações Internacionais (Universidade Nova de Lisboa)*, no. 14 (June 2007): 1–18. Pawson laments the scant attention given to this moment in Angolan history and interviews some of the common folks involved.

35. There were calls for events to be reviewed by an Angolan body like South Africa's Truth and Reconciliation Commission or by the Angolan Supreme Court. See "Verdade, justiça e reconciliação," August 2004, on the Associação 27 de Maio Web site, http://www.27maio.org/artigos.php?subaction=showfull&id=1097430804&archive=&start_from=&ucat=5&. Also see Pacheco, *Repensar Angola*, 119.

36. Tali, in *Dissidências*, 2:221, puts the number of people killed in the hundreds or even thousands and notes the highly polemical nature of other estimates and of the question in general. Orlando Ferraz, in "A convicção messiânica de Nito Alves," estimates the number killed at 30,000. Ferraz also mentions 3,000 disappeared and says that half of the highest officials in the army were terrorized or persecuted in the repression. Ferraz's article is available on AngoNotícias, an online Angolan news site, http://www.angonoticias.com/full_headlines.php?id=5485, and is included in his forthcoming book *Angola: Depois da tempestade a bonança*. An editorial in the special issue of *Folha 8*, an alternative Angolan newsweekly, May 26, 1998, 2, claims that more than 30,000 were killed. Dalila Cabrita Mateus and Álvaro Mateus, who are writing a book on the subject, also settle on 30,000 as the number. See José Pedro Casthaneira, "Golpe de 27 de Maio fez 30 mil mortos," *Expresso*, May 26, 2007; also Adolfo Maria in Pimenta, *Angola no percurso de um nacionalista*, 152–53.

37. See, for example, Pawson, "27 May in Angola"; Tali, *Dissidências*, 2:182; and the articles and commentaries on the Associação 27 de Maio Web site, http://www.27maio.org.

38. Dani Costa, "'Já estão a entregar certidões de óbito das vítimas do holocausto': Luís dos Passos ao SA," *Seminário Angolense*, May 27, 2006, http://www.semanarioangolense.com. Luís dos Passos is the founder and president of the Partido Renovador Democrático (Democratic Renovation Party).

39. Wilson Dada, "O 27 de Maio, a ambulância de Pitoco e a auto-censura," *Angolense*, May 29–June 4, 2004, available on the Associação 27 de Maio Web site, http://www.27maio.org/artigos.php?subaction=showfull&id=1087814262&archive=&start_from=&ucat=5&. In fact, attempts by the organizers of this Web site to get people to submit their remembrances and the slowness in posting even a partial list of those killed further underscores Dada's point.

40. Pawson, "27 May in Angola"; Tali, *Dissidências*, 2:20, 222–23; Tali, "'Youth in Arms'—or the Failed March to Power of the Angolan Youth 1974–1977" (paper presented at African Studies Association meeting, November 2004, Boston).

41. See for example, Carlos Pacheco, *Repensar Angola*; the special edition of *Folha 8* entitled "Era preciso o Holocausto?" no. 312, May 26, 1998; and the Associação 27 de Maio Web site, http://www.27maio.org. See also Pawson "27 May in Angola," especially 8–15, for interviews with some of the dissidents involved.

42. In particular, the party paper *Vitoria é Certa*, the daily *Diário de Luanda*, and the radio programs *Kudibanguela*, *Juventude em Luta* (broadcast by the JMPLA), and *Povo em Armas* (broadcast by the Army). By October 1976 Alves only

had allies/supporters at *Povo em Armas*, thanks to sweeps by the political police who had gotten wind of what they considered disloyal activity. Birmingham mentions that papers in Lubango, Malanje, and Lobito spread pro-Nito messages as well. Tali, *Dissidências*, 2:77, 211, and Birmingham, "Twenty-seventh of May," 559.

43. For a complete analysis see Tali, *Dissidências*, vol. 2, chaps. 10 and 14.

44. The MPLA's official response to the attempted coup is *Angola: A tentative de golpe de estado de 27 de maio de 77: Informação do Bureau Político do MPLA, 12 de Julho de 1977* (Lisbon: Edições Avante, 1977). Critiques of DISA describe it as a PIDE/DGS-like police force. It was disbanded by President Neto in 1979 following pressure from the Organization of African Unity, which had received complaints about its human rights abuses.

45. Birmingham, "Twenty-seventh of May," 556–58.

46. Tali, *Dissidências*, 2:217–18.

47. President Neto set up a Special Military Court that met secretly—so secretly, in fact, that neither verdicts nor sentences were announced publicly. See Amnesty International, "República Popular de Angola: Resumo das preocupações de Amnistia Internacional" (London, December 1982), 7–8.

48. Pimenta, *Angola no percurso de um nacionalista*,153.

49. Birmingham, "Twenty-seventh of May," 563; Pacheco, *Repensar Angola*, 53; and Tali, *Dissidências*, vols. 1 and 2. I do not mean to suggest that all dissidence in the party is a thing of the past. That is certainly not the case, but the 27 de Maio marked a certain low point. Earlier movements of dissent included the 1962 departure of Viriato da Cruz from the party, the Revolta do Leste in 1974, and the Revolta Activa, also in 1974. On the Revolta Activa, see Pimenta, *Angola no percurso de um nacionalista*.

50. Pombal Maria, "Munícipes do Sambila recordam '27 de Maio': DISA massacrou milhares . . . de jovens intelectuais," *Folha 8*, May 26, 1998, 4.

51. Birmingham, "Twenty-seventh of May," 559, and Maria, "Munícipes do Sambila," 5.

52. Maria, "Munícipes do Sambila," 4–5. Sambila is also a name for Sambizanga.

53. Pawson, "27 May in Angola," 9. Salão Faria was likely Manuel Faria's bar or that of his brother.

54. Tali, *Dissidências*, 2:66.

55. Birmingham, "Twenty-seventh of May," 556–58.

56. Interview with Filipe Zau, March 27, 2002, Luanda.

57. Birmingham, "Twenty-seventh of May," 192. One of Pawson's informants also underscored Alves's eloquence; see "27 May in Angola," 10.

58. Askew, *Performing the Nation*, 265.

59. See Birmingham, "Twenty-seventh of May," 554; Heimer, *Decolonization Conflict in Angola*; Tali, *Dissidências*, vol. 2; Cahen, "Syndicalisme urbain," 200.

60. Tali, *Dissidências*, 2:223–24. See Vera Magarreiro, "'Na prisão, todos dias pensava que ia morrer,' recorda um dos sobreviventes." *Notícias Lusofonas*, May

22, 2004, http://www.noticiaslusofonas.com/view.php?load=arcview&article=6264 &catogory=news.

61. José Eduardo Agualusa, *As mulheres do meu pai* (Lisbon: Dom Quixote, 2007), 325.

62. Thomas Turino argues that there are various cosmopolitans, among them a socialist cosmopolitan that has not yet been adequately studied. See Turino, *Nationalists*, 10.

63. Interview with António Sebastião Vicente "Santocas," November 26, 2001, Luanda. Askew's *Performing the Nation* is a study of this process and the ways it is contested and reinvented by Tanazanians.

64. Interview with Carlos Lamartine, August 20, 1998, Luanda.

65. Interview with António Sebastião Vicente "Santocas," November 26, 2001, Luanda. This point was confirmed by other musicians, including Dionísio Rocha, interview May 18, 1998, Luanda, and Chico Coio, interview February 15, 2002, Luanda.

66. Jean-Michel Mabeko Tali, e-mail message to author, September 5, 2007. See also Tali, *Dissidências*, 2:104–6 on the role of exclusion and exclusivist claims to representation.

67. Pedrito's *Comandante Gika* is another.

68. Song lyrics transcribed by Augusto Cesar Wilson de Carvalho.

69. *Angola 70's: 1974–78*, compiled by Ariel de Bigault (Paris: Budamusique, 1999), liner notes, 22.

70. Interview with Rui Mingas, January 13, 2002, Luanda.

71. Interview with António Sebastião Vicente "Santocas," November 26, 2001, Luanda.

72. Lamartine, "Caderno auto-biográfico," 9.

73. Interview with Abelino "Manuel" Faria, March 19, 2002, Luanda.

74. Interviews with Chico Coio, February 15, 2002, and Abelino "Manuel" Faria, March 19, 2002, both in Luanda.

75. Interviews with António Sebastão Vicente "Santocas," November 26, 2001, and Chico Coio, February 15, 2002, both in Luanda.

76. Interviews with António Sebastão Vicente "Santocas," November 26, 2001, and Chico Coio, February 15, 2002, both in Luanda.

77. Interviews with Carlos Lamartine, August 20, 1998 and September 3, 2001, Luanda, and Lamartine, "Caderno auto-biográfico," 24.

78. Interview with Carlos Lamartine, September 3, 2001, Luanda.

79. Interview with Carlos Lamartine, August 20, 1998, Luanda.

80. "Primeiro Festival Nacional dos Trabalhadores—Faremos da arte e do desporto um direito de todo o povo" (UNTA, undated).

81. Interview with António "Tó" Manjenje, October 4, 2001, Benguela.

82. Lamartine, "Caderno auto-biográfico, 25." Lamartine's position in the JMPLA had him at the forefront of cultural production and promotion both nationally and internationally as he directed musical groups representing Angola at cultural festivals in Libya, Cuba, and France.

83. *Angola: A Luta Continua* (MPLA, Departamento de Informação e Propaganda).

84. Interview with Jorge Macedo, May 5, 2001, Luanda.

85. Interview with Maria Luisa Fançony, October 17, 2001, Luanda. Fançony is the former program director at RNA.

86. Interview with Dr. Jorge Macedo, May 5, 2001, Luanda.

87. Interview with Carlos Lamartine, September 3, 2001, Luanda.

88. António Ole's film *O Ritmo de N'gola Ritmos* has some fabulous footage of the band Ngola Ritmos recording at the radio station just shortly after independence.

89. Interview with Maria Luisa Fançony, October 17, 2001, Luanda.

90. Interview with Carlos Lamartine, September 3, 2001, Luanda. For a literary example of the power of gossip, rumor, and unofficial discourse in this period, see Manuel Rui Monteiro, *Crónica de um mujimbo* (Porto, Portugal: Edições ASA, 1989).

91. Along with a variety of discs by those three, the following artists were included in this group, but with only one disc each: Luis Visconde, Lakes Alberto, Gildo Costa, Eleutério Sanches and Lilly Tchiumba, and Quarteto IIII.

92. Interview with Maria Luisa Fançony, October 17, 2001, Luanda, and Hodges, *Angola*, 11–12 and chap. 4.

93. Among them João das Chagas, Gilberto Júnior, Lau, Zé Neto, and Amadeu Pimental.

94. For an overview of the changes in political economy in this period see Hodges, *Angola*, chap. 4.

95. "Teta Lando aposta nos ritmos angolanos: Revitalizar músicas de 60 e 70," *Jornal de Angola*, April 6, 1998.

96. Interview with Carlos Lamartine, August 9, 2001, Luanda. Lamartine was one of the founding members of the group, along with Santocas, El Belo, Santos Júnior, Voto Gonçalves, Mulato, Vate Costa, Dina Santos, Carlos Burity, Pedrito, Artur Adriano Prado Paim and others. He said that it was founded in 1993 in response to a speech by the then minister of culture, Ana Maria de Oliveira, in which she said that "Angolan artists should make do and find their own mode of livelihood," suggesting that the days of ministerial support were over. The group was still active in 2008. See Lamartine, "Caderno auto-biográfico," 26–27.

97. Tali notes the overwhelming importance placed on participation in the guerrilla struggle in the early years of independence. A look at party leadership lists from the period shows a predominance of those who had been in exile with the struggle. See Tali, *Dissidências*, 2:240–41.

EPILOGUE

Epigraph: Interview with Chico Coio, February 15, 2002, Luanda.

1. Patrick Chabal and Nuno Vidal, eds. *Angola: The Weight of History* (London: Hurst and Co., 2007) and Tony Hodges, *Angola: Anatomy of an Oil State*

(Bloomington: Indiana University Press and Oxford: James Currey in association with the Fridtjof Nansen Institute, 2004).

2. One can tell a car's provenance by its license plates. FAA stands for Forças Armadas Angolanas, the Angolan military.

3. There has been a growth in private radio stations since 1992. But Rádio Ecclésia, the Catholic station that leads as a sometime voice of opposition in communications media, has often had its broadcasts jammed in the years in which I have traveled back and forth to Angola (roughly 1997–present).

4. Cristina Udelsman Rodrigues, "Trabalho assalariado e estratégias de sobrevivência e reprodução nas famílias de Luanda" (PhD diss., Instituto Superior de Ciências de Trabalho e Empresa, Lisbon, 2004).

5. Information about this incident is culled from the following articles: Rafael Marques, "Angola: A Death for a Song and the Triumph of Impunity," allAfrica.com, December 4, 2003, http://allafrica.com/stories/200312040283.html; Marques, "Comment and Analysis: When the People's Silence Speaks," February 26, 2004, http://allafrica.com, subscription content; and "Rappers Give a Voice to Angola's Cry for Democracy," *Financial Times*, June 17, 2004.

6. Marques, "Death for a Song."
7. *Financial Times*, "Rappers."
8. Marques, "Death for a Song."
9. *Financial Times*, "Rappers."

Bibliography

ARCHIVAL MATERIAL

Arquivo Histórico de Angola (Angolan Historical Archives), Luanda
Códices: 5268, 5686

Instituto dos Arquivos Nacionais, Torre do Tombo, Lisbon
Polícia Internacional e de Defesa do Estado/Direcção Geral de Segurança (PIDE/DGS)
Delegação de Angola. Divisão de Informação–1a Secção (DInf./1A)
Processo no. 10.05: Centro de Informação e Turismo de Angola
Processo no. 11.25.B/25: J.M.P.L.A., nt 1847
Processo no. 11.27.F: C.E.A. (Centro de Estudos Angolanos)
Processo no. 13.20.A/5: Grupo Feminino de Sta. Cecília, nt 1989
Processo no. 14.19.A/1: Emissoras Estrangeiras, nt 2045
Processo no. 14.26.A: Postos Emissores Clandestinos
Processo no. 14.29.A: Seminaristas
Processo no. 14.29.A/3: Movimento Nacional Feminino, nt 2055
Processo no. 15.03.A: Clubes e Associações, nt 2071–2072
Processo no. 15.12.A: Muçeque Lixeira, nt 2084
Processo no. 15.12.A/1: Muçeque Calemba, nt 2084
Processo no. 15.12.A/2: Jornal "Tribuna dos Muçeques," nt 2084
Processo no. 15.12.B/1: Muçeque Zangado, nt 2085
Processo no. 15.12.B/2: Muçeque Catambor, nt 2085
Processo no. 15.12.B/3: Muçeque Mulemba N'Gola, nt 2085
Processo no. 15.12.B/4: Muçeque Ilha do Cabo, nt 2085
Processo no. 15.12.B/5 Muçeque Caputo, nt 2085
Processo no. 15.12.B/6: Sambizanga, nt 2085
Processo no. 15.12.D: Muçeque Rangel, nt 2086
Processo no. 15.12.D/1: Muçeque Prenda, nt 2086
Processo no. 15.12.E/4: Muçeque Mota, nt 2086

Processo no. 15.12.E/5: Muçeque Marçal, nt 2086
Processo no. 15.29/B: Radio Tanzania, nt 2097
Processo no. 15.33.A/1: Emissora Oficial de Angola, nt 2099
Processo no. 16.14.A./1: Caminhos de Ferro de Luanda
Processo no. 16.48: Comando Geral da PSP de Angola
Processo no. 24/66: C.I.T.A, nt 9042

Serviços Centrais. Centro de Informação 2—CI(2)
Processo no. 332 SC/C1(2): Armamento, contrabando de armas, tráfico de armas
Processo no. 4313/7342 SC/C1(2): Voz de Angola

Processos Individuais
Processo no. 4844/61 SC/SR: Arminda Correia de Faria
Processo no. 121/65 DelA/PC: Arminda Correia de Faria
Processo no. 54772 DelA/Luanda Gab: Arminda Correia de Faria
Processo no. 2937/62 SC/SR: Carlos Aniceto Vieira Dias
Processo no. 2418 Del A/Subdel L/Gab: Carlos Aniceto Vieira Dias
Processo no. 112/71 Del A/PC: Lopo Ferreira do Nascimento, José Mendes de Carvalho
Processo no. 281/63 Del A/PC: Lopo Ferreira do Nascimento
Processo no. 617/61 Del A/PC: Lopo Ferreira do Nascimento
Processo no. 3752 Del A/PR: Lopo Ferreira do Nascimento

Serviços de Centralização e Coordenação de Informações de Angola (SCCIA)

Caixa no. 256: UPA-Rádio
Caixa no. 260: MPLA-Rádio (1967–74)

INTERVIEWS AND CONVERSATIONS

Interviews by the Author

Alberto Teta Lando, May 7, 1998, Luanda
Dionísio Rocha, May 18, 1998, June 2, 1998, June 12, 1998, Luanda
Carlos Lamartine, August 3, 1998, August 4, 1998, August 14, 1998, September 3, 2001, September 4, 2001, September 9, 2001, September 11, 2001, Luanda
Waldemar Bastos, April 26, 2000, Lisbon
Gaspar Agostinho Neto, January 18, 2001, Luanda
Armando Correia de Azevedo, January 25, 2001, September 11, 2001, Luanda
Barceló de Carvalho "Bonga," January 28, 2001, Luanda
Amélia Mingas, March 20, 2001, Luanda
Amadeu Amorim and José "Zé" Maria dos Santos, April 4, 2001, Luanda
Jaime de Sousa Araújo, April 27, 2001, Luanda
Elias dia Kimuezu, May 11, 2001, Luanda
Dr. Jorge Macedo, May 5, 2001, May 7, 2001, May 11, 2001, July 27, 2001, Luanda
Paulo Flores, August 2, 2001, Luanda

Raul Indipwo, August 10, 2001, Luanda
Arturo Neves, September 8, 2001, Luanda
Carlos Alberto Pimentel, October 3, 2001, Benguela
António "Tó" Manjenje, October 4, 2001, Benguela
António "Chicuta" da Silva, October 4, 2001, Benguela
Maria Luisa Fançony, October 16, 2001, Luanda
Luís "Xabanu" Martins, November 21, 2001, Luanda
Olga Baltazar, November 22, 2001, Luanda
António Sebastião Vicente "Santocas," November 22, 2001, November 26, 2001, Luanda
Alberto Jaime, December 4, 2001, December 12, 2001, Luanda
Ruy Mingas, January 13, 2002, Luanda
Albina Assis, January 17, 2002, Luanda
Chico Coio, February 15, 2002, Luanda
Efigénia Barroso Mangueira Van Dunem, February 20, 2002, Luanda
Arminda Faria, February 24, 2002, Luanda
Matemona Sebastião, February 27, 2002, Luanda
Padre Vicente José Rafael, March 4, 2002, March 6, 2002, Luanda
Carlitos Vieira Dias, March 18, 2002, Luanda
Abelino "Manuel" Faria, March 19, 2002, Luanda
Dr. Filipe Zau, March 27, 2002, Luanda
Luzia "Inga" Van Dunem, April 1, 2002, Luanda
Ricardina "Dina" Carvalho Santos, April 6, 2002, Luanda
Lourdes Van Dunem, April 9, 2002, Luanda
Miguel Frances Santos Rodolfo "Kituxi," April 17, 2002
Adolfo Maria, June 22, 2005, Lisbon
Paulo Jorge, August 2, 2005, Luanda
Holden Roberto, August 9, 2005, Luanda
Aurélio João Evangelista "Zito Calhas," August 13, 2005, Luanda

Professional Conversations with the Author

António Ole, July 9, 1998, Luanda
António Fonseca, September 11, 2000, October 30, 2001, Luanda
António Adão Paulo, Division Head, Center for Historical Documentation and Investigation, MPLA National Headquarters, Luanda, April 20. 2001
Gilberto Júnior, November 5, 2001, Luanda
Maria Francisca Jacinta, April 15–17, 2002, Luanda
Dr. Edmundo Rocha, June 16, 2005, Lisbon

Rádio Nacional de Angola, Recorded Programs

Drumond Jaime and Helder Barber, *Foi Há Vinte Anos*, interview with Amadeu Amorim, 1995
João das Chagas, *Música Angolana na Rádio*, February 28, 2002

COMPACT DISCS, AUDIOCASSETTES, AND RECORD ALBUMS

Rádio Nacional de Angola, entire collection of recorded music, 1940s–1980s.

Angola 60's: 1956–70. Paris: Budamusique, 1999, compact disc. Music selection by Ariel de Bigault and Gilberto Júnior. Text by Ariel de Bigault and Jorge Macedo.

Angola 70's: 1972–73. Paris: Budamusique, 1999, compact disc. Music selection by Ariel de Bigault and Gilberto Júnior. Text by Ariel de Bigault and Artur Arriscado.

Angola 70's: 1974–78. Paris: Budamusique, 1999, compact disc. Music selection by Ariel de Bigault and Gilberto Júnior. Text by Ariel de Bigault, Gilberto Júnior, and João das Chagas.

Angola 80's: 1978–90. Paris: Budamusique, 1999, compact disc. Music selection by Ariel de Bigault and Gilberto Júnior. Text by Ariel de Bigault, Gilberto Júnior, and João das Chagas.

Angola Freedom Songs—Recorded by the UPA Fighters in Angola. New York: Folkway Records, 1962, 33 rpm.

Bonga. *Bonga: Angola 72.* Rohnert Park, CA: Tinder Records, 1997, compact disc.

Bonga. *Bonga: Angola 74.* Rohnert Park, CA: Tinder Records, undated, compact disc.

de Castro, Urbano. *Kia Lumingo.* Silva Porto, Angola: Fadiang, Rebita, 45 rpm.

dia Kimuezu, Elias. *Xamavu.* Lisbon: Nováfrica Audiovisual, undated, compact disc.

———. *Diala Monzo.* Lisbon: Valentim de Carvalho, Ngola label, 45 rpm.

dya Kimuezu, Elias. *Os Grandes Sucessos*, vol. 1. Manaus, Brazil: Centro Cultural e Recreativo Kilamba, 2005, compact disc.

Dog Murras. *Bue Angolano.* Pontinha, Portugal: Vidisco, 2003, compact disc.

———. *Pátria Nossa.* Pontinha, Portugal: Vidisco, 2005, compact disc.

Flores, Paulo. *Recompasso.* Lisbon: N'jila Produções and Ruben Produções, 2001, compact disc.

Garda e o Seu Conjunto. *Maria Candimba.* Lisbon: Parlophone, LMEP 1054, 45 rpm.

Guerra do Popoli MPLA: Angola Chiama (Documenti e Canti dalle Zone Liberate) (War of the People MPLA: Angola Calls: Documents and Songs from the Liberated Zone). Milan, 1970, 33 rpm.

Kaboko Meu. *Na Rua de São Paulo.* Luanda: Rádio Nacional de Angola, 1978.

Lamartine, Carlos. *Histórias de Casa Velha.* Luanda: Produções RMS, 1999, compact disc.

Mingas, Rui. *Monangambé.* Lisbon: Strauss, 1994, compact disc.

———. *Temas Angolanos.* Lisbon: Strauss, 1995, compact disc.

Ngola Ritmos. *João Dumingu.* Luanda: Rádio Nacional de Angola.

———. *Muxima.* Luanda: Rádio Nacional de Angola, 1956.

N'zaji. *Destinos.* Luanda: Teta Lando Produções, 1998, compact disc.

Os Kiezos. *Os Kiezos.* Luanda: ENDIPU, audiocassette.

———. *Milhorró.* Silva Porto, Angola: Fadiang, Rebita label, 1972, 45 rpm.

Paim, Prado. *Bartolomeu.* Luanda: Companhia de Discos de Angola, 1975, 45 rpm.

Reviver Artur Nunes, vol. 2. Paris: Teta Lando Produções with authorization of ENDIPU, 1997, compact disc.

Reviver David Zé. Paris: Teta Lando Produções with authorization of ENDIPU, 1998, compact disc.
Reviver Os Kiezos, vol. 10. Paris: Teta Lando Produções with authorization of ENDIPU, 1999, compact disc.
Reviver Urbano de Castro, vol. 5. Paris: Teta Lando Produções with authorization of ENDIPU, 1998, compact disc.
Ritmos Angolanos, vol. 1. Paris: Teta Lando Produções with authorization of ENDIPU, 1997, compact disc.
Ritmos Angolanos, vol. 6. Paris: Teta Lando Produções with authorization of ENDIPU, 1998, compact disc.
Ritmos Angolanos, vol. 9. Paris: Teta Lando Produções with authorization of ENDIPU, 1998, compact disc.
Santocas. *Valódia*. Luanda: Departamento de Informação e Propaganda, 1975, 45 rpm.
Santos, Dina. *Semba Kassequel*. Luanda: Companhia de Discos de Angola, Merengue, 1975, 45 rpm.
Silva, Mário Rui. *Chants d'Angola: "Pour demain . . ."* Paris: Alliance Française, 1994, compact disc.
Soul of Angola Anthologie de la Musique Angolaise 1965/1975. Paris: Lusafrica with authorization from Teta Lando Produções, 2001, compact disc.
Tchiumba, Lily. *Angola*. Lisbon: Ovação, 1994, compact disc.
União Mundo da Ilha. *Amanhã Vamos à Procura da Chave*. Luanda: Rádio Nacional de Angola, 1978.
"Victory Is Certain!" New York: Parendon Press, 1970, 33 rpm.
Visconde, Luis. *Chofer de Praça*. Luanda: Companhia de Discos de Angola, 1974, 45 rpm.

PERIODICAL COLLECTIONS

Arquivo Histórico de Angola, Luanda

Magazine Collection

A Cidade, 1973–74
Noite e Dia, 1967–71
Semana Ilustrada, January 1969–August 1974

Biblioteca Municipal (Municipal Library), Luanda

Magazine and Newspaper Collections

Jornal de Angola (published in Luanda by the Associação dos Naturais de Angola, Anangola), 1953, 1957, 1958, and 1961
Notícia, 1967–74

Official Publications

Diário de República, 1st Series, no. 275 (November 22, 1976); no. 283 (November 30, 1979); no. 28 (July 17, 1992); no. 36 (September 9, 1992)

ARTICLES FROM THE CONTEMPORARY ANGOLAN AND PORTUGUESE PRESS

Carlos, Severino. "'Eu vi as fichas do Pacavira e do Norberto na Torre do Tombo': Alberto Neto abre o dossier PIDE/DGS." *Angolense*, February 9–16, 2002, 6–7, 24.

Castanheira, José Pedro. "Golpe de 27 de Maio fez 30 mil mortos." *Expresso*, May 26, 2007.

Fortunato, Jomo. "Da antologia musical de Carlos Lamartine: Histórias cantadas da casa velha." *Jornal de Angola*, February 20, 2000, 1–2.

———. "Entrevista com guitarrista Betinho Feijó." *Jornal de Angola*, February 6, 2000, 1–3.

———. "Entrevista com Carlitos Vieira Dias: Carlitos, da lírica dos Gingas à Banda Xangola." *Jornal de Angola*, August 8, 1999, 1–4.

———. "Entrevista com o cantor Filipe Mukenga: Tenho saudades da 'Banda Madizeza.'" *Jornal de Angola*, September 26, 1999, 1–3.

———. "Entrevista: As realidades do Mito Gaspar." *Jornal de Angola*, 2000, 1–3.

———. "Entrevista: Bonga 'tivemos sérios problemas com os assimilados.'" *Jornal de Angola*, November 19, 2000, 4–5.

———. "Entrevista: Carlos Burity, o arauto do semba." *Jornal de Angola*, January 24, 1999, 1–3.

———. "A guitarra superlativa de Botto Trinidade." *Jornal de Angola*, August 19, 2001, 4–5.

———. "Joãozinho Morgado: A melódia dos tambores." *Jornal de Angola*, April 7, 2002, 4–5.

———. "José Oliveira Fontes Pereira: A alma da dikanza." *Jornal de Angola*, June 4, 2000, 1–3.

———. "Lourdes Van Dunem: A voz do canto dolente." *Jornal de Angola*, November 4, 2001, 4–5.

———. "A magnitude simbólica dos 'Kiezos.'" *Jornal de Angola*, July 29, 2001, 4–5.

———. "Mário Gama, o baritone da voz." *Jornal de Angola*, July 16, 2000, 3.

———. "Morreu o Gaby Monteiro: calou-se mais uma voz." *Jornal de Angola*, June 18, 2000, 1.

———. "Música Popular Angolana: A banda e a maravilha." *Jornal de Angola*, October 11, 1998, 1–3.

———. "Música popular angolana: A música tradicional na consolidação do semba." *Jornal de Angola*, February 14, 1999, 1–2.

———. "Música popular angolana: Euletério Sanches, a voz do canto nostálgico." *Jornal de Angola*, March 11, 2001, 4–5.

———. "Música popular angolana: Luto—Morreu o autor de Mamã Divua Diami e Sakessa Mukongo... Adeus Avozinho." *Jornal de Angola*, January 14, 2001, 3.

———. "Música popular angolana: Moisés e José Kafala, a irmandade vocal." *Jornal de Angola*, April 30, 2000, 1–2.
———. "Música popular angolana: Os dons de Dom Caetano." *Jornal de Angola*, November 28, 1998, 1–2.
———. "Música popular angolana: Santocas, o operário da canção política." *Jornal de Angola*, July 30, 2000, 4–5.
———. "Música popular angolana: Santos Júnior, a nostalgia do Kissangela." *Jornal de Angola*, January 16, 2000, 1–2.
———. "Música popular angolana: Talentos musicais de ouvido artístico." *Jornal de Angola*, May 6, 2001, 3.
———. "Música popular angolana: Tonito, a alma entregue à música." *Jornal de Angola*, October 15, 2000, 4–5.
———. "Música popular angolana: Zé Keno, o génio de uma guitarra." *Jornal de Angola*, June 27, 1999, 1–2.
———. "Revelação: Milhorró é a música do coração do mais kota do conjunto, Adolfo Coelho ainda tem voz para cantar." *Jornal de Angola*, March 26, 2001, 17.
———. "Teta Lando: A idoneidade musical de um canto esperançado." *Jornal de Angola*, undated, 1–2.
Júnior, Gilberto. "A dimensão do semba." *Angolense*, January 8–15, 2000, 15.
Júnior, José. "Liceu falaceu há quarto anos." *Jornal de Angola*, August 19, 1998, 13.
Kyoza, Ezekiel. "Um 'Caldo do Poeira' excepcional . . . a 'Dipanda' foi lembrada por artistas engajados nos seus ideais." *Angolense*, November 16–23, 2002, 24–25.
Macedo, Jorge. "Fontinhas, compositor, tocador de reco-reco, cantor: O semba é uma criação do Ngola Ritmos." *Angolense*, March 9–19, 2002, 20–21.
———. "A música angolana e a identidade cultural." *Semanário Angolense*, April 12–19, 2003, 22–23.
Maria, Pombal. "Munícipes do Sambila recordam '27 de Maio': DISA massacrou milhares . . . de jovens intelectuais." *Folha 8*, May 26, 1998, 4–5.
Martins, Fernando. "Os Kiezos: Do bairro Marçal para a eternidade." *Agora*, August 1998, 10.
Sebastião, Nlandu Mila. "Música angolana de tradição oral." *Jornal de Angola*, January 6, 2002, 4–5.
Silva, Mário Rui. "Estórias de música em Angola (1): A história, os instrumentos e a influência da música angolana na América Latina e Caraíbas." *Austral* (TAAG Angolan airline in-flight magazine), no. 13 (August–September 1995): 15–20.
———. "Estórias de música em Angola (2): As pessoas, o meio, o tempo, figures marcantes da epoca (1875/1935)." *Austral* (TAAG Angolan airline in-flight magazine), no. 15 (January–March 1996): 33–41.
———. "Estórias de música em Angola (3): A geração dos anos 1940/50. Luanda e as suas figures mais marcantes." *Austral* (TAAG Angolan airline in-flight magazine), no. 16 (April–June 1996): 33–40.
———. "Estórias de música em Angola (4): A música suburbana luandense das suas origens até aos fins dos anos 50." *Austral* (TAAG Angolan airline in-flight magazine), no. 18 (October–December 1996): 49–57.

Valódia, Mateus (Virgílio Coelho). "Das turmas aos conjuntos musicais." *Angolense*, August 3–10, 2002, 21.

———. "Das turmas aos conjuntos musicais: Rescaldo do 'Poeira no Quintal' (2a Parte)." *Angolense*, August 10–17, 2002, 20–21.

Venâncio, António. "O 'semba' em discussão: Subsídios para a sua compreensão." *Angolense*, March 18–25, 2000, 16–17.

Vunge, Advayo. "Lourdes Van Dunem: Sou a personificação da contradição." *Figuras & Negócios*, September 30, 2000.

BOOKS, JOURNAL ARTICLES, REPORTS, AND MEMOIRS

Agualusa, José Eduardo. *As mulheres do meu pai*. Lisbon: Dom Quixote, 2007.

Alegi, Peter. *Laduma! Soccer, Politics and Society in South Africa*. Scottsville, South Africa: University of KwaZulu-Natal Press, 2004.

Allman, Jean, Susan Geiger, and Nakanyike Musisi, eds. *Women in African Colonial Histories*. Bloomington: Indiana University Press, 2002.

Amnesty International. "República Popular de Angola: Resumo das preocupações de Amnistia Internacional." London, December 1982.

Anderson, Benedict. *Imagined Communities*. London: Verso, 1996.

Angola: A tentative de golpe de estado de 27 de maio de 77: Informação do Bureau Político do MPLA, 12 de Julho de 1977. Lisbon: Edições Avante, 1977.

Askew, Kelly M. *Performing the Nation: Swahili Music and Cultural Politics in Tanzania*. Chicago: University of Chicago Press, 2002.

Averill, Gage. *A Day for the Hunter, a Day for the Prey: Popular Music and Power in Haiti*. Chicago: University of Chicago Press, 1997.

Ball, Jeremy. "Colonial Labor in Twentieth Century Angola." *History Compass* 3, no. 1 (2005). http://www.blackwell-compass.com/subject/history/section_home?section=hico-africa.

———. "'Colossal Lie': The Sociedade Agrícola do Cassequel and Portuguese Colonial Labor Policy in Angola, 1890–1977." PhD diss., University of California, Los Angeles, 2003.

Barber, Karin. *The Generation of Plays*. Bloomington: Indiana University Press, 2000.

———. "Popular Arts in Africa." *African Studies Review* 30, no. 3 (1987): 1–78.

———. "Preliminary Notes on Audiences in Africa." *Africa* 76, no. 3 (1997): 347–62.

Barnett, Don. *With the Guerrillas in Angola*. Seattle: Liberation Support Movement Information Center, 1970.

———. *Liberation Support Movement interview: sixth region commander Seta Likambuila, MPLA*. Seattle: Liberation Support Movement Information Center, 1974.

Barnett, Don, and Roy Harvey. *The Revolution in Angola: MPLA, Life Histories and Documents*. New York: Bobbs Merrill, 1972.

Bender, Gerald. "Angola: Left, Right and Wrong." *Foreign Policy*, no. 43 (1981): 53–69.
———. "Angola, the Cubans, and American Anxieties." *Foreign Policy*, no. 31 (1978): 3–30.
———. *Angola under the Portuguese: The Myth and the Reality*. Berkeley: University of California Press, 1978.
Bettencourt, José da Sousa. "Subsídio para o estudo sociológico da população de Luanda." *Boletim do Instituto de Investigação Científica de Angola* 2, no.1 (1965): 83–130.
Bhabha, Homi K., ed. *Nation and Narration*. New York: Routledge Press, 1990.
Birmingham, David. "Carnival at Luanda." *Journal of African History* 29 (1988): 93–103.
———. *Frontline Nationalism in Angola and Mozambique*. Trenton, NJ: Africa World Press, 1992.
———. "The Twenty-Seventh of May: An Historical Note on the Abortive 1977 Coup in Angola." *African Affairs* 77, no. 309 (October 1978): 554–64.
Bittencourt, Marcelo. *Dos jornais às armas: Trajectórias da contestação angolana*. Lisbon: Vega, 1999.
———. *Estamos juntos*. Lisbon: Kilombelombe, forthcoming.
Boavida, Américo. *Angola: Cinco séculos de exploração portuguêsa*. Rio de Janeiro: Civilização Brasileira, 1967.
Boxer, Charles R. *Race Relations in the Portuguese Colonial Empire, 1415–1825*. Westport, CT: Greenwood Press, 1963.
Bozzoli, Belinda. *Theatres of Struggle and the End of Apartheid*. Athens: Ohio University Press, 2004.
Brennan, Timothy. *At Home in the World: Cosmopolitanism Now*. Cambridge, MA: Harvard University Press, 1997.
Brinkman, Inge. "A canção política, as religiões e o conceito de 'cultura popular.'" Unpublished paper presented in Luanda and Mbanza Kongo, December 2003.
———. *Singing in the Bush: MPLA Songs during the War for Independence in South-east Angola (1966–1975)*. Cologne: Rüdiger Köppe Verlag, 2001.
———. *A War for the People: Civilians, Mobility, and Legitimacy in South-East Angola during the MPLA's War for Independence*. Cologne: Rüdiger Köppe Verlag, 2005.
———. "War, Witches and Traitors: Cases from the MPLA's Eastern Front in Angola (1966–1975)." *Journal of African History* 44, no. 2 (July 2003): 303–26.
Byfield, Judith. "'Unwrapping' Nationalism: Dress, Gender, and Nationalist Discourse in Colonial Lagos." Discussion Papers in the African Humanities, AH no. 30, African Studies Center, Boston University, 2000.
Cabral, Amilcar. Foreword to *The Liberation of Guiné*, by Basil Davidson. Baltimore: Penguin Books, 1969.
———. *Unity and Struggle: Speeches and Writings of Amilcar Cabral*. With an introduction by Basil Davidson and biographical notes by Mário de Andrade. New York: Monthly Review Press, 1979.

Cahen, Michel. "Syndicalisme urbain, luttes ouvrières et questions ethniques à Luanda: 1974/1981." In *"Vilas" et "cidades": Bourgs et villes en Afrique lusophone*, edited by Michel Cahen, 200–79. Paris: L'Harmattan, 1989.

Cardoso, António. *Baixa e musseques*. 2d ed. Havana: Ediciones Cubanas for the União de Escritores Angolanos, 1985.

Castelo, Cláudia. *"O modo português de estar no mundo": O luso-tropicalismo e a ideologia colonial portuguesa (1933–61)*. Porto, Portugal: Edições Afrontamento, 1998.

"Centro Emissor de Mulenvos." Centro Informação e Turismo de Angola, Luanda, August 7, 1964.

Chabal, Patrick. *Amilcar Cabral: Revolutionary Leadership and People's War*. Trenton, NJ: Africa World Press, 2003.

Chabal, Patrick, and Nuno Vidal, eds. *Angola: The Weight of History*. London: Hurst, 2007.

Chabal, Patrick, with David Birmingham, Joshua Forrest, Malyn Newitt, Gerhard Seibert, and Elisa Silva Andrade. *A History of Postcolonial Lusophone Africa*. Bloomington: Indiana University Press, 2002.

Chatterjee, Partha. *Nationalist Thought and the Colonial World: A Derivative Discourse*. Minneapolis: University of Minnesota Press, 1986.

———. *The Nation and Its Fragments: Colonial and Postcolonial Histories*. Princeton, NJ: Princeton University Press, 1993.

Cheah, Pheng, and Jonathan Culler, eds. *Grounds of Comparison: Around the Work of Benedict Anderson*. New York: Routledge, 2003.

Cheah, Pheng, and Bruce Robbins, eds. *Cosmopolitics: Thinking and Feeling Beyond the State*. Minneapolis: University of Minnesota Press, 1998.

Chilcote, Ronald, ed. *Emerging Nationalism in Portuguese Africa: Documents*. Stanford, CA: Hoover Institution Press, 1972.

Clarence-Smith, W. G. "Review Article: Class Structure and Class Struggles in Angola in the 1970s." In "Special Issue on Contemporary Politics," *Journal of Southern African Studies* 7, no. 1 (October 1980): 109–26.

———. *The Third Portuguese Empire 1825–1975: A Study in Economic Imperialism*. Manchester, UK: Manchester University Press, 1985.

Clington, Mário de Souza [Ary Kemitow Zirka]. *Angola Libre?* Paris: Éditions Gallimard, 1975.

Coelho, Sebastião. *Angola: História e estórias de informação*. Luanda: Executive Center, 1999.

Cooper, Frederick. *Africa since 1940: The Past of the Present*. Cambridge: Cambridge University Press, 2002.

———. *Decolonization and African Society: The Labor Question in French and British Africa*. Cambridge: Cambridge University Press, 1996.

Coplan, David. *In Township Tonight! South Africa's Black City Music and Theatre*. Johannesburg: Ravan Press, 1985.

da Conceição, Lourenço Mendes. "Katambore, lago seco da capital angolana." *Angola: Revista de Doutrina e Estudo*, 1966, 37.

da Silva, Elisete Marques. "Social Conditions of School Attendance and Achievement of Minors in Suburban Luanda: A Preliminary Test of Some Hypotheses." In *Social Change in Angola*, edited by Franz-Wilhelm Heimer, 194–210. Munich: Weltforum Vertag, 1973.
da Silva, António José Garcia. "Dedo na ferida." *Notícia*, June 22, 1968.
Davidson, Basil. *In the Eye of the Storm: Angola's People*. Garden City, NJ: Doubleday, 1972.
de Andrade, Mário Pinto [Buanga Fele]. *Origens do nacionalismo Africano*. Lisbon: Publicações Dom Quixote, 1997.
———. "Qu'est-ce que le 'luso tropicalism'?" *Présence Africaine* 4 (October–November 1955): 24–35.
de Barros, Maria da Luz Ferreira. "Alguns aspectos da situação socioeconómico em Angola (1961–1974)." *Africana*, no. 14 (September 1994): 41–62.
de Boeck, Filip, and Marie Françoise Plissart. *Kinshasa: Tales of the Invisible City*. Tervuren, Belgium: Royal Museum for Central Africa, 2004.
de Carvalho, Ruy. *Ana a Manda: Os filhos da rede*. Lisbon: Instituto de Investigação Científica Tropical, 1989.
de Castro Lopo, Júlio. *Alguns aspectos dos musseques de Luanda*. Luanda, Angola: Editorial Angola, 1948.
Denzer, LaRay. "Towards a Study of the History of West African Women's Participation in Nationalist Politics: The Early Phase, 1935–50." *Africana Research Bulletin* 6, no. 4 (1976): 65–85.
de Oliveira, Mário António Fernandes. *A formação da literatura angolana (1851–1950)*. Lisbon: Imprensa Nacional–Casa da Moeda, 1997.
———. *Luanda, ilha crioula*. Lisbon: Agência Geral do Ultramar, 1968.
———. "Problemas essenciais do urbanismo no ultramar: Estruturas urbanas de integração e convívio." *Boletim Geral do Ultramar* (Agência Geral do Ultramar, Lisbon), 1962, 14.
De Sousa Santos, Ana. "Aspectos de alguns costumes da população Luandense." *Boletim do Instituto de Investigação Científica de Angola* 7, no. 2 (1970): 55–71.
Dilolwa, Carlos Rocha. *Contribuição à história económica de Angola*. 2d ed. Luanda: Editorial Nzila, 2000.
Do Amaral, Ilídio. "Aspectos do povoamento branco de Angola." *Junta de Investigação do Ultramar-Estudos, Ensaios e Documentos* no. 74 (1960).
———. "Contribuição para o conhecimento do fenómeno de urbanização em Angola." *Finisterra: Revista Portuguesa de Geografia* 13, no. 25 (1978): 43–85.
———. *Luanda: Estudo de geográfia urbana*. Lisboa: Junta de Investigações do Ultramar, 1968.
dos Santos, Jacques Arlindo. *ABC do Bê Ó*. Luanda: Edições Chá de Caxinde, 1999.
Duara, Prasenjit. *Rescuing History from the Nation: Questioning Narratives of Modern China*. Chicago: University of Chicago Press, 1995.
Duffy, James. *Portuguese Africa*. Cambridge, MA: Harvard University Press, 1961.

Eduarda, Maria. "O musseque e as suas gentes." *Boletim Cultural: Repartição de Cultura e Turismo,* 1973, 17–20.

Erlmann, Veit. *African Stars: Studies in Black South African Performance.* Chicago: University of Chicago Press, 1991.

Fabian, Johannes. "Popular Culture: Findings and Conjectures." *Africa* 48, no. 4 (1978): 315–34.

———. *Remembering the Present: Painting and Popular History in Zaire.* Narrative and paintings by Tshibumba Kanda Matulu. Berkeley: University of California Press, 1996.

Fair, Laura. "Music, Memory and Meaning: The Kiswahili Recordings of Siti Binti Saad." *Swahili Forum,* September 1998: 1–16.

———. *Pastimes and Politics: Culture, Community, and Identity in Post-Abolition Zanzibar, 1890–1945.* Athens: Ohio University Press, 2001.

Fanon, Frantz. *A Dying Colonialism.* New York: Monthly Review Press, 1965.

Ferguson, James. *Expectations of Modernity: Myths and Meanings of Urban Life on the Zambia Copperbelt.* Berkeley: University of California Press, 1999.

Financial Times. "Rappers Give a Voice to Angola's Cry for Democracy." June 17, 2004.

Fonseca, António. Untitled report, pp. 1–11. Luanda: ENDIPU, 2000.

Fortunato, José, ed. *Angola: Documentos do MPLA,* vol. 1. Lisbon: Ulmeira, 1977.

Freyre, Gilberto. *Aventura e rotina: Sugestões de uma viagem à procura das constantes portuguesas de carácter e acção.* Lisbon: Edições Livros do Brasil, 1954.

———. *Um brasileiro em terras portuguesas: Introdução a uma possível Luso-tropicalogia, acompanhada de conferências e discursos proferidos em Portugal e em terras lusitanas e ex-lusitanas da Ásia, África e do Atlântico.* Lisbon: Edições Livros do Brasil, 1954.

Gagnon, Renée. "Mon Angola." *Le Maclean,* March 1976, 43–45.

———. "Les musseques de Luanda ou la civilisation du déchet version africaine." *Colóquio: Artes* (Fundação Calouste Gulbenkian, Lisbon), February 1976, 43–51.

Geiger, Susan. "Tanganyikan Nationalism as 'Women's Work': Life Histories, Collective Biography and Changing Historiography." *Journal of African History* 37, no. 3 (1996): 465–78.

———. *TANU Women: Gender and Culture in the Making of Tanganyikan Nationalism, 1955–65.* Portsmouth, NH: Heinemann, 1997.

———. "Women and African Nationalism." *Journal of Women's History* 2, no. 1 (1990): 227–44.

Gellner, Ernest. *Nations and Nationalism.* Ithaca, NY: Cornell University Press, 1983.

Gleijeses, Piero. *Conflicting Missions: Havana, Washington & Africa, 1959–1976.* Chapel Hill: University of North Carolina Press, 2002.

Gondola, Ch. Didier. "*Ata ndele* . . . et l'independence vint: Musique, jeunes et contestation politique dans les capitales congolaises." In *Les jeunes en Afrique: La politique et la ville,* vol. 2, edited by Catherine Coquery-Vidrovitch, Odile George, and Françoise Guitart, 463–87.

———. "*Bisengo ya la joie*: Fête, sociabilité et politique dans les capitales congolaises." In *Fêtes urbaines en Afrique: Espaces, identités et pouvoirs*, edited by Odile Goerg, 87–111. Paris: Karthala, 1999.

———. "*Ô Kisasa makambo!* Métamorphoses et représentations urbaines de Kinshasa à travers le discours musical des années 1950–1960." *Le Mouvement Social*, no. 204 (July– September 2003): 109–29.

———. "Popular Music, Urban Society, and Changing Gender Relations in Kinshasa, Zaire (1950–1990)." In *Gendered Encounters*, edited by Maria Grosz-Ngate and Omari H. Kokole, 65–85. New York: Routledge, 1997.

Guerra, Henrique. *Angola: Estrutura económica e classes sociais: Os últimos anos do colonialismo português em Angola*. Lisbon: Edições 70, 1979.

Hamilton, Russell. *Literatura Africana, Literatura Necessária*. Lisbon: Edições 70, 1984.

———. *Voices from an Empire*. Minneapolis: University of Minnesota Press, 1975.

Hayes, Joy Elizabeth. *Radio Nation: Communication, Popular Culture, and Nationalism in Mexico 1920–1950*. Tucson: University of Arizona Press, 2000.

Heimer, Franz-Wilhelm, ed. *Social Change in Angola*. Munich: Weltforum Verlag, 1973.

———. *Decolonization Conflict in Angola, 1974–76: An Essay in Political Sociology*. Geneva: Institut Universitaire de Hautes Études Internationales, 1979.

Heywood, Linda. *Contested Power in Angola: 1840s to the Present*. Rochester, NY: University of Rochester Press, 2000.

Hobsbawm, Eric. *Nations and Nationalisms since 1780*. Cambridge: Cambridge University Press, 1990.

Hodges, Tony. *Angola: Anatomy of an Oil State*. Bloomington: Indiana University Press; Oxford: James Currey, in association with the Fridtjof Nansen Institute, 2004.

Hunt, Nancy Rose, Tessie Liu, and Jean Quataert, eds. *Gendered Colonialisms in African History*. Malden, MA: Blackwell, 1997.

Instituto António Houaiss. *Dicionário Houaiss da língua portuguesa*. Rio de Janeiro: Editora Objectiva, 2001.

Isaacman, Allen. *Cotton Is the Mother of Poverty: Peasants, Work, and Rural Struggle in Colonial Mozambique, 1938–1961*. Portsmouth, NH: Heinemann, 1996.

Jaime, Drumond, and Helder Barber. *Angola: Depoimentos para a história recente, 1950–76*, vol. 1. Lisbon: privately published, 1999.

James, C. L. R., Grace Lee, and Pierre Chaulieu. *Facing Reality*. 1958. Reprint, Detroit: Bewick Editions, 1974.

Júnior, António de Assis. *Relato dos acontecimentos de Dala Tando e Lucala*. 2d ed. Luanda: União dos Escritores Angolanos, 1980.

Júnior, Paulo M. *Lembranças da vida*. Luanda: INALD, 1998.

Kandjimbo, Luís. *Apologia de Kalitangi: Ensaio e crítica*. Luanda: INALD, 1997.

Kapuściński, Ryszard. *Another Day of Life*. New York: Penguin Books, 1987.

Kelley, Robin D. G. *Race Rebels: Culture, Politics, and the Black Working Class.* New York: Free Press, 1996.

———. *Yo' Mama's DisFUNKtional! Fighting the Culture Wars in Urban America.* Boston: Beacon Press, 1997.

Laban, Michel. *Angola: Encontro com escritores.* 2 vols. Porto, Portugal: Fundação Eng. António de Almeida, 1991.

———. *Mário Pinto de Andrade: Uma entrevista.* Lisbon: Edições Sá da Costa, 1997.

———. *Viriato da Cruz: Cartas de Pequim, com uma entrevista de Monique Chajmowiez e um ensaio de Christine Messiant.* Luanda: Edições Chá de Caxinde, 2003.

Lamartine, Carlos. "Caderno auto-biográfico sobre a sua vida profissional, política e sócio-cultural na sociedade angolana desde o periódo colonial (1943) ao pós-independência até (1999)." Unpublished manuscript, Luanda, 1999/2000.

Lara, Lúcio. *Um amplo movimento...: Itinerário do MPLA através de documentos e anotaçoes.* Vol. 1, *Até fevreiro 1961.* Luanda: LitoTipo, 1998.

Leite, Ana Mafalda. "Angola." In *The Postcolonial Literature of Lusophone Africa*, edited by Patrick Chabal, 103–64. Evanston, IL: Northwestern University Press, 1996.

Lindsay, Lisa A., and Stephan F. Miescher, eds. *Men and Masculinities in Modern Africa.* Portsmouth, NH: Heinemann, 2003.

Lipsitz, George. *Dangerous Crossroads: Popular Music, Postmodernism and the Poetics of Place.* New York: Verso, 1994.

Lodge, Tom, and Bill Nasson, with Steven Mufson, Khehla Shubane, and Nokwanda Sithole. *All, Here, and Now: Black Politics in South Africa in the 1980s.* New York: Ford Foundation and Foreign Policy Association, 1991.

Lopes, Júlio Mendes. "Contribuição à história da radiodifusão em Angola." Rádio Nacional de Angola, Luanda, 2000.

Lyons, Tanya. "Guerrilla Girls and the Zimbabwean National Liberation Struggle." In *Women in African Colonial Histories*, edited by Jean Allman, Susan Geiger, and Nyankanyiki Musisi, 305–26. Bloomington: Indiana University Press, 2002.

Macedo, Jorge. *Gente do meu bairro, cenas e contos,* 2d ed. Havana: Ediciones Cubanas for União de Escritores Angolanos, 1985.

———. *Literatura angolana e texto literário.* Lisbon: Edições ASA for União de Escritores Angolanos, 1989.

———. *Ngola Ritmos: Obreiros do nacionalismo angolano.* Luanda: União de Escritores Angolanos, 1989.

MacQueen, Norrie. *Decolonization of Portuguese Africa: Metropolitan Revolution and the Dissolution of Empire.* New York: Longman, 1997.

Malaquias, Assis. *Rebels and Robbers: Violence in Post-colonial Angola.* Uppsala, Sweden: Nordiska Afrikainstitutet, 2007.

Margarido, Alfredo. "The Social and Economic Background of Portuguese Negro Poetry." *Diogenes* 37 (1962): 50–74.

Marcum, John. *The Angolan Revolution*. 2 vols. Cambridge, MA: MIT Press, 1969–78.
Marques, Rafael. "Comment and Analysis: When the People's Silence Speaks," February 26, 2004, http://allafrica.com, subscription content.
———. "Angola: A Death for a Song and the Triumph of Impunity." allAfrica.com, December 4, 2003. http://allafrica.com/stories/200312040283.html.
Martin, Phyllis. *Leisure and Society in Colonial Brazzaville*. Cambridge: Cambridge University Press, 1995.
Matrosse, Dino. *Memórias (1961–1971)*. Luanda: Editora Nzila, 2005.
Mattera, Don. *Gone with the Twilight: A Story of Sophiatown*. London: Zed Books, 1987.
McClintock, Anne. *Imperial Leather: Race, Gender and Sexuality in the Colonial Contest*. New York: Routledge, 1995.
Messiant, Christine. "'Em Angola até o passado é imprevisível': A experiência de uma investigação sobre o nacionalismo angolano e, em particular, o MPLA: Fontes, crítica, necessidade actuais de investigação." In *Actas do II Seminário Internacional Sobre a História de Angola: Construindo o passado angolano: As fontes e a sua interpretação, Luanda 4 a 9 de Agosto de 1997*, 808–11. Lisbon: Commissão Nacional para as Comemorações dos Descobrimentos Portugueses, 2000.
———. "L'Angola colonial, histoire et société, les prémisses du mouvement nationaliste." PhD diss., Ecole de Hautes Etudes en Sciences Sociales, Paris, 1983.
———. "Luanda (1945–61): Colonisés, société coloniale et engagement nationaliste." In *"Vilas" et "cidades": Bourgs et villes en Afrique lusophone*, edited by Michel Cahen, 125–99. Paris: L'Harmattan, 1989.
Minter, William. *Apartheid's Contras: An Inquiry into the Roots of War in Angola and Mozambique*. London: Zed Books, 1994.
———. *Operation Timber: Pages from the Savimbi Dossier*. Trenton, NJ: Africa World Press, 1988.
Monteiro, Manuel Rui. *Crónica de um mujimbo*. Porto, Portugal: Edições ASA, 1989.
Monteiro, Ramiro Ladeiro. *A família nos musseques de Luanda (Subsídios para o seu estudo)*. Luanda: Fundação de Acção Social no Trabalho em Angola, 1973.
———. "From Extended to Residual Family: Aspects of Social Change in the Musseques of Luanda." In *Social Change in Angola*, edited by Franz-Wilhelm Heimer, 211–33. Munich: Weltforum Verlag, 1973.
Moore, Robin D. *Nationalizing Blackness: Afrocubanismo and Artistic Revolution in Havana, 1920–1940*. Pittsburgh, PA: University of Pittsburgh Press, 1997.
Moorman, Marissa. "Putting on a *Pano* and Dancing Like Our Grandparents: Dress and Nation in Late Colonial Luanda." In *Fashioning Africa: Power and the Politics of Dress*, edited by Jean Allman, 84–103. Bloomington: University of Indiana Press, 2004.

Moreira, Jaime. "Como vai o mercado do disco?" *Notícia*, March 23, 1974, 22–27.
Mourão, Fernando. "Configurações dos núcleos humanos de Luanda, do século XVI ao século XX." In *Actas do Seminário: Encontro de Povos e Culturas em Angola*, vol. 1, 109–226. Lisbon: Comissão Nacional para as Comemorações dos Descobrimentos Portugueses, 1997.

———. "O contexto histórico-cultural da criação literária em Agostinho Neto: Memória dos anos cinquenta." *África: Revista do Centro de Estudos Africanos* 14/15, no. 1 (1991–92).

Movimento Democrático de Angola. *Massacres em Luanda*. Lisbon: África Editora, 1974.

Murray, Martin J., and Garth A. Myers, eds. *Cities in Contemporary Africa*. New York: Palgrave Macmillan, 2006.

"Música: Luiz Montez." *Afro-Letras: Revista de Artes, Letras e Ideias* 1, no. 1 (March 1999): 17–18.

Myers, Garth Andrew. *Verandahs of Power: Colonialism and Space in Urban Africa*. Syracuse, NY: Syracuse University Press, 2003.

Neto, Mária da Conceição. "Entre a tradição e a modernidade: Os ovimbundu do planalto central à luz da história." *Ngola: Revista de Estudos Sociais* 1, no. 1 (January–December 1997): 193–216.

———. "Ideologias, contradições e mistificações da colonização de Angola no século XX." *Lusotopie* 1997 (Paris): 327–59.

Ntarangwi, Mwenda. *Gender, Identity, and Performance: Understanding Swahili Cultural Realities through Song*. Trenton, NJ: Africa World Press, 2003.

Nunes, José António Pereira. "Inquéritos socio-económicos dos muçeques de Luanda: Salários, alimentação, habitação, mobilário e baixelas." *Mensário Administrativo Portugal*, no. 14 (1961): 161–66.

Okuma, Thomas. *Angola in Ferment: The Background and Prospects of Angolan Nationalism*. Boston: Beacon Press, 1962.

Pacheco, Carlos. *MPLA: Um nascimento polémico*. Lisbon: Vega, 1997.

———. *Repensar Angola*. Lisbon: Vega, 2000.

Pagano, Caetano. "Visit to MPLA and Their Liberated Areas," May–September 1974. International University Exchange Fund, 1974.

Parker, Andrew, Mary Russo, Doris Summer, and Patricia Yaeger. *Nationalisms and Sexualities*. New York: Routledge, 1991.

Pawson, Lara. "The 27 May in Angola: A View from Below." *Instituto Português de Relações Internacionais* (Universidade Nova de Lisboa), no. 14 (June 2007): 1–18.

Péclard, Didier. "Etat coloniale, missions chrétiennes et nationalisme en Angola, 1920–1975: Aux racines sociales de l'UNITA." PhD diss., Institut d'Etudes Politiques de Paris, 2005.

———. "Religion and Politics in Angola: The Church, the Colonial State and the Emergence of Angolan Nationalism, 1940–1961." *Journal of Religion in Africa* 28, Fasc. 2 (May 1998): 160–86.

Pepetela. *Luandando*. Porto, Portugal: Elf Aquitaine, Angola, 1990.

———. *Mayombe*. 5th ed. Lisbon: Publicações Dom Quixote, 1993.
Peres, Phyllis Reisman. *Transculturation and Resistance in Lusophone African Narrative*. Gainesville: University Press of Florida, 1997.
Pimenta, Fernando Tavares. *Angola no percurso de um nacionalista: Conversas com Adolfo Coelho*. Porto, Portugal: Edições Afrontamento, 2006.
Pitcher, M. Anne. *Politics in the Portuguese Empire: The State, Industry and Cotton, 1926–1974*. New York: Oxford University Press, 1993.
Popular Memory Group. "Popular Memory: Theory, Politics, Method." In *Making Histories: Studies in History-Writing and Politics*, edited by R. Johnson, G. McLennan, B. Schwarz, and D. Sutton, chap. 6. Minneapolis: University of Minnesota Press, 1982.
Power, Marcus. "Aqui Lourenço Marques!! Radio Colonization and Cultural Identity in Colonial Mozambique, 1932–74." *Journal of Historical Geography* 26, no. 4 (2000): 605–28.
Presley, Cora Ann. *Kikuyu Women, the Mau Mau Rebellion and Social Change in Kenya*. Boulder: University of Colorado Press, 1992.
"Pronunuciados por actividades contra a segurança do Estado mais trinta e dois indivíduos na Comarca de Luanda." *Jornal ABC: Diário de Luanda*, December 18, 1959.
Ranger, Terence. *Dance and Society in Eastern Africa*. Berkeley: University of California Press, 1975.
———. *Peasant Consciousness and Guerrilla War in Zimbabwe: A Comparative Study*. Berkeley: University of California Press, 1985.
Redinha, José. "Angola terra de folclore." *Boletim Cultural* (Câmara Municipal de Luanda), July–September 1967.
———. "A habitação tradicional em Angola: Aspectos da sua evolução." *Revista do Centro de Informação e Turismo de Angola*, 1964, 3–43.
Reuver-Cohen, Caroline, and William Jerman, eds. and trans. *Angola: Secret Government Documents on Counter-subversion*. New York: IDOC, 1974.
Ribas, Óscar. *Ilundu: Espíritos e ritos angolanos*. Porto, Portugal: Edições ASA for União de Escritores Angolanos, 1989.
Rive, Richard. *Buckingham Palace, District Six*. London: Heinemann, 1987.
Roberts, Allen F., and Mary Nooter Roberts. *A Saint in the City: Sufi Art in Urban Senegal*. Los Angeles: UCLA Fowler Museum of Cultural History, 2003.
Rocha, Edmundo. *Angola: Contribuição ao estudo da génese do nacionalismo moderno angolano (período de 1950–1964): Testemunho e estudo documental*. Lisbon: Kilombelombe, 2003.
———. *O Clube Marítimo Africano: Uma contribuição para a luta e independência nacional dos países sob domínio colonial português*. Lisbon: Biblioteca Museu República e Resistência, 1998.
Rodrigues, Cristina Udelsman. "Trabalho assalariado e estratégias de sobrevivência e reprodução nas famílias de Luanda." PhD diss., Instituto Superior de Ciências de Trabalho e Empresa, Lisbon, 2004.

Rodrigues, Deolinda. *Cartas de Langidila e outros documentos*. Luanda: Editorial Nzila, 2004.

———. *Diário de um exílio sem regresso*. Luanda: Editorial Nzila, 2003.

Rodrigues, Eugénia. *A geração silenciada: A Liga Nacional Africana e a representação do branco em Angola na década de 30*. Lisbon: Edições Afrontamento, 2003.

Samuels, Michael A., and Norman A. Bailey. "Education, Health, and Social Welfare." In *Portuguese Africa: A Handbook*, edited by David M. Abshire and Michael A. Samuels, 178–201. New York: Praeger, 1969.

Schmidt, Elizabeth. *Mobilizing the Masses: Gender, Ethnicity, and Class in the Nationalist Movement in Guinea, 1939–1958*. Portsmouth, NH: Heinemann, 2005.

Schubert, Benedict. *A guerra e as igrejas: Angola 1961–1991*. Lucerne: P. Schlettwein, 2000.

Scott, James C. *Domination and the Arts of Resistance: Hidden Transcripts*. New Haven, CT: Yale University Press, 1990.

Sebastião, Adriano. *Dos campos de algodão aos dias de hoje*. Luanda, 1993.

Shain, Richard. "Roots in Reverse: Cubanismo in Twentieth-Century Senegalese Music." In "Special Issue on Leisure in African History," *International Journal of African Historical Studies* 35, no. 1 (2002): 83–101.

Shohat, Ella, and Robert Stam. *Unthinking Eurocentrism: Multiculturalism and the Media*. New York: Routledge, 1994.

Sidaway, J. D., and Marcus Power. "'The Tears of Portugal': Empire, Identity, 'Race,' and Destiny in Portuguese Geopolitical Narratives." *Environment and Planning D: Society and Space* 23, no. 4 (2005): 542.

Simone, A. M. *For the City Yet to Come: Changing African Life in Four Cities*. Durham, NC: Duke University Press, 2004.

Smith, Anthony. *Ethnicity and Nationalism*. New York: E. J. Brill, 1992.

Soremekun, Fola. *Angola: The Road to Independence*. Ile-Ife, Nigeria: University of Ile-Ife Press, 1983.

Spitulnik, Debra. "Mediated Modernities: Encounters with the Electronic in Zambia." *Visual Anthropology Review* 14, no. 2 (Fall/Winter 1998): 68.

———. "Mobile Machines and Fluid Audiences: Rethinking Reception through Zambian Radio Culture." In *Media Worlds: Anthropology on New Terrain*, edited by Faye D. Ginsburg, Lila Abu-Lughod, and Brian Larkin, 337–54. Berkeley: University of California Press, 2002).

Strobel, Margaret. *Muslim Women in Mombasa, 1890–1975*. New Haven, CT: Yale University Press, 1979.

Tali, Jean-Michel Mabeko. *Dissidências e poder de estado: O MPLA perante si próprio (1962–1977)*. 2 vols. Luanda: Editorial Nzila, 2001.

Terretta, Meredith. "Nationalists Go Global: From Cameroonian (UPC) Village *Maquisards* to Pan-African Freedom Fighters." Paper presented at the Equatorial African Workshop, University of Wisconsin–Madison, October 14, 2006.

Troni, Alfredo. *Nga Mutúri*. Lisbon: Edições 70, 1991.
Turino, Thomas. *Nationalists, Cosmopolitans and Popular Music in Zimbabwe*. Chicago: University of Chicago Press, 2000.
"Variações da populção em relação ao censo de 1950." *Actividade Económica de Angola: Revista de Estudos Económicos*, no. 69 (May–August 1964): 206.
Vianna, Hermano. *The Mystery of Samba: Popular Music and National Identity in Brazil*. Chapel Hill: University of North Carolina Press, 1999.
Vieira, José Luandino. *A cidade e a infância: Estórias*. 3d ed. Luanda: União de Escritores Angolanos, 1977.
———. *Luuanda: Short Stories of Angola*. Translated by Tamara Bender. London: Heinemann, 1980.
———. *O nosso musseque*. Luanda: Editorial Nzila, 2003.
———. *A vida verdadeira de Domingos Xavier*. Lisbon: Edições 70, 1974.
Wade, Peter. *Music, Race and Nation: Música Tropical in Colombia*. Chicago: University of Chicago Press, 2000.
Waterman, Christopher. *Jùjú: A Social History and Ethnography of an African Popular Music*. Chicago: University of Chicago Press, 1990.
West, Michael O. *The Rise of an African Middle Class: Colonial Zimbabwe, 1898–1965*. Bloomington: Indiana University Press, 2002.
Wheeler, Douglas. "Origins of African Nationalism in Angola: Assimilado Protest Writings, 1859–1929." In *Protest and Resistance in Angola and Brazil*, edited by Ronald Chilcote, 67–90. Berkeley: University of California Press, 1972.
Wheeler, Douglas, and Réne Pélissier. *Angola*. New York: Praeger, 1971.
White, Bob W. "Congolese Rumba and Other Cosmopolitanisms." In "Musique, joie et crise dans le cosmotropole Africain," edited by Bob White, special issue, *Cahiers d'Etudes Africaines* 168, XLII, no. 4 (2002): 663–86.
White, Luise. *The Comforts of Home: Prostitution in Colonial Nairobi*. Chicago: University of Chicago Press, 1990.
Wolfers, Michael. ed. *Poems from Angola*. London: Heinemann, 1979.
Yuval-Davis, Nira, and Flora Anthias. *Woman-Nation-State*. New York: St. Martin's Press, 1989.
Zau, Filipe. *Marítimos africanos e um clube com história*. Lisbon: Embaixada de República de Angola em Portugal, 2005.

WEB SITES

Apontamentos para a história de radiodifusão de Angola (site maintained by P. Monteiro): http://www.geocities.com/dpmonteiro/radioangolahistoria.htm
Associação 27 de Maio: http://www.27maio.org/
Associação José Afonso: http://www.aja.pt
National Public Radio, *All Songs Considered*: http://www.npr.org/programs/asc/archives/20070518/

Index

Page references in italics denote illustrations.

acculturation, 44, 46, 48; dress codes and, 62; prostitution and, 49; soccer clubs and, 51
Adriano, Artur, 99, 131
Afonso, Zeca, 165
Africanists, 10–11
Africans: *assimilados* self-identified as, 45; displaced to fringes of city, 33; "double life" of, 46–47; male unemployment, 35; *mestiços*, 32, 53, 227n25, 232n92; migration to urban areas, 40, 41; of *musseques*, 28, 31; in Portuguese army, 152, 153–54, 244n74; Portuguese citizenship for Angolans, 89, 137; white immigrants and, 42. *See also* middle class, African
África Show (band), 130, 231n88
Afro-Letras (journal), 135
"afternoon sessions," 70
age. *See* generations (age groups)
agriculture, 9, 31, 41–42, 162, 211n34
Aguarela Angolana talent show, 94, 135–36
album covers, 114–15, *115*, *116*, *141*; Castro, Urbano de, *105*; Garda e o Seu Conjunto, *159*; Ho MPLA Nkango Angola, *178*; Ngola Ritmos, *158*; Ngoleiros do Ritmo, *160*; Palma, Belita, *104*
Algeria, 13, 242n46
"Alguns aspectos dos musseques de Luanda" (Lopo), 48
Alves, Nito, 172–73
Alvorada record label, 115, *115*, *116*, 158, *158*
"Amanhã vou acender uma vela na Muxima" (Ouro Negro song), 114
Amaral, Ilídio do, 32, 36, 41, 43, 47, 54; on cultural practices of *musseques*, 51; on effects of white immigration, 42; on prostitution, 49
Ambundu-Kimbundu ethnolinguistic group, 34
Amerindians, 37
Amorim, Amadeu, 52, 61, 74, 233n2; arrest and imprisonment of, 66, 125, 205n66; on "danceable" music, 116; as dancer, 121; on "João Dumingu," 124–25; on song lyrics, 112; on stylized Portuguese songs, 64. *See also* Ngola Ritmos (band)
Anangola (Association of Natural-born Angolans), 44, 57, 71, 215n83; collaborationist politics of, 66, 79; generational tensions within, 72; publications of, 73
Anderson, Benedict, 7, 11; "horizontal comradeship" concept, 108, 239n94; on imagined communities, 10, 141–42, 159–60; on print capitalism, 85, 140, 159–60
Anderson, Perry, 39
Andrade, Costa, 40
Andrade, Mário Pinto de, 39, 40, 48, 73, 199n15, 223n81
Angola, 1, 2, 5, 6–7, 17; coup attempt (May 1977), 17, 109, 166, 171–77, 249n36; daily cultural practices, 59; early socialist period, 24; ethnolinguistic groups of, 34–35; "hiatus" in music and, 166, 189; humanitarian crisis in, 21–22; market-driven economy in, 188, 190, 191; as overseas territory of Portuguese nation, 110; Portuguese (white) immigration to, 4, 32, 42–43; racism and colonial paternalism in, 20;

275

Angola (*cont.*)
  radio in, 142, 143–55, 145; reforms and everyday life, 88–93; remembrance of colonial period, 23; sonorous capitalism in, 140; transition to independence, 167–70
Angola: A Luta Continua [Angola: The Struggle Continues] (LP record), 184
Angola: Cinco séculos de exploração portuguesa [Angola: Five Centuries of Portuguese Exploitation] (Boavida), 39
"Angola Avante Revolução" [Angola Forward the Revolution] (national anthem), 121, 170, 235n39
Angola Combatente (MPLA radio program), 142, 149–55, 235n40
Angola Libre (FNLA radio program), 142, 149
Angolan Broadcasting Plan, 146–47
Angolan Center for Information and Tourism (Centro de Informação e Turismo de Angola, CITA), 20, 133, 192, 243n61; Colloquium on Radio Broadcasting, 156; PIDE infiltration of, 207n86; radio programs sponsored by, 135, 136
Angolan Historical Archives, 20
angolanidade (Angolanness), 2, 7, 54, 176; *assimilado* elites and, 123; cosmopolitanism and, 31; as counter to *portugalidade*, 40; "double life" of *musseque* residents and, 47; literary nationalists and, 39–40, 58, 209n7; music clubs and, 52, 53; petty bourgeoisie and, 24; politically partisan music and, 185; radio and, 144, 157; recording industry and, 164; semba and, 8; social scientists and, 39; song lyrics and, 112; turn away from, 17; urban elites and, 25; various cultural sources of, 138–39. See also identity, Angolan
Angolan Radio Club, 157
Angolan Women's Organization (Organização das Mulheres de Angola, OMA), 60, 77, 217n1
Anne, Saint (Santa Ana), 121–22
Anos Depois [Years Later] (Flores song), 193
anthropology, 11, 37
António, Mário, 48
"Aqui'tas" [You're Here] (Dog Murras song), 193

Araraqura (police), 128, 130
artisans, 35
Artistas de Primeira Grandeza, 188, 252n96
Asia, 10, 37
Askew, Kelly, 11, 114, 175–76
assimilados (assimilated persons), 4, 39, 42; Africanization of, 53; *angolanidade* and, 123; Angolan identity and, 40; associations of, 57; in Bairro Indígena (B.I.), 69–70; in Bairro Operário (B.O.), 61; Bota Fogo and daily life in *musseques*, 71–77; as civil status under colonial law, 59; downward social mobility of, 44–45; musicians, 63, 65, 114; old and new, 45, 67, 71, 90, 221n55; pushed out of city center, 60, 70, 74
Assis, Albina, 61, 67, 112, 244n84; on *Angola Combatente* broadcasts, 151; Bota Fogo and, 72–75; on dancing, 117; in Grupo Feminino Santa Cecília, 77, 78–79; on radio, 144; on women in music clubs, 106–7
Assis, Guilhermo, 96
Assis Faria, Manuel "Manec," 73, 107
audiences, 2, 18, 27, 101, 175; as collectivity, 137; dancing and, 115–17; European, 111; gender and, 108; for literary nationalists, 58; male musicians revered by, 23; MPLA plans for independence and, 168; *poder popular* (people's power) and, 171; Portuguese or European, 115; radio, 157; respect for musicians, 98; semba and, 139; shared taste and, 133; women as critical members of, 87
authenticity, 18, 22, 84
authoritarianism, 10
Averill, Gage, 6
Azevedo, Armando Correia de, 61, 67; arrest of, 75; Bota Fogo and, 73; on culture in reform period, 91; on *Kutonoca* show, 136–37, 167, 172; on "Milhorró," 128; on soccer clubs and politics, 72; on street festivals, 84; on unity at time of independence, 165
Aznavour, Charles, 112

Babaxi, 128
backyard gatherings, 119, 121, 133, 135, 191, 192

Bairro Cacimba, 68
Bairro Indígena (B.I.), 28, 33–34; Bota Fogo and, 71; changing social composition of, 67–71; housing in, 68, 69; parties in, 119; razing of, 70–71; *turmas* in, 97
"Bairro Indígena" (song), 70–71
Bairro Operário (B.O.), 50, 60–66, 100
Bairro Popular, 181
Baixa de Kassanje, 81, 130, 199n16
baixa (European city center), 9, 32, 33, 34, 55, 93; Angolan music in, 84; *assimilados* pushed out of, 60, 70, 74; carnival in, 95; *musseques* in relation to, 126–28, 210n16; nightclubs, 134; Teatro Nacional (National Theater), 110. *See also* Luanda
Baizinha soccer club, 71
Bakongo-Kikongo ethnolinguistic group, 34, 215n90
Baltazar, Olga, 84, 106, 220n30, 245n89
Bandung Conference, 75
Barber, Karin, 116, 133, 137
"Bartolomeu" (Paim song), 131–32
Batalha, Lomilhão, 238n81
Batalha's club, 129
Batuque record label, 164
BBC (British Broadcasting Corporation), 142
"Belita" (Adriano song), 131
Belo, Sílvia, 78–79
Bender, Gerald, 38, 39, 42, 43, 88, 215n78
Benfica sports club, 71
Benguela, 4, 31, 65, 82; factories on outskirts of, 89; music festivals under MPLA state, 182; radio in, 143, 155, 240n12; recording technology in, 161
bessangana attire, 61, 104
Bettencourt, José de Sousa, 36, 42, 43, 54, 210n17; on cultural practices of *musseques*, 51; on detribalization, 43–44; on "double life" of *musseque* household heads, 46–47, 48; on female promiscuity, 48; on *musseques* and city center, 41
Bicesse Accord, 166, 188
Bittencourt, Marcelo, 12, 57, 130, 209n7
Boavida, Américo, 39
Boa Vista soccer club, 71
Bonga, 73, 208n94
Boss, Angelo, 193

Bota Fogo soccer club, 13, 60, 65, 79, 80, 92; *assimilado* experience and, 71–77; context of social change in *musseques* and, 67; "golden age" songs and, 128; origins of MPLA and, 57; *quintal* (backyard) of, 121; *turmas* from, 97
Boxer, Charles, 39
Brazil, 11, 18, 32; independence of, 31; lusotropicalism and, 37, 38; popularity of soccer and music in, 98, 190
Brazilian music, 19, 84, 100, 120, 164; Angolan culture discovered through, 63, 64; *berimbau* instrument, 221n49; bossa nova, 161; samba, 139, 161
Brazzaville, 16, 81, 151, 155, 227n23. *See also* Congo-Brazzaville (Republic of the Congo); Radio Brazzaville
"Brinca na Areia" (Dikanzas do Prenda song), 163
Brinkman, Inge, 5–6
British colonialism, 37
Brown, James, 112
Bungo, 33

cabaret bars, 50–51
Cabinda, 45, 94, 117
Cabinda Ritmos (band), 94, 129
Cabral, Amilcar, 248n30
Caetano, Ambrósio, 86
Caetano, Dom, 118
Caetano, Marcelo, 199n11
Café da Noite: Boa música em boa companhia [Nighttime Coffee: Good Music in Good Company] (radio program), 157, 163, 244n77
Caldo do Poeira [Dust Soup] (radio program), 187
candongueiros, music on, 194
Cape Verde, 4, 13, 27; Cape Verdeans in Angola, 65, 168; music from, 19; Tarrafal prison, 58, 73–74, 125
capitalism, 166, 179, 180
capitalism, print, 85, 140, 141, 159–60
capitalism, sonorous, 7, 24, 140; "meanwhile" simultaneity and, 85, 142; nation as imagined community and, 160; recording industry and, 164; shift from print capitalism, 141
Cardoso, António, 40, 48, 58, 214n64, 222n63
Caribbean music, 118, 185, 235n32

Index ⟿ 277

carnaval (carnival), 121, 230n68; banned, 137; groups devoted to, 61, 62, 67, 95, 96; whites' interest in, 214n76
Carneiro, Higino, 192
Carvalho, Álvaro de, 143
Carvalho, Barceló de, 98, 229n64
Carvalho, Ruy Duarte de, 95
Casa dos Panfletos ("pamphlet house"), 61
Castelo, Cláudia, 11, 37, 213n54
Castro, Nitistas de, 180, 181
Castro, Urbano de, 1, 99, 169; album cover featuring, 105, 105; killed in MPLA purge, 174; music censored after coup attempt, 186, 187, 197n1; reappearance of music on radio, 187–88; songs by, 130, 131
Catholic Church, 68, 151, 224n89; celebration of Santa Cecília, 78; Our Lady of Muxima Church, 121–22; Rádio Ecclésia, 155, 157, 253n3
Cazumbi, 72
censorship, 66, 150, 154, 186
Centro Recreativo de União de São Paulo, 181
Chá das 6, 72
Chagas, João das, 154, 187, 246n103
Chatterjee, Partha, 10, 11, 13, 201n30
Chilcote, Ronald, 39
children's matinees, 72, 106, 134
"Chofer de Praça" [Plaza Chauffeur] (Visconde song), 34, 112, 126–28
cinema, 15, 84, 91, 94; music shows and, 92, 111, 135; nation and, 239n94
Cine Ngola, 92, 135
cipaios (African policemen), 152
civil servants, 44, 47, 223n81; anticolonial politics and, 125; music clubs operated by, 83, 90; as musicians, 102; music school in Luanda and, 96; reforms of late colonial period and, 91; surveillance of, 66
civil war, postindependence, 1, 5, 17, 26, 166, 182; Cold War and, 188–89; humanitarian crises brought by, 21–23; imperialist involvement in, 180; population displacement from, 194–95
Clarence-Smith, Gervase, 88, 90, 127
class, social, 3, 55, 139; colonial system and, 61; cultural production and, 59; gender in relation to, 87–88; nation inflected by, 56; *patrício* (compatriot) signifier and, 93, 108; urban experience and, 23–24, 82. *See also* elites, African; middle class, African; petty bourgeoisie; working class
Clington, Alba, 114–15, 115
Clington, Mário de Souza, 13, 114
Clube Atlético de Luanda, 71, 96
clubs, music, 9, 15, 26–27, 82; African cosmopolitanism in, 52; *angolanidade* and, 53; dress code, 108; entrance fees, 107; "family" ambiance of, 87; female musicians in, 103, 105–7; government oversight of, 133–34; growth of, 25; live music shows, 134–37; MPLA supported by club-goers, 7; opening of, 83–84; owners, 16, 52, 89, 90, 95; performance spaces, 133; private gatherings as predecessors of, 120; prostitutes in, 50, 100, 102, 106, 107, 134, 231n90; reforms of late colonial period and, 90–92; reopened as recreation centers, 181; sonorous capitalism and, 24, 141
Coelho, Sebastião, 143, 155, 240n12, 245n93; Estúdios Norte and, 157, 160, 162; radio programs of, 156, 157, 163
coffee production, 32, 59, 215n90, 222n69; Bakongo producers in revolt, 81; Luanda's urbanization and, 70; Portuguese immigrants and, 60
Cohen, Irene, 75, 77, 79
Coio, Chico, 91, 97–98, 190, 192, 228n49; in self-defense militia, 168; on songs about women, 100–101
Cold War, 5, 38, 169, 188–89
colonialism, European: Belgian, 148, 241n35; British and French, 37
colonialism, Portuguese, 10, 248n30; attempts to co-opt music, 7; Catholic Church and, 78, 122; cultural politics of, 61; history of, 12; ideology of, 31; injustice of, 22; lusotropicalist ideology and, 39; paternalism of, 20, 54; reforms and changes in everyday life, 88–93; repression exercised by, 83; revolts of 1961 and, 81, 162; songs critical of, 25, 153; violence of, 16
Cometa, João, 118
Comités Amilcar Cabral, 170, 248n29
Comités Henda, 170, 248n30
Commissões Populares de Bairro (Popular Neighborhood Commissions), 168
Companhia de Discos de Angola (CDA), 162, 163, 185

Concert Services office, 133
Concordata (1940), 78
conga music, 118
Congo, Belgian, 148, 241n35
Congo-Brazzaville (Republic of the Congo), 4, 81, 144, 148, 149. *See also* Brazzaville
Congo-Kinshasa. *See* Zaire (Congo-Kinshasa)
Congolese music, 19, 164, 245n96; Cuban influences in, 240n117; guitar styles, 113, 230n71; at private gatherings, 120, 121; on radio, 144, 148; significance of women for, 101
consciousness, political, 5, 19, 22, 76; cultural practice and, 80; music as spark of, 137
contract (forced) labor, 124, 125, 126, 211n34; death as result of, 132; forms of, 236n52; "Monangambe" poem and song, 193
contribution parties, 107, 117, 120
Coordinating Commission for Radio Broadcasting Plan for the Province of Angola, 155
Coqueiros, 33
cosmopolitanism: Brazilian music in Angola, 63; cultural sovereignty and, 140; defined, 234n14; European audiences and, 111; "hot," 85, 87; in music clubs, 52; music scene of Luanda and, 85; romantic songs and, 233n9; socialism and, 177, 251n62; songs about women and, 131
Costa, Contreiras da, 73
Costa, Idalina, 120–21, 235n37
Costa, Vate, 128, 252n96
cotton production, 81
counterinsurgency, 21, 89, 155–57
creoles, 12, 32, 58, 209n7. *See also mestiços* (culturally mixed Africans)
Cruz, Viriato da, 40, 73, 250n49
Cuba/Cubans, 5, 18, 177; Cuban forces in Angolan civil war, 169, 170, 173; cultural festivals in, 251n82; journalists, 64
Cuban music, 84, 117, 164, 186; Congolese music influenced by, 240n117; rumbas, 64, 240n117; Zairean musicians and, 208n95
Cubata, 181
Cultura [Culture] (literary journal), 40, 73

cultural sovereignty, 7, 13, 140, 176; achieved before independence, 19; coup attempt (1977) and, 175; "into nation" and, 108; MPLA plans for independence and, 168; music scene of Luanda and, 85–86, 87; *poder popular* (people's power) and, 189; production of music and, 17; transition to independence and, 171
culture: colonial paternalism and, 20; colonial reforms and, 88; politics and, 6, 10, 11, 57; Portuguese practices adopted by Africans, 51–53; state formation and, 2; transformative qualities of, 13
Cunene province, 117, 162

dancers and dancing, 16, 85, 234n26; dance parties, 117–19; *kisomba*, 119, 185, 235n32; *kuduro*, 119, 192, 193, 235n32; Latin American, 113; at private gatherings, 120; *rebita*, 8, 61, 117, 223n72; renowned dancers, 118; "traditional" Angolan dance, 117, 118; *umbigada*, 61; women in music clubs and, 106
Dar es Salaam (Tanzania), 16, 151
Davidson, Basil, 10, 39, 40
Dembos area, 65, 169
detribalization, 40, 41, 43–48, 51
development, economic, 14, 30, 46
Dia do Trabalhador [Worker's Day] (music show), 134, 135, 136
"Diala Monzo" (Elias song), 130–31
Dias, Carlitos Vieira, 163, 169, 170
Dias, Carlos do Aniceto "Liceu" Vieira, 15, 27, 105, 205n67; arrest and imprisonment of, 66, 125, 205n66; on Brazilian music, 63; semba and, 63–64. *See also* Ngola Ritmos (band)
dikanza (musical instrument), 63, 72, 73, 96, 113
Dikanza record label, 164, 246n106
Dikanzas do Prenda (band), 163
Diniz, 98
DISA [Direcção de Informação e Segurança de Angola] (Angolan Directorate for Information and Security), 173, 174, 250n44
disc jockeys *(discotequeiros)*, 20, 120, 161, 191
Discoteca de Angola (store), 162
"Dr. Neto" (song), 153

Index 279

Dos jornais às armas [From Newspapers to Arms] (Bittencourt), 57
dress (fashion), 26, 61–62, 91, 108
drums, 72, 73, 164
Duara, Prasenjit, 13
Duffy, James, 39, 49–50
duplicity *(duplicidade)*, 46–48, 51

education, 31, 36, 42, 61, 74, 88
Egypt, 142, 144
Elias. *See* Kimuezu, Elias dia
elites, African, 16, 33, 44; access to live music and, 193; *angolanidade* defined by, 25; in Bairro Operário (B.O.), 60; clandestine political activity and, 66; creole, 12; Kimbundu language and, 233n2; Liceu Salvador Correia and, 65; MPLA, 166, 192; music and social gatherings of, 120; musicians' criticism of, 24; as reading audience for literary nationalists, 58; women's cultural/political activities and, 74
elites, white colonial, 65, 70
Emancipação da Mulher Angolana [Emancipation of the Angolan Woman] (Nino and Merengues album), 182, 183
emcees, 16, 61–62, 95, 110
Emissora Oficial de Angola [Official Broadcasting Station of Angola] (EOA), 144, 150, 160; counterinsurgent radio and, 155, 156, 157
ENDIPU [Empresa Nacional do Discos e Publicações] (National Company of Discs and Publications), 162, 185
English language, 11, 37, 112, 153
Erlmann, Veit, 132
Escola do Samba, 97
Estádio Nacional Cidadela Desportiva (national stadium), 70
Estado Novo (New State), 62, 83; as developmentalist state, 37, 38; lusotropicalist ideology, 11–12, 31, 37–38, 49, 212–13n47; reform-and-repression policy, 88–89; rise to power, 3–4, 32; social science in service of, 30. *See also* Portugal; Salazar, António
Estrela Canora, 62
Estúdios Norte, 157, 160, 162, 163
ethnicity, 3, 139
ethnolinguistic groups, 34–35

ethnomusicologists, 7, 53
European Economic Community, 88
exile, 16, 19, 48; arrogance of leaders in, 92, 188; male political elites in, 56; of nationalist leaders, 31

Fabian, Johannes, 131
Fadiang (Rádio Reparadora do Bié) record company, 161, 162–63
fado music, 84
Fair, Laura, 7, 203n43
families, social science and, 41, 46–47
Fançony, Maria Luisa, 162, 186, 187, 245n88
Fanon, Frantz, 242n46
FAPLA [Forças Armadas Populares de Libertação de Angola] (Popular Armed Forces for the Liberation of Angola), 169–70
Faria, Manuel, 89, 150, 161, 181, 230n71, 238n81
fascism, Portuguese. *See* Estado Novo (New State); Salazar, António
Feijó, Betinho, 193
Ferguson, James, 18, 208n91
Ferreira, Carlos "Cassé," 187
Ferreira, Roldão, 154, 156, 244n72
festivals, 15, 84, 85, 177, 181–85
"Filhos Querem Pão" [Children Want Bread] (Dog Murras song), 194
films. *See* cinema
5 Kings (band), 112
Flores, Paulo, 8, 190, 193, 194
FNLA [Frente Nacional para a Libertação de Angola] (National Front for the Liberation of Angola), 4, 5, 57, 200n17; album recorded by, 243n55; Cohen (Irene) killed by, 75; guerrilla bases in neighboring countries, 13, 81; musicians associated with, 246n2; neutralization of, 165, 177; origins, 199n12; radio and, 142, 144, 147; revolts of 1961 and, 81; in transition to independence, 167, 168, 169, 170; war against Portuguese military, 84
Fogo Negro (band), 62, 220n30
folklore, Angolan music marketed as, 114–15, 115, 116, 158, 158, 159, 160
Fonográfica, 162, 163
Fonseca, António, 161–62, 245n93
"Fontinhas." *See* Pereira, Euclides de Fontes "Fontinhas"

Forças Armadas Angolanas (Angolan Armed Forces), 182, 253n2
Fortunato, Jomo, 16, 19, 54, 128
France, 18, 251n82
Franco, 64, 120, 149
Franco, Pedro Bonzela, 120
French colonialism, 37
French language, 11, 37, 61, 86, 112
French music, 164
Freyre, Gilberto, 11–12, 37, 49, 212–13n47
fubeiros (shop owners), 68–69, 70, 75, 168, 169, 222n63
funjada (afternoon meal), 70

Gagajeira, 181
Garda e o Seu Conjunto (band), 123–24, 158, 159
Gaspar, Mito, 177, 184
"gee vees" (GVs), 118, 161
Geiger, Susan, 11, 22, 56
gender, 3, 11, 25, 55, 219n15; as cover for political song lyrics, 125; division of domestic labor, 96; in music scene, 87–88; *musseque* population and, 35; nation inflected by, 56; urban experience and, 23, 82. *See also* men; women
General Council for Countersubversion, 156
generations (age groups), 55, 57, 66, 192, 193; "afternoon sessions" and, 70; Bota Fogo and, 72, 92; division of domestic labor and, 96; intergenerational transmission of knowledge, 96, 120, 186; literary nationalism and, 73; music and male experience, 96; music clubs and, 107; nation building and, 185; radio and, 186, 187; women's activities and, 77–79, 102, 182
geopolitics, international, 14
Gexto, 64, 66, 121
Ghana, 144, 206n75
Ginásio Futebol Clube, 60, 65, 67, 79, 238n86
Giro-Giro (music club), 55, 181, 238n81
golden age, of Angolan music, 15, 16, 19, 84; dance and, 119; MPLA Ministry of Culture and bands of, 181; nostalgia for, 189; performer-audience relations in, 192; revived on radio, 187; songs, 125–32; unity in desire for independence and, 165. *See also* music, Angolan
Gondola, Didier, 101

"Grândola, Vila Morena" (Afonso song), 165
Grupo de Reflexão de Sita Valles (Sita Valles reflection group), 170
Grupo dos Sambas, 63
Grupo Feminino Santa Cecília (Santa Cecília Girls Group), 74, 77–79, 80, 219n20
guerrilla struggle, 2, 4–5, 25, 55, 85, 108; changes in everyday life and, 92; colonial reforms and, 88; radio and, 140, 141, 153, 155–56; transition to independence, 167–70
Guinea-Bissau, 4, 13, 167, 248n30

Haiti, 6
Hayes, Joy Elizabeth, 142, 143
Heimer, Franz-Wilhelm, 39, 89
Hernandez, Francisco Xavier, 64, 220n39
HMV (His Master's Voice) record label, 118
Hobsbawm, Eric, 10
Ho MPLA Nkango Angola (Pinheiro album), 178, 178–80
Huambo Radio Club, 143, 149, 157
hungu (musical instrument), 66, 73, 96, 221n49

"Içar da bandeira" [Raise the Flag] (Neto), 15
identity, Angolan, 3, 40, 91. *See also angolanidade* (Angolanness)
Imagined Communities (Anderson), 141, 159
imperialism, 179, 180, 184, 222n64
independence: Catholic Church and, 78; dance club administration as training for, 52–53; "hiatus" in music and, 188–89; ideal of, 76; military coup in Portugal and, 165; transition toward, 167–71
India, 37
indígenas (indigenous persons, natives), 4, 42; *assimilados* and, 44, 69–70, 74; as civil status under colonial law, 59; migration to Luanda, 67; tax on, 68; upward mobility of, 70
indigenato system, 69, 89
industrialization, 89
"infrapolitics," 6
Ingombotas, 32–33, 96, 215n84, 222n69
intellectuals, 56, 61
Irmãos Kafala (Kafala Brothers), 184

Jacinto, António, 40, 48, 58, 73, 193
Jack Rumba, 118
Jaime, Alberto, 52–53, 72, 222n57; on *Angola Combatente* broadcasts, 150; on backyard gatherings, 119–20; on Bairro Indígena, 69; Bota Fogo and, 71–72; on danger of political activity, 75–77; Maxinde club and, 92; as "new" *assimilado*, 67; on women in music clubs, 106
Jaime, Cipriana, 106
JMPLA (Juventude do Movimento Popular de Libertação de Angola), 169, 177, 180–81, 242n55
"João Dumingu" (Ngola Ritmos song), 65, 124–25
Jorge, Paulo, 149
Jovens do Prenda (band), 177, 181, 185
Jovens [Youth] (band), 163
Júnior, Gilberto, 163, 187, 246n103
Júnior, Santos, 177, 181, 252n96

kabetula music, 8
Kafala, Moises and José, 177
"Kaputu" (song), 153
Kassav (band), 185, 186, 235n32
Kassequel *musseque*, 103–4
kazekuta music, 8
Kelley, Robin D. G., 8, 86
Kenya, 13
Kianda Kianazanga, 181
Kiezos, Os (band), 1–2, 15, 99, 103, 177, 185; arrested by PIDE, 129; girlfriends of band members, 99–100; MPLA Ministry of Culture and, 181; songs performed by, 128–30
Kikongo language, 112, 244n72
Kimbandas do Ritmo (band), 73
Kimbundu language, 14, 32, 62, 65, 66, 138; anticolonial songs in, 153; *assimilado* youth and, 73; band names in, 94; colonial officials' ignorance and denigration of, 111, 112, 113, 126; as lingua franca, 234n11; mixed with Portuguese, 118, 123, 128–29; at music festivals, 182; radio programs in, 154, 156, 157, 244n72; song lyrics in, 114, 116, 122, 132; songs translated into Portuguese, 110; urban elites and, 113, 233n2; valorized by musicians, 137
Kimuezu, Elias dia, 65–66, 67, 244n84; on danceable music, 116–17; as "king of Angolan music," 116; MPLA-sponsored music festivals and, 182; songs by, 130–31
Kinshasa, 16, 81, 148, 227n23. *See also* Leopoldville; Zaire (Congo-Kinshasa)
kisomba dance/music, 119, 185, 235n32
kissange (musical instrument), 113, 234n12
Kissueias do Ritmo (band), 94
Kituxi, 66, 96
Kizomba, 181
Kriptons, Os (band), 112–13
Kudissanga KwaMakamba (music club), 181, 238n81
kuduro dance/music, 119, 192, 193, 235n32
Kussunguila (radio show), 154
Kutonoca (music show), 134, 135–37, 167–68

labor: categories of, 35–36, 42; division of domestic labor, 96; free and enslaved, 32, 33; music as respectable male labor, 98; racial discrimination in, 42; urban migration and, 42. *See also* contract (forced) labor
Lamartine, Carlos, 19, 54, 90, 185, 191; Angolan national anthem and, 170; Artistas de Primeira Grandeza and, 252n96; on decline of semba, 186; on financial situation of clubs, 91–92; on girlfriends of Os Kiezos band members, 99–100; *Memórias* CD, 192; MPLA involvement of, 169, 251n82; on music festivals, 182; on prostitutes in clubs, 107; on "revolutionary" music, 177; on women's "good" reputations, 102, 106
Lando, Alberto Teta, 1, 2, 10, 19, 163, 174; FNLA and, 246n2; on musicians killed by Angolan government, 109; *Ritmos Angolanos* collection, 188; singing in Portuguese, 112
languages, 34–35, 112–13
Lara, Alda, 48, 73
Lara, Lúcio, 13, 57, 199n15
Latin American music and dance, 113, 121, 148, 161, 164. *See also* Brazilian music
Lei Orgânica do Ultramar Português (Organic Laws of Overseas Portugal), 37
Leitão, Gabriel, 64, 205n66, 220n39
Leopoldville, 148, 161, 225n4, 241n35. *See also* Kinshasa
Liceu Salvador Correia, 65

Liga Nacional Africana (National African League), 44, 57, 71, 74, 77, 232n92; *Angola Combatente* broadcasts and, 154; Catholic chapel at, 78; collaborationist politics of, 66, 79; generational tensions within, 72; musical and theatrical performances at, 121; Ngola Ritmos and, 63, 64; publications of, 73

Lingala language, 149

Lisbon, 4, 21, 32, 48, 149, 161

literacy, 7, 72, 73

Lobito, 89, 143, 161

Lobito Radio Club, 162

Lomba, Euclides da, 193

Lopes, Júlio Mendes, 156, 239n2

Lopo, Julio de Castro, 48–49

Luanda: Brazzaville in communication with, 155; as colonial capital, 113; creole elite, 12, 32; factories on outskirts of, 89; history of, 31; in late colonial period, 20; map, 29; Marginal boulevard, 19; MPLA presence in, 109, 201n36; Music Academy, 96, 123; music festivals under MPLA state, 182; music shops, 19; neighborhoods of, 28, 32–33, 208–9n2; population, 41, 194–95; Portuguese immigrants in, 4; postindependence period, 191; prostitution in, 49; radio in, 157; recording industry in, 162, 163, 164; slave trade and, 31–32; in transition to independence, 168, 169, 170; urban growth of, 31, 32; white population, 35, 41–42, 59; women of, 62; as young and male city, 102. *See also* baixa (European city center); *musseques* (urban shanty towns)

lusotropicalism, 11–12, 44, 54, 212–13n47, 213n54; album covers and, 114–15, 115, 116, 158, 158, 159; colonial possession and, 110; cosmopolitanism as response to, 18; social science and, 37–38; stylized Portuguese songs and, 64. *See also* Freyre, Gilberto

Macau, 37

Macedo, Jorge, 15, 19, 54, 206n82; on Africanization of *assimilados*, 53; on clubs and parties, 86–87; on Congolese radio, 148, 149; on Latin American musical influence, 113; on politically partisan music, 185

Maculusso, 32

"Madya Kandimba" (Garda e o Seu Conjunto song), 123–24, 131

Mãe Preta, 181

Malanje, 4

Malaquias, Assis, 166, 171

Mamdani, Mahmood, 10

Mangololo, 86

Mangueira, Efigénia Barroso. *See* Van Dunem, Efigénia Barroso Mangueira

Manguxi Brigade, 184

Manjenje, António "Tó," 183–84

Manuel, Zé, 86

Marçal *musseque*, 3, 28, 65, 68; Batalha's club, 129; Bota Fogo and, 67; as cradle of Angolan music, 195; Kissueias do Ritmo in, 94; live music shows, 136; MPLA presence in, 169; music clubs in, 100, 134; Ngola Cine and, 135; prostitution in, 50; *turmas* in, 97

Marcum, John, 12, 39

Maria, Adolfo, 149, 166, 174

"Maria Vai a Fonte" (Portuguese song), 64, 114

Martins, Fernando, 1–2, 10, 15, 185

Martins, Luís. *See* Xabanu (Luís Martins)

Marxism-Leninism, 176

masculinity, 25, 93–101

massemba dance, 117

Maxinde (music club), 55, 92, 97, 188, 237n78; origin as soccer club, 52; prostitutes in, 107; as recreation center, 181; sports team of, 134; women in organization of, 106

McClintock, Anne, 87

MCK (rap singer), 195, 196

Mdembe, Achille, 10–11

Memórias (Lamartine CD), 192

memory, 15, 119, 192

men: in carnival groups, 95; dominance in music industry, 23; dress for clubgoing, 26, 61; friendship and politics among, 75; male musicians, 87, 91, 112, 230n72; manual laborers, 35; *musseque* population and, 35; soldiers in Portuguese army, 50, 107, 130; "tragic *mulata*" prostitutes and, 48–49, 50; *turma* groups, 62, 97

"Meninas de Hoje, As" [Girls Today] (África Show song), 130, 231n88

Mensagem [Message] (literary journal), 40, 73, 214n64

Merenges, Os (band), 163, 177, 181
merengue music, 161, 164
Merengue record label, 163, 164
messianic movements, 5
Messiant, Christine, 5, 12–13, 35, 42; on "new assimilated," 45, 67, 90, 221n55; on unpredictability of Angola's past, 1, 13
mestiços (culturally mixed Africans), 32, 53, 227n25, 232n92. *See also* creoles
middle class, African, 59, 77; Bairro Indígena (B.I.) and, 67, 68, 70; as consciousness of social position, 82; values expressed in songs, 65
migration, rural-to-urban, 40, 41–43
"Milhorró" (song), 128–30
Mingas, André, 177
Mingas, Rui, 96, 98, 170, 180, 193, 229n64
Mingas, Saydi, 181
modernity, 9, 18, 54, 55, 145
modernization, 14, 30, 40, 46
"Monangambe" (Jacinto poem), 193
"Monetu ua Kassule" (song), 153
Monteiro, Manuel Rui, 170
Monteiro, Ramiro Ladeiro, 35, 43, 54, 92, 134, 145; on cultural practices of *musseques*, 51; on "double life" of *musseque* household heads, 47; as head of SCCIA, 36; on interethnic marriages, 45; on prostitution in Luanda, 50; on radio ownership, 146; on rural-to-urban migration, 41
Montez, Luiz, 135–36
Mourão, Fernando, 32, 53
Mozambique, 88, 144, 161, 184; anticolonial war in, 13, 167; students in Lisbon, 4
MPLA [Movimento Popular de Libertação de Angola] (Popular Movement for the Liberation of Angola), 1, 4–5, 9, 130; in control of state, 165, 170, 177; coup attempt (1977) and, 171, 172–76; Cuban and Soviet support for, 5; guerrilla bases in neighboring countries, 81; independence of Angola and, 83, 165; internal politics of, 166, 176; musicians in support of, 7, 17, 165, 176, 177–85, 188; musicians killed by government of, 109, 180; official historical narrative of, 5, 12; origins, 13, 57, 199–200n17, 199n12; as petty bourgeois elite, 192, 248n30; politicians of, 66, 67; politicized music festivals and, 177–85; radio broadcasts of, 142, 144, 149–55, 212n42; return of exiles (1974), 83, 165–66, 174; revolts of 1961 and, 81; in transition to independence, 167–71; urban popular culture misunderstood by, 109; war against Portuguese military, 84; as "workers' party," 174, 176, 177, 188; youth wing (JMPLA), 169, 177, 180–81, 242n55
Mudimbe, V. Y., 11
Mukenga, Filipe, 177
Murimba Show, 128, 129
Murras, Dog, 192, 193–94
Murray, Martin, 14
music, Angolan, 2, 6, 8; authenticity and, 22; at backyard gatherings, 121; collective experience and, 87; as constant presence in everyday life, 54; cosmopolitanism and, 18; cultural sovereignty and, 3, 6, 13; genres of popular urban music, 8; "hiatus" in, 166, 189; history of, 20; instruments, 63–64, 73, 113, 234n12; *kabetula*, 8; *kazekuta*, 8; marketed as folklore, 114–15, *115*, 116, *158*, 158, 159, 160; masculinity and, 93–101; mobility and reterritorialization of, 141, 164; resurgence in post-independence period, 185–88; transition to independence and, 167–70; trova, 184, 191; Western musical instruments and, 52. *See also* clubs, music; golden age, of Angolan music; song lyrics; *specific genres or styles*
musicians, 2, 83; *assimilado*, 63, 65; audience interaction with, 115; Bota Fogo and, 73; Congolese, 64; cosmopolitanism and, 18; as cultural producers, 16; cultural sovereignty and, 22; dress (fashion) and, 91; in economic hardship, 190; economic status of, 24; festivals organized by MPLA state and, 177–85; gender and, 23; "golden age" remembered by, 84; imprisoned, 125, 128; independence and, 165–66; as intellectuals, 54; killed by Angolan government, 1, 109, 174, 180; MPLA supported by, 165, 176, 180, 188; of post-independence period, 185, 193; professionalization of, 158, 161, 163; reforms of late colonial period and, 88; respect and admiration for, 97–98;

sexual double standard and, 102–3; in transition to independence, 168–69, 171; *Voz de Angola* radio and, 156–57. See also *specific musicians*
musseques (urban shanty towns), 1, 13; African cultural sovereignty in, 93; *angolanidade* in, 9; *baixa* in relation to, 126–28, 210n16; as birthplace of music and nationalism, 28; carnival in, 95; civil war between nationalist partisans in, 167; club scene in, 25; colonial social science and, 28, 30; as cultural bases of nationalism, 16; cultural practices in, 51–53, 58–59; cultural sovereignty in, 3; dance parties, 117–19; independence and, 26; literary nationalism and, 40; map, 29; "masses" of nationalist metanarrative in, 82, 147; MPLA presence in, 225n3; music clubs in, 7, 9, 97, 134; origins and social composition of, 31–36; police surveillance of, 3, 21; population figures, 41; prostitution in, 48–51; semba in, 25; social composition of, 58, 67–71; social history of, 25; street festivals, 84, 111; transethnicity in, 43–48; as transitional spaces, 138; urban migration versus immigration, 41–43; white residents of, 43, 222n63. See also Luanda; *specific musseques*
Mussulo Island, 27, 195
"Muxima" (Ngola Ritmos song), 121–22, 131, 235n40
Myers, Garth, 14

Namibia (Southwest Africa), 144, 203n48, 247n3
"Nandó." See Santos, Fernando da Piedade "Nandó"
Nascimento, Alexandre, 78
Nascimento, Lopo do, 73
nation: cinema and, 239n94; as "imagined community," 10, 26, 85, 141–42; nationalism distinguished from, 10–14; pleasure versus sacrifice in narrative of, 17
nationalism, 2, 18, 142, 192; armed struggle, 16; birthplace in *musseques*, 28; civil war and, 166; cosmopolitan, 149, 206n75; culture and, 14, 56, 218n10; division into three movements, 4; gender and, 59–60; "into nation," 8, 31, 108; literary, 30, 31, 39–40, 45;
metanarrative of, 56–57, 60, 80, 81–82, 83; MPLA institutions and, 184; *musseque* residents and, 21; nation distinguished from, 10–14; popular support for, 5–6; standard historical accounts, 3–6, 8, 71, 79; in Tanganyika (Tanzania), 11; urban areas and, 13–14; women's involvement in, 77–79
National Radio Station, 19
nation building, 6, 166, 177–85
Neto, Agostinho, 40, 48, 73, 175, 205n66; on Angolan unity, 45; in Bairro Operário (B.O.), 61; as first president of independent Angola, 61, 66; "Manguxi" nickname, 184; as poet, 15; repression following coup attempt and, 250n47
Neto, Maria da Conceição, 38, 197n4
Ngola Melodias (band), 114, 116
Ngola record label, 164
Ngola Ritmos (band), 13, 79, 80, 96, 105, 153; album cover, 158; *angolanidade* and, 52; Bairro Operário (B.O.) and, 60–66; band members, 27, 61, 125; danceable music of, 116; foundational status of, 14–15, 16, 22; literary critics on, 58; MPLA's origins and, 57; music produced in Portugal, 158; narrative of nationalism and, 16–17; as "old" *assimilados*, 67; in Ole film, 252n88; private gatherings and, 121; songs, 65, 121–22, 124–25; at Teatro Nacional (National Theater), 110; whites attracted to music of, 111
Ngola Ritmos (Macedo novel), 15
Ngoleiros do Ritmo (band), 62, 158, 160
Ngoma Jazz, 94–95
Ngongo, 13, 97
Nico, Dr., 149
Noite e Dia [Night and Day] (magazine), 20, 43
Nosso musseque (Vieira novel), 50, 231n88
nostalgia, 15, 16, 17, 22, 24, 53; for golden age of music, 189; songs of Ngola Ritmos and, 121; for time of "hiatus," 166
Notícia (magazine), 20, 162, 236n57, 244n74
Novatos da Ilha Rebita (dance group), 63
Nunes, Artur, 1, 169; killed in MPLA purge, 174, 180; music censored after coup attempt, 186, 187, 197n1; reappearance of music on radio, 188
N'zaji (band), 153, 206n81

Index ↩ 285

Okay Jazz (band), 120
Okuma, Thomas, 39
Ole, António, 15, 64, 205n67, 252n88
Organization of African Unity, 85, 250n44
Ouro Negro (duo), 114, 244n84
Ovimbundu migrant workers, 81, 215n90, 220n41
Ovimbundu-Umbundu ethnolinguistic group, 34, 216n109

Pacavira, Manuel Pedro, 150
Paim, Eduardo, 193
Paim, Prado, 131, 163
Palma, Belita, 63, 104, 105, 230n72, 232n92
pan-Africanism, 149, 200n17, 241n35
Parendon Press, 153, 243n57
Parlophone record label, 158
parties, political, 14, 167, 168, 224n87
Passos, Luís dos, 172
paternalism, colonial, 20, 54
patos ("ducks," party crashers), 120
patrício (compatriot), 87, 93, 108
patronage, 24, 192
Pawson, Lara, 175
peasants, 14, 89, 170, 248n30
Pedrito, 177, 252n96
Pepetela, 45
Pereira, Euclides de Fontes "Fontinhas," 125, 126, 205n66
Pereira, Lemos, 136
Pereira d'Eça (Ondijva), town of, 162
performance, space and, 132
Pernambuco, Joana, 118
Petanga, 86
petty bourgeoisie, 23–24, 166, 228n43; African-owned businesses, 93; "middle class" distinguished from, 82; musicians from, 102; *poder popular* (people's power) and, 171; reforms of late colonial period and, 89–90; "revolutionary" redefinition of music and, 177. *See also* middle class, African
PIDE [Polícia International e de Defesa do Estado] (International Police for Defense of the State), 83, 168, 172, 207n86, 223n80; archive of, 19, 21, 130, 144, 149; infiltration of political groups by, 75; intensified efforts of, 89; music venues frequented by, 85, 86, 129; Ngola Ritmos and, 125; radio broadcasts monitored by, 144, 146, 147, 149, 150–52, 154; raids by, 76; SCCIA in relation to, 37; song lyrics monitored by, 113–14, 125, 126
Pimental, Amadeu, 187
Pimentel, Carlos Alberto, 93, 94, 96, 111, 112, 230n71
PIM [Polícia de Informação Militar] (Military Information Police), 152
Pinheiro, Paulo, 178
Pioca, 86
Pitcher, M. Anne, 88
plena music, 161
poder popular (people's power), 170–71, 189
"Poema do Semba" [Semba Poem] (Flores song), 8, 193
police, secret. *See* PIDE [Polícia International e de Defesa do Estado] (International Police for Defense of the State)
Portugal, 4, 12, 18, 137; Angolan music produced in, 157–58; Angolan sports stars in, 98; colonial history in Angola, 31; Communist Party, 248n30; developmentalist policies, 37; economic boom and colonial reform, 88; global colonial empire of, 37; international debates on colonialism of, 85; lusotropicalist ideology in, 11–12; military coup (1974), 5, 84, 165, 167, 174, 199n11; as pluri-continental nation, 83, 148; recording industry of Angola and, 162–63. *See also* colonialism, Portuguese; Estado Novo (New State); whites, Portuguese
portugalidade (Portugueseness), 18, 38, 40
Portuguese army: Africans in, 152, 153–54, 244n74; prostitutes and, 50, 107, 130
Portuguese language, 11, 86, 110; African languages translated into, 110, 114; mixed with Kimbundu, 118, 123, 128–29; radio broadcasts in, 144, 148, 157; song lyrics in, 112, 126–27
Prenda *musseque*, 43, 174
Présence Africaine, 39
Primeiro de Maio (band), 177
prisons, attack on (1961), 79, 81, 199n15, 200n17, 224n89
Processo de 50 (Trial of 50), 4, 16, 69, 205n66; Bota Fogo members in, 74; Ngola Ritmos members as part of, 66; women's support activities for prisoners, 79
Progresso soccer club, 175
proletariat, 35, 89, 224n1

prostitution, 41, 48–51, 100, 216n109; female musicians and stigma of, 102, 107–8, 121, 235n37; music clubs and, 50, 100, 102, 106, 107, 134, 231n90; Portuguese soldiers and, 50, 107, 130
Protestantism, 45, 65, 246n3
Provincial Association of Luanda, 134

Quintal do Ritmo [Rhythm Patio] (radio program), 187, 246n103

race and racism, 4, 20, 110; *assimilados* as victims of, 44; definition of *musseque* and, 33; laws, 42; lusotropicalism and, 11, 37, 38, 49, 54; residential segregation and, 38, 42; stratification under Estado Novo, 32; in United States, 86
radio, 3, 20–21, 93, 194, 239n2; amateur radio clubs, 84; counterinsurgency and, 155–57, 243n65; as cultural technology, 141–43; foreign broadcasts, 142, 144, 147; history of radio in Angola, 143–55, 145; music reterritorialized by, 26; nation constituted by, 133, 140, 141; resurgence of music and, 185–88; sonorous capitalism and, 140; transistor radios, 92
Radio Brazzaville, 142, 146, 152–53
Rádio Ecclésia, 155, 157, 253n3
Radio Moscow, 142, 144
Rádio Nacional de Angola (Angolan National Radio, RNA), 185–87, 236n52
Radio Netherlands, 142
Rafael, Padre Vicente José, 78, 79
Rangel *musseque*, 65, 68, 96, 174; Cine Ngola and, 92, 135; MPLA presence in, 168; music clubs in, 134; *turmas* in, 97
rebita dance/music, 8, 61, 117, 223n72
Rebita record label, 163, 164
Recompasso (Flores album), 193
recording industry, 3, 84, 159–64; archives of, 20; mobility of music and, 141, 164; music as male occupation and, 103; music reterritorialized by, 26; Portuguese labels, 115; sonorous capitalism and, 140, 160
recreation centers, 177, 180–81, 185–86, 191
Redding, Otis, 112
Revolta Activa, 149, 250n49
Revolução dos Cravos (Revolution of the Carnations), 167, 176
Rhodesia, Southern, 12

Ribas, Oscar, 73, 123
Ritmo de N'gola Ritmos, O [The Rhythm of Ngola Ritmos] (Ole film), 15, 64, 205n67, 230n72, 252n88
Ritmo Jazz, 86
Ritmos Angolanos (Angolan Rhythms) collection, 188
RMS music shop, 19
Roberto, Holden, 147
Rocha, Dionísio, 19–20, 73, 135, 158, 220n30; *Kutonoca* show and, 136; on recording industry, 163
Rocha, Edmundo, 57, 225n3
Rochereau, Tabu Ley, 149
rock music, 112–13, 138
Rocks, Os (band), 112, 163
Rodrigues, Deolinda, 77, 79, 217n1
Rodríguez, Silvio, 186
"Rosa Maria" (Castro song), 131
rumba, 8, 25, 64, 117, 139
Russia, 177, 206n75

Salão dos Anjos (music club), 55, 238n81
Salazar, António, 3, 32, 167, 199n11
Sambizanga *musseque*, 65, 89, 131, 174; live music shows, 136; music clubs in, 134; Progresso soccer club, 175
Santocas, 70, 137, 177, 185, 252n96; on Congolese music, 149; "Valódia," 178–80
Santos, Arnaldo, 40, 214n64
Santos, Dina, 106, 128, 181, 232n92; Artistas de Primeira Grandeza and, 252n96; music festivals and, 182; "Semba Kassequel" song, 103–5
Santos, Fernando da Piedade "Nandó" dos, 67, 188
Santos, Jacques dos, 50, 63, 117, 120
Santos, José Eduardo dos, 66, 153, 181
Santos, José "Zé" Maria dos, 64–65, 66, 110, 116, 121, 205n66. *See also* Ngola Ritmos (band)
Santos, Manuel dos, 73
São Paulo *musseque*, 134, 161, 173
São Tomé and Príncipe, 4, 153, 236n52
Saude, Noé de, 74
Savimbi, Jonas, 5, 21, 184, 226n9
SCCIA [Serviço de Centralização e Coordenação de Informações de Angola] (Angolan Services for the Centralization and Coordination of Information), 36–37, 242n55

Index 287

Scott, James, 6
Sebastião, Arsénio "Cherokee," 195–96
Sebastião, Matemona, 86, 94–95, 115, 222n60, 229n50, 246n2
SECULT (Secretary of State for Culture), 177
Semana Ilustrada [Illustrated Weekly] (magazine), 20, 43
"Semba Kassequel" (Santos song), 103–5
"Semba Lekalo" (Castro song), 130
semba music, 7–8, 10, 97, 184; "consolidation" of, 16; decline of, 186, 191; evolution of, 117–19; life of *musseques* and, 138; *massemba* dance and, 117; Ngola Ritmos and creation of, 60; origins of, 63–64; reissued music from golden age, 19; spirit of insurgency and, 83; as symbol of Angolan nation, 193; urban experience represented by, 25
Semba record label, 164, 246n106
Semba Tropical (band), 177
sexuality, 100–101, 102, 130
shantytowns, colonial, 14
Silva, António José Garcia da, 148
Silva, Mário Rui, 19, 54, 165
slave trade, abolition of, 31–32, 35
soccer clubs, 51, 52, 57, 71; Boa Vista, 71; Progresso, 175; proliferation of, 67, 95; Provincial Association of Luanda and, 134. *See also* Bota Fogo; Ginásio Futebol Clube
Social Darwinism, 38
socialism, 5, 17, 176, 183, 184, 251n62
social science, anticolonial, 30–31
social science, colonial, 20, 24, 28, 30, 31, 34; *angolanidade* and, 39; on cultural practices in *musseques*, 51–53; on detribalization, 43–48; folkloric associations and, 62; lusotropicalism and, 36–38; reinterpretation of, 40–51; on social composition of *musseques*, 34, 36
Sociedade de Cultura Angolana, 40
sociology, 37
"Som Angolano" [Angolan Sound] (Caetano song), 118
song lyrics, 25, 138; "Bairro Indígena," 70–71; "Bartolomeu," 131–32; "Chofer de Praça," 23, 126–28; "Diala Monzo," 130–31; of "golden age" music, 125–32; "João Dumingu," 65, 124; life under colonial rule expressed in, 111–12; love songs, 112; "Madya Kandimba," 123–24; "Milhorró," 128–29; "Muxima," 122; "Semba Kassequel," 103–4; "Valódia," 178–80
son music, 118
Soremekun, Fola, 169
South Africa, apartheid, 5, 12, 42, 43; African urban music in, 226n47; Angolan whites' departure for, 167; investments in Angola, 88; military intervention in Angola, 170; record prices in, 162; UNITA supported by, 177, 180, 184; white settler rule in, 203n48
Soviet Union, 5, 183
Spanish language, 112
Spitulnik, Debra, 143, 145
Sporting (sports club), 71
sports, 25, 71, 87, 93, 95, 98. *See also* soccer clubs
state formation, 2
subalterns, 11
"Subsídio para o estudo sociológico da população de Luanda" [Elements for the Sociological Study of Luanda's Population] (Bettencourt), 41
Swahili music, 11

Tali, Jean-Michel, 12, 92, 168, 252n97; on coup of 1977, 174; on internal politics of MPLA, 176; on "revolutionary" music, 178
Tanzania, 22, 142, 175, 206n75; radio broadcasts from, 144, 146, 242n42; Swahili music in, 11
Tarrafal prison, 58, 73–74, 125
taxi drivers, 126–27, 236n54, 236nn56–57
Tchokwe language, 114, 182
Teatro Nacional (National Theater), 110
"Technique, the Causes, and the Consequences, The" (MCK song), 195
technologies, 10, 191; gender and, 87; ideologies of status and, 145; imagined community and, 85; mobility of music and, 164; recording industry and, 160–61; semba and, 139
television, 20, 185, 195, 196, 243n65
Teta Lando Produções, 19, 206n81
theatre, 12, 57; Bota Fogo and, 73, 79; Gexto, 64; Yoruba, 116
Timor, 37
"Timpanas" (Portuguese song), 64, 114

Tondoya Mukina o Kizomba [There Is a Party in Our House] (radio program), 156, 157, 163
Tonito, 73
Tops dos Mais Queridos, Os (radio program), 187
Torre do Tombo, 20–21
Trio Assis (band), 158
trova music, 184, 191
Turino, Thomas, 11, 18, 234n14
Turma do Babaxi, 97
Turma do Rico, 97
Turma dos Caboverdianos, 97
turma groups, 62, 97

Úbia, 128, 237n59
Uíge, 130
umbigada dance step, 61
Umbundu language, 86, 112, 114, 157, 182, 244n72
unemployment, 33, 42
União Mundo da Ilha, 63
UNITA [União Nacional para a Independência Total de Angola] (National Union for the Total Independence of Angola), 4–5, 57, 226n9, 246n3; Bicesse Accord and, 188; exile bases in Zambia, 13; imperialism and, 180, 184; as rebel opposition to MPLA government, 165, 177, 180, 182; in transition to independence, 167, 169, 170; war against Portuguese military, 84
United Nations (U.N.), 38, 85, 150
United States, 43, 88; black working class in, 86; rock music from, 84; UNITA supported by, 5, 177, 180, 184
UNTA [União dos Trabalhadores de Angola] (National Union of Angolan Workers), 177, 182
Urbanito, 27
urbanization, 31, 36, 55, 70

Valentim de Carvalho (record company), 162, 163
Valódia, Mateus, 97
"Valódia" (Santocas song), 178–80
"Vamos descobrir Angola!" [Let's discover Angola] (nationalist slogan), 39–40, 45, 57, 73
Van Dunem, Aristides, 73, 75
Van Dunem, Domingos, 40

Van Dunem, Efigénia Barroso Mangueira, 61, 67, 68, 71, 221–22n57; Bota Fogo and, 72–75; in Grupo Feminino Santa Cecília, 77, 78–79; on women in music clubs, 106–7
Van Dunem, José "Zé," 167, 172–73
Van Dunem, Lourdes, 63, 103, 105–6, 223n78; MPLA-sponsored music festivals and, 182; in Ole film, 230n72; as *Voz de Angola* announcer, 156
Van Dunem, Luzia "Inga," 153, 243n56
variety shows, 91
Venâncio, António, 7–8
Victory Is Certain! (Parendon Press album), 153, 243n57
Vida verdadeira de Domingos Xavier, A [The True Life of Domingos Xavier] (Vieira), 15
Vieira, José Luandino, 15, 40, 48, 214n64; *Nosso musseque*, 50, 231n88; in Tarrafal prison, 58
Visconde, Luiz, 34, 126–27
Voice of America radio, 142
Voz de Angola (Voice of Angola) radio program, 147, 150, 154, 156–57

Wendo, 149
West, Michael O., 59
Westernization, 51–52, 53
Wheeler, Douglas, 57
White, Bob W., 18, 233n9
whites, Portuguese, 20, 214n76; in "African" jobs, 127; Angolan white settlers and metropole, 203n48; as club-goers in *musseques*, 55; departure from Angola, 167; economic development benefiting, 59; *fubeiros*, 68–69, 70, 75, 168, 169, 222n63; gender equity among, 35; housing problems and, 42–43; immigrants to Angola, 32, 39, 59; in Luanda, 33; in music clubs, 97; poor, 28; radio in Angola and, 143–44, 154, 155; reforms of late colonial period and, 88; soldiers, 50, 107, 130; violence of settlers, 81; women, 35, 42, 48, 49. *See also fubeiros* (shop owners)
witchcraft, 122, 126
women, 47, 51, 62; agriculture and, 211n34; Bota Fogo and, 73; in carnival groups, 95; colonial educational system and, 74; competition among, 103–5, 123–24; criticized in song lyrics,

women (*cont.*)
121–24, 130–31; cultural and political activity of, 23, 25, 74; as cultural consumers, 80; dress for club-going, 26, 61–62; female musicians, 87, 101–2, 103–6, 104, 223n78; "good girls," 101–8; male musicians and attention of, 94, 98–101; manual laborers, 35–36; marginalization of, 25; *mulatas* (mixed-race women), 48–50; music in everyday life, 54; nationalist narrative and, 59–60; role in music scene, 60, 223n72; Santa Cecília Girls Group, 77–79; squeezed out of central marketplace, 42; white (Portuguese), 35, 42, 48, 49. *See also* gender; prostitution

working class: African American, 86; leftist currents in transition to independence and, 170–71; MPLA ruling as workers' party, 177; urban industrial proletariat, 35, 89, 224n1

writers, 40, 48

Xabanu (Luís Martins), 97, 98, 148, 230n71, 245n89; on *Angola Combatente* broadcasts, 152; in MPLA cell, 168–69; record collection of, 162

Xavarotti (music club), 191, 233n10

Xenda Hala, 62, 97

Xitu, Uanhenga, 40, 48, 58, 214n64

youth, 72, 90, 96, 201n36; legacy of coup attempt (1977) and, 172, 176; MPLA youth wing (JMPLA), 169, 177, 180–81, 242n55; music clubs and, 134–35; post-independence generations, 185; at spontaneous jam sessions, 119–20

Zaire (Congo-Kinshasa), 13, 18, 144, 162, 246n2; Angolan guerrillas in, 81; independence of, 76; Latin American music and, 164; military intervention in Angolan civil war, 170; popular painting in, 131; radio broadcasts from, 4, 142, 147, 148, 149. *See also* Congo, Belgian; Kinshasa; Leopoldville

Zambia, 4, 81, 144, 208n91; radio in, 143, 148; UNITA bases in, 13

Zangado, Mateus Pelé do, 118

Zau, Felipe, 175, 177

Zé, David, 1, 169, 175, 180; music censored after coup attempt, 186, 187, 197n1; reappearance of music on radio, 188

Zimbabwe, 11, 13, 18, 58, 197n4, 203n48

zouk music, 185, 235n32

www.ingramcontent.com/pod-product-compliance
Lightning Source LLC
Chambersburg PA
CBHW031234290426
44109CB00012B/284